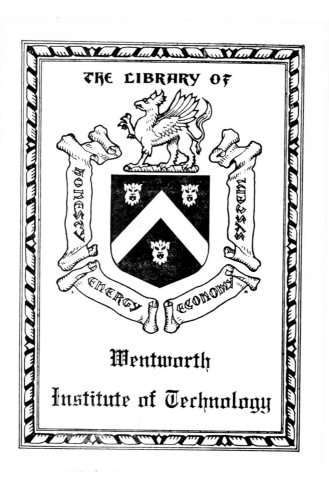

G-MEN

Hoover's FBI in American Popular Culture

RICHARD GID POWERS

SOUTHERN ILLINOIS UNIVERSITY PRESS

Carbondale and Edwardsville

Printed in the United States of America
Edited by *Daniel M. Finnegan*
Designed by *Design for Publishing, Bob Nance*
Production supervised by *John DeBacher*

86 85 84   4 3 2

Library of Congress Cataloging in Publication Data

Powers, Richard Gid, 1944–
  G-men, Hoover's F.B.I. in American popular culture.

  Includes bibliographical references and index.
  1. United States. Federal Bureau of Investigation.
2. Hoover, J. Edgar (John Edgar), 1895–1972. 3. United
States—Popular culture. 4. Criminal investigation in
mass media—United States. 5. Detectives in mass media—
United States. I. Title. II. Title: G-men, Hoover's FBI
in American popular culture.
HV8138.P68 1983   353.0074   83-632
ISBN 0-8093-1096-1

Permission to quote from the following sources is gratefully
acknowledged:

"The Director." By Jack Alexander, in *The New Yorker,* Reprinted by
    permission: © 1937, 1965.

The song "Gee, but I'd like to be a G-Man," by Harold Rome. Copy-
    right © 1940 by Chappel & Co., Inc. Copyright renewed. Inter-
    national Copyright Secured ALL RIGHTS RESERVED. Used by
    permission.

The poem from *The Saturday Evening Post,* April 17, 1943. Reprinted
    from *The Saturday Evening Post* © 1943 Curtis Publishing
    Company.

CONTENTS

ILLUSTRATIONS

ACKNOWLEDGMENTS

The late Rex Collier was a central figure at the beginning of the FBI's public relations, and his recollections, notes, and files were crucial to my understanding of what actually happened. I am grateful to him and his wife, Mrs. N. Rex Collier, for their help, their friendliness, and their patience. Former Assistant Director Cartha DeLoach and the late Assistant Director Louis Nichols guided FBI public relations during the bureau's greatest years, and I am grateful for the information and insight they provided.

The record of the FBI's impact on American culture would have been lost were it not for the fans and collectors who preserve the ephemeral materials that are the only surviving evidence of popular enthusiasm. They are the real experts on popular culture, and I found them always ready to enlighten me. I am particularly grateful to Richard M. Minter, Jim Ashton, Howard Rugofsky, Monte A. Brakefield, Conrad Somerville, and, especially, Nils Hardin of *Xenophile Magazine*. I depended on the staffs of the libraries where I worked: the Film Collection at the Library of Congress, the New York Public Library and its Performing Arts and Newspaper Annex, the Brooklyn Public Library, the New York University Library, and the Film Collection at the Wisconsin State Historical Society; thanks also to Catherine Heinze at the Broadcast Pioneers Library, Jerome Mardison at the College of Staten Island Library, and the staffs of Movie Star News and Wide World Photos. The External Affairs Division of the FBI, particularly Donald W. Moore and G. W. Gunn, were unfailingly obliging and prompt in providing me with documentation of the bureau's public relations activities and with calling useful information to my attention.

Joseph Friel, Louis Phillips, and Barton L. St. Armand discovered previously unsuspected materials for me, and Claudia Wallis helped locate crucial items. Harold Rome, Edward Sorel, David Levine, and William E. Robinson kindly gave me permission to reproduce their copyrighted work. My colleagues at the College of Staten Island, Don

Hausdorff, Edward Margolies, David Traboulay, and Fred Binder, provided ideas and encouragement; and the college's president, Edmond L. Volpe, and former dean Michael Shugrue supported this work with a research grant.

I am grateful for the aid and encouragement given this project by Ray Browne, Russel B. Nye, Tom Towers, Gerard O'Conner, J. Fred MacDonald, and Jan and Bill Cohn of the Popular Culture Association, and by Jack Salzman and David G. Hartwell. Much of this book was written while I was spending a Fulbright year on the faculty of the University of Hiroshima, and I am grateful to my colleagues there for providing companionship and ideal working conditions: Higashi Shikibu, Katsuhiro Jinzaki, Kosuke Shimura, Norifume Watanabe, Kunihiro Iwakura, and Masashi Yamamoto.

My typists, Sarah P. Sherry, Mary Geisler, Harriet Rosenberg, and Jeanne Arnold, performed wonders with my illegible drafts. The staff of Southern Illinois University Press, particularly Joyce Atwood and John DeBacher, devoted themselves to this book, and I thank them for their skill and commitment. Seymour Rudin subjected the manuscript to review by his keen eye and encyclopedic memory, to its great benefit.

Lastly, I wish to show my gratitude to my teachers at Brown University, Hyatt H. Waggoner and William G. McLoughlin, for their example and guidance; and, for their patience and encouragement, to my wife, Eileen Friel Powers, and to my father, Richard M. Powers.

INTRODUCTION

For nearly forty years J. Edgar Hoover was an American political giant, quick to anger and terrible in wrath. His Federal Bureau of Investigation was venerated like no other institution in a country where even Christianity and baseball have to tolerate disbelievers. His millions of admirers slept better knowing Hoover was on guard against crime and communism, while fear of Hoover kept millions of other Americans awake at night: fear that Hoover was putting the stamp of orthodoxy on his own brand of intolerant traditionalism, fear that his attacks on dissent were silencing free expression, fear that his dragnets for subversives had crippled freedom of political association, fear that a careless remark or youthful indiscretion uncovered in an FBI security check might ruin a reputation or destroy a career. For most Americans Hoover's FBI was a national security blanket. For a great many others the bureau was a symbol of fear.

At the same time Hoover was casting his shadow over American public life, his agents were the stars of movies, radio adventures, comics, pulp magazines, television series, even bubble-gum cards. Hollywood celebrated the FBI as the nation's crime fighting elite, the government's official anticrime strike force, by giving it exclusive possession of the nickname "G-Men," which had been for years underworld slang for all government operatives, treasury agents, postal inspectors, and military intelligence, not just FBI agents. Meanwhile the director himself broke bread with Hollywood stars and hobnobbed with the oil-well aristocracy. Hoover's arrivals and departures were chronicled in the gossip columns, his speeches were featured at rallies and conventions, his ghost-written "cases from the files" appeared in popular mass circulation magazines. The director and his G-Men were American legends. Their adventures were American mythology.

J. Edgar Hoover and his G-Men operated on two levels of American culture generally considered quite distinct, and their success depended on hidden connections between politics and popular entertainment; the bureau's reputation was kept aloft by the pressure of fantasy on politics and of politics on the public's fantasy life. It may seem improbable that a chief of the secret police should have once been a celebrity on the level of John Wayne or Billy Graham, but Hoover's popularity was undeniable, and the power his celebrity gave him made Hoover a force to be reckoned with in American life.

Hoover's power had its sources in the hopes, fears, and needs of the American public, drives that are expressed openly only in American popular entertainment. His power ultimately rested on his popular support, and as Nixon's collapse during Watergate proved, even the most powerful officeholder is impotent when that support is lost. Hoover's standing with the public let him escape the narrow confines of his job. On paper he was subordinate to the attorney general and the president, but in fact he was an independent political force. The public had such confidence in him that by criticizing him his critics lost their credibility. The public's refusal to believe anything but the best of Hoover and his men disarmed his political opponents. The "Official and Confidential" files Hoover kept on the politically powerful were the immediate restraint on Hoover's enemies, but if he had not been so popular that he could smear without being splattered himself, the blackmail files would have been blank charges.

Hoover's popularity placed him so high above the political stage that he could comment on the struggles below, interpret the action to the audience, lead the crowd in cheers and catcalls, change the script when it pleased him, and intervene magisterially whenever one of his favorites faltered, all without exposing himself to the battering of political strife. By a quirk of the public psychology, Americans saw, when they looked at Hoover, not a spokesman for a partisan political philosophy, but a suprapolitical national hero.

This book is an inquiry into the forces that turned J. Edgar Hoover into a national hero, a dynamic shaped by politics' function as a melodrama expressing (and satisfying) the collective hopes and fears of the mass society. It was popular culture, as a reflection of the political subconscious, that defined the role Hoover was to play in American life from the thirties to the seventies.

A public figure like Hoover can emerge only if important cultural needs go so long unsatisfied that they turn into public obsessions. This occurred during the early thirties: coinciding with the Great Depression, and to some extent as a result of it, national alarm over crime reached hysterical proportions. Statistics now show that there was no crime wave,[1] but newspaper headlines then told a different story. Top gangsters were national celebrities. Crime reporters treated gang wars and truces as though mobs were sovereign nations independent of society. The lives of crooks like Legs Diamond and Al Capone were written up in the same columns that covered film stars and royalty.

Believing that the police were too incompetent and corrupt to cope with the "new" breed of criminal, the public demanded a national mobilization against crime. Herbert Hoover ignored these appeals; he was fully occupied with his economic problems and unwilling (on constitutional grounds) to allow the federal government to take on new responsibilities. To calls for federal action he replied that crime was a matter for local government. With the public screaming for more law enforcement (and even martial law), civic leaders organized what amounted to a grass roots anticrime movement. When Roosevelt took office in March, 1933, this movement was still looking for a leader.

By itself, the anticrime movement would not necessarily have produced a hero like J. Edgar Hoover. For this to happen, the culture had to possess a traditional defense mechanism that simplified a complex real-life situation like the "crime wave" by making a single person the symbol of the entire problem. Because the cause, nature, and effect of crime are so complex, any realistic attempt to deal with criminal activity is unlikely to produce quick and dramatic results. But there is an opportunity for spectacular action if the public designates one notable crook the "master criminal of the age" and makes him the symbol of all rebellion against the law.

The public's habit of turning individual gangsters into symbols of crime was particularly pronounced during the thirties. It was a reflex response for editorialists to label the outrage of the hour—the Saint Valentine's Day Massacre, the Lindbergh kidnapping, the Kansas City Massacre, the Urschel kidnapping, the Dillinger jailbreak—as the "crime of the century." No sooner was the culprit killed or captured than another "mastermind of crime" was nominated to take his place as "public enemy number one": Dutch Schultz, Al Capone, Machine Gun Kelly, Bruno Richard Hauptmann, Louis "Lepke" Buchalter, and the greatest of them all, the thirties' all-American gangster, John Dillinger.

The thirties' metaphorical substitution of the part for the whole, the individual criminal for the entire crime problem, was obviously an irrational basis for national policy. On the other hand, rational solutions to the problems of the thirties did not have a very good track record, so the public, with the encouragement of its leaders, turned to mythology as an escape from politics.

Mythology is usually taken to mean irrational beliefs, but a more useful definition describes myth as the imaginative transformation of historical reality into eternal truth.[2] The myth-making mentality finds in daily events the working out of providence; it sees individuals as symbols of vice and virtue; it understands human conflict as the eternal opposition of good and evil. Myth turns the historical George Washington into Parson Weems' "Father of His Country"; it revises Abraham Lincoln's biography to make him "belong to the ages." In the thirties, mythology operated to turn John Dillinger, the "Mad Dog of the Midwest," into depression America's symbol of crime.

For the mythological process to produce a Hoover-style hero, there had to be a universally understood formula within the culture for dealing with the sort of villain who had come to represent the public's fears. Associated with that villain in the formula, there had to be a hero defined as his mortal foe. This formula and this hero would have to be found in the nation's popular culture, because popular culture is modern society's common mythology, its adaptation of the universal patterns of human myth to its own needs. In depression America there was such a formula. It was the popular crime story, and its hero was the action detective.

The careers and punishments of notable criminals had been popular entertainment in England and America ever since the development of the cheap press in the early eighteenth century and crime news had been the mainstay of the popular newspaper since the 1830s. The crime story formula treated crime as a willful attack on morality. Punishment was morality's revenge against the criminal, with its goal the restoration of the moral *status quo ante*. The formula crime story may have emerged as a functional substitute for the public punishment of criminals when that important ritual of social solidarity vanished from Western society.

A formula can be defined as the way a national culture makes a universal myth its own[3] by giving it a specific local setting and a conventional cast of national character types. In this way a formula adapts the universal myth to the national experience so that national history might be understood as an instance of the eternal struggle between good and evil.

America began to develop its own crime story formula with the publication of Edgar Allan Poe's first detective story in 1841. Poe's detective, however, was French, and the setting was Paris; not until 1872 and the appearance of the first "Old Sleuth" novel did the formula take its definitive shape. The action detective hero, as his name suggests, relied on brawn, not brains, and his adventures cast aside the intellectual puzzle of Poe's mystery detective story in favor of fast-paced action—escapes, chases, and fights, ending with a man-to-man duel against a villain evil enough to serve as a symbol of all crime.

Action detectives like Old Sleuth and Nick Carter (who first appeared in 1886) dominated the American dime novel field during the nineteenth century, and by 1900 over 250 different pulp detective series were being sold. In the early twentieth century pulp magazines featured adventures of a single detective *(The Nick Carter Weekly)* or special types of action stories *(Adventure Magazine, Detective Magazine).* Then came detective comics and detective radio shows. By the thirties the public's infatuation with the action detective had reached the obsessive level exemplified by today's television movies. Munsey's *Detective Fiction Weekly* and Street and Smith's *Detective Story* were the leading pulps among dozens of rivals. Inspector Post implored kids, from the back of cereal boxes, to join the "Post Toasties Law and Order Patrol." There were detective movies and plays. There was hardly any form of American popular entertainment that had not succumbed to the action detective formula.

There was an obvious psychological relationship between the popularity of the action detective formula in the thirties and America's alarm over the inability of real lawmen to bring real crime under control. Action detective entertainment exploited American culture's traditional romanticization of the law and its minions. Because Americans understand society as a struggle for supremacy between law-abiding people and the lawless,[4] they have come to regard legal agreements and codes (rather than history, religion, or custom) as the basis of social relationships, the glue that holds society together. This creates a mythic role for lawyers, judges, sheriffs and the whole legal tribe as the carriers of civilization to the American wilderness.

Since their cultural history and contemporary popular entertainment accustomed depression Americans to this mythological view of crime and punishment, it was natural in those unsettled times to see an apocalyptic significance in society's success or failure in fighting crime. Whenever crime, whether real or fictional, captured the public's imagination during the thirties, the popular press turned the news into a melodrama that conformed to the mythic pattern of the action detective formula. The result was that every major crime was turned into a test of whether America and its values could survive the depression.

At this stage in the myth-making process, a politician appeared with the ability and inclination to respond to the crime hysteria with a policy patterned after the action detective formula. By an inevitable process of association, the public identified this politician with the action formula detective, and credited him with the detective's heroic attributes and moral symbolism. This politician was not Hoover; it was his boss in the Justice Department, Attorney General Homer S. Cummings.

Cummings's crime program of 1933 and 1934 was the action detective formula translated into politics. He proclaimed major crimes to be "declarations of war" against organized society. He labeled celebrity criminals "public enemies," symbols of crime. He designated the FBI the federal government's strike force against the public enemies. He refurbished Alcatraz as a dungeon for any supercriminals who managed to survive the FBI's new firepower.

As far as the public was concerned, Cummings was the crime-fighting messiah the pulps and the movies had been calling for. Law enforcement groups across the country fell into line behind the attorney general; by the end of 1934 he was able to hold a mammoth Attorney General's Conference on Crime to organize local, state, and federal law enforcement, civic, religious and youth groups, and the news and entertainment industries into a single, coordinated movement under his own command.

How conscious was Cummings of the mythological aspects of his campaign? The New Deal's administrative style (Cummings called it "government in action") made public mobilization an end or a means in all its large-scale programs, a strategy that grew out of Roosevelt's conviction that public demoralization (the "fear" of his inaugural address) caused by the depression was as dangerous as the depression itself. Mobilization of the public is probably never possible without recourse to myth and ritual; in any case the New Deal's most publicized programs, the NRA and the CCC, featured parades, enlistment drives, uniforms and encampments, all governed by the metaphor of a nation that had declared war against the depression. Cummings's mythologization of crime fighting differed from the rest of the New Deal's programs only by being more forthright, spectacular, and successful.

Cummings was assisted in decking out his program in the trappings of myth and ritual by Justice Department publicists like Henry Suydam, Courtney Ryley Cooper, and Rex Collier. They had crime-reporting backgrounds that automatically inclined them to tailor Justice Department publicity to fit the formulas that had worked for them in daily journalism. The result was that during 1933 and 1934 the Justice Department was at the center of a new national myth-in-the-making, with gangsters like Machine Gun Kelly, Pretty Boy Floyd, Baby Face Nelson, and John Dillinger cast as formula villains and Attorney General Cummings as the action detective hero come to life in Washington.

When the public locates real-life cultural rituals as satisfying as Cummings's extravaganzas (this satisfaction, according to functionalist sociology, is the secure feeling of group strength produced by collective action), it calls upon the popular entertainment industry to provide reenactments of those events so that it can re-experience them at its leisure. Because the big cases of 1933 and 1934 were still fresh in the public's mind, the entertainment industry could not depart too far from the historical record, but because popular entertainment had to satisfy a mass audience, writers had to bring into sharp focus whatever aspects of the cases resembled formula detective stories, and they had to eliminate anything that departed from the formula. This process of making historical events fit a popular formula required that characters and facts be added and subtracted, enlarged and reduced, combined and recombined until history resembled myth and, because of the impact of popular entertainment on the public's imagination, myth replaced the events of history.

A funny thing happened to Homer Cummings's crusade on its way to becoming a myth: Homer Cummings disappeared. To fill his role as the leader of the crusade, the nation's symbol of law enforcement, popular culture selected J. Edgar Hoover. This *coup de théâtre* was simply the logical result of a strict application of the action detective formula to the events of 1933 and 1934.

When Hollywood pared the Justice Department's crime crusade down to the bare essentials, it turned out that only three items proved necessary for it to function as formula entertainment, and the attorney general was not one of them. The formula needed a villain vicious enough to be cast plausibly as a threat to the nation; this would be a composite gangster based on Machine Gun Kelly, John Dillinger, Pretty Boy Floyd, and Baby Face Nelson. There had to be an action hero who combined the customary savvy and strength of the traditional sleuth with a new crime-fighting style suited to the new style public enemy; this, of course, was the G-Man. Only one thing more was required. The action hero needed someone, a father-figure, to recruit him for the anticrime war; train him in the FBI's new crime-fighting tricks; back him up with science, reinforcements, and advice; order him into battle; and then, when the fighting was over, explain the significance of the slaughter to the audience. For this job the FBI director was perfect. He combined a close, personal, almost fatherly relationship to the G-Man (which the attorney general lacked) with an impressive rank and title that had a resonance, particularly in Hollywood, of complete authority.

With the director handling the mythic role of father to the G-Clan, the attorney general, who stood in relation to the G-Man as a metaphorical grandfather, could be dispensed with. Just as in the World War II combat movie the whole chain of command could be represented by the figure of the top sergeant, the G-Man formula made the director stand for the entire process that translated public alarm over crime into a command to the G-Man to rub out the public enemies.

The most important single force in creating this popular entertainment image of the G-Man was the Warner Brothers film *G-Men,* starring James Cagney, that appeared in 1935. This film adopted the G-Man/Public Enemy/FBI Director formula, as did all the other G-Man pictures that slipped through a loophole in the Movie Code's ban on gangster movies in 1935; so did all the radio shows, comics, pulp magazines, and bubble-gum cards that capitalized on the public's enthusiasm for their new heroes.

By the end of 1935 American popular culture had a new and militant symbol of the law to counterbalance against the symbol of "modern crime." The chief of the G-Men was another John Wayne, a celebrity presumed to possess in real life the heroic qualities he displayed on the screen. Hoover had become, according to the persistently critical *Nation* magazine, "box office."[5]

Since Hoover's power came from his popular culture image, he could maintain that power only by continuing to project that image. After 1935 the action detective image controlled Hoover: he succeeded when he was able to act in the style expected of an action detective; he failed when he did something out of character.

Hoover became the nation's popular authority on communism and the symbol of cold war Americanism after World War II because he purveyed his anti-Communist views in terms of the action detective formula. He equated communism (as well as socialism and "pseudo-liberalism") with crime. Soviet agents and domestic Communists were the old public enemies in more dangerous guise. The G-Man was the hero of a new edition of the old formula: spy-smasher as well as gang-buster. The old G-Man formula had assigned the director the job of interpreting the nature and significance of the public enemies' crimes, and so the public, still guided by the formula, looked to Hoover for an analysis of the Communist menace and the best strategy for hunting down Reds. In books like *Masters of Deceit* Hoover added the role of thought policeman to his repertory of detective hero poses.

But Hoover's image as the top G-Man meant that he could never be anything *except* the top G-Man. Whenever he did anything inconsistent with that image he was ignored. His action detective image sabotaged his life-long effort to build a coordinated nationwide drive against crime, the sort of movement that Cummings had been on the verge of creating when popular culture dethroned him.

Hoover's theories about the causes of crime turn out to be, on close examination, quite at variance with his "machine gun criminologist" rhetoric. He saw crime as stemming from society's failure to transmit the proper cultural values to the young, and so he believed that real headway could be made against crime only by strengthening moral education in the family, with government, church, school, and public opinion supporting, but not supplanting, the efforts of parents. Hoover campaigned throughout his career to build cooperation between parents, churches, schools, civic organizations, and law enforcement. His message went unheeded because the public paid attention only to words and actions in accord with his action detective image, activities that also created friction between the FBI and the local authorities he had to work with.

Hoover's G-Man image also contributed to the decline of his reputation during the sixties and its complete collapse after his death in 1972.

Hoover's popularity depended on the public's confidence in the action detective formula as a way of making sense out of current events. In the sixties Hoover began to encounter a new type of enemy who had rebelled against the law out of conscience—Daniel Berrigan, Martin Luther King, civil rights workers, anti-war activists, and, sometimes it seemed, the whole student generation. These new "fugitives" who populated the FBI's Most Wanted List could not easily be passed off as formula villains. Hoover's implausible attempts to explain the unrest of the sixties in formula terms made the whole G-Man concept seem irrelevant.

Almost as fatal to the FBI myth was the elderly Hoover's subtle recharacterization of the G-Man hero (in movies like *The F.B.I. Story* and television's "The F.B.I.") as a mature family man, a symbol of decency more than an action hero. This redefinition puzzled the public, but it developed logically from Hoover's almost-despairing conviction that only a last-ditch defense of traditional American values could save America from crime and communism. The G-Man's new image in the fifties and sixties as a moral paragon made the FBI fatally vulnerable when bag jobs, wiretapping, and political dirty tricks that might have been expected from the old hard-boiled action hero were discovered to have been the work of Hoover's late-model, God-fearing G-Men.

From 1924 until 1972 J. Edgar Hoover reigned as FBI director. For the last thirty-eight years of his tenure he was a popular culture hero whose whim made Washington tremble. A democracy can allow no one the prolonged and untrammeled power that Hoover's popular reputation gave him, so one lesson taught by Hoover's career has been to ensure, by legislative safeguard, that no director of the FBI will ever again acquire such power.

J. Edgar Hoover's career as the G-Man hero also has a cultural significance that extends beyond his value as a horrible example to civil libertarians. A half century ago Franklin D. Roosevelt, Homer Cummings, J. Edgar Hoover, John Dillinger, Pretty Boy Floyd, and Baby Face Nelson collaborated with Warner Brothers, James Cagney, *G-Men Magazine*, Phillips H. Lord (of "Gangbusters"), and the American press to create a new American legend, a myth that was so exciting and so satisfying that for nearly forty years we kept J. Edgar Hoover under glass, feeding his vanity, tolerating his foibles, excusing his failures. We allowed him to do anything except change, as though by hanging onto him we could hang onto the relief we had felt when the G-Men gunned down Dillinger and we knew at last that the nation was going to come through the crisis of the depression poor but honest, its laws, its values, and its pride intact.

G-MEN

1

The Public Enemy and the American Public:
Prelude to the New Deal

Depression America invented the G-Man because it had to. The G-Man was the country's solution to a crisis in American popular culture produced by the depression, aided and abetted by prohibition. The public enemy, one of the most powerful, dangerous, and ambiguously fascinating figures in American cultural history, was the symbol of this crisis.

The myth of the public enemy, like all myths, was compounded from the culture's hopes, fears, and desires (and, of course, from a few facts as well). The public enemy captured America's imagination during the twenties and thirties because, with the efficiency and persuasive force that are the reason for myth's power, the myth of the public enemy helped Americans understand their times and what was happening to their society. Oppressed by a sense that prohibition and the depression were draining American society of discipline and order, popular culture sought to explain the national plight as the work of a new breed of criminal. Once the image of the public enemy had been pieced together from the careers of the most famous criminals of the day, the myth took on a life of its own, persuading Americans that the authorities had neither the brains nor the courage to cope with what seemed to be a calculated rebellion against society. Once the myth of the public enemy had gained currency it persuaded Americans to interpret every outbreak of crime as further evidence of social demoralization and moral decline. This meant that for Americans to emerge from their state of psychological depression they would have to find another and more hopeful myth to take the place of the myth of the public enemy.

The public enemy was a collective representation of the criminals prohibition had turned into celebrities: Johnny Torrio, Dion O'Banion,

Hymie Weiss, and Klondike O'Donnel in Chicago; New York mobsters like Dutch Schultz, Mad Dog Coll, and Legs Diamond; and scores of other big name gangsters throughout the country. Dwarfing them all in the public imagination was Al Capone, the frog-shaped boss of the "Chicago firm." Capone was the premier symbol of crime during Herbert Hoover's administration. His wealth and political influence, his wide-open defiance of the law, and his highly publicized wars, life style, and loutish personality combined to create the image of a criminal who was more than a match for anything law-abiding society could pit against him.[1]

The gang wars that attended Capone's rise to power over the Chicago underworld, together with the law's obvious impotence, convinced America that a new breed of criminals had freed itself from the control of the law. Wide-open gambling, bookmaking, and prostitution rings were bad enough, but the gang wars gave the mobs the appearance of formally organized armies belonging to underworld states; Chicago's legitimate city government looked as ineffectual as the League of Nations.[2]

By the end of the twenties Capone had become a monument on the Chicago scene. All criminal activity in town and in the surrounding suburbs was under his control. Whenever the pie was sliced in government or business in Illinois, Capone had to be taken care of.[3] He enjoyed the status of a quasi-civic leader: the official welcoming party for Mussolini's goodwill ambassador in Chicago included the mayor's representative—and Al Capone.

Capone was colorful copy, so reporters sought him out. When a church group in Chicago complained that Capone got more newspaper space than it, an editor patiently explained that Capone was better copy than the average minister. Capone defended himself in the press by claiming that his activities may have been illegal, but they were not wrong; the law, the prohibition law anyway, was wrong, and he was only giving people what they wanted: "I'm a public benefactor . . . . Some call it bootlegging. Some call it racketeering. I call it a business. They say I violate the prohibition law. Who doesn't?"[4]

There were law-abiding citizens who agreed. A Chicago rabbi said Capone's organization was "based on a policy that may be good for all time and should be a forerunner for what society as a whole ought to do with its maladjusted and antisocial. They will simply have to be drafted into the social system. . . . Statesman-like governments will have to learn . . . from the Chicago firm [as the Capone gang was called] that to rebuild the nations of the world they will have to draft those men who, after all, are only the products of our way of living."[5]

Capone was a major celebrity in the popular culture of the twenties. His suburban headquarters was an attraction on the tourist bus tour of

Al Capone (1899–1947) had photographs taken from this profile so the scars on his left cheek would be hidden.

Chicago: "Castle Capone," the guides called it. Seven books about Capone were published between 1929 and 1931 (including Fred D. Pasley's classic *Al Capone: The Biography of a Self-Made Man*) and there was a one-shot illustrated magazine called *Al Capone on the Spot*. An Edgar Wallace play about Capone called *On the Spot* ran on Broadway in 1931.

Capone did his best to turn his reputation into a business asset. He saw the practical value of a good public image, and he realized the danger a super-gorilla reputation posed to his operations, so he tried to manipulate public opinion in his favor. He became friendly with the most famous crime reporters of the time; the *Chicago Tribune*'s Jake Lingle, who was murdered in 1930 (very likely on Capone's orders), was a go-between serving Capone in his dealings with corrupt politicians. When the Saint Valentine's Day Massacre story broke in 1929, the *New York Post*'s Jack Kofoed got an exclusive interview with Capone because Kofoed was a houseguest at the gangster's Palm Beach estate. Capone also cultivated the Hearst chain's star crime reporter, Jack Lait. Capone used Lait, Lingle, Kofoed, and other reporters to get his side of a story out to the public before reformers could mobilize the city against him, and he fooled many Chicagoans into regarding him as a modern Robin Hood. He set up soup kitchens for the unemployed and told his reporter friends about his gifts, tips, and charities.

The papers printed the same kind of gossip about Capone that they peddled about Hollywood stars: "Capone loses eleven pounds"; "Capone doesn't go to church Sundays"; "Capone picks the Cubs to win the 1930 flag." On slow news days Capone was always good for a quote: "The trouble with women today is their excitement over too many things outside the home. A woman's home and her children are her real happiness. If she would stay there, the world would have less to worry about the modern woman."[6] Many of the Capone stories sound too good to have been true: reporters could recycle almost any old gangster story by hanging it on Capone.

By 1930 Al Capone was known around the world as the new symbol of crime in America—crime accepted matter-of-factly as an intrinsic part of society, a force in American life that government was powerless to control. He was a national celebrity, not because he was admired but because he was grudgingly accepted as representative of his city and of his time. Like it or not, Americans had to recognize Al Capone and the powerful forces he symbolized as important additions to the American scene. At the end of the decade a Chicago school of journalism voted him "one of the ten outstanding personages of the world—the characters that actually made history."[7] In light of all this, Al Capone's freedom from prosecution was an incitement to civic cynicism, irrefutable proof that government could no longer function as the guardian of the law. This meant the government was losing the moral prestige that law enforcement confers on governmental authority.

Capone was the foremost symbol of crime during Herbert Hoover's administration, but there were many other celebrity hoodlums who were almost as well known. Dutch Schultz's battles against his under-world rivals in New York got almost as much press as the Chicago blood baths. During 1928 and 1929 Schultz's war against Legs Diamond for control of the New York beer racket was headline news. The New York nightclub set adopted the lean, well-dressed, and handsome Diamond as its pet. The newspapers turned Diamond's career into a multi-chapter cliffhanger as he was cut, shot, and blown up by Schultz's boys. In August, 1930, Diamond decided that he needed rest and recu-peration so he set off on a tour of Europe to get out of the Dutchman's reach. Country after country refused to admit him; editorial writers made the point that foreign governments at least could keep Diamond out while American authorities could do nothing about him at all.

During 1931 the New York papers were in a lather over Vincent "Mad Dog" Coll, who was also trying to take over Schultz's beer empire. During an East 107th Street gun battle against Schultz's men Coll killed a five-year-old boy and wounded four other children. The state destroyed its case against Coll by putting a perjured witness on the stand, and Coll walked away a free man. The episode seemed an unbe-lievable miscarriage of justice; Coll's lawyer, Samuel Leibowitz, became the personification of the criminal "mouthpieces" (or "lawyer crimi-nals," as J. Edgar Hoover called them) who had succeeded in castrating the law.

The public saw the Diamond and Coll cases as clear demonstrations of the law's weakness because, while the law could do nothing about Diamond and Coll, Dutch Schultz could. Schultz told reporters that he was taking over the case and would make sure that Coll got what he deserved. In 1932 Schultz's gang caught Coll in a telephone booth and machine-gunned him to death.

When Diamond returned from exile, he abandoned New York City to Schultz and tried to take over the upstate bootlegging rackets. In Oc-tober 1932, Schultz's gang murdered him while he slept in his Albany apartment. Once again the underworld had shown that it ruled itself and brooked no interference from the law. In a phrase that helps make the symbolism later attached to the FBI's cases understandable, the New Haven Register said that gangland murders like Diamond's were "crime's most daring gestures, and fairly make the entire social fabric of the land tremble in anticipation of a possible extension of gang rule to wider and still wider areas of life."

Capone, Schultz, Coll, and Diamond became major public figures during Herbert Hoover's administration because they were seen as symbols of what was happening to American civilization. According to England's *Manchester Guardian,*

When a set of criminals can announce publicly their intention of killing one another, and carry out that intention in the full glare of newspaper publicity, the general prestige of those responsible for law and order must inevitably suffer. . . . The fate of a Jack Diamond is without significance in itself. The social attitude toward him is significant of much. All the machinery of law exists in America, but the thing does not work properly. It does not work properly because the public conscience does not function as it should. . . . The gangsters are an inconsiderable proportion of the population in America, but they carry on their activities unchecked, and the only reason for that can be that at bottom the public does not mind them, does not feel that what they do is wrong. You cannot blame the police in such a case. The police are merely the instruments whereby the public sense of what is right or wrong expresses itself.[8]

Political pressure on Herbert Hoover to do something about Capone became too great to resist after the publisher of the *Chicago Daily News* led a delegation to the White House with hair-raising stories about Big Al's power in the Windy City.[9] The much-maligned president thereupon did manage to put Capone behind bars, but the public's reaction to the way he did it shows that Hoover had failed to grasp the fact that crime in America was no longer simply a problem in law enforcement. Gangsters like Capone fascinated the public because they posed a political challenge to the government's authority and a moral challenge to American culture's solidarity and its confidence in its value system. Instead of confronting this moral and political crisis, the Hoover administration hauled Capone into court and nailed him on a pair of technicalities: criminal contempt and income tax evasion.[10]

In 1932, using the tax laws to attack organized crime was a new technique that puzzled the public. When Capone got a ten-year sentence for his income tax conviction in 1932 the papers ridiculed the government. The *Boston Globe* wrote, "It is ludicrous that this underworld gang leader has been led to the doors of the penitentiary at last only through prosecutions on income tax and liquor conspiracy charges." The *Washington Star* complained that "no matter how satisfactory will be the eventual incarceration of Capone in a Federal prison for the failure to make an income tax return as a technical means to the end of getting him in jail, there will remain the sense that the law has failed."[11]

The public wanted justice, not technical and legalistic justice, but a poetic justice that took into account moral, and not merely legal, guilt. The nation wanted to see Capone punished in a way that would demonstrate the law's victory over crime. Because Capone was a symbol of crime, the public wanted a symbolic, as well as a legal, victory.

The nation's impotence against the devils it knew—celebrity public enemies like Capone—was bad enough. Even worse was the sense of futility and defeat when a major crime went unpunished in which the authorities could not even discover the identity of the criminal who had mocked and scorned the law. The most devastating instance of crime's function as a symbol of national demoralization during the abject last months of Herbert Hoover's administration was the futile search for the kidnapper of Charles Lindbergh's infant son.

The twenty-month-old son of the famous flyer was snatched from his Hopewell, New Jersey, home on March 1, 1932, and the hunt for his kidnapper lasted for two and a half years. Not until Bruno Richard Hauptmann was arrested in September, 1934, tried the following year, and electrocuted in 1936 did the case stop making news. The media turned "the crime of the century" into what the irreverent H. L. Mencken called the "greatest story since the resurrection." The case was not only a classic human interest story that laid bare the soul of America's most admired family. Lindbergh was an emblem of everything Americans most admired about their national character. "Lucky Lindy" was a symbol of a kind of success irresistible to Americans— one man, armed only with grit and know-how, betting his life against nature, and winning fame, riches, and a beautiful girl.[12] Lindbergh was the American dream incarnate, so an injury to him was an assault on the dream at a time when Americans had precious few dreams to sustain them. The kidnapping was not merely a crime; it was a national tragedy. From the first news flash until the switch was pulled at the Trenton death house four years later, the case was never understood as an isolated crime against one private citizen by an individual criminal. It was an attack on the nation by the underworld, and so the nation's leaders were looked to for a response appropriate to the national significance of the crime. Instead of action, however, Herbert Hoover gave the country lectures about states' rights and the constitutional limits on federal jurisdiction.

Since kidnapping was a symbol of all crime, the public refused to believe the Lindbergh case was the work of a lone criminal; even after Hauptmann's capture the country was convinced that he must have had accomplices with connections in the underworld. It is likely that a large segment of the public will always search for a criminal conspiracy whenever a crime attains mythic proportions. Since they are interpreting crime as the handiwork of "the army of crime," they must find a link between the actual perpetrators and the rest of the organized underworld. Thus the *New York Herald Tribune* said the kidnapping was "a challenge to the whole order of the nation. . . . The truth must be faced that the army of desperate criminals which has been recruited in the last decade is winning its battle against society."[13] Foreign papers said the crime proved that this "army of desperate criminals" was already running the country. "For the first time in modern history," wrote the *London Daily News*, "we are confronted with an organization directed by men of personality, courage and genius, who are above the law. What is behind these crimes? . . . how is it that nobody, from the highest to the lowest, apparently, is safe in the United States?"[14]

For the first few days after the kidnapping attention was focused on the local investigation headed by Colonel Norman Schwartzkopf of the New Jersey State Police, assisted by thousands of volunteers. When nothing was found, the papers quickly concluded that outsiders must be involved, creating the opportunity for a spontaneous nationwide mobilization. Cops everywhere announced that they had reason to believe that the baby was hidden somewhere in their jurisdiction. Citizens around the country phoned in clues and shadowed suspicious-looking strangers. A Valley Stream, Long Island, airplane club contributed its flying time to the search. The Cambridge, Massachusetts, district attorney and police chief were convinced the baby was in Boston. Chicago's Secret Six detectives raided a rooming house to follow up a Lindbergh clue. Mexico began special searches of all trains, ships, and cars entering the country.

With the whole country joining in the hunt, citizens looked to Washington for leadership. Congress was already considering laws making kidnapping a federal capital crime, and so the first Washington stories featured the bill's sponsor, Senator Patterson of Missouri. But since Patterson did not have the political stature to represent the whole nation, pressure mounted on Herbert Hoover to intervene.

Hoover's first response was to release a statement that he had authorized the Bureau of Investigation, the Postal Inspector, the Secret Service, the Prohibition Unit, and the Washington metropolitan police to cooperate with the New Jersey State Police if so requested, with federal cooperation coordinated by J. Edgar Hoover. Attorney General Mitchell's announcement was actually intended to limit federal authority as much as to indicate concern: "Although there is no development to suggest that the case is within Federal jurisdiction, agents of the department will keep in close touch with State authorities on the chance that the perpetrators of the crime in this or in some other activity may have touched Federal authority." In other words, federal aid would not actually be delivered until evidence turned up that a federal law had been broken.

The administration also made it clear it was not overly enthusiastic about making kidnapping a federal offense. "Bills are pending," Mitchell added, "to make transportation of kidnapped persons across state lines a federal offense. Because of budget limitations and recent reductions in appropriations for detective forces in the department, I have not felt able to recommend such legislation, but I have no objection to such a measure if Congress desires to pass it."[15] A few days later Mitchell warned the public not to expect too much from new federal laws.[16]

Washington's half-hearted leadership did not impress anyone. Some began to suggest that more progress could be made by private individuals without the blundering interference of the police and the government. Frank Loesch of the Chicago Crime Commission visited the President and announced that the federal agencies were helpless. "What I believe is needed to eradicate this growing menace to our lives," Loesch said, "is the formation of a *private* organization operating all over the country. It should be along the lines of the secret six in Chicago. No police officer can be retained without it being known. Even the Secret Service officers are known. You have to fight this business in a different way. Private individuals could band together to find out who is back of these rings. The organization should be perfected in each state and then organized into a national body."[17]

The *Washington Post* also thought that the Lindbergh case proved that citizens would have to fight crime on their own because there was no effective anticrime leadership forthcoming from the authorities: "Public authority as now constituted is impotent. Vigilance committees should be organized in every community to cooperate with the law authorities. . . . The people must be their own law enforcement system or be subject to the crime enforcement system. So long as they fail to organize for the common defense, they are assisting the crime system to flourish and destroy all."[18] Will Rogers suggested that the tradition of lynching public offenders should be revived.[19]

As the hunt went on there were those who proclaimed that the kidnapping proved the entire nation lay under a curse of communal guilt. A *Minneapolis Journal* editorial declared that "the baby's blood is also on the hands of the average American citizen because of his long complacency to crime."[20] Citizens began to beat their breasts and wonder whether it was their lack of support for the law that had weakened it to the point where public standards could no longer restrain greed and violence. This sense of being implicated in the breakdown of standards helped create pressure for a cathartically violent attack on crime as a way of purging the nation of guilt, a pressure that would be vented by the G-Men in the gangster wars of 1933 and 1934. For the time being, however, the nation, bereft of strong leadership, could only call for a revival of national values. According to the *New York World-Telegram*:

God knows why little Charles Lindbergh was murdered, but indirectly the wicked, wanton, causeless crime can be attributed to the wise-cracking, jazzed-up, hypocritical age in which we live—an age that pays racketeers for protection, that elects crooks to office on the ground that they are smart politicians, that outlaws bootleggers, buys their goods at exorbitant prices, and then claps them in jail when they fail to pay income taxes on the profits they make [referring, of course, to the Capone case].[21]

Editors claimed that the kidnapping was a just punishment for America's departure from traditional values. "Sobered by this awful experience," the *Indianapolis News* wrote, "and with the springs of sympathy stirred as never before, the American people should kneel down in a new devotion to the laws of God and the faith of our fathers."[22] The *New York Evening Post* said, "Let us all firmly resolve that this shall be the high mark of crime in the United States; that we shall first clear out the evil thing that is breaking respect for law and financing wickedness, and that we shall then go on to put justice into our courts and the fear of God into our criminals."[23] According to the *Richmond Times Dispatch*,

This brutal, hideous, unthinkable crime constitutes a challenge to law and order that cannot be underestimated. The Lindbergh crime will bring to a head, this newspaper believes, the entire question of whether the United States is to be swept along in a tide of lawlessness, or whether, finally aroused, the lawless are to be beaten into hiding, if they cannot be stamped out of existence. The law enforcement agents of the United States have received the supreme challenge. What will be the result—will the United States be governed by law or lawlessness?[24]

The shock of the Lindbergh case led to calls for collective action on the national level, and these came close to describing the "new look" FBI the New Deal would unveil one year later. "This crime," wrote the *Camden [New Jersey] Courier-Post*, "shows that America needs a system of state 'Scotland Yards'—with a central organization at Washington."[25] The *Philadelphia Record* urged that the police systems of all the states be unified into "one incorruptible central agency [that] can supervise our national battle against organized crime."[26] Only one thing would turn back the criminal assault, said John J. Cochran of Missouri on the Senate floor: "the fear of Uncle Sam."[27]

Commercial popular entertainment could not fail to reflect the extent to which the depression public had turned crime into a symbol of national demoralization. The nation's fascination with the public enemy was seen as a harbinger of society's failure to defend itself against an impending moral breakdown. As with newspaper accounts of celebrated crimes, gangster movies of the pre-Roosevelt depression showed that the image of the public enemy had become deeply embedded in the popular imagination as a symbol of national defeat and despair. More than that, the gangster movies also showed that American popular culture had come to regard the public enemy as not only a reproach against the present, but also as a preview of what the future held in store for America if public morale and the nation's commitment to traditional values and institutions continued to decline.

Even before the depression a few movies had upended the old formula of crime and punishment to make audiences identify with criminal heroes. Ben Hecht (author of the script for the classic Capone film *Scarface*, 1932) wrote a story for Joseph Von Sternberg in 1928 called *Underworld*. Hecht said he "decided to skip the heroes and heroines, to write a movie containing only villains and bawds. I would not have to tell any lies then."[28] In 1928 Hecht was the odd man out, but after the economy collapsed, "villains only" became the rule in crime movies. Hollywood began to cast stars as criminals in films that treated the law with contempt, hostility, and derision.

First came a cycle of prison pictures in 1930, films like *The Big House* (1930), *Convict's Code* (1930), *Ladies of the Big House* (1931), and *20,000 Years at Sing Sing* (1932). At first these movies simply exploited the exoticism of the prison world—frame-ups, riots, and the hot squat—but as the novelty wore off the prison became a clichéd metaphor for life in depression America. In a typical prison picture the hero is in jail because he was framed. He has no quarrel with the notion that crime should be punished or with the authorities' right to punish it. The problem is that the cops got the wrong guy. This situation was obviously full of significance for an audience that was out of work, because the depression was also getting the wrong guy.

As the depression worsened, so did the national morale; prison pictures were no longer adequate expressions of the public's alienation from authority, so in the next cycle of depression crime pictures the heroes were no longer innocent victims of injustice; they were outlaws on the prowl. The first example of this ominous turn in public mood was one of the most famous pictures in film history, *Little Caesar* (1930), starring Edward G. Robinson as Caesar Enrico Bandello, a Capone-style Chicago gangster. According to a film historian, *Little Caesar* established "the conventions of what was to all intents a new genre."[29] In the America depicted by the gangster movies that followed *Little Caesar* the authority of the law had all but disappeared. The economic debacle had destroyed the moral authority of priest, policeman, politician, and plutocrat; the most plausible claimant to their abandoned station at the helm of society was the mobster.

Little Caesar's Chicago is the legal no-man's land that Johnny Torrio found and Al Capone conquered. Little Caesar rises by being more daring and self-disciplined than his gangster rivals. The only enemies worth his attention are rival gangsters, and the only authority he acknowledges is the "Big Boy." The police are only minor obstacles to be

Edward G. Robinson in Little Caesar *(1930).*

ignored, bought off, or killed. In fact, the law is such a dim offscreen presence in *Little Caesar* that the story could seem plausible only if the audience accepted the notion that there really was an organized American underworld outside the reach of the law with the power to infiltrate legitimate society and conquer it. The success of *Little Caesar* showed that audiences during the pre-Roosevelt depression had no trouble with that horrific premise.

The gangster movie was so faithful to depression America's demoralized self-image that critics recognized Robinson's Little Caesar as a representative hero of the era. The *New York Times* called him a modern "figure out of Greek epic tragedy, a cold, ignorant, merciless killer, driven on and on by an irresistible lust for power, the plaything of a force that is greater than himself."[30] Like all pop culture heroes who capture the public imagination, Little Caesar was able to give expression to the characteristic emotions of his age, but there was a difference. Little Caesar's predecessors—cops, detectives, sheriffs—all had legitimate roles in the social order. Little Caesar was an outsider. When America identified with him, it too stood outside the law.

On the heels of *Little Caesar*'s success, more than fifty gangster pictures swaggered into the theaters in 1931, movies like *The Gang Buster*,

Scandal Sheet, The Vice Squad, Hush Money, Star Witness, Undercover Man, and *The Docks of San Francisco*.[31] Among them was a picture that made cultural history by combining the contemporary mythic power of the gangster formula with the raw energy of one of the most dynamic performers ever to appear on film, James Cagney. This was *Public Enemy,* in which Cagney, as gangster Tommy Powers, created the definitive characterization of the untamed criminal as the new American hero.

"When Cagney gets down off a truck," a critic wrote in 1932, "or deals at cards, or curses, or slaps his girl, or even when he affords himself or her the mockery of sweetness, he is, for the time being, the American hero, whom ordinary men and boys recognize as themselves."[32] Cagney played Tommy Powers as the classic American good-bad boy, Tom Sawyer with a snap-brim fedora and a cigarette instead of a straw hat and a corncob pipe. Tom Sawyer, however, was only a make-believe rebel. Tommy Powers was the real thing—a thief, a bully, and a killer.

Little Caesar's unassimilated Italian ethnicity, with his Old World

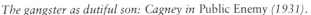

The gangster as dutiful son: Cagney in Public Enemy *(1931).*

dignity and ascetic life-style, set up barriers that kept American audiences from completely identifying with him. Cagney's youthful vitality created an immediate bond with the audience. Whether Cagney was showing off a new car, being measured for his first custom-fitted suit, or killing his first man, his magnetism implicated the audience in his irreverent sneers at authority. In *Public Enemy* audiences were made to identify with Tommy Powers because of his criminality, not in spite of it. Powers hates all the standard symbols of middle-class morality, ridiculing patriotism (he tells his respectable brother that fighting rival gangsters is no different from war: "You didn't get those medals holding hands with the Germans"), laughing at education ("school just teaches you how to be poor"), and sneering at romance. The movie's symbol of the law is a fatuous Officer Burke wringing his hands over Tommy's "dhurty" rackets.

The reason for *Public Enemy*'s impact (besides Cagney's charisma) was that it had an almost documentary flavor. Its story was a thinly fictionalized dramatization of the Chicago gang wars the national press had turned into folklore. One example: a hoodlum friend of Tommy's dies after a fall from a horse, so Tommy buys the horse and kills it. A Chicago gangster named Louis "Two Gun" Alterie actually had executed the horse that killed Nails Morton, one of Dion O'Banion's North Side mobsters.

The gangster movies' documentary references to real-life personalities and events made these pictures' departures from the familiar crime-and-punishment formula all the more disturbing to conservative spirits. Crime pictures had always been ritualistic affirmations of poetic justice: rewards for the worthy, punishment for the guilty. Popular entertainment had never neglected the intrinsic interest of crime, but within conventional plot formulas the principal function of a crime was to justify the criminal's legal extirpation. The criminal existed only so the law could load him with responsibility for society's ills and then purge the nation of evil by consigning him to oblivion.

Like the conventional crime movie, the gangster movie also ended with the death of its criminal hero, but his doom was handled in a way that drained the formula of its ritual significance. In *Public Enemy* Tommy Powers is murdered by rival gangsters, his death a triumph, not for the rule of law, but for the law of the jungle. In *Little Caesar* Edward G. Robinson *is* killed by the police, but they are so unattractively portrayed that it is impossible for audiences to identify with his executioners. Warner Brothers showed that it recognized the subversive effect of *Public Enemy* by nervously tacking a printed title to the film's final frames: "The end of Tom Powers is the end of every hoodlum. 'The Public Enemy' is not a man, it is not a character, it is a problem we all must face."

Cagney with Jean Harlow in Public Enemy.

The public's simultaneous fascination with real-life celebrity criminals and with gangster movie heroes showed that the country had indeed turned the "public enemy" into a symbol of the nation's "problems." The law's inability to come up with a dramatic solution to the "problem" symbolized by Tommy Powers (or Al Capone) meant, metaphorically, that America's moral values might not survive the economic crisis. The new symbolism attached to the criminal during the pre-Roosevelt depression might be called the "myth of the public enemy," and for political leadership to regain the confidence of the public, leaders were going to have to enforce the law within the context of this new mythic framework.

The gangster movies of 1930–1933 were, of course, a symptom of America's crisis of confidence, not the cause of it. Nevertheless, cultural leaders responded to the gangster movies with a wave of censorship that finally produced the Legion of Decency and the enforcement of the previously-disregarded Film Production Code in 1934. Half of the Chicago censor's cuts during 1930 and 1931 were for "showing disrespect for law enforcement." In New York State 29 percent of the scenes cut dealt with crime, while another 27 percent were for excessive violence or disrespect for the government.[33] The fate of *Scarface* (1932; produced by Howard Hughes and directed by Howard Hawks), the bloodiest of all the gangster films, shows how aware the censors were of the gangster movies' significance. *Scarface* served up forty-three murders as it followed Al Capone's career from the death of Big Jim Colosimo through the Saint Valentine's Day Massacre, tossing in a few non-Capone episodes (like the murder of Legs Diamond) for good measure. It was so violent and amoral that the Motion Picture Production Code, which was a rubber stamp for the producers until 1934, withheld its seal of approval. When Hughes released it anyway, the individual state boards went to work cutting up the film.[34]

The film's original ending had Capone, played by Paul Muni, shot down in the streets by the police. Though this was more punishment than Capone, then languishing in Leavenworth, had really gotten, it was not enough. The censors insisted that Muni be tried in court and hanged, and so a new ending was shot. They also cut out most of the gunplay and made Hughes add the phrase "Shame of a Nation" to the title and a statement at the end that read: "This is an indictment against gang rule in America and the careless indifference of the government. What are you going to do about it?"

Nobody knew. The ridicule that greeted Herbert Hoover's campaign against Al Capone showed that the country's political leadership had not yet discovered an answer to the symbolic significance crime had lately acquired. Until the New Deal revived the nation's confidence through federal action, the crime scare would continue to be an index of Americans' fear that their society and its values were crumbling. The gangster movies' amoral crime-without-punishment formula showed that American audiences could not yet imagine a symbol of the law with enough charisma to counterbalance the anarchic power the criminal displayed in the new myth of the public enemy. There were legal answers to criminals like Capone, but until the country had regained its morale, no one could deal with his symbolic meaning.

With headlines and Hollywood both proclaiming the authorities' powerlessness against crime, and with Washington failing to provide law enforcement leadership, the depression public tried to come up with its own answer to the real and symbolic menace of the gangster. During the years from 1930 to 1933 a grassroots anticrime crusade grew in America, a mass movement without a leader or a plan of action. By the time Roosevelt took office, this movement had become a permanent fixture on the American scene, presenting an unprecedented opportunity for anyone who would seize it.

As time passed, out of the chorus of demands for action there emerged a handful of proposals that comprised the depression public's own anticrime program. Since the plans were the public's own, the public was obligated in advance to support them and any politician who adopted them. As the war against crime entered the public domain, Everyman became his own criminologist. Letters to the editor called for a return to public hangings and floggings; other readers darkly suspected that prison walls were concealing golf courses and other delights concocted by moonstruck penologists for their clients. The press gave a respectful, or at least an interested, hearing to almost anything anyone had to say about crime. Daily newspapers always had room for the newest panacea, as long as it was sufficiently bizarre or bloody-minded.

The prescriptions varied with the point of view. Dentists wrote in to blame crime on bad teeth. Endocrinologists thought the culprit was the ductless gland. Wets blamed dry law; dries blamed the lax administration of the Volstead Act. Clergymen said the answer was a return to Sabbath blue laws. There were even some who blamed the whole mess on tobacco and coffee.[35]

Just about everyone agreed there had to be stricter laws and tougher punishments. There were regular stories about whippings in Delaware, Michigan, Canada, and England, where the lash was still legal. A Brooklyn grand jury hoped that "with the use of the whipping post these culprits will soon fade from our community."[36] A former police commissioner of New York City called for "public application of the lash and exile to a criminal colony like the French Devil's Island for habitual offenders."[37] Proposals for an American Devil's Island were especially popular. William L. Love of Brooklyn introduced a bill in the state legislature in 1930 for a special prison in New York reserved for the exemplary punishment of celebrity prisoners.[38] Another popular

demand was for generous application of the "third degree." President
Hoover's criminal justice fact-finding group, the Wickersham Commission, denounced police brutality in 1931, but law and order advocates
replied that a strong-arm policy was the best way to keep criminals off
balance. Mayor Walker of New York complained that he had ordered
"strong, athletic cops [to] round up gangsters in their own districts and
beat them before their own people," but that when "New York City
police tried this system they were arrested for assault and battery."[39]

Newspapers applauded the new "swing of the pendulum of opinion
against sentimentalism and the coddling and pampering of prisoners,"[40]
while legislators experimented with new laws to round up criminals
before they committed their crimes. Several local jurisdictions passed
so-called "public enemy laws" modeled on New York's 1931 legislation, which decreed that "a person who, with intent to breach the peace
or whereby a breach of the peace may be occasioned, is engaged in
some illegal occupation or who bears an evil reputation and with an
unlawful purpose consorts with thieves and criminals or frequents unlawful resorts, is guilty of disorderly conduct."[41] These laws gave police
the authority to round up supposed gangsters and racketeers. Even
though these cases were usually dismissed in court, the laws gave legislators a chance to show they were on the job whenever the public went
on an anticrime binge. New York State Commissioner of Corrections
Dr. Walter N. Thayer called for a "National Public Enemies Act."
Judges, he said, should be able to jail "an individual with a known
record who consorts with known criminals and has no visible means of
support." He argued that

Every sizeable community has persons who have no visible means of support,
but live well, who have criminal records and consort with known criminals. Yet
society must wait until a crime has been committed. . . . When circumstances
are to their liking we gaze into a gun held by a man we knew was a criminal but
who the law would not permit us to hunt. Any city can be cleared of known
criminals in 48 hours if the hands of the police are unshackled and if the powers
that be will assure them of backing and support. It would be doubly ensured if a
public enemy act could be not only enacted but enforced.[42]

The so-called Baumes Laws in New York State were another popular
model for legislation during the pre-Roosevelt depression. New York
State Senator Caleb H. Baumes had sponsored a package of twenty stiff
crime-control measures in 1926 that, among other things, imposed a
mandatory life sentence for conviction of a fourth felony (the "three-
time loser law"). The trouble was that judges and juries refused to
convict minor criminals when they knew the three-time loser law would
come into play, while the public could not understand why the law had

not put all habitual criminals behind bars permanently. The same public that screamed for the law to be imposed across the board, however, was appalled every time a small-time shoplifter or bootlegger went to jail for life.[43] Despite the law's demonstrated ineffectiveness, it was an important symbol of depression America's commitment to the fight against crime.

There were even calls for martial law, at first from the lunatic fringe, but after 1933 from prominent public figures. Warden Lewis Lawes of Sing Sing called for a "modified martial law by presidential proclamation pending adoption of a constitutional amendment and legislation eliminating state lines as far as the war on criminals is concerned." He also claimed that he "could stamp out racketeering in sixty days if he was a Mussolini."[44]

The most radical proposal to emerge from this anticrime hysteria was from Gordon Evans Dean, then assistant to the chairman of the American Bar Association's committee on law and criminology and later chief of public relations for FDR's Attorney General, Homer Cummings. Dean published an essay in the *Journal of the New York County Grand Jurors* that called for a revival of the ancient English custom of outlawry:

In early English history, the proclamation of outlawry was the method of legalizing the killing by private persons of those who refused to submit themselves to the law. . . . The subject of outlawry does not deal with the voluntary adventures of a Jesse James or a Tracy or an Al Capone. Rather it deals with a technical legal procedure by which men, since early Anglo-Saxon times, have been placed outside the law, . . . their goods forfeited and their lives taken. . . . Outlawry probably had its origins in the legalized process of summary justice meted out to a criminal taken in the act. . . . He was *ipso facto* an outlaw. It was a type of justice we now associate with Mr. Lynch. . . . It was the duty of all citizens to pursue an outlaw and knock him on the head as though he were a wild beast.[45]

Dean thought that a proclamation of outlawry might be useful, not because it would solve the crime problem, but because the authorities needed to do something to satisfy the public's demand for drastic action. "Kidnappers and other dangerous criminals have become so defiant in the United States that even conservative citizens are becoming convinced that eventually they must be suppressed summarily."

Grassroots fear of crime led to grassroots mobilization. Anticrime civic associations sprang up, some with specific platforms and goals, others simply as demonstrations of support for tough law enforcement. Sometimes these demonstrations attained giant proportions. For instance, during the manhunt for Mad Dog Coll a mass meeting in Madison Square Garden on August 24, 1931, was attended by twenty thousand New Yorkers who heard messages from Governor Roosevelt and gangbusting Judge Samuel Seabury, as well as a harangue from Marine Corps General Smedley Butler, who, as head of a municipal anticrime drive in Philadelphia, had spent 1924 in a frustrating attempt to wipe out crime. Butler said that politicians were to blame for the epidemic of lawlessness: "Some of your public officials have betrayed you. When you put moral cowards and hypocrites in office, you are bound to have trouble."[46]

By 1931 the government's failure to provide anticrime leadership had made vigilante organizations almost respectable, perhaps because they were intended more as symbolic gestures than as real threats of extralegal action. The American Legion was organizing and arming its members as police auxiliaries. John Haynes Holmes, a founder of the American Civil Liberties Union, joined the well-known liberal rabbi, Stephen S. Wise, in a call for citizens' groups to force the authorities to act against crime: "The first thing to be done is the organization of a vigilance committee of fifty to one hundred men and women to give counsel, support and heartening to such public officials as are not in collusion with the gangsters and racketeers and their office-holding confederates."[47]

The Lindbergh kidnapping in 1932 produced its own surge of grassroots anticrime organizations. The Boy Scouts organized a crime-fighting crusade,[48] and on July 11, 1932, a New York minister called for the churches to create a national youth organization against crime: "Believing as we do that the kidnapping and murder on March, 1932, of a baby, symbol of all that men hold dear, constitutes a challenge to Americans of all creeds and races to uproot from the soil of our society the weeds of crime and disloyalty, . . .[we] call for a crusade for law and order which will restore to America the spiritual, dynamic and social integrity upon which the nation was founded. . . . Youth of all creeds and races can join hands in a united effort and common cause."[49]

One reason for the tremendous political success of the New Deal's crime program was the common fear that ran through all these calls for more law enforcement: the belief that the increase in crime was a symptom of national disunity, so that only a rebirth of unity could overcome lawlessness. The Roosevelt administration was astute enough to understand the connection between social solidarity and law enforcement, and in the war on crime that began in 1933 the New Deal exploited this relationship with spectacular political results.

Responding to the pleas of the grassroots anticrime crusade, local elites set up anticrime strike forces independent of the local police (who were often seen as allies of the criminal element). The Chicago Crime Commission (which had existed since 1919 but began to draw national attention after the Crash) was the model for many of these autonomous anticrime units.[50] The commission was a creation of the Chicago Association of Commerce and was made up of a hundred Chicago lawyers, bankers, and businessmen, with its own staff of investigators, statisticians, and clerks. Its most famous contribution to law enforcement lore was the Public Enemies List, begun in April, 1923, with Al Capone holding top billing. The Chicago Crime Commission also captured the public's imagination with its Subcommittee for the Prevention and Punishment of Crime,[51] popularly known as The Secret Six because its members kept their names secret to guard against reprisal. The Six forced prosecutors to bring cases against protected gangsters and got the Justice Department to send Eliot Ness's team of "Untouchables" to Chicago to harass the Capone organization. In 1931 Hollywood capitalized on the public's fascination with this mysterious (and therefore romantic) outfit by producing a film called *The Secret Six,* starring Clark Gable and Wallace Beery. Cities across the country set up their own versions of Chicago's Six. Newark, New Jersey, had its Committee of One Thousand;[52] the New York City Board of Trade formed its Secret Six in 1931,[53] and an "Anti-Gang Rule League of America" was organized on December 19, 1930, as a national Secret Six to put pressure on unenthusiastic local police.[54]

All this commotion had an inevitable impact on American public opinion. By the time Roosevelt took office, the country was used to the idea that some sort of national mobilization was going to be necessary if the country was going to survive its "war" with the organized underworld, and by 1932 the metaphorical notion of a war against crime had lodged in the public's mind as the normal way of describing what was happening. This metaphor was, of course, a self-confirming prophecy: every kidnapping was additional proof that criminals were at war with society; conversely, even the most trivial crime became significant when it was seen as evidence of a general uprising of the underworld. For example, when a pistol-packing dentist in New York chased a gang of burglars out of his house, an editorial claimed that "the United States is practically in a state of warfare against the forces of gangdom and banditry. It is shocking to realize that since the declaration of war, April 6, 1917, the United States has lost, through murder and crime in our own borders, three and a half times the 50,280 American lives lost in the World War." The problem, the same writer continued, was that "the criminal courts of this nation have become in effect a protection to the criminal through the web of technicalities, objections to evidence, delays, appeals, straw bond, parole, and pardon at the disposal of unscrupulous criminal lawyers." He concluded that the public could expect no protection from the courts or the government; citizens would have to buy guns and practice using them.[55] On another occasion the

St. Louis Star wrote that society must "put the crooks and their legal and political pals in a group, proceed against them as common enemies of society, and organized crime will be wiped out."[56]

Herbert Hoover desperately needed to show the public that he was still in charge, but he passed up the chance to lead this crusade in search of a leader. With newspapers demanding "a nationwide revolution against the gangster and hoodlum rule,"[57] Hoover referred the matter back to the states. In a 1930 speech he rejected federal legislation and urged instead "a more widespread public awakening to the failures of some local governments to protect their citizens from murders, racketeering, corruption and other crimes. . . . Every state has ample laws that cover such criminality. What is needed is the enforcement of those laws, and not new laws. Any suggestion of increasing Federal criminal laws in general is a reflection on the sovereignty and the standing of state government."[58]

Hoover was handcuffed by principles which were opposed to anything that might undermine American society's self-government. A leader will not lead if he does not believe in the necessity of leadership. Regardless of principles, however, for a leader to reject his followers' call for leadership in anything is probably an act of political suicide.

Even if Herbert Hoover had wanted to respond to the public's call for law enforcement leadership, he probably would have failed. With the depression deepening, he did not have the resources to create a new law enforcement agency, so he would have had to turn to one of the two existing investigative units large enough to be considered for the job, the Prohibition Unit of the Treasury (after 1930 the Justice) Department or the Bureau of Investigation, and there were serious objections to either of these alternatives. The Prohibition Unit, with its twelve hundred dry agents in 1933 (the Bureau of Investigation had 266 special agents and 60 accountants that year), was huge by pre-New Deal standards, and it was already absorbing two-thirds of the federal government's budget for criminal justice.[59] The unit had its hands full without being given any additional responsibilities, and the president could not ask it to spare time from its prohibition enforcement duties without alienating the dries, his last remaining bloc of political supporters.

Even if it had been politically possible to give the Prohibition Unit the assignment of leading a federal anticrime crusade, to make the dry agent the symbol of a national war on crime would have been unthinkable. The Prohibition Unit had a well-merited reputation for corruption, and its agents were popularly regarded as no better than the bootleggers they were supposed to be fighting. In 1930 the *Baltimore Sun* commented that "the announcement of a Federal war on criminality would have electrified the country fifteen years ago [but] it arouses no excitement whatever today because of the failure of Federal government agents to enforce the Volstead law."[60]

It would obviously have been possible for the president to repackage the Justice Department's tiny Bureau of Investigation to turn it into the symbol of a federal law enforcement drive (and that is exactly what FDR did in 1933), but Herbert Hoover was not the man to do it. Hoover was thoroughly familiar with the bureau, its history, and its director; and his personal experience had made him far more alert to the harm a freewheeling bureau could do than to any possible benefits.

As Warren Harding's secretary of commerce, Herbert Hoover had seen an administration destroyed by the Bureau of Investigation's corruption and incompetence, and he did not intend to give history a chance to repeat itself in his administration. He knew that J. Edgar Hoover had been named director of the bureau in 1924 expressly to keep the bureau small and out of sight, and he had reappointed the director because he had done that job so well.

It was an ironic accident of history that President Hoover, who desperately needed an opportunity to demonstrate leadership, should have been so adamantly opposed to utilizing the Bureau of Investigation. The Bureau had been created precisely for the purpose of getting presidents out of public relations jams by defusing public anxiety over media-inflated crises like the "threat" of the public enemy.

The Bureau of Investigation had been founded in July, 1908, by Theodore Roosevelt during a dispute between the president and Congress over the investigation of a congressional scandal.[61] Roosevelt had discovered that some of his political rivals (in both parties) had gotten involved in a corrupt public land scheme in Idaho. The Justice Department had no detectives of its own, so Roosevelt borrowed Secret Service agents from the Treasury Department. The Interior Department's investigatory agency, the General Land Office, could not be used because it was implicated in the scandal.

The guilty congressmen were, of course, willing to do anything to head off this investigation, and even innocent congressmen wanted to block it because there was no telling what Roosevelt might do if given the chance to even old scores, particularly if he had an army of detectives helping him dig up dirt. Just before adjourning for the summer, therefore, Congress tried to cripple the land frauds investigation by prohibiting the Justice Department from "borrowing" detectives from other agencies.

Instead of retreating, Roosevelt accused Congress of obstructing justice. He issued an executive order to Attorney General Bonaparte to create a "Bureau of Investigation" within the Justice Department. Congress denounced Roosevelt for creating a secret police force for his own

political purposes, but soon several of liberty's most strident congressional defenders were on trial as a result of the investigation they were
denouncing.[62]

The Bureau of Investigation was thus founded to provide a fast political payoff. Its job was to collect facts about Roosevelt's congressional
enemies to help keep them in line, a function that might be called "elite
discipline." The bureau also gave Roosevelt the opportunity to score
points with the public as its champion against the lawless; this can be
called "symbolic politics." The bureau continued to work on these two
levels until 1924, and, after its revival under FDR, it resumed these
functions until its reputation collapsed once again after J. Edgar
Hoover's death in 1972.

The Bureau of Investigation let Theodore Roosevelt pose as a symbol
of law and order in 1908,[63] and it offered his successors a convenient
and effective way to strike similar poses whenever new issues emerged
to disturb the public's sleep. Its public function was to calm the public
by fighting crime in whatever symbolic form the popular mind might
imagine it.

For two years after the 1908 Idaho land fraud cases, the bureau had
nothing to do except investigate crimes on Indian reservations. Then in
1910 a bizarre hysteria developed that forced the government to make
another foray into the world of symbolic politics. This was the famous
White Slave Scare. In an almost classic instance of a mass delusion, the
sensational press convinced the public that prostitutes and their pimps
had just about taken over the country. The town whore was, according
to the press, part of a gigantic conspiracy. Stanley W. Finch, then head
of the Bureau of Investigation, told Congress that only a federal law
against prostitution could save the country, because "unless a girl was
actually confined in a room and guarded there was no girl, regardless of
her station in life, who was altogether safe. There was need that every
person be on his guard, because no one could tell when his daughter or
his wife or his mother would be selected as a victim."[64]

For authorities to point out that there was no white slavery conspiracy would have been to make light of the public's underlying fear that
traditional sexual morality was under attack, so Congress passed the
1910 Mann Act to show that it too was alarmed about changing moral
standards. The government was thus able to show that it was doing
"something" about this cultural crisis by symbolically opposing the
symbolic expression of the public's fears. Years later J. Edgar Hoover
gave the game away by saying the intent of the Mann Act was to mount
an attack on "the problem of vice in modern civilization."[65]

The bureau enforced the Mann Act by arresting prominent individuals whose cases could be counted on to generate publicity. The prize
victim was Jack Johnson, the unpopular black heavyweight champion.[66]

The Mann Act experience taught the bureau that by defending popular morality one becomes identified with popular morality. Popular morality's defender *becomes* popular morality in the minds of those who cannot distinguish between a thing and its representation.

The bureau's next important assignment was to lead the Slacker Raids of April–September, 1918, and the Red Scare Raids of the winter of 1919–1920. In the Slacker Raids the underlying fear was of military unpreparedness, and the symbol of this fear was the "slacker," or draft dodger; the bureau's response was to round up everyone it could find of draft age in several large cities and hold them until they could produce their draft cards. In the Red Scare Raids the predominantly foreign-born members of the Communist party were the symbols of the fear of revolution, and so the bureau rounded them up with the intention of deporting them aboard transports nicknamed "Soviet Arks." The bureau's dragnets were carried out in the glare of frenzied publicity. In the Slacker Raids seventy-five thousand men in New York City alone were arrested, and hundreds of thousands nationwide, though the bureau itself admitted afterwards that only one out of every two hundred turned out to be a draft dodger. In the Red Scare raids ten thousand were arrested; only thirty-five hundred were prosecuted and fewer than seven hundred were finally deported.[67] Both cases represented a capitulation to public hysteria by the government and a pervasive contempt for civil liberties by the Bureau of Investigation.

The Red Scare raids were J. Edgar Hoover's first important Department of Justice assignment. Hoover had joined the Justice Department in 1917, one year after he graduated from law school. He had supported himself in law school as a clerk in the Library of Congress where, according to friendly biographer Ralph de Toledano, "he exceeded the call of duty by mastering for himself the intricacies of card-index systems, an expertise which he took with him to the F.B.I." Hoover's wartime work in the Justice Department consisted of reviewing the applications of aliens who wanted to join the American armed forces.

When Congress reacted to the 1919 hysteria over radicalism and "anarchists" by ordering the administration to do something about the Reds, Attorney General A. Mitchell Palmer set up an antiradical task force in the Justice Department called the "General Intelligence Division" and placed twenty-four-year-old Special Assistant to the Attorney General J. Edgar Hoover in charge of it. Hoover had to provide the attorney general with information about communism to use in preparing legislation and to draw up lists of radical organizations and individuals as targets for action should Congress or the president so decide. He buried himself in Marxist-Leninist literature and interviewed dozens of Communists. He was perhaps the first government official to make an in-depth study of the Russian Revolution and domestic Marxist communism. In 1919 he wrote the first official government study of communism, his *Report on Radicalism,* thus laying the foundation for his later reputation as the chief theologian of American pop anticommunism.

The reports Hoover wrote as head of the GID defined, once and for all, his characteristic political outlook. For Hoover communism was simply the latest outbreak in "the eternal rebellion against authority,"[68] and like crime, it was an attack on the collective sentiments and values that were the basic sources of solidarity in any culture. From the beginning to the end, Hoover's ideology was the ethnocentric American tradition of Christianity and free enterprise; cultural unity was for him the highest of all the political virtues. In 1939 he defined democracy as the "dictatorship of the collective conscience of our people,"[69] meaning that the danger of both crime and communism was their threat to the cultural consensus. The Red Scare Raids taught Hoover that outbreaks of crime and communism had to be countered by reassuring the public that the common values of society were safe and secure—and that the most effective way of doing this was to create a symbol of the threat and then destroy it.

A year after taking over the GID Hoover had the names of over four hundred fifty thousand supposedly radical individuals in his files, all cross-referenced according to the elaborate system that would later be the basis of the bureau's investigative procedures. When Palmer gave orders in 1919 to round up the Reds, these files provided the information and Hoover provided the coordination.

The bureau's campaign against the Communists during the winter of 1919–1920 was of one piece with its war against vice in 1910: it was a campaign to defuse a threat to the national consensus through ritual action. Even before the G-Man days of the thirties, the bureau was the government's chosen instrument for mobilizing a pageant of popular politics to dramatize the government's determination to do something about the latest target of public wrath: vice, disloyalty, communism, or crime. Whether or not this sort of symbolic crime-fighting discouraged would-be villains, it was at least an effective way of temporarily strengthening social solidarity and heightening the popularity of the officials in charge of the revels.

Herbert Hoover had witnessed the bureau's public relations triumphs in 1918, 1919, and 1920, and he had seen them turn to ashes in the subsequent senatorial investigations. He had seen the bureau pilloried for its scandalous behavior in 1924 during the investigation of the Teapot Dome affair, in which it had tried to cover up Interior Secretary Albert Fall's crimes by framing Fall's chief accuser, Senator Burton Wheeler of Montana.[70] Herbert Hoover was therefore impressed with the wisdom of Coolidge's attorney general, Harlan Stone, who appointed J. Edgar Hoover director of the Bureau of Intelligence in 1924 with orders to cease all general intelligence duties and to turn the bureau into "a fact-gathering organization" whose "activities would be limited strictly to investigations of federal laws."[71] With that the Bureau of Investigation (and Hoover with it) faded from view.

For the next nine years J. Edgar Hoover worked tirelessly in obscurity to make sure that the Bureau would do nothing except investigate violations of federal laws. Since there were few federal laws to investigate until the expansion of federal authority under the New Deal, Hoover had plenty of time to perfect the administration, discipline, and control of his slimmed-down organization. It is not quite true to say that the bureau did nothing from 1924 until 1933; what it did do (Ku Klux Klan investigations, for example, and enforcement of the antipeonage laws in the South), however, it did quietly, efficiently, and inconspicuously—and President Hoover was perfectly content to keep it that way.

With Herbert Hoover refusing to provide the grassroots anticrime movement with federal leadership, the public, thwarted in its desire for a real-life mobilization against crime, had to make do with vicarious vengeance against the public enemy. Popular entertainment of the pre-Roosevelt depression prospered by serving up violent rituals of crime and jury-less justice. Chester Gould's Dick Tracy became famous as a plainclothes avenger in the funnies who meted out the poetic justice the public vainly looked for in the news pages. Chester Gould's comic had the advantage of the artist's unique draftsmanship and wild imagination, but the strip's topicality was the major reason for its huge success. Tracy gave the public the kind of performance they weren't getting from real cops. Gould gave credit to current events for creating the conditions that made his comic a hit: "Tracy was a symbol of law and order who could dish it out to the underworld exactly as they dished it out—only better. An individual who could toss the hot iron right back at them along with a smack on the jaw thrown in for good measure." A sales pitch for the comic said that Tracy was "the prototype of the present hero [the gangster] but on the positive side. An antidote to maudlin sympathy with society's enemies, he creates no glamor for the underworld. Children love this character and parents and teachers approve of him."[72]

Since popular culture consists in large part of fantasy projection and wish fulfillment, popular entertainment often predicts the kind of political action it will take to defuse the public's anxieties. Popular artists like Gould had detected a taste for the hot-lead and machine-gun style of law enforcement as early as 1931. The public had moved far beyond its leaders in tolerance for violence against lawbreakers. In their fantasies

Highlights of Dick Tracy's career, which began in 1931.

the public had already rejected Herbert Hoover's legalistic style of law enforcement.

Hollywood even went beyond Dick Tracy in giving the public a taste of revenge against its criminal tormentors. Movies made during the last months of Hoover's administration and the first months of FDR's show that the public was indulging in fantasies of direct, extralegal action against crime. Beginning early in 1933, and lasting until 1934, a cycle of vigilante movies followed the gangster films into the theaters. *This Day and Age* (1933), *Gabriel over the White House* (1933) and *The President Vanishes* (1934) dispensed with all the legal niceties and let the public participate in imaginary lynchings of public enemies.

In *This Day and Age* a public enemy (Charles Bickford) beats a murder rap with the help of his shyster lawyer (another favorite stock villain of the early depression). Taking the law into their own hands, the town's teenagers kidnap Bickford and force him to confess at a rally enlivened with torches and high school cheers. "We haven't got time for rules of evidence," the young vigilantes tell him as they lower him into a pit full of rats. The movie's producers may well have intended its audiences to recall the real-life Junior Division of the Crusaders then being organized in New York City to fight crime.[73] A film historian wrote about *This Day and Age* that "what was new in the film was the seriousness of the crowd's rage against a lack of control, a void in authority. . . . Legality was presented as a barrier to the truth. In his courtroom scene [director] DeMille used a montage of law books, objections being raised, and fingers pointed to show how due process was in fact a symptom of social illness; it had become a shield for shysters."[74]

Walter Lippmann called *Gabriel over the White House*, produced by William Randolph Hearst's Cosmopolitan Pictures, "a dramatization of Mr. Hearst's editorials."[75] The movie had the president (Walter Huston) respond to the depression crime wave by sweeping Congress aside, declaring martial law, and then mobilizing the nation for a war on the gangs. One scene could have been a dramatization of an editorial cartoon that appeared a thousand times during the early depression years: the stereotypical black sedan of gangdom sweeps by the White House and sprays it with bullets, a striking instance of how the national anxiety over crime had coalesced into an image of a criminal attack on the paramount symbol of the nation. This movie's president does not mutter about the Constitution. He rounds up the gangsters, hauls them before impromptu courts, then stands them before the firing squad. The film was one of the six best box office draws of April, 1933.[76]

Kidnapping was the most highly publicized crime of the pre-Roosevelt depression because it was a direct attack on the home, the country's grassroots symbol of security and traditional values at a time when both were threatened. In *The President Vanishes* the president (Arthur

Byron) has given up hope that crime can be controlled by conventional methods. He mulls over the alternatives and decides on martial law. Fearing that the public would see this as a dictatorial grab for power, he engineers a call for the suspension of liberties by staging his own kidnapping. The resulting uproar gives the administration a chance to lead the country in an all-out crusade against crime.

Mob action movies, in the context of the calls for direct action against crime during Herbert Hoover's administration, were a symptom of the public's impatience with conventional law enforcement. Long before the New Deal unveiled its crime program the public had a pretty fair idea of the kind of law enforcement it wanted. And that was what it got.

By the time Roosevelt took office, the cultural materials that coalesced into the myth of the G-Man had all been assembled: popular fascination with rituals of crime and punishment, both in the news and in entertainment; an accepted interpretation of crime as an attack on the nation and its values; a passion for vengeance against larger-than-life criminals as symbols of crime; and a hunger for mass involvement in anticrime action. Above all, the crime hysteria of the pre-Roosevelt depression had convinced the country that only Uncle Sam could deal with the crime problem now that it had become a symbol of national decline. When Franklin D. Roosevelt entered the White House, therefore, a pre-defined hero role already existed for someone on the federal level to step into. All Roosevelt had to do was to give the word.

2

The Crime War of the Thirties:
The Myth of the Gangster

The New Deal turned the nation's accumulated frustration into political capital by using the grassroots anticrime movement's ideas for its law enforcement program. Far from coming up with a conceptually new anticrime policy, the administration appropriated the movement's favorite ideas—new federal laws, new kinds of prisons, and, above all, the myth of an epochal struggle between lawful society and an organized underworld. The G-Man hero was born as Hollywood shorthand for this government policy of adopting pop culture's law enforcement fantasies as a guide for official action.

Though Franklin D. Roosevelt took office promising action, his choice of attorney general showed that law enforcement action was low on his list of priorities. To head the Justice Department, he chose Senator Tom Walsh, a just-married, seventy-four-year-old senator who was planning a "two month to ten week" honeymoon away from Washington immediately after the inauguration.[1] Walsh's selection made no sense if Roosevelt wanted the Justice Department to organize programs as dramatic as those planned by his other agencies. His choice of Walsh also showed that Roosevelt had no particular concern for the fate of the Bureau of Investigation or its director, J. Edgar Hoover. Walsh hated Hoover and loathed the bureau. The Montanan had served on the Senate Judiciary Committee that investigated the Justice Department's role in the Red Scare Raids of 1919–1920[2], and he had led the questioning of Attorney General A. Mitchell Palmer. Again and again he heard the attorney general defer to the young man who was sitting beside him: "I cannot tell you. . . . If you would like to ask Mr. Hoover, who was in charge of this matter, he can tell you."[3] Though Hoover claimed he was only obeying orders, Walsh was convinced Hoover was guilty of a "manifestation of man's inhumanity to man" when "justice for a season bade the world farewell."[4]

Nor was the Red Scare the only score Walsh had to settle with Hoover. In 1924 Hoover's bureau had tried to frame Walsh himself during the Teapot Dome scandals. When Burton Wheeler, Walsh's senatorial colleague from Montana, uncovered illegal sales of the naval oil reserves at Teapot Dome by Harding's secretary of the interior, Albert Fall, the Republican administration tried to block Wheeler's investigation by indicting him on trumped-up charges of corruption. The Bureau of Investigation was given the job of gathering evidence against Wheeler at a time when Assistant Director J. Edgar Hoover was in charge of day-to-day operations. Tom Walsh was Wheeler's defense counsel and discovered that Hoover had sent agents to Montana to see if they could dig up anything on Wheeler or on Walsh.[5] Walsh had reason enough to want to fire Hoover. As the inauguration approached there were rumors that Walsh was planning to do just that, but it was a pleasure Walsh was not to enjoy. On March 2, 1933, on the way to the inauguration, he died of a heart attack in his pullman car.

Walsh's death jeopardized plans for the dramatic display of "government action" Roosevelt was scheduling for Inauguration Day, March 4, 1933. Roosevelt had deliberately kept the country in suspense about his program, spurning Herbert Hoover's offer to join him in any bipartisan efforts during the interregnum. Roosevelt wanted to start his administration with a sign of a clean break with the past, and the proclamation of a bank holiday shutting down the financial system was to be the most dramatic sign that the country had entered a new era. In order for this unprecedented action to have a semblance of legality, Roosevelt needed an opinion from the attorney general that this would be within his prerogatives under a 1917 monetary law. To ensure that the opinion would be ready on Inauguration Day, Roosevelt huddled with Secretary of State-designate Cordell Hull and released the name of a stand-in nominee for attorney general. The man was Homer Stillé Cummings.

The sixty-three-year-old Cummings was a loyal Roosevelt political operative who had already been rewarded with the governorship of the Philippines. His own elective career had gotten no further than three terms as mayor of Stamford, Connecticut, and an unsuccessful run for the U.S. Senate in 1916.[6]

Homer Cummings took office as temporary attorney general with no mandate except to take care of Justice Department housekeeping until a permanent appointment could be made. As he went to work on the prosaic task of preparing the papers for the bank holiday, however, events had been set into motion that would make the bespectacled, owl-faced, accidental attorney general one of the most famous men in America.

Attorney General Homer Stillé Cummings, architect of the New Deal's war on crime.

Nothing in Cummings's background tagged him as a budding crime-buster. Cummings did have extensive experience in criminal law and a knowledgeable interest in criminology and penology, but he also had a record as a scrupulous civil libertarian alert to the danger of debasing justice to appease public hysteria.[7] Nor did Cumming's boss in the White House have a past that indicated a desire to become a crime crusader. Roosevelt had belonged to the National Crime Commission during the twenties, but as governor of New York he had fought for repeal of the three-time-loser law, one of the grassroot anticrime crusade's pet panaceas. During the presidential campaign Roosevelt had steered clear of law and order topics, confining himself to platitudes about reforming parole procedures and improving rehabilitation in the prisons. Roosevelt came into office in 1933 bound by no promises except a pledge to repeal prohibition. He certainly had not committed himself to a war on crime.

But while neither Cummings nor Roosevelt started by intending to lead an anticrime crusade, there were forces at work in Washington that in retrospect made it almost inevitable that the Justice Department would eventually launch a war on crime. As the New Deal unveiled its program for combating the depression, something close to a war fever took hold of the cabinet. The Agriculture Department proclaimed a "war" on farm surpluses and rural poverty. The CCC was "fighting" youth unemployment and soil erosion. The NRA was "marching" against low prices and destructive competition. Sooner or later the martial fervor was going to infect the Justice Department's ribbon clerks and paper shufflers.

Roosevelt's inaugural address was a call to arms boiling with military metaphors: the nation was to "move as a trained and loyal army willing to sacrifice for the good of a common discipline." The nation needed leadership, and he was going to provide that leadership: "In the event that the Congress shall fail . . . and in the event that the national emergency is still critical, I shall not evade the clear course of duty that will then confront me. I shall ask the Congress for the one remaining instrument to meet the crisis—broad Executive power to wage war against the emergency, as great as the power that would be given to me if we were in fact invaded by a foreign foe."[8]

There was a remarkable consistency in the military style of Roosevelt's administrators, and Homer Cummings could not have helped being impressed and influenced. Each of Roosevelt's agency heads developed his own programs; all employed military imagery to mobilize their constituencies. The agency that set the style for the young New Deal was General Hugh Johnson's National Recovery Administration. Johnson, a West Point cavalry officer who had served as Bernard Baruch's assistant during the World War, turned the NRA into a crusade that mobilized the energy and imagination of the nation as nothing had since the Great War. Every large city held an NRA parade to kick off its recruitment drive, with citizens marching behind the flag and the NRA's Blue Eagle emblem. Businesses subscribing to their industry's code got permission to put the Eagle on their advertising and their windows. Individuals were given Blue Eagle lapel pins. Riding the crest of the public's joy at finally being able to "do something," Johnson supervised some seven hundred industrial codes governing everything from automobiles to burlesque. Averaging a speech a week, Johnson was the national drill sergeant, cajoling and threatening his raw recruits with horse-soldier invective.[9]

The NRA lasted until May, 1935, when the Supreme Court declared it unconstitutional. As an economic nostrum the NRA was a bust. Business revived only slightly, unemployment stayed high, and the industrial codes helped foster monopolies. Despite its ineffectiveness, however, the NRA gave the public what it wanted: involvement, leadership—and action.

According to novelist Leo Rosten (writing in 1935), national morale revived under Roosevelt because he offered the country "the altruism of a noble cause [and] the cameraderie of participation in mass activity. . . . There is the melodrama of flags, pageants, parades, extravagant oratory, and the glorious thrill of being worshipped by mothers, sweethearts, and the multitudes that line the boulevards." The New Deal's political success owed much less to the administration's relief and make-work programs than to Roosevelt's talent for invigorating his dispirited country with the emotional equivalent of armed combat. "We are waging a war," Rosten continued, "a war against unemployment, against social insecurity, a war for social justice. There was in the Blue Eagle, the codes, the honor rolls, the public stigmatizing of the New Deal all the panoply of a military campaign and a holy crusade."[10]

During 1933 and 1934 Roosevelt suspended normal political activity as a threat to the nation's fragile solidarity. He abolished traditional Democratic party functions like the Jefferson Day dinners and endorsed only nonpartisan events open to Republicans as well as Democrats. He fostered a cult of personality around himself and his family as a way of transcending party and class differences. A charity for crippled children was allowed to hold a nationwide Roosevelt birthday celebration to raise funds. His fireside chats were cast as reunions of the national family.

The common goal of all the New Deal programs was the revival of national solidarity,[11] and a military style was their unifying characteristic. The New Deal was trying, Roosevelt said, "to cement our society, rich and poor, manual worker and brain worker, into a voluntary brotherhood of freemen, standing together, striving together, for the common good of all." He was trying to create the "unity of purpose that is best for the nation as a whole . . . among many discordant elements," with the government serving as "the outward expression of the unity and leadership of all groups."[12]

Cumming's first speech as attorney general urged compliance with Roosevelt's recall of gold from private ownership. "It was the patriotic duty," he announced, "of those still hoarding gold to turn it in to the Treasury." Then came the threats. He told the press that he had ordered the Bureau of Investigation to prepare a list of gold hoarders, and that "ten thousand names had already been collected." (An echo of the "ten thousand public enemies.") He had no patience, he said, "with those who hold out in defiance of their government, and I brand them slackers." "Slackers" was World War I slang for draft dodgers, conjuring up the spectre of dragnets, summary imprisonment, and mob action. "Not one person who can be located will escape investigation. . . . They will be held up to scorn before their fellow citizens."[13]

Another early New Deal program Cummings defended was the NRA. He threatened legal terror against anyone who wore Johnson's Blue Eagle without first signing the pledge. Privately he told Johnson that actual prosecution would be divisive and self-defeating. "Enforcement was to be largely psychological," he admitted, "rather than legalistically punitive."[14]

Cummings's experience during the first hundred days of the New Deal convinced him that all of the New Deal programs depended for success on the public's confidence in the government; anything one department did to revive public confidence increased the chances for success in all the other departments. His earliest speeches show that he was being drawn to a concept of law that measured success by the contribution a measure made to social solidarity. The function of the law, Cummings said in a speech later that summer, is "to cement, and not to strain, the bonds of affection that exist between the people and the government they have erected."[15]

The first hundred days convinced Cummings that the New Deal was more than a government: it was a political movement whose essential philosophy was "government in action." "Our experience has shown," Cummings remarked in a 1935 address, "that what might have appeared to be public indifference was, largely, the apathy of the disillusioned, resulting from the frequent failure of public authorities to supply the service and the type of leadership to which the American people are entitled. Once a reasonable course of action has been projected, and representatives of federal, state, and local interests have been brought together for concerted action, public opinion is inspiringly spontaneous in its support of the common objectives."[16]

Cummings's first step towards defining a role for the New Deal Justice Department was to assert federal leadership of the grassroots law enforcement movement. During the spring of 1933 almost any citizens' group with an interest in the crime problem—the International Association of Chiefs of Police, the American Legion, the Daughters of the American Revolution—heard from Cummings. By mid-1933 Homer Cummings had become the most conspicuous figure in the anticrime movement. Anticrime rallies during the Hoover administration were populist demonstrations against the government; Cummings's presence transformed them into mass demonstrations of support for the New Deal and the anticrime program he was promising. He sent a telegram to a youth-against-crime rally at New York's Carnegie Hall on June 2, 1933, that was typical of the message he was delivering to the country during this period: "Any public gathering to further the ends of law and order and to strengthen the safeguards of the citizen in his guaranteed rights under constitutional government has a meaning and a message to all worthy citizens. Racketeering must not be permitted to thrive in a land of ordered liberty. It must be set down as a national menace, the existence of which negates lawful grants and guarantees to all citizens."[17]

In 1933 the United States Flag Association organized an anticrime drive whose purpose was "to arouse public opinion to support local efforts to eradicate criminals and racketeers" and "to build up an attitude of mind tending toward the eradication of lawlessness . . . through education of school children." The drive was kicked off on July 4, 1933, with "a declaration of freedom from crime" distributed to schools and youth groups.[18] For the next few months there was a busy schedule of events culminating in an October leadership conference in Washington with former Secretary of War Patrick Hurley as chairman. Hurley's keynote address announced that "a civic war on crime, in which the general enlistment of the American people will be sought, will be formally declared and a mass offensive will be planned. . . . What has been lacking among citizens up to now is a coordination of civic effort, a leadership which will unite citizens into a tremendously powerful force against which the scarlet army of crime cannot survive."[19] Hurley's speech was followed by hearings on topics like "The Press and Crime," "Motion Pictures and Crime," "The Negro and Crime," and "We Are at War." The plan was for participants to go home and organize support for law enforcement in their local communities.

Herbert Hoover would either have resented the Flag Association crusade, or he would have ignored it and so allowed the energy it stirred up to dissipate. Cummings's reaction was to bring the Association's drive under the umbrella of his anticrime program. FDR accepted the honorary chairmanship of the effort, and Cummings spoke on the NBC radio series sponsored by the Flag Association. Cummings's speech (titled "Predatory Crime") placed the administration's seal of credibility on the pop culture myth of a ritual struggle between society and an organized underworld. The country was, he said, "confronted with real warfare which an armed underground is waging upon organized society. It is a real war which confronts us all—a war that must be successfully fought if life and property are to be secure in our country." He promised that the New Deal would lead the country to victory in this war: "Organized crime is an open challenge to our civilization, and the manner in which we meet it will be a test of our capacity for self-government. It has been said that popular government is organized self-control. This is the kind of government which our forefathers set up and it is my confident belief that we shall not be recreant to our great heritage."[20]

Cummings's aggressive public relations offensive gave direction and leadership to the citizens' groups that had complained of Herbert Hoover's inaction and incompetence. Homer Cummings's Justice Department joined the public in demanding action against the lawless, with the attorney general at the head of the protesters. Citizens would continue to be involved in law enforcement activities under the New Deal, but the controversy about crime became a public dialogue between the nation and an attorney general who promised to use the ideas generated by the discussion to fashion the federal government's law enforcement policy.

Cummings also used his appearances before citizens' anticrime groups to stress the importance of public involvement in the war on crime. "The Department of Justice and the government," he repeatedly proclaimed, "must have public support to make its drive against gangsters a success."[21] Citizens had a moral obligation to stay informed about what the government was doing against crime, and to applaud the efforts of officialdom.

Cummings's speeches in the spring of 1933 helped create a consensus that he should take over leadership of the movement. The most prominent leaders of the law enforcement community lined up behind Cummings, and local law enforcement officials began to ask the federal government to coordinate the national effort. Frank Loesch of the Chicago Crime Commission, who had given up hope in the government under Herbert Hoover, asked the Justice Department to take over this Public Enemies List.[22] Local leaders notified Cummings that they would support the president if he had to declare martial law to deal with the threat of crime.[23]

More evidence that Cummings had succeeded in positioning the federal government at the head of the anticrime movement came in the increasingly frequent calls for Cummings to create an elite federal police force. In July, 1933, a columnist wrote that "it is my judgement that federal action is the only solution. Uncle Sam with his long arm can reach over extraditions now necessary between states . . . I favor a national police force for investigation and prosecution. The detectives of the United States will be like its soldiers. They will never know their next point of call. They will operate under centralized orders from Washington. They will have at their fingertips a complete international identification bureau. They will use radio, telegraph, telephone, photographs, fingerprints, Bertillon measurements—use in fact every science known to criminal detection." Once there was a national police force, he continued, "crime will be against society, not against a country or a city or a state. Prosecution will be by society, not by politically controlled organizations dependent for a living upon the votes of a few communities. . . . Then solution of crime will be sure in the vast majority of cases, prosecution will be genuine and speedy and efficacious."[24] The faith of the thirties—which was also the myth of FDR and the New Deal—was that the nation, if only it could unite, could accomplish anything it set its mind to.

By July, 1933, Cummings's position as the leader of the law enforcement movement was well enough established for him to begin to unveil the administration's program. The federal government, he announced, was readying a package of new laws that would "arm" the nation against racketeers. "Racketeering has got to a point where the government as such must take a hand and try to stamp out this underworld army. The preying of this army on the organized public must be stopped."[25]

For the rest of July the Justice Department talked up the idea of a "super police force," and at the end of the month Roosevelt announced that he had ordered Cummings to "report on the advisability of creating a super police force to check the growth of organized crime."[26] Throughout July there were rumors about the identity of the chief of this super police force. There was one report that J. Edgar Hoover would be sacked and Louis R. Glavis, chief of the Interior Department's investigators, brought in. Another rumor had one of James Farley's pals from New York City heading the new "crime bureau." On July 30, however, headlines announced the President's decision: "J. EDGAR HOOVER HEADS NEW CRIME BUREAU—DIVISION CREATED BY ROOSEVELT WILL WAR ON KIDNAPPERS AND RACKETEERS."[27]

There was less to this "new" crime bureau than met the eye. It was actually an amalgamation of three pre-existing agencies: the Prohibition Bureau (which had been transferred to the Justice Department in 1930), the Bureau of Identification, and Hoover's own Bureau of Investigation. The Prohibition Bureau was slated to disappear with the demise of prohibition, and Hoover was already in charge of the Identification Bureau, so the new Division was really only the old Bureau of Investigation with a new name and new publicity. Roosevelt and Cummings were launching their "war on crime" with the same 226 agents J. Edgar Hoover had been keeping out of sight since 1924, and there was no indication that the president or the attorney general intended to call up any reinforcements. All Roosevelt and Cummings had done was to put a new label on an old bureau, suggesting that they regarded the crime problem primarily as a crisis in public relations. The goal of the "new" crime program was to create a "new psychology" of confidence in the law and in society's ability to defend itself. Whenever Cummings discussed his new federal police force during its first weeks in existence, he did so in the context of public relations. He had decided to create an elite law enforcement agency, Cummings explained, because "at last public opinion has been sufficiently aroused to be of real assistance in the nation-wide drive. The Federal attack will have many ramifications. The first purpose is . . . to acquaint the public with the facts, to reinforce its demand for upholding the law."[28] The mere fact that FDR had created a federal police force demonstrated that the new administration had accepted the responsibility of providing anticrime leadership, thus laying to rest the fear that Washington did not have the courage to confront this threat to the nation.[29]

Shortly before naming J. Edgar Hoover as director of his super police force, Cummings had introduced Joseph B. Keenan, a gangbusting Ohio prosecutor, as his assistant in charge of the Criminal Division of the Justice Department. Cummings announced that Keenan would be in charge of the crime war—determining tactics, directing field operations, and prosecuting the major cases—reporting directly to Cummings. Hoover's super police force was described as a "mobile detachment" reporting to Keenan.[30] Cummings hoped that this command structure would ensure that the Division of Investigation's cases would be seen as part of the Justice Department's overall program, so that political credit generated by the federal war on crime would accrue to the whole administration, and not merely to the agents involved.

At the beginning of the Justice Department's anticrime crusade everyone had his assigned role. Cummings focused the attention of the public on selected cases as battles between society and the underworld. Keenan prosecuted these cases, while Hoover provided the legwork and muscle. Cummings wove each big case into a continuing Justice Department saga, an adventure cycle that demonstrated the solidarity of society, the strength of the law, and the potency of the government.[31] The NRA, the CCC, and the AAA were waging *their* wars against the depression, and Homer Cummings's Justice Department was giving the country a war against an even more dramatic villain, the public enemy.

The first headline adventure in Homer Cummings's crime war was the Kansas City Massacre. On June 17, 1933, a prisoner in handcuffs accompanied by seven lawmen (four Bureau of Investigation agents, a McAlester, Oklahoma, police chief, and two Kansas City detectives) stepped off a train at Kansas City's Union Station. The prisoner was

Frank "Jelly" Nash, an escaped convict on his way back to the federal prison at Leavenworth.

Nash was a big man in the Midwest underworld with famous friends like Machine Gun Kelly, Alvin Karpis, Doc Barker, and Verne Miller. Nash's arrest set off an underworld panic: he knew too much for his pals to risk his being interrogated. Three gunmen were waiting for Nash and his captors at Union Station: Verne Miller was the leader. Adam Richetti was there also, but the identity of the third man is still a mystery. The bureau has always claimed that it was Charles "Pretty Boy" Floyd, and, though Floyd always denied any involvement, on that assumption the bureau hunted Floyd to his death.

As the lawmen opened the door of their car, the Miller gang, all armed with machine guns, stepped out of hiding. The lawmen went for their guns and the machine guns opened fire. In an instant four lawmen, including Special Agent Raymond J. Caffrey, were dead. Two other special agents were badly wounded, and Frank Nash lay dead on the ground, killed in the first burst.

Cummings immediately recognized the propaganda potential of the incident. He issued a statement that he "accepted the murder of a Department of Justice agent among the victims as a challenge to the government and ordered the entire government to work on the case. . . . The slaying of Raymond J. Caffrey, the Department of Justice man, was accepted by Attorney General Cummings as outright defiance of a government agency which gangdom has long respected."[32]

In all the big cases of 1933 and 1934 the media focused on Attorney General Cummings as the leader of the federal war on crime. Cummings led the press in publicizing the cases as important episodes in a battle in which authority, symbolized by the Justice Department and Homer Cummings, invariably triumphed. As the crime war continued, Cummings provided a running commentary from the Justice Department that underlined the epic significance of it all.[33] On July 12, 1933, for example, when a John J. O'Connell of Albany was kidnapped, Cummings turned the Justice Department loose on the case and proclaimed "It is almost like a military engagement between the forces of law and order and the underworld army, heavily armed. It is a campaign to wipe out the public enemy, and it will proceed until it succeeds."[34]

A few weeks later, news of the most sensational kidnapping of the Roosevelt years reached Washington. On July 22 George "Machine Gun" Kelly, his wife, and their gang had abducted Oklahoma City oilman Charles F. Urschel and demanded a $200,000 ransom. FBI publicists later turned this case into one of the most important episodes in the bureau legend, the case in which they won their name of "G-men"; but while the case was in progress it was Homer Cummings, busy building up public support for his crime crusade, who turned it into a test of strength between society and the underworld. It was Joseph Keenan, as Cummings's assistant, who turned the trial into a ritualistic triumph for the national government over the "army of crime": Keenan told the jury that "the interest of the nation is focused on the drama now coming to a close in this courtroom. We are here to find an answer to the question of whether we shall have a government of law and order or abdicate in favor of machine gun gangsters. If this government cannot protect its citizens, then we had frankly better turn it over to the Kellys, the Bates, the Baileys [Kelly's accomplices] and the others of the underworld and pay tribute to them through taxes."[35] The FBI later rewrote the history of these cases to make Hoover and his special agents the featured heroes, but while they were in progress, Homer Cummings was the undisputed star.

Actually Hoover's bureau was only one of Cummings's ploys to move the Justice Department to the front of the law enforcement movement. Another idea that Cummings appropriated from popular culture was the "super prison" for the super criminals his "super police" were catching. Spectacular escapes like Frank Nash's from Leavenworth made a new maximum-security federal prison a sensible idea, but the proposal's chief attraction to Cummings was its publicity value. The public wanted proof that the government was getting tough, so adopting the popular notion of an American Devil's Island was a made-to-order way of giving the country what it wanted.

On August 1, 1933, just two days after naming Hoover to lead the Division of Investigation, Cummings sent a memo to Assistant Attorney General Keenan: "In the agenda of things to be considered, when we get around to it, would it not be well to think of having a special prison for racketeers, kidnappers, and others guilty of predatory crimes, said prison to be in all respects a proper place of confinement? . . . It would be in a remote place—on an island, or in Alaska, so that the persons incarcerated would not be in constant communication with friends outside."[36] Cummings learned from the director of the Bureau of Prisons, Sanford Bates, that the army was willing to give him the military prison in San Francisco Bay. By October 12, 1933, Cummings, speaking on the Flag Association's radio series, said he was building a jail for convicts with "advanced degrees in crime," a kind of post-graduate penal colony. Among the first guests, he said, would be Machine Gun Kelly and Harvey Bailey (one of the Urschel kidnappers); Al Capone would be lodged there as soon as special accommodations were ready. Alcatraz, he explained, would be a symbol of the New Deal's determination to use whatever means might be necessary to repress crime: "Here may be isolated the criminals of the vicious and irredeemable type so that their evil influence may not be extended to other prisoners who are disposed to rehabilitate themselves."[37] A few months later Cummings sent the first "post-graduates" from other prisons to Alcatraz; Al Capone joined them there soon after.

As the public reaction to the government's prosecution of Al Capone showed, the country was demanding that criminals be given new and more impressive punishments for their crimes. Setting up Alcatraz satisfied this demand, and gave American popular culture a new symbol of the ultimate penalty short of death which captured the public imagination and became an instant part of American folklore and popular entertainment.[38]

Cummings preserved the momentum of his anticrime program by announcing something new—like the "Division of Investigation" or the "super prison"—every six months or so, heralding each new addition to the program as another breakthrough in law enforcement. He used whatever case the department was working on as a reason for supporting the administration's newest brainchild. Years afterwards only the cases would be remembered, while the "law enforcement innovations" the cases had been used to publicize were forgotten, but the crimes and Cummings's proposals were originally two sides of the same coin. Popular culture has come to regard the Dillinger case as the climax of the thirties war against the gangsters, but one reason Dillinger became as famous as he did was that Cummings and Roosevelt used him to generate support for their law enforcement proposals of 1934, the Attorney General's Twelve Point Crime Program.

Cummings had promised the country comprehensive new laws to arm the federal government against the underworld for battle in what he called "the twilight zone" between federal and local jurisdiction. Finally on April 19, 1934, Cummings announced that he was placing before Congress twelve recommendations for strengthening federal law enforcement.[39] His proposals included measures against interstate racketeering, transportation of stolen goods, interstate flight to avoid prosecution, assaulting federal officers and robbing banks; there was also a collection of amendments to the criminal code that strengthened the hands of prosecutors, and a prohibition on the sale of machine guns and concealable weapons. Cummings's proposals were incorporated in twenty-one bills passed by Congress during the late spring and summer of 1934. Among them was a bill permitting FBI agents to carry weapons and make arrests.

Roosevelt and Cummings presented the 1934 crime control bills as a dramatic response to John Dillinger's rampage through the Midwest during the spring of 1934. When Dillinger escaped from an FBI ambush near Little Bohemia, Wisconsin, in April, 1934, the headlines announced that the "NEW DILLINGER KILLINGS STIR THE PRESIDENT AND HE ASKS QUICK ACTION ON CRIME BILLS." "Aroused by the latest escapades of bandit John Dillinger, President Roosevelt has requested early pas-

sage of a sheaf of bills greatly enlarging the police powers of the Federal
Government. . . . One of the measures would bear directly on Dillinger's Wisconsin clash. This bill would make it a Federal crime to kill
an officer of the Federal government."[40] Cummings used the same incident to demand funds from Congress for planes, armored cars, and four
hundred more agents.

During 1933 and 1934 Homer Cummings's personality and political
rhetoric united the various fronts of the administration's war on crime.
He spaced each of his proposals to have an incremental effect on public
opinion. By mid-1934 the country had become used to a constant barrage of new anticrime measures coming out of the Justice Department.
More than anything else this constant barrage of law enforcement publicity, personally orchestrated by Homer Cummings, *was* the 1930s war
on crime. Only later did popular culture's need for myths and action
heroes remove Cummings from the central position he actually occupied in this war and expand the FBI's role until the bureau finally
eclipsed the rest of the crime crusade in the public's memory.

When Roosevelt signed the Crime Control Laws on May 18, 1934, he
made it clear that the administration's intent was to mobilize public
opinion against crime, and not simply to unleash the Division of Investigation against the gangs. The *Times* ran the headline "ROOSEVELT
OPENS ATTACK ON CRIME SIGNING SIX BILLS AS 'CHALLENGE'—HE CALLS
ON PEOPLE TO JOIN WAR ON UNDERWORLD." In his remarks at the signing ceremony he described the impact he hoped the laws would have on
public opinion:

These laws are a renewed challenge on the part of the Federal Government to
interstate crime. They are also complementary to the broader program designed
to curb the evildoer of whatever class. In enacting them the Congress has
provided additional equipment to the Department of Justice to aid local authorities. Lacking those new weapons, the Department has already tracked
down many major outlaws and its vigilance has spread fear in the underworld.
With additional resources I am confident that it will make still greater inroads
upon organized crime.

I regard this action today as an event of the first importance. So far as the
Federal Government is concerned, there will be no relenting. But there is one
thing more. Law enforcement and gangster extermination cannot be made completely effective so long as a substantial part of the public looks with tolerance
upon known criminals, permits public officials to be corrupted or intimidated
by them or applauds efforts to romanticize crime.

Federal men are constantly facing machine gun fire in the pursuit of gangsters. I
ask citizens, individually and in organized groups, to recognize the facts and
meet them with courage and determination.

I stand squarely behind the efforts of the Department of Justice to bring to book
every lawbreaker, big and little.[41]

Roosevelt's sweeping claim that the Justice Department now had the power to "book every lawbreaker, big and little" effectively slammed the door on public demands to transfer all police power to the federal government. The Crime Control Laws of 1934 restricted federal responsibility to the "box office" crimes of the era—kidnapping and bankrobbery—and made sure that Washington was not saddled with the impossible task of dealing with local crime or offenses committed by politically protected criminal organizations. Cummings had a mandate from Congress to pick and choose his cases; he could thus commit the federal government to attacks on the criminals whose conviction promised the greatest publicity payoff and he could avoid the kind of local crime that was impossible to eradicate. He established a policy that J. Edgar Hoover adhered to for the rest of his career—he would accept combat with celebrity criminals who had become symbols of the crime problem, but he would refuse any formal responsibility for the crime problem itself.

By the end of fall, 1934, Cummings's federal enforcement edifice was all but complete. Intense public support for federal law enforcement, generated by a stirring series of Justice-Department-versus-Public-Enemies adventures, had rallied the entire law enforcement community behind Cummings's leadership.[42] Each element in his program—his "super police," Alcatraz, his Twelve Point Crime Program, his war against the gangsters—had been presented as part of a drive to unify American law enforcement and provide the police with the public support he said would make the movement irresistible. All that remained was for him to establish a formal structure that would bind together the informal law enforcement confederation that was held together only by Homer Cummings's personality and leadership.

In December, 1934, Cummings summoned the American law enforcement establishment and representatives of major citizens' groups to Washington to discuss a law enforcement alliance.[43] This was the Attorney General's Conference on Crime, meeting December 10–13, 1934, attended by over six hundred delegates: state attorneys general, United States marshals and attorneys, police chiefs and commissioners, and representatives of over seventy organizations, including bar associations, labor unions, churches, educational associations, philanthropic organizations, and the entertainment industry. The conference was intended to mark the birth of a permanent and unified national law enforcement alliance.

FDR opened the conference with a call for a sustained law enforcement crusade that would enlist the entire nation, especially "the genius of the younger generation." The conference's task was "to build up a body of public opinion, which, I regret to say, is not in this day and age sufficiently active or alive to the situation in which we find ourselves. I want the backing of every man, woman, and every adolescent child in every state of the United States, and every county in every state—their backing for what you and the officers of law and order are trying to accomplish." Roosevelt congratulated Cummings for what he had already done to create such a movement: "The country knows that under his leadership we are getting better results than ever before."[44]

More than two hundred proposals were submitted for the consideration of the conferees. Cummings focused the discussion on two questions: how public opinion could be rallied and maintained in support of the movement, and how the American law enforcement community could be reorganized into a harmonious and efficient system.[45]

The press and the entertainment industry were nervous about their bad reputations as glorifiers of crime, so they were eager to cooperate in "molding public opinion to demand the end of crime." Carl E. Milliken of the Motion Picture Producers Association and radio news commentator H. V. Kaltenborn promised to do their best to build public support for the police.[46]

The conferees also decided that it was the duty of law enforcement officials to publicize themselves and their work so that the public would identify with the law. In Cummings's closing address he said, "There is the question of public support. This will involve the proper interpretation of the work of officials to the public, so that the people may be informed of what is going on, and why, to the end that a healthy morale may be developed which will strengthen the work of honest officials, and so affect the psychology of our people that there will be a universal abhorrence of crime and a fixed determination to eradicate it."[47]

Cummings's rationale for the high-powered publicity campaign he had been engineering was his conviction that the ultimate weapon against crime was the public's respect for the law, respect that depended upon the manipulation of public opinion. Publicity was therefore an integral and essential part of law enforcement. The priority J. Edgar Hoover later gave to public relations had its origin in Homer Cummings's concept of law enforcement as a national movement totally dependent on public support for its success.

Public support without effective organization soon evaporates, so the conference discussed the coordination (but not unification) of the nation's police. Cummings persuaded the conference that local police departments should be "coordinated" through an interlocking series of compacts. The federal government should serve as a "clearing house for information" and an "authoritative moving force for continued activity." The Justice Department would be responsible for interstate crime, filling in the gray area between local jurisdictions. Cummings told the conference that the Justice Department should not "extend activities in violation either of constitutional limitations or the customs of our people. The motive is to attempt to meet a need which has long existed, and to assist, complement and serve the law enforcing agencies of America."[48]

As a symbol of this coordination Cummings proposed (and got the conference's approval for) a "West Point of Law Enforcement," a "national scientific and educational center" in Washington for training police officers. This police academy was to be the capstone of his coordinated national law enforcement system. Far more than a police school, it was to be a "national institute of criminology" and a "bureau of crime prevention." It would

assemble, digest, and translate into practical form reports of improvements in the various branches of the administration of criminal justice, . . . educate civic organizations in different parts of the country as to the nature of these materials, their availability, and how they may be used locally to improve the administration of criminal justice and to help in the prevention of delinquency and criminality . . . and conduct a training school. . . . A primary concern of the proposed new unit of the Department of Justice will be the development of methods for dealing effectively with young pre-delinquents and delinquents for the purpose of checking crime at its source.[49]

The proposed law enforcement institute was to be a symbol of the cooperation Cummings was trying to develop between all elements of the law enforcement community.

The conference heard Cummings emphatically reject a monolithic national police force, not just because of the political risks it entailed for the administration, but because such a policy would have changed the nature of his crusade. In the spirit of the New Deal Cummings preferred to rely on high morale and a sense of common purpose rather than formal structure. For Cummings, the mobilization of the population was not merely a means to an end; it was an end in itself, a way of repairing the tattered social fabric and self-confidence of the country. Public support and high morale within the law enforcement community sustained by crime-fighting publicity would be a substitute for a more formal kind of unification.[50]

Homer Cummings's Crime Conference of December, 1934, was the anticrime movement's peak,[51] the pause before the decline. Even while Cummings was triumphantly presiding over his crime conference, movie studios in Hollywood and editorial offices in New York were beginning to turn the FBI, rather than the Justice Department, into the symbol of the movement. While the media's glorification of the G-Men was sapping the vitality from the grassroots anticrime movement, Cummings had to devote more and more of his energy to the administration's confrontation with the Supreme Court. By 1937 he was the principal strategist and lobbyist for Roosevelt's court-packing plan, and when that was defeated, his political influence was at end. J. Edgar Hoover was left as the leader of the anticrime movement, or what remained of it, in the eyes of Congress and the nation.

But soon, with Cummings in eclipse, very little was left of the anticrime movement. The FBI's media-inflated reputation was resented by other law enforcement groups, while the focus on G-Man dramatics transformed the public from participants in a crusade to spectators. Homer Cummings himself had singlehandedly held the movement together in his dual status as a political figure in the New Deal and a symbol of the law. The cross-fertilization between Roosevelt's mobilization of American society and the crime crusade was what had briefly turned law enforcement into a national cause. With Cummings out of the picture, Hoover was left adrift as a symbolic leader with no movement to lead.

The two years J. Edgar Hoover served Homer Cummings as a faithful lieutenant were decisive in forming his ideas about law enforcement policy. From Cummings, Hoover learned to see his role as one of shaping and guiding public opinion, first in support of law enforcement, later in support of the values of "Americanism." He adopted many of Cummings's methods: speeches at law enforcement meetings, radio addresses to the public, cooperation with civic anticrime groups. He tried to turn the FBI itself into the agency for the coordination of local law enforcement that Cummings had dreamed of, and he substituted his own FBI National Academy for Cummings's West Point of Law Enforcement.[52]

Hoover continued Cummings's policy of trying to build support for the law by providing dramatic confrontations between symbols of evil (public enemies) and symbols of good (G-Men). When the momentum of Cummings's crusade slowed, Hoover tried to revive it by substituting new public enemies—Nazi spies, Communists, Black Panthers, the New Left, even Martin Luther King—for the gangsters of the depression. Above all, Homer Cummings's example gave J. Edgar Hoover the lifelong goal of leading a national law enforcement movement sustained by popular enthusiasm. For the next forty years, however, instead of national law enforcement policy and a coordinated national drive against crime, the country got the myth of the G-Man.

3

Hollywood and Hoover's Rise to Power:
The Myth of the G-Man

At the end of 1934 Homer Cummings was the nation's unchallenged symbol of law enforcement. For two years he had been giving the Roosevelt administration a spectacular run of public relations triumphs. He had managed to restore the nation's confidence that crime was under control by bagging trophies like John Dillinger, Machine Gun Kelly, Pretty Boy Floyd and Baby Face Nelson.

One year later Homer Cummings had been completely displaced as the public's favorite cop by his subordinate in the Justice Department, J. Edgar Hoover. The adulation that carried Hoover into power was based on the Justice Department's gangbusting exploits of 1933 and 1934, but at the time of those front-page adventures the public had never seen Hoover play anything but a supporting part to Homer Cummings's lead. Tom Wicker has said that J. Edgar Hoover wielded more power, and wielded it longer, than any man in American history,[1] but that power did not spring spontaneously from the real accomplishments of the FBI. It was based on popular entertainment's accounts of those events in a wave of G-Man stories, movies, and radio shows that began in 1935. Hoover's emergence as the symbolic leader of American law enforcement was a vivid demonstration of public opinion's power to reshape political realities in the United States, and the popular arts' power to determine what the public believes.

Homer Cummings's success resulted from his insight that the thirties' crime problem was not so much a crime problem as a political crisis.[2] The alarm over the supposed crime wave was a symptom of a more general fear: that under the impact of the depression, American society would no longer be able to enforce the rules that held it together. This incoherent dread took the tangible form of a morbid preoccupation with the sensational, but basically trivial, depredations of a handful of media-inflated thugs.

Since Cummings diagnosed the crime wave as a political problem, he sought its cure through political action. His law enforcement policy was designed to involve all citizens in a national crusade that would give them a sense of the law's vitality and strength. Police officials and citizens' anticrime groups were enlisted in a federally led drive, while unorganized citizens were invited to participate vicariously in the spectacles of public combat Cummings staged between the FBI and big-name gangsters.

The enthusiasm that greeted Cummings's program proved he had been right. The panic over crime had been a plea for leadership that would defend national solidarity; the public had been ready to follow anyone who would provide it with a mass movement of national unity.

As long as Cummings could control his anticrime movement, it was a priceless political asset for the New Deal. But by the beginning of 1935 his crusade had grown so popular that it was out of control. It had taken on a life of its own, becoming legend as much as fact.

In February, 1935, word reached Cummings that a movie about the Justice Department was being filmed in Hollywood. The news made him nervous. He may have suspected that J. Edgar Hoover was striking out on his own after publicity, because in February Hoover wrote the attorney general a memo, evidently in response to a query from Cummings, affirming that "no representative of Warner Brothers Studios has ever contacted our Los Angeles office or contacted my office relative to any information desired for the making of any picture pertaining to the activities of this Division."[3] The movie Cummings was grilling Hoover about was G-Men;[4] whether or not the attorney general knew it at the time, he had good cause for worry. G-Men was the first important piece of popular entertainment based on the history of the FBI (there had been several radio programs during 1934). It was the first wave in a flood of G-Man glorification that would radically alter the balance of power in the Justice Department.

In February, 1935, Cummings could not have had much information about the film, since the final script of G-Men was not finished until February 14. One month later the shooting was well under way, and Cummings's curiosity had shifted to alarm. In March the Department of Justice began issuing a series of statements about the film to refute the studio's claim that it was an authentic record of the federal crime war. On March 23 Cummings issued a press release that disassociated the department from the movie:

It has been brought to the Department's attention that a motion picture newspaper has published an article stating that the Department has designated a former agent of the Federal Bureau of Investigation to act as technical advisor in connection with various motion picture productions said to be in course of preparation on the Pacific coast which purport to depict Department activities. Any statement in motion picture publications to the effect that the Department has authorized any person to furnish technical advice or assistance is untrue. The Department has approved no motion picture scenario or production purporting to deal with its work.[5]

In April *G-Men* was previewing throughout the country, accompanied by a massive publicity campaign that proclaimed it "THE FIRST GREAT STORY OF THE MEN WHO WAGED AMERICA'S WAR ON CRIME."[6] Warner Brothers notified the public that the studio had "performed a patriotic service by showing how one branch of the government's law enforcement agencies will wipe out gangland." Advertisements tried to make seeing the movie a patriotic duty: "Officials believe that the last hold of the criminal mobs on the imagination of the public will be broken by this picture, which shows criminals as they are—and how helpless they are when the government really starts after them."

Local theater owners were urged to stress the documentary and semiofficial character of the film. Properly handled, the studio advised, the film could be turned into a civic event with a parade and a speech by the chief of police. Lobby displays should include "firearms, tear gas bombs and submachine guns" on loan from the local police, who should also be asked to set up fingerprint apparatus in the lobby to fingerprint audience volunteers as "part of the city's war on crime."

The Justice Department continued to undercut Warner Brothers' claims of official status for the film. On April 27 *Motion Picture Daily* ran a story under the headline "JUSTICE FILMS GET WASHINGTON FROWNS":

Films based on the exploits of Uncle Sam's secret service have fallen under the ban of the men they seek to glorify. Edgar J. Hoover [*sic*] head of the bureau of investigation of the U.S. Department of Justice, has instructed his agents throughout the country not to attend preview showings of pictures with a secret service theme and to refuse any statements whatsoever regarding them. The operatives are permitted, however, when asked to comment to say merely that such pictures are not authorized by the Department of Justice. Hoover's order points out that the department has not sanctioned any films of this type.[7]

When the movie proved to be a resounding success[8] despite the Justice Department, the FBI was flooded with fan mail about the picture. Hoover had his office respond with a stock reply: "This Bureau did not cooperate in the production of *G-Men*, or in any way endorse this motion picture."[9]

Why was the Justice Department so concerned about *G-Men?* First of all, for reasons of bureaucratic prudence Hoover could not have openly endorsed the movie. The bureau still had many powerful enemies from the bad old days of the Wilson and Harding administrations. They would have loved to prove that Hoover had taken money appropriated for criminal investigations and spent it on publicity. On April 10, 1936, one of Hoover's most persistent foes, Senator Kenneth McKellar of Tennessee, told Hoover that the G-Man movies "virtually advertised the Bureau, because your picture was shown in connection with them frequently . . . and apparently . . . they were advertisements of your Department. I was just wondering what sums of money, if any, were contributed by the Department, or if we are contributing any to that." Hoover replied: "Not a cent has been spent in that sort of advertising. As a matter of fact it has been more or less objectionable to the Department, some of this publicity that has appeared in the motion pictures. . . . We have, in every instance, registered our objection. We cannot control it. Of course, we have indicated our official disapproval."[10]

Throughout his career J. Edgar Hoover wrote memos "for the record" to be produced later if necessary, so his comments on *G-Men* might simply have been the groundwork for a future defense of the bureau, evidence that the FBI had not bankrolled Hollywood's G-Man boom. But Hoover's characteristic concern for being able to defend his bureau against congressional criticism does not explain why he went beyond mere neutrality to show active disapproval of a film so sensationally useful to the bureau—the film, in fact, that put the FBI on the map of American popular culture.

The most likely explanation for Hoover's behavior is that Attorney General Cummings himself objected to *G-Men* and made hostility to the movie a Justice Department party line imposed from the top.[11] *G-Men* seemed to be a valuable piece of war-on-crime propaganda that could only have aided the Justice Department's efforts. Only from the unique point of view afforded by the attorney general's office would it have been possible to foresee the disruptive effect this film could have on the Justice Department's chain of command.

It also seems certain that the Justice Department's condemnation of *G-Men* was specifically aimed at that particular film, and *not* at anticrime pictures in general. Just a few months before he began his campaign against *G-Men,* Cummings had asked leaders of the radio and movie industries at his Washington Crime Conference to publicize law enforcement to arouse public opinion against crime.[12] Warner Brothers was thus fully justified in expecting publicity aid and official endorsement from an attorney general who had told them that it was the industry's civic duty to produce just this type of film. Only his alarm at what *G-Men* might do to his anticrime movement could have made

Cummings withdraw his blanket approval of anticrime movies and disown this film in the public press.

Only Cummings himself would have realized at once what was wrong with *G-Men*, because there was nothing the matter with anything in the film; the trouble was with what was not in the film, or rather who was not in the film. Here was a picture about Homer Cummings's war on crime. Here were filmed dramatizations of the Justice Department's fights with Dillinger, Floyd, and Nelson; here was an account of the new laws and powers that Homer Cummings had given the FBI. Here, in short, was a fast, exciting story of the anticrime crusade Cummings had created and led for the past two years. Insofar as a short fictional film could be complete, it appeared to be the complete story of Homer Cummings's days in Washington—except there was no Homer Cummings, no attorney general at all. *G-Men* was a glorification of the FBI, not as Homer Cummings had created it, an agency firmly under the control of the attorney general, but as it would become—a highly independent force led by a popular hero who received his mandate directly from the public, a force responsible only to the public, free from any effective political supervision. Such a national police force had been dreaded by all critics of the bureau since it had been formed in 1908, and for Cummings to watch Hollywood turn his FBI into just such an extragovernmental police force must have been hard to endure.

The story of *G-Men* was melodrama itself: a gang of crooks pursued by the FBI tries to bring the federal government to heel by kidnapping an agent's girlfriend. Only the verve of Jimmy Cagney's performance as the G-Man hero keeps the plot from seeming completely preposterous, and even his abilities cannot totally rescue the premise. What made *G-Men* one of the hit movies of 1935 was the glimpse it gave of a new breed of heroes in action—college-educated cops with new scientific tricks and a no-holds-barred strategy for dealing with hoodlums.

Cagney plays Brick Davis, a young lawyer who joins the FBI when his law-school roommate is gunned down while on assignment for the bureau. Cagney's Davis is tough, smart, and brash—exactly the same character, as many critics have pointed out, that Cagney played four years before in *The Public Enemy;* now he was cracking wise on the side of the law.[13] For character development the film depends on a collection of clichés—the nightclub dancer who loves Cagney but loses him to his new FBI career; the tough instructor at the bureau who hates Cagney when he first meets him but is won over by his bravery, loyalty, and daring; the instructor's sister who resents Cagney at first for coming on too strong, but falls for him in the end.

Years later Hoover's assistant director in charge of public relations, Louis Nichols,[14] complained that Cagney had played the agent as too much of an individualist. The bureau, said Nichols, was a "we" organ-

Cagney as Special Agent Brick Davis in G-Men *(1935).*

ization. (In his satirical *No Left Turns* former agent Joseph Schott claimed that the "we" were Hoover and his deputy, Clyde Tolson).[15] Nichols's reservations notwithstanding (and they only prove you can't please everybody), there was nothing in Cagney's characterization to wrinkle the Justice Department brow. If anything, Cagney's Phi Beta Kappa agent was too good to be true. For example, when a political boss tries to hire Cagney to defend a flunky who "got drunk last night and beat up his old lady," Cagney throws him down the stairs, saying indignantly, "Do you think I'd defend a guy like that? I'd rather beat his brains out. I don't want the case. It smells." After he tosses the "greaseball" out, Cagney explains, "I don't happen to like shysters, and that takes in blackmailers and ambulance chasers too."[16]

Neither could *G-Men* be faulted on the technical details it showed of FBI procedures. The picture labored to re-create scenes that the Justice Department had already made famous through publicity photographs. There were shots of the Justice Department Building; the camera peered through microscopes at bullets and fingerprints; the audience was brought into the FBI gym for boxing and judo instruction and was given a tour of the pistol and machine gun ranges. The film tried for a newsreel-like effect in its coverage of FBI procedures: the script called for reproduction as "accurately as possible" of the widely published photograph of a line of G-Men at machine gun practice, specifying that the guns should be "roaring while Marine Corps sergeants are working with the men." A "grim faced operative" at the firing range demonstrates the determination of the G-Men trainees by firing straight into the camera with the muzzle close to the lens.

These "documentary" episodes in *G-Men* were so popular that they became obligatory features of all subsequent FBI pictures. Inspired by these movies, visitors to Washington began to ask to see the real FBI laboratories and firing ranges, and Crime Records Division chief Louis Nichols had to begin organized daily tours of the facilities,[17] tours that are still among the most popular tourist attractions in the capital. Hollywood, Washington, and the public all liked these tours, and for the same reason: for the space of the film, or the time of the tour, citizens could share the agent's indoctrination and point of view, vicariously becoming agents themselves. This was exactly the kind of public involvement with police work that Homer Cummings had been working for two years to create.

Warner Brothers' publicity touted *G-Men* as a "shot-by-shot dramatization of gangdom's Waterloo,"[18] and in fact scriptwriter Seton Miller and director William Keighley did piece the plot together by cutting and pasting the most famous crime headlines of the previous two years. Of course a lot of touching up was necessary to compress two years of history into two hours of film. The Justice Department had corralled famous gangsters from all over the country during 1933 and 1934, and the only thing they had in common was that they were all famous. In order to turn their adventures into a coherent story the producers had to allow themselves a certain amount of freedom with the facts.

The villains of *G-Men*, Leggett, Gerard, and Collins, are modeled after the three most famous hoodlums of the early thirties: script notes describe them as "dangerous types . . . Leggett is the Pretty Boy Floyd type . . . Gerard, the 'Baby Face' Nelson type . . . and Collins the Dillinger." Actually Dillinger and Nelson had been for a short time members of the same gang. Floyd may have helped them rob a South Bend, Indiana, bank on June 30, 1934, shortly before Dillinger's July 22 death.[19] This tenuous relationship was enough for Seton Miller. He made the three the leaders of a close-knit gang, and then had the gang stage the two most famous shootouts in FBI history: the Kansas City Massacre of June 17, 1933, and the battle between the Dillinger gang and the FBI at Little Bohemia, Wisconsin, on April 22, 1934. Besides re-creating these two historical events, the movie has the gang rob the Federal Reserve Bank in New York and five small midwestern banks.

The film's intent was to improve on history by turning the great crimes of 1933 and 1934 into the unified assault upon society by an "army of crime" that was a 1935 pop culture convention, even though this dramatic unity was lacking in the historical events themselves. No one ever tried to connect Dillinger or Nelson with the Kansas City Massacre, while even Floyd claimed he had nothing to do with it. The film has Gerard (the "Baby Face Nelson type") stage the massacre to rescue Leggett (the film's Pretty Boy Floyd) from FBI custody. Though Frank Nash was really killed along with his FBI captors, Leggett manages to escape so that Cagney can catch him and personally take charge of his delivery to Leavenworth.

With their Pretty Boy Floyd in custody, the movie G-Men track the Dillinger and Nelson "types" to a Wisconsin lodge owned by the reformed mobster who helped Cagney through law school. Here again the film had to doctor history. The real assault on the Little Bohemia, Wisconsin, hideout of the Dillinger gang had been a monumental fiasco. Special agents under the command of Chicago chief Melvin Purvis and Assistant Director Hugh Clegg had rushed the lodge in the dark; while they were blundering in ditches and tangling themselves in barbed wire, watchdogs gave the alarm and the gang escaped through an undefended rear porch. In the confusion the agents opened fire and shot two hapless guests at the lodge who had chosen the moment of the FBI's attack to wander out to their car. One was killed and the other wounded. After escaping from the lodge, Baby Face Nelson killed one FBI agent and wounded another. The bureau's entire haul consisted of three terrified girls who had followed the gangsters to Wisconsin. Purvis was disgraced, and Hoover, who had gone to the press with the news that he had Dillinger surrounded, was humiliated.

The "affair at Little Bohemia," as Melvin Purvis called it in his autobiography,[20] was still fresh in the public's mind, and so Hollywood could not turn it into a complete triumph for the FBI; the movie did, however, absolve the bureau of any guilt for Dillinger's escape. The film shows no FBI confusion. Through no fault of the agents the gang's watchdogs sense their approach and start barking. No movie G-Men are killed in the raid, and with the exception of the "Dillinger-type" all the gangsters are killed or captured. The only innocent citizen killed is Cagney's old mobster friend, and he only because the Dillinger-type uses him as a human shield.

After tricking Cagney into shooting his own pal, the gangster kills the nightclub dancer who was Cagney's girlfriend before he joined the Bureau. Then he kidnaps Cagney's new girl, the sister of his FBI instructor.

These atrocities justify Cagney's obsessive pursuit of the Dillinger-type by giving him a revenge motive. The death of "Dillinger" is justified because it is the only way the girl can be freed.

Dillinger's capture actually had become an obsession with Hoover and the FBI. This gave rise to some criticism after Dillinger's death, because Dillinger's only federal crime had been interstate transportation of a stolen car—not quite a capital offense. Others said that the bureau could have taken Dillinger alive if it had wanted, while still others faulted the bureau for endangering the public in the final battle at the Biograph theater, where two women were wounded by stray FBI bullets.

It would have been risky for Warner Brothers simply to have restaged Dillinger's death at the Biograph. The studio had already violated the spirit of a Motion Picture Producers Association edict that "no picture on the life or exploits of John Dillinger will be produced, distributed, or exhibited by any member. This decision is based on the belief that . . . such a picture could be detrimental to the best public interest."[21] Re-creating the ambush at the Biograph would have violated the Production Code ban too flagrantly, so *G-Men*'s writers invented their own death scene for Dillinger, and in doing so, whether by necessity or by choice, they neatly answered all the objections to the way Dillinger had really died. They made Dillinger's death simply the inevitable outcome of melodramatic conventions—a friend's death has to be avenged; a heroine has to be rescued. Legal technicalities are dispensed with by moving the Dillinger case from the level of legal guilt or innocence to the stage of melodrama.

Besides reshaping the Kansas City and Little Bohemia incidents and Dillinger's death to suit their purposes, *G-Men*'s producers pulled in bits and pieces of other famous cases. The Lindbergh kidnapping is alluded to by having the movie's Pretty Boy Floyd captured when he passes a marked banknote. Every detail of the Lindbergh case was so famous that the audience would have picked up the reference to Bruno Richard Hauptmann's slip in using a marked bill at a Bronx gas station. The movie gives the impression that the trick was standard FBI procedure, when in fact the registered gold certificates had been placed in the Lindbergh ransom package at the insistence of Treasury Department Secret Service Chief Elmer Irey. A few years after *G-Men* had appeared, a journalist taking the public tour of the FBI headquarters would note that among the exhibits was a display explaining how marked bills had led "us" to Hauptmann, thus turning the film's error into "fact"—that the Lindbergh case was entirely an FBI operation.[22]

In *G-Men* the marked bill is discovered not at a gas station but at a flower shop. This allowed the film to recall another famous case, the flower shop murder of Chicago mobster Dion O'Banion by the Capone organization. Another sequence has the movie's FBI director set up a public enemies list to dramatize his attack on gangsters. The first names on the list, of course, are the movie's villains; but the next three names, "Van Ober" and "George and Fred Barret," would have made the audience recall the names of Dillinger's notorious friend (Homer) Van Meter and the two sons of Ma Barker, Doc and Fred Barker.

Throughout the thirties the public believed that there *was* a public enemies list, although Cummings and Hoover, sensitive to charges that they were ignoring the vast majority of criminals to concentrate on a few celebrities, steadfastly denied that there was a scoreboard. All "10,000 Public Enemies," they insisted, were being chased just as hard as Dillinger.[23] The public enemies list does seem to have been a creation of Justice Department reporters who borrowed the idea from the Chicago Crime Commission's famous list, because not until the fifties did the bureau itself begin its own "Most Wanted Fugitive Program." By showing the FBI director himself with the public enemies list, the film made the FBI conform, not to reality, but to the image created by the extravagant stories of the era's flamboyant crime reporters.

Whenever the movie used historical details they were invariably "improved" to turn the bureau into an infallible instrument that meted out to the unjust their just deserts. The FBI was the movie's *deus ex machina* that reordered history's confusion to suit the requirements of poetic justice. The sensational 1933 trial of Machine Gun Kelly and his wife for the kidnapping of Oklahoma oilman Charles Urschel is referred to, but the episode is altered so that the culprits get the penalty they would have had if movie audiences, instead of judges and juries, punished crimes. *G-Men* shows a teletype message to the FBI director telling him that "the Tulsa kidnappers" of "Borden" had been convicted and sentenced to death, a far more satisfying conclusion artistically than the life sentences handed down to the real kidnappers.

All the historical inaccuracies in the film moved reality in the direction of the public's beliefs and desires, so they seem to have gone unnoticed. The movie reviewer of *Literary Digest,* for example, wrote that "the action of 'G-Men' follows the Federal hunt of the late John Dillinger and his colleagues during three years with remarkable fidelity to known facts."[24] *G-Men* and other films like it gave the FBI credit for what the public wished had happened rather than measuring its performance by what actually had happened. As early as 1935 the FBI had become a fantasy projection of the public's desire for vengeance against criminals. Since Homer Cummings's own public relations efforts had promoted the same kind of legend-building, it is unlikely that the film's historical inaccuracy would have bothered him.

Homer Cummings felt threatened, but not because Jimmy Cagney made an unsatisfactory G-Man, or because the movie was an inaccurate portrayal of FBI procedures, or because the film habitually departed from the historical record. Homer Cummings was a politician, and in 1935 crime-fighting was politics—politics for big stakes. Homer Cummings would have judged *G-Men* by its political impact, by the effect that it might have on the public's image of himself, his Department of Justice, and, finally, on the public's support for the New Deal. By these standards the attorney general must have seen at once that *G-Men* was, for him and for his program, a major political disaster.

The New Deal's crime policy was ultimately based on the public's acceptance of the attorney general as the national symbol of law enforcement. The attorney general was the human link between the public's crusade against crime and the New Deal's political program of national unity; by assuming leadership of the national anticrime movement Homer Cummings had made crime-fighting one of the most politically productive of all of the New Deal programs. As each successive public enemy fell before federal bullets or heard the doors of Alcatraz or Leavenworth clank behind him, the country saw more proof that the Roosevelt administration had succeeded in reestablishing order in the depression- and prohibition-disordered country. So much effort had gone into building the public image of the attorney general and so much political benefit had been reaped from Homer Cummings's role as a public symbol that Cummings would have judged *G-Men* by the role that it assigned to the attorney general in the nation's war on crime.

He must have been astounded by what he saw. The historic part that Homer Cummings had played in conceiving, organizing, and leading the federal crusade against crime was handed over to a man who was, both in fact and in public image, Cummings's unquestioned subordinate in the Justice Department: the director of the FBI. In *G-Men* the FBI director is a barely disguised J. Edgar Hoover. The script describes "Bruce J. Gregory" as a "strong-faced man of about thirty-nine [precisely Hoover's age in early 1935] very young for his important post." All of Cummings's accomplishments, even some of his very words, were assigned to the FBI director. Not only had Warner Brothers rewritten history; the studio had engineered a departmental coup d'état.

In 1933 Homer Cummings had made the Kansas City Massacre the pretext for proclaiming the federal government's anticrime crusade. He had publicized the crusade by administrative reorganizations that upgraded the Bureau of Investigation to the status of a Justice Department division and established a federal prison for top criminals at Alcatraz. After a year of incessant anticrime publicity he had gone to Congress with his package of anticrime measures, and then he had skillfully exploited the uproar over John Dillinger to speed the bills through Congress during the spring and summer of 1934.[25]

G-Men telescopes history by having the Kansas City Massacre spark not only the war on crime but the laws that armed the FBI a year later.

The movie's re-creation of the Kansas City Massacre is quickly followed by a series of newspaper headline dissolves: "RAILWAY STATION MASSA-CRE—4 OFFICERS SLAIN, 2 WOUNDED," "MACHINE GUNS BUTCHER OF-FICERS," and so on, until the relation between the filmed incident and the actual crime is firmly established. The headlines are immediately followed by a shot of the Capitol building and an interior shot of a congressional committee room in which a group of "serious-faced" Congressmen are listening to a "grim" and "earnest" speech by FBI Director Gregory:

"The state police cannot combat these criminals . . . neither can city police! The law prevents them from following criminals across state lines! With the automobile and aeroplane, these gangs can get from one state to another in a few hours. The Department of Justice is handicapped! . . . A Federal Agent can't carry a gun! He can't even make an arrest without getting a local warrent first! Gentlemen, . . . if you will back us by national laws with teeth in them . . . that cover the whole field of interstate crime, . . . that let us work to full effect with state police agencies, . . . these gangs will be wiped out."

After a suspenseful pause, the chairman of the committee asks Gregory, "What laws do you need most?" Gregory's reply is an outline of the Attorney General's Twelve Point Crime Program Cummings had submitted to Congress in the spring of 1934. "Make bank robbery and kidnapping federal crimes!" Gregory tells Congress.

"Make it a federal crime to kill a Governmental Agent . . . to flee across the State Line to escape arrest or to escape testifying as a witness. Arm Governmental Agents . . . and not just with revolvers! If these gangsters want to use machine guns—give the Special Agents machine guns . . . shotguns . . . tear gas and everything else! This is war! Understand . . . I don't want to make them a group of quick-trigger men, but I do want the underworld to know that when a Special Agent draws his gun, he is ready and equipped to shoot to kill with the least possible waste of bullets!"

From the committee room the scene shifts to a joint session of Congress, and then to another series of newspaper dissolves: "GOVERN-MENT DECLARES WAR ON CRIME . . . CONGRESS RUSHES THROUGH NEW CRIME LAWS . . . DEPARTMENT OF JUSTICE STARTS DRIVE."

As he watched this scene, Homer Cummings might have sensed control of the FBI slipping from his grasp. The movie had taken the message he had delivered to Congress and had put it in the mouth of another man. Cummings knew too much about public opinion and its manipulation—he had done almost nothing else for two years—not to realize the significance of this deft substitution of FBI director for attorney general.

Whether the movie was cause or effect—and in popular culture the two are impossible to separate—a momentous shift was taking place in the public's image of his bureau. The FBI's image was no longer a reflection of Washington realities. It was a projection of Hollywood formulas, and these formulas dictated that Cummings's historical role be handed over to J. Edgar Hoover.

The movie redefined the FBI agent as the latest incarnation of a century-old stereotype in popular entertainment, the action detective hero. The characterization of the action detective required him to operate outside the cumbersome institutions of the government and the law. An attorney general was not only irrelevant, but counterproductive in this formula, because he would have linked the G-Man hero to the system the action detective had been created to bypass.

The action detective formula did leave a role for the director, however. The G-Man was different from other action detective heroes because he had scientific training and could call on the FBI with its nationwide organization and elaborate scientific facilities to reinforce his individual derring-do. The director was needed to play the role of organizer and leader of the G-Man's team; he was trainer, adviser, and father-figure to the youthfully impetuous hero. He could play this role in the formula, however, only if he and his bureau, like the G-Man himself, kept their distance from the rest of the bureaucracy. Therefore the makers of *G-Men* changed the FBI from a conventional government agency existing within the normal structure of a chain of command which carried out policies determined by constitutional superiors. The movie G-Men and their director got their mandate, not from the president, not from the attorney general, but from the nation itself, represented by an extraordinary joint session of Congress.

G-Men and the films that followed it short-circuited the link between the attorney general and the people Homer Cummings had laboriously forged. Hollywood's G-Man pictures showed an FBI director who had entered into a compact with the public; this alliance would not be dissolved, despite the strains of the years, until after J. Edgar Hoover's death.

After 1935, in reality as on film, the attorney general faded from the public's image of federal law enforcement. Hollywood had done something Hoover would not have dared, something that Cummings could not prevent—it had turned the top G-Man into a star and it had demoted the director's boss to an offscreen nonentity. One expert in the star-making business, a Hollywood producer, years afterward stated: "Hoover is a star in his own right. I felt much as I did when I met Cary Grant—that this is a special person."[26] Once Hoover's stardom had been conferred, no one who depended on the public's good will (and by definition that included presidents and attorneys general) could afford to cross Hoover within his field of acknowledged supremacy. Hoover's power was given to him by the public, not by his superiors, and only the public could take it away. *The Nation,* one of Hoover's most persistent critics, complained on November 28, 1970, that "Hoover has gone his own stern way, and no President has had the wish or guts to bring him in line or retire him. . . . Mr. Hoover has got away with it . . . [because] he's box office . . . and he has been box office longer than anyone else, even John Wayne. . . . You can fight City Hall once in a while, and win, but you can't beat box office."[27]

After *G-Men* J. Edgar Hoover and his FBI could no longer be understood in terms of political science and criminology. From 1935 on, the G-Man's business was show business.

4

The G-Man and the Censors:
G-Man Movies and the 1935 Ban on Movie Gangsters

James Cagney was the movie G-Man who turned the FBI agent into a pop culture hero, but he was not the only Hollywood Special Agent of 1935. That year G-Man movies took the country by storm; there were seven of them in 1935, all trumpeted as spontaneous tributes to the country's newest idols: *Public Enemy's Wife; Public Hero Number One; Whipsaw; Mary Burns, Fugitive; Let 'Em Have It; Show Them No Mercy;* and, of course, *G-Men.*

Hollywood sold these pictures as its contribution to the national anticrime movement. "SEE UNCLE SAM DRAW HIS GUNS TO HALT THE MARCH OF CRIME" ran the ads for *Public Hero Number One. Public Enemy's Wife*'s ads featured a picture of its star G-Man, Pat O'Brien, shaking hands with J. Edgar Hoover. A studio urged exhibitors to turn the opening of a G-Man film into an anticrime rally with the theme "THE UNITED STATES DECLARES WAR ON CRIME": "All the various agencies engaged in the protection of the public—mayors, police chiefs, city officials, bankers, newspaper editors—should be contacted for their opinions and cooperation. Get their statements on 'Crime Does Not Pay' after private previews. Will the mayor issue a proclamation of an 'Anti-Crime Week' with [the] picture to be mentioned?"[1]

Behind all the patriotic ballyhoo, however, Hollywood had some very practical reasons for the 1935 blitz of FBI movies, reasons close to the industry's pocketbook. After two decades of complaining about Hollywood's exploitation of crime and violence, the censors had finally cracked down. A new censorship code, imposed at the end of 1934, had placed an outright ban on Hollywood's most profitable product, the gangster film.

Only by requesting specific exemption from the anti-gangster film rule to make a small number of "tributes" to the FBI could the filmmakers produce any violent crime pictures in 1935, and that exemption lasted only that one year. Not only did that abrupt prohibition against any violent crime pictures except those glorifying the FBI account for the flood of G-Man pictures in 1935, but it also helps explain their extraordinary impact. The American public, thoroughly addicted to movie violence, had suddenly had its supply cut off. The FBI movies gave Americans their last glimpse of the gangsters, albeit as corpses at the feet of triumphant G-Men. At a critical point in the cultural life of depression America, the G-Man movie was the most violent—and therefore the most popular—act in town.

Ever since *The Great Train Robbery* in 1903, traditionalists had been blaming movies for the progressive collapse of traditional morality. The result was censorship, beginning in 1909 in New York City, followed by Pennsylvania in 1911, then spreading throughout the rest of the country. In an attempt to defuse pressure for a nationwide official system of censorship, Hollywood created the National Association of the Motion Picture Industry in 1919. This had two functions: "first, placate the critics; second, try to block censorship."[2]

Until 1934 Hollywood's strategy of warding off meaningful national censorship by promising "self-regulation" was successful. In 1921 the studios hired Will Hays to run the Motion Picture Producers and Distributors Association of America censorship office. In 1927 Hays issued thirty-eight "don'ts" and "be carefuls" which the studios pledged to observe. In 1930 the industry weathered another storm by commissioning Father Dan Lord of Catholic Action and Martin Quigley of *Motion Picture Daily* to write a code of ethics for the movies, the Motion Picture Production Code, which the studios promptly ignored. For the filmmakers "the code and the Hays Office were tidy bits of camouflage behind which they would continue to do what they wished."[3] They particularly wished to continue to make the gangster movies that had been among their most profitable products since 1930.

Hollywood had been able to get away with the farce of self-regulation because censors could point to no objective proof that movies really were corrupting the country. Hollywood claimed the gangser movies, far from producing unsettled conditions, simply reflected America's inability (or unwillingness) to do anything about gang rule.

In 1933 Hollywood's enemies were finally able to make a scientific case for censorship documented by experimental as well as biblical evidence, and their new call for censorship coincided with the new national mood of confidence and support for the law stimulated by Homer Cummings's anticrime crusade. A few years before, one of the leaders of the censorship forces, William H. Short of the National Committee for the Study of Social Values, had decided that "the absence of an adequate and well-authenticated basis of fact has probably had much to do . . . with preventing agreement of civic-minded forces of the country on policies and programs of action for dealing with the problems of the screen."[4] He got a grant from the Payne Study and Experiment Fund to come up with the "well-authenticated basis of fact" that would get the censors the laws they wanted. In 1933 the results were ready, twelve volumes of surveys, statistics, and conclusions. Two of these volumes made an especially deep impression on the public: *Movies, Delinquency, and Crime* by Herbert Blumer and Philip Hauser, and a popular summary of the whole Payne project, *Our Movie Made Children* by Henry James Forman.

Blumer and Hauser's book was newsworthy because it based its case on interviews with convicts who explained how gangster movies had turned them into criminals. One prisoner said, "In my opinion it is a bad thing for young boys to go to the movies and see pictures showing men stealing. I saw a picture and thought I could do the same thing." Another said that "crime pictures led me to go crooked. Gambling and crook pictures led me to try to be a big shot. Movies had shown me the way of stealing automobiles and the charge for which I am now serving sentence." Still another told Blumer and Hauser that "the movies in my childhood were the principal cause of my downfall."[5]

The authors buried whatever qualifications and reservations they had about movies as a cause of crime in the footnotes. One note, for instance, pointed out that in one sample of 258 inmates, only 11 percent thought that movies had influenced their careers while 75 percent thought they had had no effect (14 percent did not respond).[6] The interviews themselves, which seemed conclusive proof of the link between movies and crime, were what made the headlines.

The Payne Foundation knew that public policy is shaped not by scientific research, but by the public's interpretation of that research, so a journalist, Henry James Forman, was commissioned "to resolve all hesitations, dramatize dry research findings and place the scholars's data firmly within the structure of familiar moral and social ideologies."[7] The resulting book, with the provocative title of *Our Movie Made Children*, created a sensation. Forman's conclusion was simple and direct: movies were "not merely a school, but a university of crime."[8]

In 1933 Americans were looking for scapegoats, and so *Our Movie Made Children*'s readers were ready to believe and to act. A film historian reports that "the Forman book was [probably] catalytic in persuading the industry" finally to enforce the tough code of ethics it had only pretended to adopt in 1930.[9]

Hollywood had been able to fend off censorship before because its critics had not created alliances with politically potent pressure groups. The 1934 drive was successful because two groups with political and moral clout—the Roman Catholic bishops and the professional associa-tion of the nation's chiefs of police—decided to support the censorship campaign.

The bishops started their drive with a sermon by the new apostolic delegate to the United States, Monsignor Giovanni Cicognani. "Cathol-ics are called," he announced late in the summer of 1933, "by God, the Pope, the bishops and the priests to a united and vigorous campaign for the purification of the cinema, which has become a deadly menace to morals."[10] The bishops organized the Episcopal Committee on Motion Pictures in November, 1933; and in April, 1934, they established their mass-membership division, the Legion of Decency. Within a few weeks seven and one-half million American Catholics had taken its pledge:

I wish to join the Legion of Decency, which condemns vile and unwholesome motion pictures. I unite with all who protest against them as a grave menace to youth, to home life, to country and to religion.

I condemn absolutely those salacious motion pictures which, with other degrad-ing agencies, are corrupting public morals and promoting a sex mania in our land.

I shall do all that I can to arouse public opinion against the portrayal of vice as a normal condition of affairs and against presenting criminals of any class as heroes and heroines, presenting their filthy philosophy of life as something acceptable to men and women. . . ."[11]

Soon this was shortened into a version which simply condemned "indecent and immoral pictures and those which glorify crime and criminals."[12]

When Protestant, Jewish, and civic groups, alarmed by the findings of the Payne researchers, supported the bishops, Hollywood tossed in the towel late in 1934. The producers agreed to abide by their 1930 code and to submit to a censor who could deny distribution to films that broke the rules. Joseph I. Breen, an ex-reporter already employed as an assistant to Will Hays, was hired to fill this job. At long last Hollywood was committed to real and substantial regulation of its pictures.

This production code all but outlawed the gangster movie. The pre-amble stated that "the intent of the Code is . . . to insure above all that crime will be shown to be *wrong* and that the criminal life will be loathed and that the law will *at all times prevail.*" [Italics in the original.][13]

More than anything else it had been the star quality of the actors who played the movie gangsters—Cagney, Robinson, and Muni—that had made gangster movies look like celebrations of crime. The code ordered that "criminals should not be made heroes, even if they are historical criminals."[14] This meant that criminals could neither be the objects of sympathy ("The treatment of crimes against the law must not make criminals seem heroic and justified"),[15] nor could they be "heroes" in the show business sense of having the most lines and scenes. This meant that stars would no longer be cast as criminals, since stars naturally got the fattest parts. Criminals would be played by extras or typecast heavies like Barton MacLane or Edward Pawley.

The code not only took away the gangster's star billing, but it stripped him of his favorite props: "the use of firearms should be restricted to essentials" and "the flaunting of weapons by gangsters or other criminals"[16] was forbidden. Worst of all, the code stated that gangsters had to turn in their machine guns, as much a part of their characterization as the cowboy's six-shooter: "There must be no display, at any time, of machine guns, sub-machine guns, or other weapons generally classified as illegal, in the hands of gangsters or other criminals."[17]

The code also decreed that the bad guys had to be dead or in jail by the end of the picture; they could not even kill a few cops before they bit the dust: "law enforcement officers should not be shown dying at the hands of criminals."[18] Gangsters could no longer scare the daylights out of the leading lady ("the words, gestures and actions of the criminal and the reaction of his victim to threats and intimidation by means of violence should not be presented on the screen")[19]; thugs could not reveal their character by wiping out crowds of extras ("action suggestive of *wholesale slaughter* of human beings will not be allowed by criminals in conflict with the police; in any conflict between warring factions of criminals; or in public disorder of any kind").[20]

Whole classes of crimes like kidnapping and arson were now off limits. The few crimes that the code would still allow could not be portrayed graphically ("details of crimes must never be shown"). The code also took away the basic motivation for most movie manhunts; the hero could no longer avenge the death of his buddy or the kidnapping of his girlfriend: "revenge in modern times shall not be justified."[21]

If *The Public Enemy* had had to dodge and weave its way through the code, it would have been a mere shadow of itself. Everything that had stirred the audience—machine guns, mass murders, cop killing, dynamite—had been ruled out. Worst of all, Officer Burke, not Tommy Powers, would have had to be the star, even though there was as yet in 1935 no ordinary cop American audiences could seriously envision as an action hero or a romantic lead.

It would have been too dangerous in 1934 or 1935 for Hollywood to have tried to evade its code of self-regulation once again. The next step surely would have been government censorship. Nevertheless, the studios still wanted to make gangster movies because they still wanted the cash those movies brought in. The producers needed a loophole. J. Edgar Hoover's FBI, with an assist from the International Association of Chiefs of Police (the IACP), gave them that opening.

The IACP was just as worried as the bishops about movie-made criminals, but the police chiefs were worried even more about their movie image. They felt Hollywood's portrayal of cops had hurt law enforcement self-confidence and morale and had made the public reluctant to cooperate with the law. "Moving pictures mould public opinion," they said. "The old comedy cops of silent screen were portrayed as unintelligent policemen. . . . One of our first tasks in this country, if we are ever to defeat the criminal, is to create a public opinion in favor of cooperating with the police."[22]

At its 1934 convention the IACP appointed a committee to persuade Hollywood that "the screen should not be contributory to crime and, second, that the treatment of police characters and stories on the screen should be handled in a true light."[23] This committee found Hollywood eager to cooperate. If the old gangster pictures had hurt the police, the producers suggested, how about some new gangster pictures to help the police repair their public image?

As evidence of its new pro-police attitudes, Hollywood showed the chiefs an MGM short subject series called *Crime Does Not Pay*. The films used a formula later popularized by radio's "Gangbusters"— each installment had a real-life police officer introducing a dramatization of a case he had investigated. The first installment, *Buried Loot*, opened with the "MGM Reporter" announcing he was "a man with a message . . . the message that crime does not pay. You can't beat the law. The cards are stacked against you. . . ." This was the first of two dozen *Crime Does Not Pay* episodes MGM made between 1935 and 1939, all variations on the theme that "organized society cannot be beaten."[24]

Crime Does Not Pay was shown as a sample of the new crime movies Hollywood was eager to make. The police chiefs were impressed, and their chairman reported that he had been "agreeably surprised to find that the industry has gone much further in these regards than I had suspected. They have not been satisfied with a negative attitude but are keying all crime stories to emphasize the lesson that *crime does not pay*. . . . The details and Code principles used in this attempt are exhaustive and, in my opinion, largely effective."[25]

Hollywood's gamble was that if it served up a new series of gangster pictures focusing on the exploits of idealized and heroic cops, the law enforcement profession's enthusiasm would overwhelm the protests of critics outside law enforcement. The most logical candidate for the role of supercop was the G-Man.

Buried Loot *(1935), first installment in MGM's* Crime Does Not Pay *short subject series. Robert Taylor* (center) *in his screen debut.*

In later years there was a good deal of jealousy between Hoover's FBI and the local police community, but at the end of 1934 the reputation of the bureau among police was at its peak. Even before Cummings had publicized the FBI, its technical services had become indispensable to local police departments. Cummings's anticrime publicity had also given the local police something they needed even more than fingerprint collections, crime laboratories, and crime statistics: that was the sparkling vision of Hoover's well-groomed and college-educated agents as a public image for all law enforcement. A historian of American law enforcement wrote that by late 1934 "J. Edgar Hoover, the evangelist against crime, was also a symbol of police professionalism. No police officer was held in higher esteem by the newly emerging cadre of police professionals."[26] The same police officials who were embarrassed by movie policemen wrote that "we need just what J. Edgar Hoover is giving us—an efficient group of well-trained policemen who are capable of trailing down the facts about our criminals and who, if need be, can meet the law-breaker with the same kind of weapons he uses against society."[27]

Since the nation's police had accepted the G-Men as ideal self-images, Hollywood calculated that they could be lured into endorsing movies glorifying the FBI, even if the new movies were basically the same old crime films the police chiefs had been complaining about. The studios asked for an exemption from the antigangster rules so that they could make a new kind of crime film "in the public interest." The censors knew that G-Man pictures would be in *prima facie* violation of the code, but they voted to let the studios "make a limited number [of gangster pictures] from this new angle, namely Government activity in fighting crime."[28]

The chiefs' reaction to the G-Man movies proved that Hollywood had been right. A prominent police chief bragged that "a committee of the International Association of Chiefs of Police appointed to confer with the Motion Picture Producers and Distributers of America brought about a definite change in the sentiment induced by the movies. Gangster pictures, with sentiment definitely in favor of the criminal, were replaced by the 'G' men pictures which induced the public to applaud the efforts of the police."[29]

The G-Man pictures of 1935 that established the public image of Hoover's FBI were the direct result of this short-lived (until September, 1935) exemption from the production code. It might even be said that Hoover's power had its origin in that exemption. At a moment when the country was rediscovering its pride and unity, when it was hungry for stirring dramatizations of its government's victory over public scapegoats, the only film heroes who were allowed to wage war against truly dangerous contemporary villains were the G-Men.

The movies that brought about the G-Man's apotheosis in 1935 were not the result of political manipulations by Hoover or anyone else, nor was it Hoover's record in the Justice Department that made Hollywood decide to turn his men into heroes. The G-Men movies were the result of an irresistible force—the depression public's demand for exciting crime entertainment and Hollywood's hunger for the profits to be made from catering to that demand—colliding with an immovable object—the antigangster provisions of the movie production code buttressed by public opinion led by the Catholic bishops and the chiefs of police. The movie G-Man was the most obvious solution to this impasse, the easiest way of establishing an equilibrium between unquenched demand and restricted supply.

All good things must come to an end, however, and finally it was the British who rang down the curtain on the G-Man cycle. The British Board of Censors sent their American counterparts a note of protest in 1935 complaining that "there is a new type of film being introduced here from America, or, may I say, an old type in a new garment, namely a revival of the "gangster" film which purports to show the determination of the Federal Government to stamp out gangster activities. . . . In the new variation the whole of the gangster's gamut of murder, kidnapping, robbery with violence, arson, etc., are just as prominently portrayed as of yore. I consider that the cumulative effect of this type of film is highly undesirable."[30]

The British thought that the production code had meant business when it said that there would be no more gangster films, and so they demanded an explanation. Mindful of the importance of the British market, the Production Code Authority finally gave notice in September, 1935, that "crime stories are not to be approved when they portray the activities of American gangsters, armed and in violent conflict with the law or law-enforcement officers."[31] And that was the end of the original run of G-Man movies.

There would, of course, be more FBI pictures, but they would have no gangsters for the movie G-Men to chase—villains would have to be racketeers, spies, Communists, and Ku Klux Klansmen. Armed gangsters would not be seen again until after World War II's war movies had relaxed the code's stand against film combat. The depression public's last memory of the gangsters, therefore, would be their extermination at the hands of Hoover's men.

Though the G-Men and the gangsters were exiled from the Bijou after 1935, they had by no means vanished from popular culture. In 1935 the G-Man craze overflowed from the movie theaters, deluging the radio, the comics, and the pulp magazines. With a little help from the bishops, the police chiefs, and Hollywood, the G-Man had turned into a pop culture star.

5

The G-Man and the Public:
The Cultural Function of the Action Detective

The sequence of events that turned the FBI agent into a pop culture hero in 1935 would have had little lasting effect on American life if there had not already been a well-accepted role in American culture for the G-Man to play. But there was a role, one that had been occupied for a hundred years by one of the most durable figures in American popular culture—the action detective hero. By casting the FBI agent in this role, Hollywood invested the G-Man with the heroic attributes the action detective had taken a century to acquire. The detective hero had gripped the public imagination for so long because American culture relied on him to satisfy some of its most important psychological needs. After 1935 Hollywood assigned these tasks to the FBI.

America's fascination with the fictional detective hero was almost one hundred years old in 1935. The first popular accounts of detectives appeared shortly after the formation of the first professional detective agencies: around 1827 in England (the memoirs of the Bow Street Runners) and around 1829 in France (the memoirs of Vidocq). These early detective stories were eagerly read in the United States, where Edgar Allan Poe wrote the first fictional detective short story in 1841. This was "The Murders in the Rue Morgue" in *Uncle Sam*, the first of the American "story papers" that would prosper largely because of the detective stories they supplied.

Standard histories of the detective story have focused on what Poe called the story of ratiocination, or what has come to be known as the mystery: a startlingly intelligent hero guiding the reader through a maze of clues, finally picking a devious murderer out of a crowd of equally likely suspects. This tradition includes masters like Arthur Conan Doyle, Dorothy Sayers, Agatha Christie, Ellery Queen, and Rex Stout;

and it is the tradition that has attracted the attention of intellectuals. For every reader of Sherlock Holmes, however, hundreds once read Old Sleuth, Cap Collier, or Nick Carter. For every Dorothy Sayers fan there were dozens who read *Shadow Magazine* or Doc Savage. For every Rex Stout addict there are thousands who follow Mike Hammer.

The mystery story has been collected and chronicled and reprinted, but no such care has been lavished on the action detective story.[1] They were seldom saved, and when a rare Nick Carter or Old Sleuth can be found, the cheap basswood pulp crumbles upon reading, but it was in the fragile volumes of these he-man stories that the popular (as opposed to the highbrow) image of the detective was born. It was the pulp magazine detective, not his highbrow mystery counterpart, who was the mass audience's favorite sleuth.

The mystery story's appeal has been analyzed in detail by critics like Edmund Wilson[2] and William Aydelotte.[3] They have concluded that mystery readers seek a substitute universe with fixed and reasonable laws in which all events are significant (because they are clues), a realm in which knowledge is power since it is brainwork that finally solves the case. Since the mystery universe replaces action with thought, it is a paradise for the intellectual.

Some of this applies as well to the action detective story, except that in popular crime stories knowledge is not power. Power is power. As George Orwell observed, the action detective story tends to be a celebration of the power principle.[4] It is not that complex plots never occur in action stories, but when they do, they work differently than in the mystery. The reader does not come to the action story to unravel a puzzle in the footsteps of the detective; he wants to see the hero overcome ordeals; sometimes these ordeals are intellectual, but usually they are physical: beatings, gunfights, and chases. The action detective's plots do not have to be logical, and they do not even have to be solved completely by the end of the book. The action detective does not untie the Gordian knot—he cuts through it with a secret knife hidden inside a trick decoder ring. When action detectives face mysteries, they overcome them with strength and trickery, not science. They use science only as a superior sort of mumbo-jumbo, like the rest of their gimmickry: ventriloquism, disguise, specially equipped cars, and the oriental martial arts.

In the action detective story the hero has to capture criminals whose identities, methods, and motives may be known to the reader and the hero from the very beginning. Every episode of the story is meant to display the detective's heroism by demonstrating the difficulty of his task. The action detective story is a travesty on the epic form: a series of ordeals that exist only to be overcome by a hero whose omnipotence the reader envies and identifies with. The action hero represents his

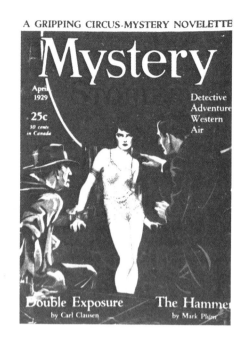

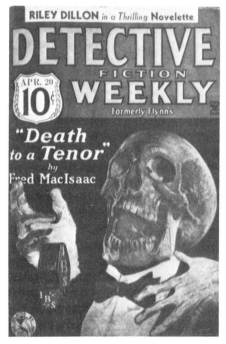

The myth of the action detective hero reached its peak in the adventure pulps.

culture, and so his triumphs demonstrate that culture's ability to repel all challenges. His adventures are rituals that prove the strength of his society's values and the weakness of those who oppose them.

The mystery story focuses on the process of solving the crime while the action detective story centers on the capture of the criminal. This makes the political symbolism of the action story more powerful than the mystery's, and it relates the action story more closely to the ritual of crime and punishment. There are other differences. Mysteries tolerate ambiguities and eccentricities in their heroes; they tend to be odd types, even defiant nonconformists. In the action story the hero is a pure projection of the audience's fantasies of power, and so he has to embody the culture's most admired traits. In a pluralistic society he will tend to be drawn only from the most admired class or ethnic groups. The requirement that the action hero represent the dominant elite reinforced Hoover's own racial and religious prejudices. Not only did Hoover allow precious few nonwhites or non-Christians in his FBI, but during the sixties he specified that applicants "look like agents" by conforming to the "Zimmy image" (*i.e.*, that they look like Efrem Zimbalist, Jr., star of "The F.B.I." television show).

In the mystery story the criminal's motive is one of the puzzles, so to preserve suspense, it, along with the villain's identity, has to be a secret. In the action story, however, the villain's black heart is motive enough; the only justification the hero needs for pursuing him is the eternal hostility of good for evil, reinforced by the desire to revenge injury or insult. The action detective story is, in short, an entirely different genre from the mystery, even though they both have detective heroes. A hundred years of popularity demonstrates how strong the attraction of this action detective formula to the mass audience has been.

There were many action detective heroes in America during the nineteenth century, but the first to become famous as an individual star was Old Sleuth. He was supposedly the "Giant Detective" narrator of the *Old Sleuth Library* of detective stories that originated in 1872 in *The Fireside Companion*, George Munro's popular New York story paper.[5] The second great American action detective was Old Cap Collier, likewise the "author" of the *Old Cap Collier Library* of stories.[6] The greatest of all the action detectives was Nick Carter, who first appeared in Street and Smith's *New York Weekly* in 1886.[7] Nick Carter was created by John Coryell and then appeared in over two hundred adventures written by Frederick Marmaduke Van Rensselaer Dey. (As late as 1943 there was a "Nick Carter, Master Detective" radio show, and today there are new paperback adventures of a new Nick Carter.)

The action detective was enormously popular from the start. By the 1880s he had displaced the cowboy as the most popular hero in the Beadle and Adams dime novel library. By 1900 the Aldine Company had over two hundred fifty different action detectives in its stable, including "The Demon Detective," "The Jew Detective," "New York Nell, the Girl-Boy Detective," "Fritz, the Bound-Boy Detective," "Old Stonewall, the Shadower," "Lynx Eyes, the Pacific Detective," and "Old Electricity, the Lightning Detective."[8] The action detective's popularity and durability were so great that he survived the medium that had made him famous. At the end of the century the story papers were replaced by weekly pulp magazines devoted either to the adventures of a single detective (e.g., *The Nick Carter Weekly*) or to several types of action stories (*Adventure, Detective*). During the second decade of the century the action detective entered the comic strips (the first was *Hawkshaw the Detective*). The great action detective of the twentieth century, Dick Tracy, arrived in 1931, and a year later "True Detective Mysteries," the first radio detective show, went on the air. By 1930 the public's infatuation with the detective hero was almost an obsession. Munsey's *Detective Fiction Weekly* and Street and Smith's *Detective Story* and *Shadow Magazine* were competing with dozens of others on the newsstands. On the back of cereal boxes Inspector Post implored kiddies to join the Post Toasties Law and Order Patrol. Later in the thirties there would be a "Sherlock Holmes" radio show and others starring Dick Tracy and Charlie Chan. The thirties would end with Superman and Batman joining Captain Midnight on the radio. The popularity of the formula shows no signs of flagging today, with odd mutations like medical detectives as stars of television adventure programs.

From the very beginning action detective stories were fast and violent; they depended on constant, brutal action to hold the reader's attention. By the 1930s the action detective formula had made room for a little more sex than in the nineteenth century, but otherwise the G-Man movies were faithful to the violent spirit of the original. In the first Old Cap Collier story, for instance, the hero

Gets into a fight (plain)	5 times
Fights four or five men at once	7 times
Is shot at or attacked with knives or bludgeons	12 times
Is blown up	Once
Escapes poisoning	Once
Is buried alive	Once
Is caught in a steel trap disguised as a chair	Once
Number of men he beats "to a jelly"	2 times
Number of men he hurls through the air	21 times
Number of men he would have hurled through the air, but refrained, for fear of making a noise, and instead choked him [sic] until he was black in the face	Once[9]

NEW NICK CARTER WEEKLY

Issued Weekly. By subscription $2.50 per year. Entered as Second-class Matter at the N. Y. Post Office, by STREET & SMITH, 79-89 Seventh Ave., N. Y.

No. 465   NEW YORK, NOVEMBER 25, 1905.   **Price, Five Cents**

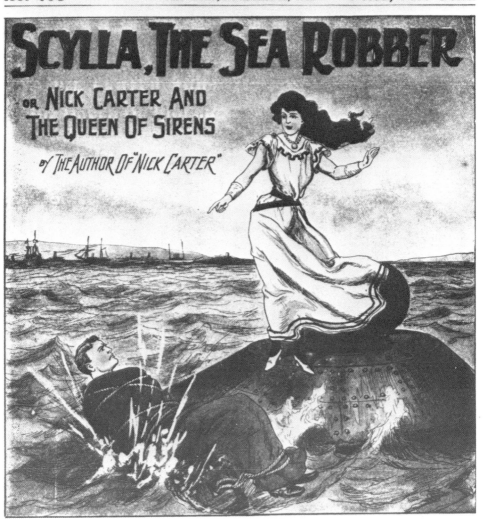

SCYLLA, THE SEA ROBBER

OR NICK CARTER AND THE QUEEN OF SIRENS

BY THE AUTHOR OF "NICK CARTER"

Nick Carter, the G-Man hero's most famous action detective predecessor.

Modern weapons technology let the G-Man fight even more spectacular battles than these, but essentially FBI movies followed the pulp stories in using the crime and punishment formula to tie together a pyrotechnic sequence of violent explosions climaxed by a final apocalyptic shootout.

The plot device that was the trademark of the G-Man detective hero was the disguise, a way of placing the hero in perilous predicaments while dumfounding villain and audience alike. This too the pop culture G-Man owed to his action detective ancestors. The prototypical disguise scene in pop culture was in Tom Taylor's *The Ticket-of-Leave Man* in 1851. That play had the hero penetrate a robbers' den wearing the rags of a derelict. There he lies unconscious until, at the last possible moment, he leaps to his feet and, Odysseus-like, sheds his rags, stupefying the crooks by announcing himself as "Hawkshaw, the Detective." An early Cap Collier story had its hero don these disguises (an incomplete list):

1. A fat Dutchman.
2. An elderly man with gray hair.
3. A countryman, very elaborate.
4. A tramp.
5. A sandwich man.
6. A cabman.
7. A cavalier at a masked ball.
8. An oysterman.
9. The oysterman reversed—that is, the clothes turned inside out, with the addition of black whiskers and a wig. This was done at great speed and in a time of special stress. The author does not give a name to the character assumed; perhaps the disguise was that of a fisher for scallops.
10. As "the man he saw in the woods."
11. Elderly broker or "merchant."
12. A "country merchant."
13. A middle-aged peddler.
14. An organ grinder.
15. A ship captain. Old Cap Collier seems to have liked the ship captain, for he wore the costume for two or three hours without change.
16. "A rough."
17. The "one he wore in the den of thieves."
18. Another quick change, in which, apparently, he was disguised as nothing in particular, or merely a human being, for the author does not describe what it represented.[10]

A bit extreme, perhaps, but this was the sort of virtuosity the public had come to expect of a "giant detective."

The title, Master of Disguise, belonged to the champion action detective of all time, Nick Carter, and his creators tried to give him an undercover identity in each story that was even more ingenious and incredible than the last. No one, not even the pop culture G-Man, has ever come close to matching Nick's disguises: "He would cheerfully run the choppers over his hair, stain his teeth, and torture his ears with gold wire. And when he became a hunchback, ... even when he took the last garment from his back you had difficulty in spotting that the hump was a dummy."[11] Nick's special trick was to disguise himself as the man he was chasing. "None of Nick's disguises were ever detected. Whatever misfortunes befell him, they were never the result of faulty disguise."[12]

As an action detective the G-Man had to start putting on disguises too, even though the bureau characteristically relied on civilian informants instead of FBI agents for undercover work. Hoover rarely put even his fictional agents into disguises. This was because an undercover agent had to rely on his own wits and courage to survive, an idea antithetical to the organization man image Hoover was promoting. In Hoover's officially approved FBI entertainment the G-Man was hardly ever alone; he was part of a team controlled by commands issued by the nerve center in Washington.

The reason the disguise plot so frequently figures in action detective stories is that it frees the audience's imagination for the kind of role playing intrinsic to formula entertainment. The proliferation of masks and alter egos destroys the audience's sense of fixed identity and replaces it with a maze of roles within roles. This is carried to an extreme in fantastic variations on the action formula in which the hero himself, Superman, Batman, or the Shadow, can be understood as a dream of his "civilian" alter ego—Clark Kent, Bruce Wayne, or Lamont Cranston.

The hero's disguises invite the audience to take on a variety of psychologically satisfying roles: most obviously the all-powerful, all-conquering detective, but also the victim, the killer, and the innocent suspect. Each role has its own kick. As the detective, the fan can flex his imaginary muscles in a fantasy of violent revenge against officially approved scapegoats. As the villain, he can safely vent his frustrations against respectable morality and social discipline. As the victim, he experiences first persecution and then, when the criminal is brought to justice, liberation.

Disguise capitalizes on the ambivalence of popular attitudes toward authority. While he identifies with the hero on an undercover assignment, the fan can rebel against society while protected from guilt by the knowledge that in the end he will throw aside his disguise and rejoin the forces of justice. When audiences in the thirties became undercover G-Men, there was an added dividend. The fan could pretend to be an official symbol of the nation, a consecrated guardian of national values who was defiling himself as a gangster, a Nazi, or a Communist-for-a-day, before redeeming himself (and thereby the nation, as well) in the final scene.

During the anti-Communist hysteria of the forties and fifties Hollywood was able to use the undercover G-Man formula as a pop culture
ritual of exorcism. In *I Was a Communist for the F.B.I.*, Matt Cvetic
(Frank Lovejoy) disgraces himself in the eyes of friends, relatives, and
family to carry out his FBI undercover assignment as a Communist
agitator. Only he and the audience know he is actually a patriot doing
his duty. The audience shares his loneliness and the shame of forbidden
thoughts, actions, and associations. When Lovejoy finally sheds his disguise and destroys his Communist ex-comrades in a Senate hearing,
there is the relief of a ritualistic return to the fold. Like Arthur Miller's
ex-Communist in *After the Fall*, Lovejoy and the audience are able to
become socially acceptable again after the pollution of (pretended) disloyalty. By having the G-Man pretend to be a public enemy or traitor,
Hollywood could provide a ritual affirmation of cultural orthodoxy and
national unity. The undercover G-Man figured in hundreds of these
rituals on screen and radio after 1935: the most fearful deviance of the
day gave the G-Man his latest disguise.

Of the G-Man movies that Hollywood served up in 1935, only *G-
Men,* because of the verve of Cagney's performance, is still remembered
today. Nevertheless, although *G-Men* was the picture that made the FBI
the national symbol of law enforcement, the forgotten FBI pictures of
1935 did something no less important. By running the screen G-Man
through all the familiar routines of the action detective hero they turned
him into a B-movie cliché. By the end of the year Americans had gotten
used to the idea that the G-Man was everything the action hero had
ever been. The pictures that followed *G-Men* into the theaters—*Public
Enemy's Wife; Public Hero Number One; Whipsaw; Mary Burns, Fugitive; Let 'Em Have It*; and *Show Them No Mercy*—by their very medi-
ocrity registered the fact that American popular culture had accepted,
with no further explanations necessary, the FBI agent as the modern-
day action detective.

G-Men had gone to great lengths to claim that it was a factual dramatization of Justice Department operations. The other 1935 G-Man
films pretended to be nothing more than what they were—standard
action detective melodramas. Their ads promised audiences the same
sex and violence as the now-outlawed gangster movies. MGM's *Public
Hero Number One* dutifully advertised itself a tribute to the FBI, and
then leeringly promised an exposé of the love lives of the new heroes:
"WHAT ARE THEY LIKE? HOW DO THEY CARRY ON UNCLE SAM'S RELENT-
LESS WAR TO END CRIME? MUST THEY KEEP LOVE OUT OF THEIR DANGER-
OUS LIVES?"[13] *Public Hero Number One*, whose villain, played by Joseph Calleia, was modeled (rather loosely) on John Dillinger, featured a
jailbreak, a run-in with a "crime doctor" (played by Lionel Barrymore),
and a shootout at a movie theater, all recalling Dillinger's career. These

historical tidbits were incidental, however. The film's G-Man hero, Chester Morris, was really just Old Sleuth in a three-piece suit and a snap-brim hat, chasing the same sort of crooks that action detectives had been after since dime novel days.

Public Hero Number One had the old disguise plot combined with another relic of dime novel days, a romance between the undercover hero and a bandit queen (recostumed as a gun moll). Chester Morris disguises himself as a convict so that he can share gangster Calleia's cell. The plan is for them to break out together so that Calleia will lead Morris to the gang's hideout. The plot was complicated by having Morris fall in love with Calleia's sister, played by Jean Arthur. *Public Hero Number One* worked well enough to be remade in 1941 as *The Get-Away*, with Dan Dailey the gangster, Donna Reed his sister.

MGM's second G-Man feature of 1935, *Whipsaw*, also had its detective hero put on a disguise and fall in love with a bandit queen. *Whipsaw* also tried to capitalize on the success of *It Happened One Night* by incorporating an imitation of Clark Gable and Claudette Colbert's cross-country romance. Spencer Tracy is *Whipsaw*'s G-Man in disguise, Myrna Loy the gun moll. They run off with Loy's gang's loot and stumble into a series of "screwball" adventures that end with them in love. The film closes with Tracy promising to wait for Loy until she gets out of the pen.

Warner Brother's *Public Enemy's Wife* also showed Hollywood's ingenuity at finding a love interest in the unlikeliest places: "THE PUBLIC ENEMIES ARE RUBBED OUT OR LOCKED UP" read its ads, "BUT WHAT ABOUT THE GIRLS THEY LEFT BEHIND: The Stark Naked Truth About the Crime War Widows Left Stranded by Their Mates in the Wake of History's Greatest Manhunt."[14]

At the beginning of *Public Enemy's Wife* Margaret Lindsay has just gotten out of prison after a three-year sentence for "harboring" her gangster husband, Cesar Romero. "She hadn't known he had been public enemy number one, but the law had not believed her." She goes to Reno for a divorce from the still-imprisoned Romero even though he has sworn to kill anyone who takes his place. There she falls in love with a socialite also in Reno "for the cure." When society reporters print her picture in a story about the engagement, Romero breaks out of jail breathing fire.

Romero's escape humiliates the Bureau, so the G-Men swear to get him "if it costs the life of every man in the department." In accordance with the FBI's pop culture image, there is no suggestion that the bureau or its director take orders from anybody. Like all self-respecting heroes, they do whatever they like. The director comes up with the idea of disguising special agent Pat O'Brien as Margaret Lindsay's fiancé (who has run off to Europe "until the whole thing blows over"), using him as

Pat O'Brien (left) as an undercover G-Man in Public Enemy's Wife *(1935).*

bait to capture Romero. Despite the opposition of his real-life girlfriend, O'Brien agrees to go through with a sham marriage to Lindsay to goad Romero into making his move. Guests at the wedding have machine guns under their coats, and the newlyweds shove their beds to the opposite sides of their honeymoon suite and sleep with a screen between them: more influence of *It Happened One Night*. O'Brien inevitably falls for Lindsay and tries to resign from the bureau so that he can really marry her. While he is in Washington handing in his resignation, Romero swoops down and kidnaps his ex-wife.

Using authority possessed only by movie G-Men, O'Brien places the whole state under martial law. When the government agents surround the gangsters' hideout, Lindsay breaks loose, shrieking that she loves O'Brien. Romero shoots her, and then the G-Men open fire on Romero's gang, "bowling them over like ten pins in a bowling alley." Upon Lindsay's recovery the G-couple resume their interrupted honeymoon. The closing shot shows the honeymoon suite with the two beds pulled up alongside one another. *Public Enemy's Wife* made no attempt to recreate FBI procedures or to document real cases. Pat O'Brien was simply the stereotyped action detective hero appropriating the most popular plot clichés of the day.

After the production code forced the movie G-Men to hunt non-gangster villains, Hollywood had to latch onto each passing fad to keep the movie version of the bureau in business. RKO's *Border G-Men* (1938), for example, cashed in on the Gene Autry-inspired vogue of the singing cowboy by disguising special agent George O'Brien as the leader of a country and western band. His assignment was to track down crooks selling guns and horses to "enemy agents." The film had an unusual finish, with O'Brien lassoing the villain from an escaping get-away speedboat. In 1935, however, producers did not have to strain after originality; they simply repeated the same formulas with different sets and stars. Paramount's *Mary Burns, Fugitive,* for example, cast Wallace Ford and Kernan Cripps as the G-Men, with Sylvia Sydney forced into the role of a gun-moll against her will.

The 1935 G-Man movies' exemption from the antiviolence provisions of the production code let these films stir audiences with the kind of bloody violence against public offenders that would not be equalled until the *films noirs* of the late forties or the revenge films of the seventies *(Death Wish, Lipstick,* and *Dirty Harry).* The most violent of all the 1935 G-Man movies was Twentieth Century Fox's *Show Them No Mercy.* This film was written by Kubec Glasmon, scriptwriter for Cagney's *Public Enemy* four years earlier. In *Public Enemy* the police were losers, and Cagney's Tommy Powers could jeer at them with impunity. Now the gangsters were the losers, and in *Show Them No Mercy* they existed only to be hated, tortured, and destroyed. The movie was based on the recent kidnapping of Washington lumber tycoon J. P. Weyerhauser's grandson, whom the kidnappers had buried alive for safekeeping. Once again Cesar Romero was the sadistic leader of a gang of villains so vicious that one of his men (Bruce Cabot) sets fire to fellow gangster Edward Brophy. The film revels in the gang's psychological disintegration under the relentless pressure of an FBI manhunt; at the climax one of the hostages grabs a machine gun and empties it into Bruce Cabot's chest.

Hollywood also took advantage of the production code's G-Man exemption to treat audiences to other horrors forbidden in ordinary films. For example, there were scenes with crime doctors—facelifts without anaesthesia, razor-erasing of fingerprints, and kitchen-table amputations. These were based on the exploits of crime doctors like Joseph P. ("Doc") Moran and Dr. William Loesser, who had become famous during the Dillinger manhunt. These doctors were simply transplanted mad scientists from the horror movies. In the Edward Small/ United Artists production of *Let 'Em Have It,* the movie's Dillinger-like villain pulls off his bandages after his facelift to discover that the treacherous plastic surgeon has branded the criminal's initials on his forehead for all the world to see.

Let 'Em Have It also gave its audience the kind of procedural details which would later be the hallmark of official FBI entertainment but which were often lacking in the unofficial 1935 G-Man films. G-Man Richard Arlen's tours through headquarters in *Let 'Em Have It* seem ploddingly paced today, but in 1935 the audience had an almost superstitious reverence for the "scientific criminology" the Justice Department and its publicists were selling as a magic cure for crime. Audiences were so enthusiastic about fingerprinting, for example, that theaters gave audiences a chance to be fingerprinted in the lobby as a way of enlisting in the anticrime crusade. In 1936 the real FBI imitated Hollywood by launching a drive to get citizens to send their fingerprints to the bureau. John D. Rockefeller, Jr., was the first volunteer; his prints were lifted by Hoover himself.

Besides Justice Department propaganda, there was another reason that movie G-Men spent so much time playing with scientific gadgets. Action detectives had always carried ingenious crime-fighting tools. Audiences had learned to expect spy cameras and bullet-proof cars from them long before anyone had heard of the FBI. By showing off the G-Man's gadgets, popular entertainment was helping the G-Man conform to the action detective stereotype.

Once the 1935 G-Man films had adapted the G-Man to the action detective model, J. Edgar Hoover's niche in American public life no longer depended on the measurable success of the Bureau's efforts against crime. Movie G-Men, like the traditional action detectives, were no longer real men fighting real criminals; they were symbols of the law performing ritual exorcisms of the public's demons. After 1935 the public would idolize the G-Men for the same reasons audiences had always idolized action detectives.

And why had the public been so fascinated for so long by the action detective formula? What do people still get from crime entertainment that can explain the persistent popularity of what is, after all, an utterly predictable routine peopled by predictable character stereotypes? The question is important because the transformation of the real FBI agent into a fictional action detective suggests that whatever role the action detective had come to play in American popular culture, the FBI agent had taken over his job.

One explanation for crime entertainment's popularity may be found in its historical origins. Presumably people have always been interested in crime, but popular narratives about crime and criminals had their start in the cheap one-page ballads sold as souvenirs to the crowds that gathered for the public executions held outside London's Newgate Prison in the early eighteenth century. These Newgate broadsides, which were later collected in the famous volumes of the *Newgate Calendar*,[15] purported to be autobiographical accounts of the temptations that had led the criminal into crime, a gory description of the crime itself, and an appeal to the reader to avoid the condemned man's fate by profiting from his example. Almost any example will show the typical didactic intent. For instance, one began, "Good people all I pray draw near, / And my sad history you soon shall hear / And when the same I do relate / I trust you will a warning take."[16]

Crime entertainment's psychological relationship to public executions can be seen not only in its origin as part of the execution spectacle, but also in the fact that crime literature's great growth in the nineteenth century occurred simultaneously with the decision to hide punishment from public view. Crime entertainment originated as a reenactment of execution spectacles for the enjoyment of those who had attended or as a substitute for those who had been absent or were too far away to see clearly. Crime literature, beginning with nineteenth century crime "exposés" like Eugene Sue's *Mysteries of Paris*, Ned Buntline's *Mysteries of New York*,[17] and crime magazines like *The Police Gazette*,[18] filled the gap left in popular culture when the legal process, under the influence of middle class sentimentality, stopped providing the real thing.

If the connection between crime literature and the spectacle of public punishment is valid, then an understanding of the satisfactions the public derived from those displays in earlier times should reveal the cultural function of detective fiction. The classic explanation is Emile Durkheim's.[19] For cultures to survive, Durkheim argued, they must remain united. To preserve their unity, cultures stage regular communal spectacles that rekindle the groups' sense that they are communities, and not merely collections of individuals. He called these ceremonies rituals. Among the most important of these solidarity-affirming spectacles, he singled out the ritual of crime and punishment. "As soon as the news of a crime gets abroad," Durkheim wrote, "the people unite," because a crime, by offending the collective conscience ("the totality of beliefs and sentiments common to average citizens of the same society"), reminds the citizens that they actually have a collective conscience, that they do form a moral community.[20]

The criminal himself provides law-abiding citizens with another opportunity to unite, this time against a symbol of rebellion against the collective conscience. One of Durkheim's American disciples wrote that "hostility toward the lawbreaker has the unique advantage of uniting all members of a community in the emotional solidarity of aggression. While the most admirable of humanitarian efforts are sure to run counter to the individual interests of very many in the community, or fail to touch the interest and imagination of the multitude, ... the cry of thief or murder is attuned to profound complexes, lying below the surface of competitive

AWFULLY AVENGED OUTRAGE AND MURDER BY A BAND OF NEGRO RUFFIANS, FOLLOWED BY THE LYNCHING OF THE GANG, AT MT. VERNON, IND.

1.—BRUTAL ASSAULT ON THE WOMEN. 2.—SHOOTING OF OLD HARRIS AFTER HIS MURDER OF DEPUTY SHERRIF THOMAS. 3.—THE INCENSED CITIZENS BREAKING INTO THE JAIL. 4.—ATTACK ON OLD HARRIS IN THE CORRIDOR. 5.—LEADING THE PRISONERS TO EXECUTION IN THE COURT HOUSE YARD.—SEE PAGE 21.

From The Police Gazette, *Oct. 26, 1878.*

individual effort, and citizens who have separated by divergent interests stand together against the common enemy."[21]

And just as the crime and the criminal help unite a society, so does the institution of punishment. Durkheim says that punishment "is the sign . . . that collective sentiments are always collective, that the communion of spirits in the same faith rests on a solid foundation. . . . The essential function of punishment is not to make the guilty expiate his crime through suffering or to intimidate possible imitators through threats, but to buttress those consciences which violations of a rule can and must necessarily disturb in their faith."[22] Taken together, then, the crime, the criminal, and his punishment combine to form a powerful ritual of cultural solidarity.

In modern society most of the traditional institutions that once unified cultures have lost their hold on the popular imagination—religion, folk-mythology, patriotic ceremonies, and political pageantry. The ritual of crime and punishment is, along with war, one of the last surviving ways for modern cultures to produce the feeling that society is more than an accidental collection of individuals, that it is a united community.

As the system of criminal justice becomes ever more encumbered by bureaucracy and complex procedures, however, the clarity of the ritual connection between crime and punishment is blurred until it finally vanishes in a maze of due process. The public then has to turn to fictional accounts of crime and punishment to get the offense-and-revenge catharsis that the real criminal justice system used to provide in the days of simple, speedy trials and public execution. Poetic justice—in which crime never pays and the guilty are always punished—finally survives only in the vicarious realm of cops-and-robbers entertainment.

Durkheim's theory would predict that calls for public rituals of crime and punishment, real ones, if possible, or, failing that, vicarious rituals in the pulp magazines and on the screen, should be particularly strong whenever the public is being awakened to a new consciousness of its solidarity and collective strength. FDR's revitalization of American confidence, therefore, should have produced a demand for strong, even brutal dramatizations of the age-old ritual of crime and punishment. And that is just what happened.

Crime literature's origins in real crime and punishment explain not only the popularity of stories about crime and criminals, but those that celebrate "heroes of the law," the ancestors of the action detective. "A social group," wrote a British anthropologist, "can only possess solidarity and permanence if [there is] . . . some more or less concrete object . . . which can act as the representative of the group. So it is the normal procedure that the sentiment of attachment to a group shall be expressed in some formalized collective behavior having reference to an object [for example, the detective hero] that represents the group itself."[23]

The crowds who struggled to witness the death agonies of criminals soon became equally fascinated by the valiant lawmen who had managed to capture these monsters. Even before the first detective agencies and police forces had been organized, the dynamics of popular ritual had created a cultural role for the hero of the law.

The first of these pop culture heroes in the English-speaking world was Jonathan Wild, "the Thief-Taker General of England," who was both the Al Capone and the J. Edgar Hoover of the first quarter of the eighteenth century.[24] At that time there were no magistrates with enough jurisdiction to cope with four large underworld gangs and hundreds of petty highwaymen and muggers who were terrorizing London. (The novelist Henry Fielding did not found the prototypical London police force, the Bow Street Runners, until 1749). Therefore Wild established a service with offices at the Old Bailey, offering to recover stolen goods for a price well below their market value. As a natural sideline he developed into a detective, or "thief-taker." Soon he destroyed the major gangs of London, bringing hundreds of street criminals to Newgate for execution. By 1723 he had the crime situation under control; he reached the pinnacle of his law enforcement career when he arrested Jack Sheppard, the most famous highwayman of the period, the era's John Dillinger. Then, unexpectedly, Wild himself was arrested in February, 1725. His Lost Property Office had been unmasked as a fencing operation for booty brought to him by his own criminal gang, which had taken over the London underworld after he had cleared the field by hanging his rivals at Newgate. There Wild himself was hanged on May 24, 1725.

Wild was commemorated by some twenty pamphlets published within a year of his death, including Daniel Defoe's anonymously published *A True and Genuine Account of the Life and Actions of the late Jonathan Wild, Not made up of Fiction and Fable, but taken from his Own Mouth, and collected from PAPERS of his own writing* (1725). In 1742 Henry Fielding titled his disguised attack on Robert Walpole *The History of the Life of the Late Mr. Jonathan Wild the Great*. There were dozens of other biographies of Wild, who was the original of all the "crime czars" other nervous ages have suspected of secretly controlling organized society. Wild's rapid decline from popular hero to villain would often be repeated in the history of crime news and entertainment, with J. Edgar Hoover's own reputation following the same pattern: from "Public Hero Number One" to the crazed enemy of the civil rights movement depicted in the television docudrama *King*.

These metamorphoses of heroes of the law into public enemies are not too hard to explain. Crime and punishment stories cast their spell over the popular imagination despite the monotony of their invariable formulas because the public's identification with the law is never completely unambiguous. The audience's "Wilder" impulses identify with the criminal's violence against society; the more melodrama indulges these antisocial impulses, the more completely will they be purged by the criminal's inevitable doom. Because the purgation takes place on the unconscious level, Aristotle called this "catharsis without enlightenment," or "poetic justice." When the popular audience's identification with the law weakens, as it did during the sixties and seventies in America, the audience's loyalty fails to shift from the villain to the hero when the law finally triumphs; on the contrary the audience resents the hero's victory as one more manifestation of malevolent power crushing the rebellious individual.

As soon as official police forces came into existence, first the Bow Street Runners in 1749, then Sir Robert Peel's Scotland Yard in 1829, their officers were turned into celebrities by the popular press and into action heroes by the writers of popular fiction. Just as the "Newgate novels" improved upon real crime and punishment by streamlining them into ritualistic form, semifictional Bow Street memoirs such as John Wright's *Mornings at Bow Street* and *More Mornings at Bow Street* (1825 and 1827) and Scotland Yard memoirs like the *Recollections of a Detective Police-Officer* by "Waters" (William Russell) quickly appeared to reshape real detectives into figures of popular mythology.[25]

The real-life detective who became the definitive model for the action detective hero was the man upon whom Poe later based his path-breaking fictional detective, Dupin. This was Eugene Vidocq, founder of the French *Sûreté* (national detective force). Before his legal career commenced, Vidocq had been a thief, a circus performer, a galley convict, and a jail-breaker. His career after switching to the side of the law was even more spectacular, at least as he told the story himself in his enormously popular autobiography. In his eighteen years on the job he claimed to have arrested twenty thousand criminals.[26] In his memoirs (published in 1829, four volumes totaling sixteen hundred pages) he portrayed himself as "a master of disguise . . . never worsted in a fight and rarely refused by a woman."[27] His talent for self-dramatization established Vidocq in the popular mind as the very image of the "ideal detective."

Besides being the original model for the action detective, Vidocq's life also offers another foreshadowing of J. Edgar Hoover's career. Vidocq was famous more for the stories he told in his memoirs than for his actual role in French history. Similarly, Allen Pinkerton, the most famous American real-life detective of the nineteenth century, probably was more famous for the eighteen volumes of casebooks his ghostwriters turned out from 1873 until 1886 than for anything he did as a detective.[28] When Hoover began issuing his own ghost-written casebooks (*Persons in Hiding* in 1938, *Masters of Deceit* in 1958, along

"A consultation was held, in my private parlor, over the business offices of the Agency, No. 45 South Third Street."

Allen Pinkerton, *from his casebook* The Mollie Maguires and the Detectives *(1877).*

with scores of magazine articles and several movies), these literary performances seemed incongruous to many, but only because his critics did not know the popular tradition of the "great detective" who has always been a storyteller as well as a hero. One of J. Edgar Hoover's cultural roles after 1935 was to be the "great detective" of his day, the official narrator of action detective stories to the American public.

Most discussions of the detective hero's appeal have been on the level of social science theory or literary criticism. For example, George Orwell thought that the action detective stories' fan's "admiration for the police is pure bully-worship. A Scotland Yard detective is the most powerful kind of being he can imagine, while the criminal figures in his mind as an outlaw against whom anything is permissible."[29] Another writer saw the action detective as "a sort of democratic scourge, a cleaner of community sinks." He quoted Mickey Spillane's Mike Hammer: "In the end the people have their justice. They get it through guys like me."[30]

A series of experiments performed by psychologist Lotte Bailyn in 1959 is the closest anyone has come to a scientific investigation of why audiences are fascinated by characters like action detectives, whom she called "aggressive heroes." Bailyn found that a child attracted to aggressive hero entertainment tends to have a "passive" personality: "The problems in his own life have not led to speculation, since these problems are not his fault; he can do nothing about them."[31]

She found that this passivity, which may arguably have been the characteristic experience of the depression, makes the child eager to escape into the more exciting world of action entertainment: "One may conceive of the mass media as providing a substitute world into which one may escape from the problems and tensions of life." She argues that the frustration of not being able to solve real-life problems (the depression, for example) makes the audience seek relief in the solution of make-believe problems: "Energy resulting from tension within the child is directed towards temporary solutions of problems having no bearing on the problems as such. Escape, . . . in becoming habitual, tends to preclude more realistic and lasting solutions."

When the fan returns to the real world, he tends to interpret it in terms of the aggressive hero fantasies he has found so rewarding: "Furthermore, the person for whom the mass media provide a habitual form of escape may so orient himself to the world of the media . . . that he will incorporate the values and behavior patterns of this world."[32] Bailyn also found that the fan of aggressive hero entertainment sees the world in stereotypes of good and evil. "His attitude will be put in these terms: people in general will fall into black and white categories—a fiat stemming from the media world reflected in his imagination."[33]

All of Bailyn's insights help explain the popularity of crime entertainment, but particularly her final observation. The aggressive hero fan, she found, tends to be "extrapunitive"—to look outside himself for solutions to personal problems, typically through the vicarious punishment of a scapegoat. This suggests that the mass audience, which as a normal occurrence finds it is troubled by problems that have causes and solutions outside of its immediate control, will seek vicarious relief in entertainment featuring stereotyped good and evil characters and plots that let the audience release its extrapunitive desires. When Bailyn asked her media-addicted children to choose their favorite action characters, they named Superman, detectives—and the G-Man.[34]

A hundred years of presiding over popular rituals of cultural unity had won the action detective a spot at the very pinnacle of America's pantheon of pop culture heroes. By turning Hoover's men into action detectives, the 1935 cycle of G-Man pictures invested the FBI agent with the heroic aura it had taken the fictional detective a century to acquire; these pictures made the G-Man the inheritor of the cultural role the action detective had so successfully played in American popular culture.

6

The FBI Formula and the G-Man Hero:
The Battle over Control of the FBI's Public Image

Hollywood's G-man hero—the formula detective with a Justice Department badge—was a far cry from J. Edgar Hoover's notion of the ideal G-Man. Hoover, like Cummings, wanted to lead a coordinated national anticrime movement, with the FBI as the model, teacher, inspiration, and technical advisor for the whole law enforcement community. Since Hoover's prescription for what ailed American police forces was "professionalism" (scientific techniques and rational organization), the FBI agent had to be seen as a symbol of this professionalism. Hoover wanted the public to see the G-Man as a scientifically-trained organization man, not a lone wolf operative with a quick trigger finger and the action detective's bag of tricks.

Hoover obviously had nothing against having his G-Men become public heroes. The trouble was that the public was putting the wrong G-Man up on a pedestal—not the official G-Man, the symbol of FBI "professionalism," but the celluloid G-Man, simply the latest incarnation of the archetypal American action hero. This pop culture G-Man was as rebelliously individualistic and anti-intellectual as any other hero of American popular culture.

Sitting back and letting his bureau be manipulated for someone else's profit was not Hoover's style. From 1935 until the end of his career, J. Edgar Hoover fought with the American entertainment industry for control over the FBI image. The G-Man's popularity he eagerly accepted and jealously guarded as vital in creating public support for law enforcement. He never gave up trying to remold the pop culture G-Man in his own image, however, to keep him from becoming the defiantly nonconformist action hero American popular culture wanted; Hoover's goal was to turn him into a symbol of security, order, and domesticity—family man, scientist, and bureaucrat as much as square-jawed, two-fisted crime-fighter. His ambition was to get the public to accept the official and orthodox image of the bureau—which might be called "the F.B.I. formula"— instead of the pop culture G-Man. Hoover's answer to the pop culture G-Man first appeared in a series of magazine articles in 1933 and 1934, articles that were collected in 1935 in the first book published about the FBI. These articles and this book provided Hoover's later publicists with a well-thought-out public image for the FBI. They also gave Hoover a strategy for publicizing the bureau and motivation for subordinating FBI law enforcement functions to the care and feeding of the FBI's public image.

When he was finished, Hoover had turned the FBI into one of the greatest publicity-generating machines the country had ever seen. In 1933, however, when the publicity drive began, Hoover was starting from scratch. From 1924 until 1933, the bureau hardly had any public relations at all. Hoover had run a stripped-down bureau that, under guidelines imposed by Harlan Stone, confined its activities to "investigations . . . made at and under the direction of the Attorney General."[1]

In one area only did Hoover move aggressively to publicize the bureau before 1933. This was his politically innocuous drive to turn the bureau into a center for scientific criminology. In 1925 he opened a fingerprint repository and identification laboratory at the bureau and offered its services to police forces across the country. To establish his credentials in the fight to get official funding for what would be the Division of Identification and Information, Hoover published an article on "Criminal Identification" in the November, 1929, issue of the *Annals of the American Academy*.[2] (Congress gave Hoover the funds he wanted in June, 1930.)

In 1930 Hoover inaugurated the *Uniform Crime Reports,* based on statistics furnished by local police. This was intended to determine "whether or not there [was] . . . a crime wave and whether crime [was] . . . on the increase," information useful both to the local police and to Hoover in their annual battles of the budget. In September, 1932, the FBI began sending local police the predecessor of today's *F.B.I. Law Enforcement Bulletin,* and in November, 1932, the bureau offered local police the free use of its crime laboratories. All this made the bureau known and admired throughout the higher echelons of the law enforcement community, but to the general public and, more importantly, to Congress, Hoover remained practically unknown.

Hoover would eventually prove himself one of the most skilled manipulators of public opinion in American history, but during those "quiet years" he was something of an innocent about publicity. An episode in the fall of 1929 illustrates this naïveté, and also marks the beginning of Hoover's drive to create a reputation for the Bureau that would extend beyond the boundaries of the law enforcement profession. A nurse in Washington, D.C., was discovered dead on her bedroom floor, her pajama cord knotted around her neck. The coroner concluded that the woman, who had a history of suicide attempts, had taken her own life. The case would have been closed except that a District of Columbia policeman denounced his colleagues and the coroner and claimed they had covered up a murder. Since the integrity of the police, the district attorney, and the local administration were all under suspicion, the Justice Department ordered the Bureau of Investigation to conduct an impartial inquiry.[3]

By now the "McPherson Murder Mystery" was a newspaper circus. When the chief of the bureau's Washington office tried to maintain security by lying to the press, the reporters chose *Washington Star* reporter Rex Collier to complain to Hoover. Collier told Hoover all he had to do was to tell the reporters that if they printed names of the suspects, it would impede the investigation; Collier said that then they would not print the names, because the press had as much interest in solving the case as he did. Hoover was surprised by Collier's willingness to cooperate and promised to straighten things out. The next morning there was a new inspector on the case and the press was given almost too much information. The FBI's investigation, incidentally, concluded that the nurse *had* committed suicide and that there was nothing to the allegations of police corruption.

Soon afterwards Hoover called Collier to thank him. The conversation turned to the difficulties Hoover had just had with Congress over his appropriations. Hoover said that he had just been testifying before Congress and one of the congressmen had asked him why he was there, since the Secret Service had testified the week before. The chairman had to tell the congressman that the Bureau of Investigation and the Secret Service were not the same.[4] Collier told Hoover the problem was that the Secret Service was well-known, but that nobody knew anything about the Bureau. He told Hoover that if the director gave him some interesting cases he could turn into stories, the bureau would become better known. Hoover said he had some good cases and told his top assistant, Clyde Tolson, to provide Collier with a memo on the Osage Indian case. Collier ran it as a full page story in the *Star* and then went on to write many other stories about the bureau, which appeared first in the *Star* and later nationwide in papers affiliated with the North American Syndicate.[5]

The Osage case that Collier worked up from Tolson's memo turned out to be one of Hoover's most valuable literary properties.[6] It was a story about a Fairfax, Oklahoma, banker who had become wealthy by murdering oil-rich Osage Indians in a complicated scheme to acquire their mineral rights. This was one time the G-Men went undercover;

FBI agents posed as cattle buyers, insurance salesmen, oil prospectors, and even Indian herb dealers to assemble the evidence that sent Hale to jail for life on January 29, 1929.

Hoover's working relationship with Rex Collier blossomed into a lifelong friendship, but it would seem that the articles Collier wrote about the FBI before 1934 hardly made a dent in the public's ignorance about the director or his men. When Homer Cummings finally ended the bureau's nine-year exile from the spotlight in July, 1933, by naming Hoover to lead the government's new "super police," the press wrote him up as a new name and a fresh face. *Newsweek,* assuming its readers had never heard of him, identified him as "Hoover—the one who is in the Department of Justice."[7] As late as 1934 newspapers would mis-identify Hoover as "the Head of the Secret Service."

Hoover's reputation grew so spectacularly after Cagney's *G-Men* that later observers were hard put to explain what had happened. By and large they assumed that someone in the Justice Department, perhaps Hoover himself, had decided to turn the director into a celebrity. In 1937 *The New Yorker* ran a profile on Hoover that claimed the Kansas City Massacre had convinced Hoover that "the mere quieting down of the kidnapping and bank robbery scare was not enough but that an actual crusade was needed. . . . Someone had to become the symbol of the crusade, and the Director decided that, because of his position, it was plainly up to him."[8] The trouble with this theory is that until *G-Men* rewrote history, Attorney General Cummings was "the symbol of the crusade." *The New Yorker,* like the public, seems to have remembered the movie's version of the gangster wars instead of the events themselves.

A second theory about the Hoover build-up had Cummings deciding to make a hero of the director. Drew Pearson claimed Cummings told him around 1934 that "the best cure for kidnapping was to build up the F.B.I., not only in actual strength but in the strength of public opinion behind it. If the underworld came to believe the F.B.I. was invincible, Cummings argued, there would be less kidnapping." Cummings asked various Washington reporters, including Pearson, to suggest a public relations man who could do the job, and they suggested a newsman named Henry Suydam. "He was appointed and did a terrific job. He really went to town with Hollywood, the radio industry and everybody else to make the F.B.I. invincible. . . . Within a year he had transformed Hoover, previously a barely known bureaucrat, into an omnipotent crimebuster whose name was familiar to every American. . . . After the head start Henry gave Hoover he had no trouble with his public relations."[9]

Pearson's story also does not square with the facts. The Justice Department's publicity drive had been kicked into high gear by Homer

Cummings a year before Suydam arrived at the Justice Department in 1934. For that matter Hoover himself, under the tutelage of Rex Collier, had already begun on a small scale the kind of institutional promotion that would allow him to capitalize on the 1935 Hollywood G-Man boom. During the winter of 1932–1933, for example, Hoover cooperated with the producers of a radio program known as "K-7" that dramatized FBI case histories and played up the bureau's scientific methods. Assistant Director Louis Nichols, who later handled Hoover's public relations, recalls that he first became interested in the bureau as a result of hearing that program on his way to law school.

Rex Collier and Louis Nichols both claim that Suydam, far from trying to publicize Hoover and the FBI, was retained by Cummings to build up the attorney general and the Justice Department at the expense of Hoover and the FBI. Hoover treated Suydam as an enemy, not an ally. When Suydam began advocating a new Justice Department "Bureau of Crime Prevention" in 1936, Hoover saw Suydam's plan as a threat to the FBI and engineered his departure from the Justice Department.[10]

The bureau's own public relations efforts had only limited impact on the public until Hollywood turned the G-Men and their director into pop culture heroes. But when the public and the mass media came out of the movie theaters itching to learn more about the bureau, Hoover was ready for them with his own version of the FBI story, a fully-fashioned myth that integrated all the bureau's activities into a unified saga, complete with a hero and a moral message. This was the official FBI formula, which Hoover offered to the public as an alternative to the entertainment industry's "unrealistic" portrait of the FBI agent as a pulp detective hero. The man who created this official myth of the FBI for Hoover was a writer named Courtney Ryley Cooper.

Cooper was a flamboyant free-lance writer from Kansas City who specialized in crime stories. He had been sent to the bureau in the early summer of 1933 by *American Magazine* to see if he could find a story there. He did. Cooper wrote twenty-four stories about the bureau between 1933 and 1940 (all but one in *American Magazine*), three books (*Ten Thousand Public Enemies,* 1935; *Here's to Crime,* 1937; and *Persons in Hiding,* 1938) and four movies (*Persons in Hiding,* 1939; *Undercover Doctor,* 1939; *Parole Fixer,* 1940; and *Queen of the Mob,* 1940).

Cooper was the first writer to organize all the activities of the FBI into one coherent story with all the parts contributing to the impressive effect of the whole. Instead of simply writing up FBI cases or procedures, Cooper looked for ways to link one episode to the next. Because he saw a chance for a whole series of stories on the bureau instead of just one piece, he could not treat each case simply as a complete story in itself; he had to look beyond each for the "big story" that gave the individual case its interest and significance. Once Cooper had seen that there really was a big story at the bureau, he drew on his experience as a hack writer of pulp adventure stories, action formula movies, and newspaper crime features to keep his audience's noses glued to the page, giving them a judicious mixture of mystery, action, struggles between clear-cut good and evil, and rapid shifts of scene to exotic locales. His pulp experience had taught him also that an adventure story had to have a hero who could carry the reader along on fantastic flights of ego-projective identification. For Cooper there was no such thing as a story without a hero, and the hero of this story was going to be J. Edgar Hoover. There was, for Cooper's purposes, no other way to do it.

Cooper's first piece on the FBI appeared in the August, 1933, issue of *American Magazine*.[11] This was the first story about the bureau in a mass circulation magazine. Here, in the company of formula stories by Rafael Sabatini, Max Brand, Rex Stout, and Agatha Christie, Cooper began work on the FBI formula that would be the pattern for a generation's FBI adventures, a formula that J. Edgar Hoover would himself use, not only in his own books and speeches, but as a blueprint for the actual program of his bureau.

"Getting the Jump on Crime" was topped by a half-page photo of Hoover working studiously at his desk. The caption identified the subject as "J. Edgar Hoover, who developed the United States Bureau of Investigation" (Cooper had problems with changes in the bureau's name: already it was the Division of Investigation and in 1935 it would become the FBI). The four-thousand-word article began with a kidnapping in North Carolina and closed with a nationwide manhunt for the killer of an FBI agent. The stories showcased the range of talents of "this army of fighting detectives, detectives who always get their men." The kidnap episode featured a Rube Goldberg contraption of electric eyes and buried wires; a second case displayed the bureau's ability to coordinate complex investigations from one coast to the other as agents predicted their quarry's behavior from a detailed reconstruction of his *modus operandi*. Cooper connected the two cases together by showing how a chain of information and command tied the agents in the field to their commander in Washington, "the master detective who simply does not conform to any picture of the average crime chaser"—J. Edgar Hoover.

This master detective, Cooper announced, had created an "amazing police force" unified by "an enthusiastic spirit of team play all through the Bureau. . . . The organization became as tightly knit as a baseball team—and Hoover was coach, just as he became the sponsor of the real bureau baseball team, which won local championships. . . . And always before every subordinate is the lure of a place on that big map which hangs on the Director's wall, where push pins, each with a name tag, denote the various Special Agents of the bureau as they are moved about in accordance with their assignments."[12]

Cooper's story painted a picture of a crime-fighting machine whose effectiveness (omnipotence, really) all depended on Hoover: his care in selecting and training his agents, his skill in leading them, the technical facilities he had built to interpret the evidence his field agents brought in. The feats of agent derring-do, the miracles of crime lab wizardry, the criminal convictions—all went to prove the genius of the master detective behind the scenes who pulled all the wires, shuffled his agents' assignments, barked orders over the telephone and flashed signals over the teletype.

Cooper made Hoover's agents conform to the image of the action detective, but only up to a point. The difference was that Cooper's agents were never on their own. They were always part of the FBI team. Cooper's strategy was to give J. Edgar Hoover and the FBI organization all the credit for anything an individual agent did. If a special agent was a walking crime laboratory it was because Hoover equipped his agents with "more paraphernalia than ever a dramatist dreamed of for a stage detective: a six-inch magnifying glass, a Stillson wrench, a hammer, files, cold chisel, sealing wax, binoculars, hand saw, knife, notebook, seven or eight tubes of various colored powders, a camera with its own electric light, so devised that a person need only aim it at any object and trip the shutter! Add to this, a steel tape measure, soft-faced rubber tape for the transference of fingerprints, flashlight with extra battery, and other tools, and you have the equipment of one of the U.S. Bureau of Investigation men."[13] The G-Man knew about all the latest scientific crime-fighting techniques because Hoover insisted that his special agents "never stop studying crime. . . . In the Bureau of Investigation, no education is ever finished. Every man works on the rule laid down by Hoover: 'Always figure that the guy you're after knows more than you do. Then he'll never catch you asleep at the switch.' "[14]

Cooper's story also had the romance of far places, with "Bureau of Investigation men in Alaska, following a trail of clues that lead to the slayer of a murdered miner. Or another agent in Arizona, working on an Apache Indian murder case, waiting in stoical silence, as patiently as ever a red man had waited. . . . Or still another agent, at a gangster's funeral in the East, mingling with killers."[15] Cooper had material here for a hundred adventure thrillers.

The "big story" Cooper used to tie together all his adventure stories was that Hoover was using the FBI to unite American law enforcement into one cohesive and effective force. For this reason "criminals hate the bureau with a viciousness only thwarted crime can know."[16] Cooper's FBI turned every case into a test of strength between "crime" and a

newly invigorated American justice that was organized and on the
march, quickened by the vitalizing spirit and intelligence of J. Edgar
Hoover. Hoover's special agent was a new type of American hero.
Larger than life, he was "not an individual. Every officer of the Bureau
of Investigation represented the full power of American Justice, in 'getting his man.' "[17]

In each of his articles Cooper selected a batch of FBI adventures that
illustrated one of the bureau's crime-fighting techniques or one of
Hoover's theories about crime. The conclusion Cooper's readers were
to draw from the sum total of all these cases was that the G-Men were
collectively the greatest detectives of all time. Their trainer, leader, and
resident crime philosopher had therefore to be the master detective of
them all, "the most feared man the underworld has ever known."

"Crime Trap," the second of Cooper's *American Magazine* stories,[18]
was published in November, 1933, with Hoover listed as the author.
It used a tour of the bureau's fingerprint collection as an excuse to
spin a few yarns illustrating how criminals had been trapped by the
bureau's deltas, whorls, and loops. Cooper topped off his lecture-
demonstration with one of Hoover's prize cases, the capture of a
bankrobber named Jake Fleagle in 1928, based on evidence of an
unidentifiable single print left behind in his getaway car. Circumstan-
tial evidence connected some other suspects to the crime, and with so
much hysteria surrounding the case (the bankrobbers had killed the
bank's president and the town doctor) their conviction seemed certain.
Hoover doubted that the police had the right men, however, and he
turned that single fingerprint into an obsession within the bureau.
Since a single print could not be classified, Hoover had his men
memorize the print so that if they ever came across it in their normal
routine, they would recognize it. And finally Hoover's hunch paid off.
As an agent peered through his microscope, "suddenly the smudges on
the paper beneath the microscope ceased to be such. There was
murder in those lines and whorls, the bark of guns, a white-haired old
man standing alone against a bandit gang, firing shot for shot until the
guns of the murderous crew had cut him down."[19]

Courtney Ryley Cooper's early stories about Hoover were lively,
forceful, and well-written, sprinkled with vivid depictions of autopsies,
visits to abortionists, and cracks about gun molls who were "good
lays"—the kind of colorful crime lore that would be forbidden to
Hoover's tightly-edited writers of later years. As Cooper wrote these
early FBI stories, he experimented with ways of organizing his enormous treasure trove of FBI material with a controlling image that would
give some overall shape to the FBI story. He refined some approaches,
repeated them, and turned them into habitual routines. The FBI formula
Cooper finally perfected consisted of a story focusing on one single FBI

technique as a thread upon which to string series of adventure stories while the spotlight rested on Hoover as the central intelligence and unifying force behind the nation's anticrime crusade.

One idea Cooper had to discard was the concept of the FBI as a national police force. In his earliest stories Cooper would start by announcing that a "nationwide war has been declared on organized crooks, kidnappers and gangsters. Mr. Hoover is the front-line commander. Recently appointed Director of the new Division of Investigation, he is virtually the chief of a new and powerful national police force.'[20] A few months later, however, Cooper was coming out against "nationalization of police," saying that "a separate national police force might be difficult or even impossible to establish. Probably it would involve changes in the Constitution and other obstacles."[21] This signaled the end of the debate within the Justice Department over whether the New Deal should push for a national police force, with Hoover arguing against a federal takeover of all police activity. Cooper turned his FBI formula into a justification for Hoover's sophisticated (and self-serving) alternative to a national police force: his vision of the FBI as a strike force of super detectives dealing only with super-criminals. In lesser cases the FBI would merely lend "non-political assistance," and so the local police would still have to cope with the great mass of crime in the nation. This kind of federal law enforcement leadership, Cooper argued, would be constitutionally "no more difficult than Federal aid in road-building."[22]

Cooper's *Ten Thousand Public Enemies,* which appeared simultaneously with Cagney's *G-Men,* was the first book ever written about Hoover's FBI.[23] In it Cooper used his final version of the FBI formula to tie everything he had learned about the FBI into one coherent, fast-paced story that had a hero, plenty of villains, and a plot full of suspense. He had by now perfected his portrait of the FBI as a crime-detection machine with a disciplined army of evidence gatherers who reported back to a scientific evaluation and testing facility in Washington headed by "the most feared man the underworld has ever known," and he had plenty of stories about the gangsters the top G-Man had put in prison or the morgue. The trouble was that all these stories had been told before, either by Cooper himself or by others in the growing tribe of FBI writers. That meant Cooper was going to have to come up with still another angle. Cooper was also going to have to figure out a way to make the great gangsters and the tricks Hoover used to nab them meaningful to the shop girls, farm boys, and peaceful citizens who were supposed to buy his book. He was going to have to bring all these famous crimes right into his readers' homes.

To do this Cooper had to invent a general theory of American crime that made every crime story he told part of a unified saga of American law enforcement, a theory that would also provide a plausible justification for the kind of headline-hunting FBI Hoover had created. Cooper's solution to this problem in *Ten Thousand Public Enemies* gave the FBI not only an image but an ideology, an ideology that made public relations the most important of all the bureau's activities. Thus Cooper gave the FBI two weapons as important as any to be found on the bureau firing range: a powerful strategy for building up the FBI's public image and a powerful reason for implementing that strategy.

Ten Thousand Public Enemies captured its readers' attention with the assertion that "out of every forty-two persons in the United States one is either a convict, an ex-convict or possessed of a police record of arrest." Cooper calculated that "out of these three million there were ten thousand whose capture means that raiding officers must be prepared with machine guns, automatic rifles and perhaps tear-gas guns. . . . These are America's Public Enemies."[24] He played on his readers' fear of physical contamination by describing crime as a sort of social disease. "The dreamy-eyed manicurist who files away so enthusiastically at your nails," he wrote, "may be thinking only of closing time, when she can hurry to meet the man whose 'moll' she will eventually become. . . . It is almost certain that the very instruments which shape your fingernails have performed the same service for men who have known the cell block and the mess hall of prisons."[25]

Crime, Cooper wrote, was everywhere. "Common citizens should realize that Crime is not something which exists in dark corners and far away places. It rubs elbows with us, often it lives next door to us. It is in a position to strike us at any moment, steal our money, kill or abduct our loved ones, and take away our pleasures of life, substituting only grief and loss and suffering."[26] Hoover liked this image well enough to quote it verbatim in speeches throughout his career.

Cooper tried to make his readers feel additionally threatened by famous gangsters by relating the big shots to the small-time criminals who "lived next door." Public enemies were "the post graduates of crime, while local neighborhood badmen "might be called the general student body. . . . The dangerous criminal becomes such by a process of education. In practically every instance, he begins in a petty way, slowly becoming more vicious, until at last he is classed as a mad dog."[27]

Cooper used the images of the "roots" of crime and the "school" of crime to fit his account of America's "mad dogs" into a narrative organized by Homer Cummings's metaphor of an "army of crime." As Cooper told the story of this army of crime, he gave the names of hundreds of criminals, together with detailed biographies of dozens of them, all the while looking for themes that let otherwise unrelated criminals serve as illustrations of one of the Bureau's selling points. For example, he admitted that Wilbur Underhill, an Oklahoma hijacker and bankrobber with the nickname of the "Tri-State Terror" was small-time compared to Al Capone, but he linked their careers by claiming that "both Capone and Underhill were at one time merely members of the three million small timers from which graduate the Ten Thousand. . . . No one knows which man out of the tremendous number of candidates will become the one who, seemingly within a short time, takes his position on the first page as a national menace."[28] In other instances Cooper linked criminals together because their capture showed the effectiveness of one of Hoover's crime-fighting innovations. For example, after a description of Hoover's "Single Print File" Cooper observed that "an identification here means that one of the true enemies of society has been found in a crime with the possibility of an arrest to follow. Or perhaps I can better illustrate by borrowing an incident from the lives of several men who will be dealt with at more length in another part of this volume."[29] With that the reader becomes part of an FBI posse tracking down Pretty Boy Floyd.

Nearly half of Cooper's book was taken up by an extended narrative that wove nearly every famous public enemy case of 1933 and 1934 into a seamless web of villainy, using every trick of melodrama—coincidence of time and place, residence in the same prison, mutual acquaintances, shared girl friends—to show how a chain of evil linked each gangster into a vast criminal conspiracy. In Cooper's account of the gangster era all the big names—Frank Nash, Verne Miller, Fred Barker, Pretty Boy Floyd, Baby Face Nelson, Machine Gun Kelly, John Dillinger—merged into an outline of an archetypal public enemy locked in eternal (and losing) battle with a superhuman detective organization headed by an almost superhuman director.

Popular culture characteristically blends diverse historical personalities and events into general stereotypes of good and evil pitted against one another in melodramatic rituals that foster and celebrate cultural unity. Probably the only way to interest a popular audience in history is to reduce reality to a ritualistic formula. In any case that is what Courtney Ryley Cooper did with the gangbusting era. His formula was different from, for instance, the plot of Cagney's *G-Men* in that Hollywood's G-Man formula revolved around an action detective hero, while Cooper's FBI formula had a bureaucratic organization at its center; the individual agent was only a cog in a machine.

Cooper intended his survey of American crime in *Ten Thousand Public Enemies* to demonstrate how the internal structure of the army of crime (the "roots" and the "school") corresponded to J. Edgar Hoover's vision of the FBI's role and organization. *Ten Thousand Public Enemies* showed that the FBI was the negative image of the criminal army it was designed to fight. Cooper's selection of cases proved that "organized crime, as imagined by the average person, with a super-criminal at its

Publicity for The Street with No Name.

A scene from the FBI-authorized Street with No Name *(1936)*.

head, and underlings taking the orders, is largely a myth." According to Cooper, criminal "organization amounts to just this: a reputable man knows where to get reputable things done, and a crook has the same kind of knowledge in the field of criminality."[30] After a wealth of illustrations showing how the most famous gangsters in the country depended on the support of obscure local supplies of criminal services, Cooper concluded that "to rid ourselves of the big criminals, it is necessary to uproot the whole field."[31]

Cooper's thesis stood conventional thinking on its head. "The American citizen," Cooper wrote, "seems to possess a childlike faith in the theory that all crime is run by a guiding genius, and that if the brains of a plot be put in prison, then the problem of law enforcement is solved. The view is idiotic." The truth was that crime "thrives because it has a foundation . . . composed of the fences, the bond salesmen, the doctors, the lawyers, the merchants, the automobile salesmen, the women confederates, the hideout owners, and a hundred and one other forms of a supporting background which lives on crime while crime thrives upon it."[32]

Cooper's theory that the superstructure of national crime (Dillinger et al.) rested on a foundation of local crime unified the otherwise unrelated episodes of his book. The implication was that big-time gangsters existed only because local police were failing to deal with local crime. Cooper was trying to refute the popular assumption that local criminals were controlled by top crime figures; this would imply that local crime flourished because of the FBI's failure to put big-time crooks out of business. Cooper argued that there would be no celebrity criminals if the local police arrested the small-time criminals who supported the public enemies.

That sounded like a case for a federal takeover of law enforcement. Not at all. Actually, local law enforcement was ineffective because it was hobbled by an unholy alliance between corrupt politicians and local criminals. "The FBI," Cooper wrote, "is not superhuman. It is merely free of entanglements."[33] Local police chiefs had to take orders from crooked officials, while Hoover had insulated the bureau from politics, hiring and promoting strictly on the basis of education and merit. FBI agents were more effective than local cops because of their superior training and backup facilities, but also because they investigated their cases with no obligation to anything except Hoover's standing orders to "chase facts."

If the FBI were turned into a national police force with the overall responsibility for national law enforcement, Cooper explained, Hoover would have no choice but to staff it with personnel from the existing forces. This would give criminals and corrupt politicians the same foothold in the bureau they already had on the local level. And even if a national police force could somehow be recruited from untainted applicants, the strict standards of organization and control that Hoover maintained in his elite bureau would become impractical in a force of several hundred thousand. A national police force, even under the leadership of the FBI, would not redeem American law enforcement; it would only destroy the bureau. The bureau had to remain separate from the local police if it were going to remain a model for the reformation of local law enforcement. So what were the answer to the crime problem?

The answer, said Cooper, was for Hoover's FBI to go on doing what it was already doing. The bureau should continue to take over cases only when a federal law was violated, but more laws should be created to trigger federal intervention whenever crime crossed a state line. The FBI should remain independent from local law enforcement, Cooper said, but "communities should be granted the right of appeal, when they believe their police forces have become so entangled that they no longer serve as guardians of the public. To that end, there should be state enforcement bureaus, under the direction of the State's Attorney General, empowered to take control, conduct investigations of police units, and substitute for the district attorney if laxity has been discovered. Failing in this, the community should have the right to appeal to the Federal Government."[34]

The bureau should continue to provide services to the police that were beyond the capabilities of any local force: its fingerprint files, its collections of criminals' *modi operandi,* and its facilities for identifying automobiles, guns, bullets, and blood. It should offer its statistical services to help local police understand their own problems in the context of national conditions. The bureau should also coordinate and lead national manhunts once a criminal escaped local jurisdiction. Each step in Cooper's argument was illustrated with still more cases from the files.

The FBI's ultimate significance, Cooper wrote, would be as a catalyst for the regeneration of American law enforcement, and only when the FBI model was adopted throughout the country would American crime-fighting finally become effective. For this to happen, of course, the police would need to know what the bureau was doing and how it was doing it. One way this could happen would be to invite "any city in the country to send its best men to Washington, there to take the same training in the Department of Justice that now is given the regular Special Agents." Shortly thereafter Hoover managed to turn Cooper's proposal (which was, of course, modeled on Homer Cummings's similar idea at his 1934 conference) into reality, with the establishment on July 29, 1935, of the FBI's National Academy. Cooper's idea was for the academy to expose the police to the FBI's theories and methods;

thus a "nucleus of educators will have begun, which will eventually spread to the entire country. They can then become educators of their own departments. When this system enters law enforcement work and is received by citizens as a necessity to be supported by their votes, crime will truly begin to slide down hill."[35]

Cooper's grandiose vision of the FBI's mission meant that the real meaning of every FBI case was the contribution it could make to getting the public (and the police) to adopt the bureau as the model for all law enforcement agencies: to learn its methods, accept its help, and follow its leadership. The force that would persuade the public and the police to do all this would be the image of the FBI as an incorruptible, unbeatable, scientific organization of master detectives. Cooper's ultimate weapon against crime, then, was the FBI image, which meant that publicity should be considered the bureau's most important product. An FBI case was not really closed until it had been made a part of the towering public relations edifice that was the FBI image.

The publication of *Ten Thousand Public Enemies* was an event second only to Cagney's *G-Men* in determining the fortunes and future of the FBI. Courtney Ryley Cooper's portrait of the FBI was decisive in shaping the bureau's self-image; and, in turn, that self-image determined forever after what the FBI did and how it presented itself to the public.

For the first time all aspects of the FBI's operations had been unified into one coherent image. The formula Cooper created was so well-organized, so logical in the way that it made every part of the bureau contribute to the impressiveness of the whole, that it became the model for all future FBI publicity, even when public interest later shifted from gangsters to Nazi spies and then to Communist subversion. FBI-approved publicity for the rest of Hoover's life closely followed the formula of *Ten Thousand Public Enemies*—Cooper and Hoover's *Persons in Hiding*, Frederick L. Collins's *F.B.I. in Peace and War*, Don Whitehead's *F.B.I. Story*, FBI-approved radio and television programs like "War Against Crime," "This is Your F.B.I.," and "The F.B.I.," and the FBI headquarters tour. J. Edgar Hoover's speeches, no matter what the occasion, were miniature condensations of the book, imitating *Ten Thousand Public Enemies* not only in structure but in hard-boiled pulp magazine style.

In later years many critics of the bureau, among them a few frustrated former agents, complained that Hoover's FBI was the servant of its public relations image rather than a master crime-fighting agency. Agents resented being made to concentrate on cases that would provide the headlines and statistics to support Hoover's claim that the bureau was forever becoming more efficient and effective.[36] This criticism of Hoover's hunger for the headline showed that the original justification for FBI publicity had been forgotten—by the public and perhaps even

She's the **WOMAN** behind the **KILLER** behind the **GUN!**

J. EDGAR HOOVER* *tells her amazing story in*

"PERSONS IN HIDING"

LYNNE OVERMAN · PATRICIA MORISON · J. CARROL NAISH · JUDITH BARRETT

A Paramount Picture · Directed by LOUIS KING · Screen Play by William R. Lipman and Horace McCoy

Director of Federal Bureau of Investigation

REIGN OF TERROR!

Ruled by a Queen of crime . . . ten times tougher than the toughest man!

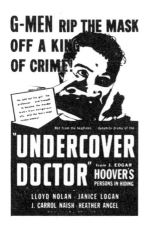

G-MEN RIP THE MASK OFF A KING OF CRIME!

Hot from the headlines . . . dynamite drama of the

"UNDERCOVER DOCTOR" *from J. EDGAR* HOOVER'S PERSONS IN HIDING

LLOYD NOLAN · JANICE LOGAN
J. CARROL NAISH · HEATHER ANGEL

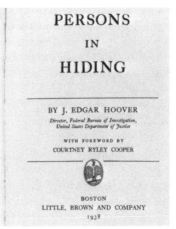

Based on
J. EDGAR
HOOVER'S
Book, Persons in Hiding

"QUEEN OF THE MOB"

A Paramount picture with
RALPH BELLAMY
BLANCHE YURKA
J. CARROL NAISH
JEAN CAGNEY
WILLIAM HENRY
RICHARD DENNING
Directed by James Hogan

PERSONS

IN

HIDING

BY J. EDGAR HOOVER

*Director, Federal Bureau of Investigation,
United States Department of Justice*

WITH FOREWORD BY
COURTNEY RYLEY COOPER

BOSTON
LITTLE, BROWN AND COMPANY
1938

Persons in Hiding *(1938), ghost-written for Hoover by Cooper,
was turned into three motion pictures.*

by the FBI. *Ten Thousand Public Enemies* had not only given the bureau an image, but also a reason for building that image. Neither
Cooper nor Hoover ever proposed that the FBI by itself ought to try to
rid the country of crime. Their original program called for the FBI to
lead the police and the public against crime. The FBI was therefore
doing its job only when its activities were encouraging the public to
support the law and to demand honest and effective law enforcement.
The FBI's proper role was to capture headlines, not crooks; an FBI case
could not be considered a success until it had been turned into a lesson
on how crime could be fought and beaten. Cooper's vision of the FBI's
law enforcement role, therefore, justified the bureau in publicizing its
activities and churning out books, movies, and radio and television
shows about them. The FBI had almost a sacred duty to blow its own
horn.

Since the FBI was supposed to be a model and an inspiration for
American law enforcement, Cooper's book encouraged Hoover to become a preacher spreading the gospel of scientific law enforcement,
standing before the nation as a "symbol of police professionalism" and
the "newly emerging cadre of police professionals." In this role Hoover
won the admiration and gratitude of the police themselves and their
most important professional association, the International Association
of Chiefs of Police.[37]

Ten Thousand Public Enemies ended with Cooper, like the other lay
criminologists of the depression era, blaming crime on the public's failure to support law enforcement. "It is society, meaning ourselves," he
wrote, "which, by its sodden attitude on election days, has allowed
many police departments to drift into the hands of politicians. It is
society which furnishes the juries that more often acquit than convict,
even while the judge seethes on his bench at the freeing of a man
palpably guilty. . . . Those who transgress do so because society has
made that transgression possible. Until society changes its viewpoint,
the criminal will certainly make no concessions."[38] Cooper helped convince Hoover that the battle against crime had to be fought in the arena
of public opinion. Law enforcement, as it was understood by Cooper,
Hoover, and most of the public during the thirties, depended on public
attitudes; that theory made publicity and propaganda indispensable aspects of police work. In 1937 two of the nation's most respected policemen, August Vollmer and Alfred E. Parker, wrote a study of law enforcement that concluded, as had *Ten Thousand Public Enemies*, that
"public opinion is a strong deterrent, and when you have the public
conscience and public opinion well organized there is bound to be
progress."[39]

After 1935 Hoover began to turn himself into a kind of covertly
Confucian teacher linking public ethics to private morals. In the 1970s

this made his homilies on "Crime and the American Home" seem anachronistic, but during the 1930s this kind of preaching was widely appreciated as essential to effective law enforcement. Chiefs Vollmer and Parker were only stating the conventional wisdom (which Hoover endorsed) when they wrote that "we cannot attain respect for law until we build family integrity. If more parents taught their children respect for authority, crime would gradually disappear."[40]

The FBI formula Courtney Ryley Cooper fabricated for Hoover in *Ten Thousand Public Enemies* was a sort of perpetual-motion publicity machine. It gave the FBI a mechanism for combining all its activities into one clear, coherent, attractive public image, and it made that image the key to Hoover's goal of leading and regenerating American law enforcement. The crucial role of public relations in the FBI formula justified doing whatever seemed necessary to nourish and maintain that image—indirectly by covertly crushing "enemies" of the FBI like Martin Luther King, *The Nation* magazine, or anyone else who threatened to discredit or debunk the FBI image; directly by churning out a flood of pro-FBI propaganda: press releases, speeches, magazine articles, movies, radio programs, and television shows.

When Cooper arrived at the bureau in 1933, the Research Division was only a tiny operation that turned out the few publications Hoover issued for the law enforcement community. After Cooper had convinced Hoover that public relations was actually the bureau's most important job, the Research Division expanded until, under the name of the Crime Records Division, it may finally have become the single most important unit in Hoover's FBI. Crime Records was Hoover's face to the world, handling the bureau's public relations with Congress, the White House, the law enforcement community, and the public. The two men who shaped and headed the Crime Records Division from 1935 until 1970, first Louis B. Nichols and then Cartha DeLoach, were Hoover's right-hand men, enjoying ranks subordinate only to Hoover's own and that of his lifelong associate director, Clyde Tolson. As Sanford J. Ungar noted, under Hoover the Crime Records Division was not simply "a typical public relations office but rather [was] . . . a part of the bureaucracy responsible for calculating and acting aggressively upon the bureau's best interest at any given moment."[41]

For all its strengths, however, Cooper's FBI formula contained, from the point of view of popular culture, a flaw that would hamper and eventually cripple Hoover's effort to use the FBI image to lead and remold American law enforcement. The problem was that Cooper's FBI formula did not contain within itself any mechanism for generating or sustaining public identification with the bureau. It was an effective instrument for capitalizing on public fascination with the FBI as long as current events and commercial G-Man entertainment were stirring up that interest, but it was itself incapable of producing the sort of public identification with the FBI that had been the source of Hoover's political and cultural power.

Hollywood had turned Hoover's FBI into a band of national heroes by portraying the special agent as popular culture's favorite figure of projective fantasy, the action detective. The official image of the FBI agent as he operated in Cooper's FBI formula, however, was hardly that of an action hero. Pop culture creates audience identification with action heroes like the G-Man by using them as embodiments of the public's most cherished cultural fantasies: absolute freedom, irresistible power, total self-reliance. The pop culture G-Man had all these qualities. He was a free agent who settled his own scores and saved his nation in the process. The G-Man was a fantasy of power for Americans locked in the ego-denying confines of anonymous bureaucracy and buffeted by forces they were powerless to overcome, to affect, or to withstand. The FBI's official formula offered the public no such food for projective fantasy. On the contrary, the special agent in the FBI formula was the antithesis of the action hero. He was faceless and anonymous, and repelled the sort of projective fantasies that the G-Man formula encouraged.

That created a dilemma for Hoover: depart too far from the G-Man formula in his public relations and risk forfeiting the public identification with the FBI that had turned the director into a national celebrity; depart too far from Cooper's FBI formula and jeopardize his dream of reforming American law enforcement along the lines of the scientific and professional model of the FBI. Would Hoover manage to manipulate popular culture, or would popular culture manipulate Hoover? That was the issue in Hoover's struggle for the next forty years to control the FBI's public image: a war between the G-Man formula and the FBI formula for what was the soul of Hoover's FBI—its public image.

7

The FBI Formula and John Dillinger:
A Case Study of Bureaucratic Heroism

J. Edgar Hoover used Courtney Ryley Cooper's formula to turn his entire bureau into the collective hero of the great public enemies cases of 1933 and 1934: Machine Gun Kelly, Pretty Boy Floyd, Baby Face Nelson, and, above all, John Dillinger. These cases gave Hoover a unique historical opportunity to turn himself and his men into pop culture legends. While Hoover was not responsible for the country's fascination with celebrity criminals during the depression, and while he had not played the leading role in turning the anticrime movement into a ritual of national unity, he was imaginative enough to realize that Hollywood had given him a once-in-a-lifetime chance to turn his obscure agency into a major cultural force; and with the help of Courtney Ryley Cooper, he developed a strategy for accomplishing this feat. To bring this about Hoover had to overcome American popular culture's habit of looking for individual action heroes in the great gangster cases; then he had to find a way for the entire bureau to share the country's gratitude for the national pride the victories over the public enemies had stimulated.

Hoover used Cooper's FBI formula to reshape public opinion to suit his ends, and he worked hard to persuade (or force) the news media and the entertainment industry to use his formula when they wrote stories based on the public enemies cases. With the entertainment industry Hoover's success was less than complete, but with the mass media his command of the FBI files (and briefing rooms) let him succeed in forcing newsmen to adopt the FBI formula, since that was the treatment most likely to lead to more choice FBI tidbits later on. Hoover worked throughout his life trying to make sure news stories about his bureau reflected the FBI public relations line. His greatest success was in the biggest FBI adventure of them all: the John Dillinger story.

John Dillinger was so central to the myth of Hoover's FBI that the case still gripped the director's imagination forty years after the gangster died. No matter what the topic of discussion, sooner or later Hoover would steer the conversation towards Dillinger. In 1967 top officials from the National Security Agency came to Hoover to ask him to resume the illegal surveillance techniques (illegal entry, mail opening, and electronic bugging) he had recently curtailed; their fifteen-minute appointment stretched to two and one-half hours while they heard "more than they wanted to about John Dillinger, 'Ma' Barker and the 'Communist Threat'."[1] One of Hoover's assistant directors recalled that "Hoover had a thing about Dillinger. If he were alive today and you went to see him, he'd tell you about Dillinger. The older he got the more he talked about Dillinger, Ma Barker, and all those old cases of the thirties. He would talk on and on about this stuff, which I guess is understandable, and is no criticism, but that's the way it was."[2] Hoover turned his office into a kind of Dillinger museum. A visitor in 1937 provided this description:

In the anteroom . . . the most compelling decorative object is a startling white plaster facsimile of John Dillinger's death mask. It stares, empty-eyed from under the glass of an exhibit case. . . . Grouped about the mask are souvenirs of the memorable night when the spectacular outlaw was cornered and shot down. . . . There are the straw hat he was wearing, a wrinkled snapshot of a girl which was fished from his trousers pocket, and the silver rimmed glasses he was wearing to heighten his disguise, one of the lens rims snapped by a bullet. There is a La Corona-Belvedere cigar he was carrying in his shirt pocket that summer night, still banded and wrapped in cellophane. . . . There is an almost unholy shriek of triumph in these stark, simple objects.[3]

Any irreverence about the Dillinger case moved Hoover to wrath. A doctor once wrote Hoover a friendly letter suggesting that the bureau ought to get rid of the more morbid Dillinger displays. Hoover blew up; the displays stayed, the doctor went on the bureau's "No Contact List."[4] Hoover's persecution of the social critic Harry Elmer Barnes during World War II may have had more to do with Barnes' criticism of the FBI's performance in the Dillinger case than with his pro-German sympathies.

In good times and bad Hoover's bureau liked to invoke the name of its all-time number one public enemy. Hoover felt the bureau had not only earned its spurs when it erased Dillinger, but had put the American public permanently in its debt. Thirty years after Hoover's death one of his assistant directors was still saying that the reason for the bureau's phenomenal success under Hoover was that "we did the job. We got the Dillingers and the Machine Gun Kellys."[5]

Hoover seemed to believe that Dillinger's relics were occultly responsible for the bureau's remarkable good fortune after the gangster's
death. "A tourist is dull-witted," wrote a reporter during the thirties, "if
he fails to comprehend, as he gapes at the [FBI museum] display cases,
that he is looking upon the rude implements and superstitious talismans
of a barbarous race that is slowly perishing under the relentless impact
of a superior one."[6] As FBI trainees today stalk through the Quantico,
Virginia, pistol range, one of the life-size targets that pop up bears the
unmistakable sneer of John Dillinger, which might well be regarded as
the bureau's adaptation of the sort of ritual warrior tribes use to initiate
their recruits into the mysteries of their clan's power.[7]

At a time when the Hearst papers dominated popular journalism,
Dillinger was the ultimate Hearst story, with so much publicity that
there seems to be no theme in the mass of verbiage. Actually, however,
there was a pattern in the great mass of Dillinger lore during the
thirties. The Dillinger story passed through three stages on its way to
becoming part of the FBI legend. The first of these legends prevailed
while Dillinger was still alive. This treated his life as an adventure story
pure and simple, with no sermonizing about Dillinger's sins or their
punishment. The second legend was born the night of Dillinger's death
at the Biograph Theater on July 22, 1934. The stories that made up this
legend were not so much about Dillinger himself as about his meaning
in a new national morality play. Dillinger was no longer a person but a
symbol of evil, proof that crime did not pay.

The final legend was the work of J. Edgar Hoover. He managed to
capture the force of the Dillinger saga, using it to fuel the mythologization of the bureau. In the months following Dillinger's death the full
propaganda value of the story was not fully exploited until Hoover
grabbed it. The papers were making Melvin Purvis, special agent in
charge of the Chicago office of the FBI, the hero of the Dillinger case.
The cultural impact of an individual hero like Purvis, however, would
be of no lasting political significance; if that heroism could be diffused
throughout the entire institution, on the other hand, it would survive
the individual and continue to buttress the organization when he had
vanished from the scene. Hoover managed to institutionalize the victory
over Dillinger, trapping the fast-escaping mythic steam of the case to
inflate the prestige of the entire FBI. Popular culture on its own had
turned the Dillinger case into a crime-and-punishment ritual that followed the G-Man formula. It was Hoover, acting through his publicists,
who persuaded the public to substitute the FBI formula as the orthodox
interpretation of the Dillinger story. That coup may well have been
J. Edgar Hoover's greatest public relations triumph.

Born in 1903, Dillinger was the son of an Indianapolis grocer; he quit
high school after one semester and started getting into trouble.[8] He

The inside story of
DILLINGER
AT LAST

By AVERY HALE *Special* | *Investigator for TRUE DETECTIVE*

True Detective, *December, 1934.*

(Top) Five studies of Public Enemy Number One from the cradle to his grave in the Dillinger family plot at the Crown Hill Cemetery, Indianapolis

I SEE where they're buryin' Dillinger today, Boss."
I stopped shaving and turned to look into the shiny brown face of the porter.
He held a copy of the *Plain Dealer* brought aboard when the west-bound Southwestern Limited stopped at Cleveland at 7.00 a.m. on a steaming morning last July.
"Yes," I replied. "The country should give the Department of Justice three cheers."
"That's what I say," said the porter. "He certainly was one bad man, that Dillinger fellow, Boss."
I nodded, turned and looked out of the window of the smoking compartment. The

Southwestern Limited was roaring through the Indiana countryside, two hours to Indianapolis, the first stop of my long journey over the Dillinger trail to marshal the facts the newspapers hadn't printed about America's Public Enemy Number One—the truth about John Dillinger from the cradle to a pool of blood in an alley alongside a third-run Chicago movie-house.
The sprawling farms of the Hoosier State, melting into the hot horizon, were crisp and rust-colored, the toll of the great drought. But the good folks who killed the parched earth had forgotten for the time about the long-dry skies; they thought of

(Above, and left) The automatic Dillinger drew too late. He reached for this gun when realization came that he had been trapped

joined the navy, deserted, and got married. In September, 1924, twenty-one years old, Dillinger held up the grocery store in Mooresville, Indiana. It hardly seemed the start of a great criminal career. He and his accomplice, the umpire of the local baseball team, panicked, beat up the grocer, and ran away without a cent. Arrested almost immediately, Dillinger took the prosecutor's promise of leniency and pleaded guilty. He got ten-to-twenty years and actually served nine of them. His pal hired a lawyer and went before a different judge, who gave him two years.

When Dillinger became famous ten years later, many people thought he had gotten a raw deal. Extenuating details like these tended to blur the clarity of the FBI formula, so Hoover had to declare them irrelevant: "After the demise of John Dillinger," he said, "many trusting souls came to his defense on the basis that he had been embittered by a long sentence while his companion in the crime was given a shorter one. This is not true. . . . Dillinger was a cheap, boastful, selfish, tight-fisted, plug-ugly, who thought only of himself."[9]

Dillinger made two good friends in jail, professional bank robbers Harry Pierpont and Homer Van Meter, and he wrangled a transfer when they were moved to the state prison at Michigan City, Indiana. There he met two more future members of his gang, John Hamilton and Charles Makley. These five, with Pierpont, the most experienced and smartest, as the leader, decided to team up when they got out. But first they had to get out.

Dillinger's behavior suddenly improved. The parole board was impressed and released him on May 22, 1933. Then he had to get his friends out. He robbed a couple of banks, bought guns with the loot and tossed them over the prison wall to his pals. Before Pierpont could get to the weapons, other inmates turned them over to the warden. The next batch of guns went into a barrel of thread bound for the prison shirt factory; this time the plan worked. On September 26, 1933, the Pierpont gang broke out, but now Dillinger was back in jail. The police had caught him visiting a girl friend. On October 12 the gang broke into the Lima, Ohio, jail, killed the sheriff, and set Dillinger free. Then they began to rob banks. The John Dillinger story had begun.

The whole Midwest was the gang's hunting ground as they raided banks in Ohio, Indiana, Wisconsin, South Dakota, and Iowa. Though Harry Pierpont was the gang's undisputed leader, Dillinger caught the public's fancy: he wore a jaunty white straw boater, traded quips with the tellers and customers, and made an athletic leap over the tellers' barrier his personal signature, even when there was an open gate close by. The original Dillinger gang stayed intact for only three months, but that was enough to make them national celebrities. They robbed banks, raided police arsenals, and ranged from Florida to Arizona. By December, 1933, both Chicago and Indiana had special "Dillinger Squads" hunting for him full-time. Newspapers combed their files and searched the Indiana countryside for background material on Dillinger. Detective magazines stuffed their pages with the exploits of the "Dillinger Gang," which they promoted as a twentieth-century version of the Jesse James and Cole Younger gang.

A photograph in *True Detective Magazine* finally led to their capture on January 23, 1934, in Tucson, Arizona. That was the end of the original Dillinger gang. Pierpont was extradited to Ohio, where he was executed for the murder of the sheriff during the Lima jail break. Dillinger was sent back to Indiana for killing a policeman during an East Chicago bank robbery. This set the stage for the most famous of all Dillinger's exploits, one of the most celebrated feats in the annals of American crime.

The news media and local politicians turned Dillinger's arrival at the Crown Point, Indiana, jail into a carnival. The sheriff at Crown Point, a woman named Lillian Holley, gave reporters the run of the jail. One of the photos showed Sheriff Holley and the district attorney smugly leering at each other, while Dillinger, his arm draped comfortably over the attorney's shoulder, grinned sardonically at the camera as though amused at the trouble the picture would cause after his escape. And,

Above: Tucson fireman William Benedict (right), who identified the Dillinger gang.

Left: Dillinger with the wooden pistol he used in the Crown Point break. Photograph courtesy of Wide World.

Dillinger at the Crown Point jail with Prosecutor Robert Eskill and Sheriff Lillian Holley. Photograph courtesy of UPI.

incredibly, he did escape. Producing a wooden pistol carved from a broken washboard, he scared the guards into releasing him, stole Sheriff Holley's car, and headed for Illinois.

Dillinger's wooden pistol became an instant pop culture icon, a symbol of law enforcement idiocy and incompetence. Dillinger realized he had finally evened the score with the police, the wardens, and the judges, and to make sure they did not get off the hook, he gave his father a photograph of himself with the wooden pistol in one hand, an unmistakably real machine gun in the other. From this point on Dillinger seemed to be bent on turning himself into a legend by leaving a trail of documents to serve as the raw material for mythology. For example, he wrote to his sister:

Dear Sis—I am sending Emmett my wooden gun and I want him to always keep it. I see that Deputy Blunk says I had a real forty five that's just a lot of hooey to cover up because they don't like to admit that I locked eight deputys and a dozen trustys up with my wooden gun before I got my hands on the two machine guns and you should have seen their faces Ha! Ha! Ha! Don't part with my wooden gun for any price for when you feel blue all you will have to do is look at the gun and laugh your blues away Ha! Ha![10]

The joke was on the police, and the whole country was laughing at them. One historian reported that the "portion of the public which writes letters to the papers was largely pro-Dillinger, or at least anti-authority."[11]

People everywhere were talking about Dillinger. They were looking for him everywhere. Pretty soon they were seeing him everywhere. The *Chicago Tribune* reported that "Mr. Dillinger was seen yesterday . . . in a State Street store in Chicago; negotiating for a twelve-cylinder car in Springfield, Illinois; buying a half-dozen sassy cravats in Omaha, Nebraska . . . and strolling down Broadway swinging a Malacca cane in New York. He also bought a fishing rod . . . in Montreal, and gave a dinner . . . in Yucatan, Mexico. But, anyhow, Mr. Dillinger seems to have kept very carefully out of London, Berlin, Rome, Moscow, and Vienna. Or at least if he did go to those places yesterday he was traveling incog."[12] According to *Time*, "If John ('Killer') Dillinger has really been at all the places he was reported to have been in the last month, he must leap along the central plains like a demented Indian's ghost."[13]

With Pierpont gone Dillinger put together a new gang. Their first job was the bank in Sioux Falls, South Dakota, and it was a beauty. John Hamilton went into town first and let it be known that he was a Hollywood producer planning to shoot a gangster movie the next day. On March 6, 1934, witnesses saw an "actor" holding the whole police department at gunpoint while the "cast" of gangsters looted the bank and raced away. Dillinger had made fools of the police again.

By now the FBI had joined the hunt. After escaping from Crown Point, Dillinger had stolen Sheriff Holley's car and had driven it across the Indiana-Illinois state line, a federal offense. The FBI's Dillinger man-hunt, however, was a fiasco from the start—and almost until the end. Dillinger ruined the reputation of every local and state police force he went up against. He almost ruined the FBI's.

Twice the bureau had Dillinger in its grasp; twice he slipped away. Soon after the FBI entered the case, two agents located the apartment in Saint Paul, Minnesota, where he was recuperating from wounds gotten in a Mason City bank robbery. The G-Men walked up to the front door and knocked. Dillinger's girl friend answered and stalled the agents in the hall, giving Dillinger time to grab a machine gun and blast his way past the startled agents. On the second occasion the FBI had Dillinger's family farm staked out. Again the bandit outwitted the G-Men and slipped past the guards for a family reunion while the FBI watched outside.

The bureau's joint operations with the local police were ruined re-peatedly by cops leaking the plans to their reporter pals. Once special agents were waiting in ambush for Dillinger while newsboys around them shouted, "U.S. lays Dillinger trap around Starks Building."[14] While the hunt went on, Dillinger continued to ridicule the police. When he and Homer Van Meter ran out of guns, they took over the police headquarters in Warsaw, Indiana, and looted the armory. The nation looked on and laughed.

Finally the bureau got the lead it had been hoping for. On April 22, 1934, an informant tipped the FBI in Chicago that the whole Dillinger gang was holed up in a resort called Little Bohemia in northern Wiscon-sin. There was no time for any sort of carefully plotted operation. Melvin Purvis, chief of the bureau's Chicago office, piled his agents into a chartered plane and landed at an airfield fifty miles from Little Bohe-mia. He commandeered some cars and drove off into the night with agents riding on the running boards and the windows bristling with machine guns. Back in Washington J. Edgar Hoover called in reporters and announced that Dillinger was surrounded and couldn't get away. The press should get ready for good news. [15]

There was to be no good news for Hoover that day. As the confused agents crashed blindly through the underbrush, watchdogs began to bark and lights flashed on. Three of the lodge's guests, drunk and terrified by the artillery their big-city drinking buddies had suddenly sprouted, raced out of the lodge and the G-Men started shooting. One of the guests was killed; another was badly wounded. From inside the lodge a new and murderous member of the Dillinger gang, Baby Face Nelson, sprayed the woods with machine-gun fire. Outside all was con-fusion. Dogs were barking and the wounded were screaming. Agents were hung up on brush and barbed wire; there was random firing in all directions. Meanwhile Dillinger and his gang slipped out the back and disappeared into the dark. Baby Face Nelson ran into two agents a little while later and killed one of them. Purvis was left with the girls the gang had left behind, a shot-up lodge, a dead agent, and a dead civilian. Despite advantages of surprise and numbers, the FBI had surrounded most of the nation's top fugitives in one place, had announced their capture in advance, and had come away empty-handed. In Washington there was talk of demoting Hoover; a petition from Wisconsin called for Purvis's dismissal "at least until Dillinger is caught or killed."[16]

Dillinger may have signed his own death warrant by humiliating the Bureau. Already the Indiana State Police's Dillinger Squad had vowed to shoot Dillinger on sight. Now the FBI could salvage its reputation only by killing him. Assistant Attorney General Joseph B. Keenan "thumped his desk wrathfully " and swore, "I don't know where or when we will get Dillinger, but we will get him. And you can say for me that I hope we will get him under such circumstances that the Government won't have to stand the expense of a trial."[17]

The FBI's image and Hoover's job were now on the line, so Hoover sent Inspector Samuel P. Cowley with a special Dillinger squad to reinforce Purvis's Chicago office, telling Cowley, "Stay on Dillinger. Go everywhere the trail takes you. Take everyone who ever was remotely connected with the gang." Hoover ordered Cowley to "take him alive if you can but protect yourself,"[18] but Attorney General Cummings said that the policy was, "Shoot to kill—then count to ten."[19]

It was small consolation at the time, but the Little Bohemia incident made the federal government look so bad that it helped Roosevelt ram the attorney general's Crime Control Package through Congress. Roosevelt claimed the FBI needed wider jurisdiction and the right to carry weapons and make arrests if it was going to have a chance against Dillinger.[20]

Little Bohemia turned the Dillinger case into a comedy. The *Washington Star* ran front-page cartoons ridiculing Attorney General Cummings; one showed Dillinger complaining to Cummings that the government's reward of $10,000 was an insult. Another had Dillinger offering to turn himself in if Cummings would split the reward with him.[21]

Once again there were bogus reports that Dillinger had been spotted in faraway places. An English innkeeper overheard four of his customers using "strange slang" like "chief" and "okay," so he phoned the police to say, "I have Dillinger here. His whole gang." The "gang" turned out to be four American Rhodes Scholars on their way to Oxford.[22]

As far as the public was concerned, the Dillinger case was at this stage a light-hearted adventure with comic overtones, and the media avoided discussion of any moral aspects of the story that would have

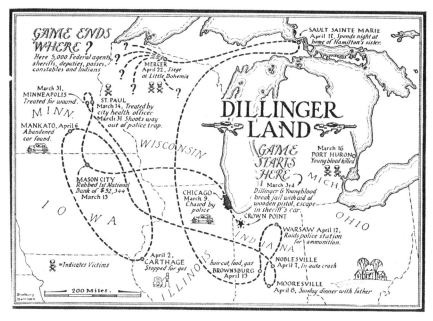

After Little Bohemia Time *portrayed the Dillinger manhunt as a party board game. Reprinted by permission from* Time, The Weekly Newsmagazine; *copyright 1934, Time, Inc.*

spoiled the fun. On May 7, *Time* magazine ran a four-page Dillinger feature with the headline "BAD MAN AT LARGE" over a detailed summary of "Desperado Dillinger's" career.[23] There were three pages of photos with captions self-consciously loaded with gangster-movie clichés: "UNDER THE GREENWOOD TREE lived Robin Hood. And John Dillinger stopped to rest . . . spending but not collecting the wages of sin . . . TO BE PLENTIFULLY LOVED and diligently hunted is the lot of desperadoes."

Time's story was laid out to look like a game it called "Dillinger Land," with a map of the Midwest for a board. Crown Point, Indiana, was labeled "Game Starts Here," and a dotted line marked Dillinger's trail, with skulls wherever cops or robbers had been killed. The trail led to Little Bohemia, then branched out in all directions, each possible trail ending in a question mark: "THE LAST BULLET . . . will lodge at a spot marked X on future maps. . . . At the end of the long trail—marked by crosses for dead policemen, Federals and gangsters—on top of the last X will lie John Dillinger, corpse."

While Dillinger was still alive, reporters on his story rarely used the crime-and-punishment formula. His was the greatest adventure story of the time, so Dillinger was turned into an all-American hero with an all-American background and all-American ambitions. *Time*'s story quoted Dillinger's father: " 'JOHN IS A GOOD BOY . . . he has horse sense.' So said a 70-year-old father. . . . 'John is a country boy and likes to get back here once in a while for good green vegetables and home-cooked meals.' "

Since adventure heroes are idolized for their strength and courage—qualities that have little to do with morality—during this phase of his legend Dillinger was often compared to other classic heroes of American folk adventure. The same story had a picture of the youthful Dillinger and a caption that read, "GREAT DESPERADOES from little urchins grow. When John Dillinger was 10 he, like Tom Sawyer, was a poor country boy. Sometimes he may have dreamed of being another Abe Lincoln or Jesse James. . . . [but not]that he would achieve a great unwritten odyssey: Through the Midwest with a Machine Gun."

Tom Sawyer, Jesse James, Abe Lincoln, Odysseus—all names to stir the imagination of readers identifying with the heroes of adventure fantasy, heroes famous for hoodwinking friends and foes. In the adventure formula morality is simply irrelevant, particularly when the hero is the trickster whose archetype in classical literature is Odysseus, and who later appears as the confidence man, the horse-trader and the used-car salesman. Audiences identify with trickster heroes because they are, like all popular heroes, winners, but also because they beat enemies who are stronger, richer, and more respectable, humiliating them and their pretensions to social and moral superiority. While John Dillinger was robbing banks he was the trickster hero, like young Abe Lincoln using tall tales to outsmart rival lawyers, or Tom Sawyer conning his pals into whitewashing a fence. The police, the prosecutors and the FBI were all Dillinger's dupes, and the public enjoyed the show. An Indianapolis paper printed a letter from a reader who may have spoken for many of Dillinger's admirers: "I am for Dillinger. Not that I am upholding him in any of his crimes; that is, if he did any. Why should the law have wanted Dillinger for bank robbery? He wasn't any worse than banks and politicians who took the poor people's money. Dillinger did not rob poor people. He robbed those who became rich by robbing the poor. I am for Johnnie."[24]

Dillinger had succeeded in turning his life into a living legend, but for that legend to survive, Dillinger would have to keep on living. The trickster hero is by definition indestructible, his dupes endlessly gullible. But something was about to happen that would prove that this trickster could be tricked himself, and that there were limits to his gulls' gullibility: the G-Men were about to kill him. Since the myth of Dillinger as the trickster hero was soon to be defunct, popular culture was going to have to find a new angle on the Dillinger story.

On July 21, 1934, Anna Sage, the famous "woman in red," came to Purvis with a proposition. She was the madam of an Indiana brothel, and the government was trying to deport her to her native Rumania for morals offenses. In return for a promise to halt the proceedings, she was willing to hand over one of her house's regular customers, her friend John Dillinger. Purvis and Sam Cowley promised to do what they could.

The next day, Sunday, July 22, Sage's call came through. The G-Men set up their ambush at Chicago's Biograph Theater, where Dillinger planned to see a movie with Sage. Purvis told his men: "Gentlemen, you know the character of John Dillinger. If . . . we locate him and he makes his escape it will be a disgrace to our Bureau."[25] At 10:30 P.M. Purvis, peering into each face as the audience surged through the doors, at last saw Dillinger: "I struck the match and lit my cigar. The men knew that Dillinger had been identified. . . . Dillinger was surrounded. I was about three feet to the left and a little to the rear of him. I was very nervous; it must have been a squeaky voice that called out, 'Stick 'em up, Johnny.' "[26] A second later Dillinger was dead, and within hours he had been transformed from a popular trickster into a symbol of the futility of rebellion against society. A new pop culture formula had taken over.

Hearst's tabloid in New York, the *Daily Mirror,* frontpaged a picture of Dillinger's corpse with the caption:

The arm of the law collects its Toll! For months John "Snake Eyes" Dillinger evaded the dragnet of the law. . . . Police could not catch him. Walking away from a Chicago movie house, Dillinger was mowed down the same way he did his victims—without warning. Our ex-Public Enemy No. One is shown here on a slab in the ice box section of the Chicago morgue. Those who prey on mankind should keep this picture in mind. It symbolizes the fate that awaits them. "YOU CAN'T WIN."[27]

Inside the paper there were more pictures of Dillinger's body with the headline " 'ICE BOX CAGES HUMAN COBRA'." The lead of the top story began, "A monstrous freak was the attraction here today—a cross between a mad dog and a cobra. It went by the name of John Dillinger and walked like a man until dead."[28] Another story focused on the $7.70 John Dillinger carried when he died: "So he died with about $7.70. In all my multifarious experience with the men who steal fortunes, they have always died with just about $7.70."[29] The rest of the paper was crammed full of Dillinger features: a scorecard listing Dillinger's crimes and victims, pictures of his gun, and more pictures of his corpse. The next day's centerfold had more Dillinger pictures, some of them close-ups of his wounded face, and the caption: "Old Saw that Crime Doesn't Pay can be Epitomized No Better Than By These Photos—Take a Good Look."[30]

The media swung so violently against Dillinger because reporters had to come up at once with a new lead for the Dillinger story without much time for careful reflection. Popular culture never simply describes

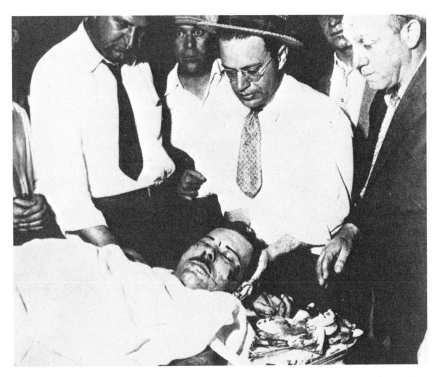

Dillinger's death turned the newspapers' adventure story into a subject for editorial sermons.

"what happens": it processes current events by fitting them into an interpretive context that tells the public why the news is interesting. While Dillinger was alive, each new development was a fresh surprise, another trick played on the law, and so the ultimate source of interest was that nobody knew how the story would turn out. For suspense to be enough to keep the story moving, each day had to generate series of new possibilities, each ending with a question mark, so that the unwritten final sentence of each episode was "to be continued." Once the suspense was over, the adventure formula ground to a halt. Once the trickster had been tricked, his characterization was obsolete. Now reporters had to come up with a new gimmick to make the Dillinger story meaningful.

They did not have to look very far. The death of a criminal was the standard cue for the oldest routine of them all, the traditional crime-and-punishment formula. In a matter of hours Dillinger was designated a ritual victim, the latest illustration of the law's inevitable triumph over crime. He was the transgressor whose punishment repairs the moral order and restores the rule of right.

While Dillinger was still free, the crime-and-punishment formula was unusable, because until Dillinger was captured, it did not help the cause of law and order to emphasize the symbolism of the case: his career was proving that crime was superior to the law from the standpoint of both fun and profit. As one Indianapolis editorial had wailed, "The laws and police of Indiana and neighboring states seem helpless to catch and punish him."[31]

Now that Dillinger's run was over, the moral symbolism of his career was a little more satisfactory. Hearst's editorial was typical of pop culture's new and moralistic reaction to Dillinger's death:

Mr. Dillinger knows now that no individual, no matter how clever and ruthless he may be, can wage war successfully on a hundred and twenty-three million people. . . .

There will be general congratulations also that Dillinger was not spared to hire some smart criminal lawyer to spare him from the death penalty and then to get him pardoned or paroled after he had served a few years of his time. . . .

As long as justice can be perverted by stupid rules of procedure, by political prosecutors, and by unscrupulous attorneys, this country will have its share of Dillingers—and the only way to deal with them will be to shoot them down as mercilessly as this modern Jesse James was disposed of in the streets of Chicago.[32]

No longer a sardonic adventurer, Dillinger was now the personification of evil, the greatest of modern criminals, the all-time public enemy number one. The *San Francisco Chronicle* called him the "arch-criminal of the age."[33] Death had, so to speak, depersonalized Dillinger, and had worked an even greater transformation on his executioners. The erstwhile comedy cops were now heroes who had provided "a hundred and twenty-three million" Americans with vengeance against a criminal waging "personal warfare against society." Popular culture had spontaneously ritualized Dillinger's death, presenting J. Edgar Hoover with the greatest public relations challenge and opportunity of his career.

Rituals exist to weld a population of individuals into a united people, and that is what was happening in the wake of Dillinger's death. At this moment the culture customarily begins looking for the hero who has provided the new-found sense of strength and security. The danger Hoover faced was that this credit would go to the individual FBI agents who were in on the kill, thus depriving the case of any lasting institutional significance. Hoover would have to keep pop culture from turning the case into an action detective story; his hero could not be an individual G-Man; it would have to be the whole FBI. He would have to convince the public to adopt Courtney Ryley Cooper's FBI formula, not the G-Man variation on the action detective story, as the definitive interpretation of John Dillinger's cultural meaning.

A legend had died at the Biograph, and Chicagoans flocked to the theater. Some dipped their handkerchiefs in the blood while other enterprising citizens tried to sell "authentic" bloodstain souvenirs. Reporters interviewed the long parade of sightseers trailing through the morgue—a woman said, "I wouldn't have wanted to see him except I think it's a moral lesson."[34]

The big story the day after Dillinger's death was the search for the hero of the new Dillinger saga. Who was "the man who got Dillinger"? For Jack Lait of the Hearst chain the prime candidate was whoever fired the fatal bullet, so he scurried around at the inquest sniffing every gun he saw. When Inspector Sam Cowley shook him off, Lait had his hero: "The man who has the deepest notch in his gun in the world," Lait's story announced, was, "Samuel A. Cowley."[35] Actually Cowley had not even fired his pistol, and in line with Hoover's goal of spreading credit throughout the bureau the FBI made a deliberate decision not to identify the bullets in Dillinger's body. They wanted his death to be regarded as a "firing squad" execution with the entire bureau as the executioner. (According to the FBI's own folklore, the death bullet had been fired by Agent Charles Winfield.)[36]

Most papers did not bother about death bullets. They thought the hero obviously had to be the G-Man in command of the ambush, Melvin Purvis, so within hours Purvis was a new national hero. To qualify Purvis for his new glory newspapers tended to inflate his rank in the FBI hierarchy. The *New York Evening Journal* called him "Chief of the Chicago Office of the Department of Justice's Division of Investigation" with a picture of him at his desk "after successfully 'getting' his man, John Dillinger."[37] The *Journal* also ran a series of Dillinger pictures laid out like a movie filmstrip titled "Underworld Melodrama—in Three Scenes—(A U.S. Production directed by Melvin Purvis)."[38] The media's need for a hero quickly made Purvis more famous than Hoover. Papers even called him "Chief of the Federal Bureau of Investigation."[39] *Time* ran a picture of Purvis shaking hands with Homer Cummings with the caption "Melvin Purvis and Friend."[40] When Purvis killed Pretty Boy Floyd in October the *New York Evening Journal* headlined its story, "And Again Melvin Purvis Triumphs."[41]

As the hero of pop culture's action detective formula treatment of the Dillinger case, Purvis so eclipsed the rest of the FBI that the media ignored Hoover and the bureau and glorified Homer Cummings as the ace G-Man's immediate boss. Stories generally called Purvis a "Department of Justice" man and the case a "Department of Justice job." In Chicago Hoover found himself overshadowed by Purvis; in Washington, by Cummings. The *Washington Star* ran a story on the shooting that included a background profile on Cummings. The story, "Attorney General Becomes Superpoliceman for Nation," mentioned Hoover only as one of Cummings' appointees.[42] Radio networks went to Cummings for a statement claiming credit in the case for the Justice Department. After congratulating himself, Cummings said, "In the removal of Dillinger, however, let a somber warning be spread among all the denizens,

Heroes of the hour: Melvin Purvis with Homer Cummings. Photograph courtesy of Wide World.

big and little, of the underworld. Let it be noted that the Federal Army of Justice is upraised in protection of the law. Dillinger's capture is not the end. It is only a fresh beginning."[43]

As far as the public could tell from these first stories about Dillinger's death, J. Edgar Hoover and the rest of the FBI had had no part in the Biograph ambush. Hoover was quoted growling that Dillinger "was just a yellow rat that the country may consider itself fortunate to be got rid of. There are other rats to be gotten, however, and we are not taking any time off to celebrate Dillinger."[44] He sounded like an outsider trying to grab credit from the country's newest hero, Melvin Purvis, ace G-Man.

Hoover had his work cut out for him. He was going to have to reduce Purvis from a hero to a pawn. He was going to have to shift the real drama in the case from Chicago to Washington. The new Dillinger story, to fit the pattern of the FBI formula, would demonstrate that Hoover had led and coordinated the whole operation from his office in Washington, and that Purvis had only followed Hoover's orders.

Hoover's strategy for persuading the public to adopt the FBI formula's version of the Dillinger story was to open the bureau's files to reporters who adopted the bureau line. The first analysis of the Dillinger case to use the FBI formula was a six-part syndicated newspaper feature written by Hoover's old friend, Rex Collier.[45] Collier's thesis was that "Hoover himself had directed the nation-wide search by long distance telephone from his office at the Department of Justice."[46] Collier sought to prove that Dillinger's capture was the payoff at the end of a nationwide campaign coordinated by Hoover. It was Hoover's scientific facilities in Washington that had evaluated each new lead. It was Hoover who had instructed Purvis and the other field agents on their every move. The operation could not have succeeded, Collier argued, except for Hoover's supervision, encouragement, and intelligence.

As Collier told the story, the FBI was such an unstoppable investigative machine that once it entered a case the conclusion was foreordained. The FBI's procedures were so scientifically thorough that the bureau was bound, sooner or later, to turn up the clue that would crack the case. Since the outcome was determined in advance, it was irrelevant to single out any particular agent as a hero or any particular lead as the key to a case. If one agent failed, another would succeed. If one clue led up a blind alley, another would lead to paydirt.

With the help of this theory Collier could downplay the importance of the "woman in red." She was an embarrassment to Hoover because her help seemed to make the solution of the case depend on a lucky break instead of scientific research. The way Collier told the story, Sage's information was not crucial because if she hadn't led the FBI to Dillinger, the FBI would have caught him with its foolproof scientific methods. In Collier's scenario Dillinger was dead the minute the bureau had come into the case. This made Dillinger's theft of Sheriff Holley's car, and not Anna Sage's tip, the key to the case, because it had been that interstate car theft that brought the FBI into the investigation. Until Dillinger made that mistake, Hoover's men had waited impatiently for Dillinger "to knock the chip off their shoulders by violating some federal law."[47] According to Collier, Dillinger had always dreaded the FBI: "Dillinger always had a wholesome respect for the G-Men—those college bred agents marshalled by J. Edgar Hoover into the Government's far-flung undercover agency. The Federals . . . were not open to 'propositions,' they used brains as well as brawn and State Lines meant nothing to them. And most important of all, they never gave up on a case."[48]

The FBI formula made any details that detracted from the FBI's performance—the fiasco at Little Bohemia, the murky details surrounding Anna Sage's past, the bargain struck between her and Purvis, and the bystanders wounded at the Biograph—irrelevant. The real meaning of the case was that Hoover always got his man. Once the bureau entered the case, Dillinger was doomed and he knew it. The exact circumstances of his death, the name of the man who had pulled the trigger, the tip-off that put Dillinger on the spot—these were quibbles that dwindled into insignificance before the grand scope of the FBI's operations.

The principal obstacle to getting the public to buy the FBI formula of the Dillinger case was Melvin Purvis. As long as he was in the spotlight, the public would not abandon pop culture's formulation of the case as an old-fashioned, one-on-one battle between a hero of the law and a symbolic criminal. Purvis had to go.

In the months immediately following Dillinger's death, however, Purvis got even more glory. After Dillinger the newspapers designated Pretty Boy Floyd, wanted by the FBI for his supposed part in the 1933 Kansas City Massacre, as public enemy number one. Purvis took personal charge of the case, tracked Floyd down, and killed him. Then he set out after the next public enemy number one, Baby Face Nelson. As the FBI closed in, Nelson managed to shoot Special Agent Herman Hollis and mortally wound Sam Cowley, now a roving inspector assigned to public enemy cases. Purvis rushed to the bedside of the dying Cowley, got a deathbed identification of Nelson, and then called in the reporters to tell them he had taken "an oath in Cowley's blood" to avenge him; "IF IT'S THE LAST THING I DO, I'LL GET BABY FACE NELSON" ran the headlines from coast to coast.[49] That was too much for Hoover. He pulled Purvis off the case and sent Inspector Hugh H. Clegg to take over.[50]

That ended Purvis's FBI career. He quit during the summer of 1935 and wrote a book about his adventures called *American Agent*. Naturally Purvis's book made him the hero of the Dillinger case. Hoover got so angry that he changed Purvis's resignation to a termination "with prejudice"—a bad conduct discharge. Purvis went to Hollywood, where he became head of the "Post Toasties Law and Order Patrol." Later he became the announcer for an unsanctioned G-Man radio show called "Top Secrets of the FBI," where he was introduced as "the man who got Dillinger." In 1960, nearly forgotten by the public, he committed suicide, supposedly with the same gun he had carried that night at the Biograph.

Even though the FBI's official formula treated the entire bureau as the hero of the Dillinger story, there still had to be someone in charge at the Biograph. With Purvis out of the bureau and in disgrace, Sam Cowley fit the bill perfectly. First, he was dead, so there was no danger that he would turn his glory to personal advantage. Secondly, by honoring one of its martyrs, someone who had given up his life for the FBI, the bureau would be honoring itself. Third, since Cowley had been Hoover's personal representative on the Dillinger case, any credit Cowley got flowed directly back to Washington without being absorbed by the agents in the field. For these reasons it became permanent FBI policy to tear down Purvis as a glory hound and build up Cowley as the epitome of the corporate G-Man hero. In a 1938 FBI casebook that Courtney Ryley Cooper ghosted, Hoover said, "It was Sam Cowley . . . who deserved the credit. . . . His control was supreme in the Chicago region. . . . It was he who mapped the campaign, working from a secret office with unlisted telephones, and it was this campaign which led to Dillinger's death." Without mentioning Purvis by name, Hoover reduced him to the level of a decoy: "While the newspapers turned the full glare of their spotlight upon the regulation Field Officer of the Bureau, Sam Cowley continued to work without their knowledge in a secret headquarters, where . . . the Special Agents of the Special Squad could come and go without interference."[51]

Purvis was a nonperson in later FBI accounts of the Dillinger case. In Hoover's *Persons in Hiding,* for example, he was not even mentioned, and the prejudice at the bureau against Purvis endured as late as 1975, when former Assistant Director Louis B. Nichols was still saying, "Purvis was doing a lot of free-wheeling on his own and he was in water over his head. Sam Cowley was the guy who actually handled the Dillinger case and Purvis was a figurehead."[52] But bureau regulations then (and now) required the ranking officer at the scene personally to take charge of an arrest. Cowley was at the Biograph, to be sure, yet it was Purvis who positioned the agents, issued the orders, and personally attempted to put the collar on Dillinger. If Cowley was in charge, he did not act the part.

There was nothing Hoover could do about the first news stories printed about the bureau's big cases. These usually followed pop culture's G-Man formula by focusing on an individual agent like Melvin Purvis as the action detective star of the melodrama. But when writers came to the bureau for follow-up feature stories on the cases, or for commercial dramatizations of them, Hoover was in a position to make sure writers followed the FBI formula. These writers needed new angles on the cases and Hoover had a monopoly on material that could produce new angles. Hoover would spoon-feed reporters "new" information on how the bureau had solved the cases. This new information usually lured the reporters into requesting more information about the techniques the bureau had used to evaluate the clues and to bind the culprit in a noose of facts, all but ensuring that the stories would follow the FBI formula, since the reporters could demonstrate the importance of the new material only if they showed how the FBI had used these advanced techniques to solve the cases. As time passed, Hoover also learned which reporters could be trusted to follow the FBI formula, and he gave these friends of the bureau the inside track on FBI newsbreaks, a priceless asset for reporters on Washington assignments.

One example of how Hoover steered writers in the desired direction occurred in 1935, when Phillips H. Lord, the phenomenally successful producer of radio's "Seth Parker," came to Hoover with a proposition for a multiple-episode series of FBI adventures for radio. Hoover put Rex Collier, a charter friend of the bureau, in charge of the project. The result was "G-Men," a radio show that faithfully adhered to the FBI formula. The first episode, aired on July 20, 1935, was "The Life and Death of John Dillinger."

The show started with an affidavit of its official status. Acting as announcer, Lord told the audience that

This series of *G-Men* is presented with the consent of the Attorney General of the United States and with the cooperation of J. Edgar Hoover, Director of the Federal Bureau of Investigation. Every fact in tonight's program is taken directly from the files of the Bureau.

I went to Washington and was graciously received by Mr. Hoover and all of these scripts were written in the department building. Tonight's program was submitted to Mr. Hoover who personally reviewed the script and made some very valuable suggestions.[53]

As a result of Hoover's pressure on Collier and Lord, the "G-Men" Dillinger episode was not really about Dillinger. Its subject was the FBI's army of scientific detectives who were leading an unstoppable national crusade against crime. When the writers had facts that supported this thesis, they were used. When the facts were inconvenient, they were discarded and others were invented to take their place.

Collier made sure that the "G-Men" Dillinger program followed the same line he had already developed in his syndicated feature stories. The break in the case did not depend on Anna Sage's tip. The key to the case was Dillinger's fatal blunder of driving a stolen car across state lines—then "the G-Men went into action." The show's first scene was a dramatization of Dillinger's two jailbreaks. Lord and Collier may have started here instead of with Dillinger's bank robberies so that they could underscore the symbolism of Dillinger as a rebel against the law itself, thus justifying the FBI's treatment of him as a symbol of lawlessness. The second scene was set in a doctor's office and dramatized the well-known incident in which Dillinger's heart stopped during a plastic surgery operation. The point of this was to show that the FBI's relentless pursuit had so terrorized the once-fearless Dillinger that he was willing to risk death to throw them off his trail.

A voice: "You can't tell how this operation's goin ter turn out. You may croak.

Dillinger: What's the difference? Ain't the G-Men hot on me—I can't sleep—They're everywhere—might's well croak now, if I can't get them off my trail.

Second Voice: You're right boss. When them guys get started, they don't stop.

Voice: You know he ain't been the same since the G-Men started. Wakes up in the middle of the night—starts on for a new place.

Doctor Cassidy: He's got the jitters.

The next scene shifts to Washington and veers sharply away from the facts to demonstrate the way the case should have been solved. Since the solution to the real Dillinger case was not exactly a textbook illustration of scientific criminology, Collier and Lord invented a new solution, and very nearly a new case. Anna Sage does not figure at all in this official version of the Dillinger story. Instead the break comes when an agent finds a fingerprint and ships it off to Washington, where Hoover's scientists identify it as belonging to one of Dillinger's girl friends.

Back in Chicago, Inspector Sam Cowley, who is very definitely in charge of *this* Dillinger manhunt, has the girl followed until she leads them to Dillinger's apartment. Agents search the room and find movie stubs, giving Cowley the idea of stationing agents at nearby movie theaters. This gives Cowley a chance to demonstrate another of the bureau's techniques: a slide lecture to show his agents the changes in Dillinger's appearance they should expect because of his recent plastic surgery.

By the time the show gets to the scene at the Biograph, Collier and Lord have brought the FBI and Dillinger together without any "woman in red," without any lucky breaks, without any FBI foul-ups, without any help from local police. The radio G-Men have caught Dillinger the way he should have been caught—by an inexorable, step-by-step application of the FBI method.

The show contains only one hint that Purvis was present at the Biograph: "I just put Nellis up against the door to smoke a cigar," Cowley tells his agents. "The only way to identify Dillinger is by the back of his head—and being by the door, Nellis will get the first look. As soon as he sees him, he will lower his cigar." The original draft of the script did not even contain this disguised reference to Purvis, but Lord decided that Purvis's signal with his cigar was too well-known to leave out, so he penciled it in just before the show went on the air. "Nellis has spotted Dillinger," Cowley tells his men. "See—he has lowered his cigar. . . . Watch him . . . he's looking around . . . he's wise something is up. . . . He's got his gun—duck." There is a shriek, a shot, and Cowley walks over to the corpse: "Let's see him—yes, Dillinger's dead—He had it coming to him. Pick up his gun Jerry; he'll never use that again."

Lord and Collier ended the program with another tribute to the FBI: "You have just been listening to a dramatization of the hunt for John Dillinger by our G-Men. I want to add that, not only do our G-Men get the criminal, but they also get everyone connected with the crime. Every criminal mentioned tonight and all persons known to have aided and protected Dillinger, are dead or have been convicted. There were 26 of them." Then the sign-off:

The Chevrolet Motor Company offers this series of radio programs in the hope of extending entertaining knowledge about the work of the Federal Bureau of

Investigation of the Department of Justice [the original script had only the words "Department of Justice"; the reference to the FBI was written in pencil in what appears to be Hoover's own writing] and in the belief that it may increase, by spreading that knowledge, the effectiveness of this arm of the federal government service. England has its Scotland Yard, Canada its Northwest Mounties, but never has there been a crime detection organization to compare with that of our own G-Men . . . Crime doesn't pay—the G-Men never give up the hunt.

A year after the "G-Men" Dillinger episode, Hoover endorsed an official FBI comic strip. It was called "War on Crime," and it claimed to be "True Stories of G-Men Activities—Based on the Records of the Federal Bureau of Investigation—Modified in the Public Interest.[54] Once again Hoover called on Rex Collier to help popularize the FBI legend. This time Collier described Dillinger's adventuresome career before the FBI entered the case by means of a flashback, as if to say that the case became significant only when Hoover took over. The theft of Sheriff Holley's car is again the lapse that turns the hunt into a contest between Dillinger, pictured as a simian-browed, stubble-faced monster, and a well-organized team of individually anonymous agents given group identity by a uniform of snap-brim hats, double-breasted suits and trench coats. Once again Purvis has been written out of the script, and his role, including his cigar signal, is handed over to "an agent" acting under the direction of Sam Cowley. Cowley, as the FBI's designated hero in the case, is the only agent identified by name, and Collier underscored the fact that Cowley outranked the other agents because he was Hoover's personal representative in the field: "Director Hoover of the FBI assigned his trusted aide, Sam Cowley, to the hazardous job of recapturing Dillinger. (Hoover): 'We have full authority now, Cowley, You're in charge of the hunt.'"

Collier made the comic follow the FBI formula by tying every important step in the case to one of the FBI's technical procedures, which the strip's artist, Kemp Starrett, sketched in Dick Tracy "Crime Stoppers" style. This time Collier managed to incorporate Anna Sage into the formula by having the bureau offer a reward for Dillinger's capture, followed by a sketch of Sage reading the ad, then by a frame showing the woman spilling her story to Sam Cowley. This turned a fortuitous accident into the outcome of a well-thought-out FBI plan. By the time Dillinger went down before FBI bullets, "War on Crime" had again turned his death into evidence that the FBI had perfected a foolproof method for dealing with public enemies. In the Hoover-edited version of the Dillinger story the case proved that the FBI method worked.

By 1936 the FBI formula's interpretation of the Dillinger case had made such a deep impression on American popular culture that all Hoover had to do was to mention Dillinger and the public drew the proper conclusion. Dillinger had been turned into the FBI's prize

The death of Dillinger according to Hoover. From Rex Collier's authorized War on Crime.

Dillinger as the prize exhibit in Hoover's trophy room. From War on Crime.

trophy. The last frame of the Dillinger episode in "War on Crime" showed a roomful of tourists gawking at a glass-topped display case in FBI headquarters: "Dillinger's gun and other 'relics' of the midwestern mad dog are now in the FBI crime museum at Washington—a grim object lesson for would-be criminals."[55]

It was a grim lesson for criminals, a morale-building one for the nation. It was for providing such lessons and not simply for killing Dillinger or building better crime traps that Hoover became one of the indispensable Americans of his generation. Like the master detectives of the past, his success owed as much to his storytelling skill and the pleasures it provided as to his detective wizardry.

With all due credit to Hoover's public relations genius, there were other cultural forces at work that helped him steer pop culture away from action detective treatments of his big cases and in the direction of the FBI formula. The legend of John Dillinger as a trickster actually was an anachronism even while the bandit was living it. The myth of the gangster as popular hero belonged to the pre-FDR depression years, when uncontrollable crime was a graphic symbol of an economy and a society out of control. In 1934 Dillinger was already a throwback to the time when a criminal's career seemed to be the last gasp of the American dream, and the moral anarchy of the underworld seemed to be a prediction of the nation's future.

By 1934 the nation's confidence had rebounded and the country was enjoying a sense of solidarity that it had not known since World War I.

America was ready for rituals of national unity like the morality play of Dillinger's death, Hearst's "U.S. Production Directed by Melvin Purvis." Hoover would have had nothing to work with if popular culture itself had not turned Dillinger's death into a spontaneous celebration of good triumphant over evil, although, from Hoover's point of view, pop culture had cast the wrong man as the hero. The country seized on Melvin Purvis with his squeaky voice and diminutive build as a kind of Frank Capra hero, proof that ordinary citizens, provided they stuck together, could lick anything and anybody, even John Dillinger, the age's chosen symbol of social disintegration.

Luckily for Hoover, the country needed more from a hero than Melvin Purvis could provide. Purvis was the image of the individual who comes through because of pluck and luck. Dillinger was a "symbol of crime in our times," however, and so the country needed to know that his capture, symbol of the revitalization of the law, was based on more than tips and lucky breaks. The public needed proof that, as Hoover said in a 1937 speech, "there is no magic in efficient law enforcement, no Sherlock Holmes theorizing or fictional deduction, but . . . before science all things must fall, including the ramparts of criminality."[56] Since the public wanted to believe that a new and magical antidote to symbolic crime had been discovered, Hoover's revision of the Dillinger story was not merely tolerated—it was applauded.

It does not seem as obvious today as it did in the thirties that the exemplary punishment of criminals automatically diminishes crime, but there can be no doubt that the fear of crime can be as corrosive to civic life as crime itself, and the manner in which a society punishes criminals can reduce the fear of crime. At a time when the country was desperate for reassurance and eager to be rid of its fear, J. Edgar Hoover and his publicists developed a formula for turning notable criminals like John Dillinger into proof that crime was under control and that the nation's virtue was intact. For this he and his bureau were richly rewarded.

When the public is in the mood for cultural reassurance and moral uplift from the government, it makes celebrities of leaders like Hoover, who can tell the stories and stage the rituals that give the public the sense of solidarity it wants. But as the years pass and the moral lessons once attached to those crime-and-punishment fables are forgotten, the public tends to return to the value-free identification with the action hero and his adventures that typified the first stage of the Dillinger legend.

When Americans recall the Dillinger story today, they do not remember it according to the FBI formula. The Smithsonian Institution reports it still gets inquiries about the gigantic Dillinger organ it supposedly preserves in an oversized jar of formaldehyde. The original image of Dillinger as the trickster supreme still has potent appeal; his symbolism as a rebel against authority evidently qualifies him as a sexual hero in the popular mind. The popular hero's association with the vital forces may also account for the rumor that Dillinger's death was a gigantic FBI hoax. In 1970 Jay Robert Nash, a violent Hoover-hater, offered "proof" that the FBI shot the wrong man at the Biograph and covered up the mistake to avoid embarassment. Dillinger was, Nash claimed, "a pragmatic but spectacular escape artist [who] eluded the law in the end."[57] Hoover issued an angry statement that the book was "completely inaccurate regarding the death of Dillinger. The book is full of falsehoods. The identity of Dillinger was established by fingerprints."[58]

The rumor that "Dillinger lives" was part of American counterculture during the sixties, part of the drive to sabotage the prestige of the power structure. A lively fantasy novel of the period made Dillinger the mastermind behind the assassinations and turmoil of the sixties. He stands for eternal opposition to the FBI and everything it represents.[59] There is even a Dillinger museum in Nashville, Indiana, dedicated to preserving his memory.[60]

Popular culture has also rescued the FBI's "figurehead" in the case, Melvin Purvis; his cigar has again become part of American folklore. In the 1973 movie *Dillinger* Purvis carries a box of cigars, a gift from a murdered agent. Every time he kills a public enemy, he ceremonially lights up another stogie. In the made-for-television film *Kansas City Massacre,* Purvis is portrayed as an old-fashioned gentleman who pursues his quarries with a strict regard for fair play and a high regard for his enemies' bravery and chivalry. At the end of the movie he even lets Pretty Boy Floyd escape to continue the chase another day.

The Dillinger story's metamorphoses from the adventure formula to the crime-and-punishment formula, then to the FBI formula, then finally back to the adventure formula exemplifies several principles of popular culture. The popular audience's desire to identify with action heroes seems to be the basic dynamic in popular culture; this desire exists before any moralistic use of a story and endures after the moral lessons have been forgotten. The audience's identification with action heroes aims at pure ego-gratification, fantasies of power, daring, courage, and, in the case of the trickster, anarchy. Anything that restrains these fantasies, like morality, contradicts the basic dynamic of formula entertainment, and so tends to be discarded at the first opportunity.

It also seems likely that the adventures of action heroes can be turned into culture-affirming rituals only when the culture is in the mood for such affirmation. When the country had been unified by the New Deal and wanted to express its solidarity by identifying with the authorities, it was willing to let popular culture adapt the Dillinger case to fit the requirements of the crime-and-punishment ritual and to let Hoover further adapt it to fit the FBI formula. When the sense of cultural unity subsided, as it did during the sixties and seventies, the public rejected formula entertainment in which rebellious individuals were defeated by the authorities. The audience preferred to identify with cultural rebels against symbols of authority like J. Edgar Hoover.

Orchestrating effective political rituals is a creative art which cannot be turned into a science. J. Edgar Hoover during the thirties and forties took risks to make FBI propaganda out of the news while it was still hot—and while the corpse was still warm. Eventually he lost that daring. He stopped trying to build up new legends about the FBI and tried to make do with what he already had. Formulas and rituals are conventional, they are repetitive, but they also have to be continuously renewed. The FBI formula needed a constant supply of new situations, new heroes, new villains, each one essentially like the last, but each one slightly novel. As the old Hollywood cliché has it, formula entertainment has to be "the same, but different."

Hoover was also generally successful in rewriting the other famous gangster cases of the thirties to fit the specifications of the FBI formula. By the time the decade was over, Hoover had managed to turn the FBI formula into popular history, and the public had come to believe that the public enemies had existed only to prove that the FBI was unstoppable. For the next forty years Hoover felt that all he had to do was to evoke Dillinger's name (or Machine Gun Kelly's, or Ma Barker's) and he had fully justified the bureau and its role in American life—and for most of the public he was right.

But while Hoover was able to impose the FBI formula on newspaper reporters, he was unable to match his success when it came to popular entertainment. There, unless an official FBI relationship with the production gave him real leverage, producers were more likely than not to shrug off his advice and stick to their tried-and-true action detective formulas—which in this case became the G-Man formula Hoover detested. As far as popular history was concerned, J. Edgar Hoover won the battle of the formulas. His efforts to control the FBI's image in popular entertainment, however, were not nearly so successful. To discover the limits of his power over the public image of the bureau, we have only to turn from the headlines and open the newspapers to the comics pages.

8

Hoover's Assault on Popular Mythology:
The Comic Strip G-Man

Hoover had to learn the hard way that popular attitudes are not simply based on the "facts," even when these facts are vouched for by authorities as highly respected as Hoover himself. In great measure the public reformulates those facts in the light of popular mythology; reality, as the public perceives it, is a projection, then, of popular fears and desires. Hoover could control the facts, as he proved when he rewrote the popular history of John Dillinger and other public enemies. Popular mythology, though, eluded his grasp; Hoover was to discover that he was powerless to manipulate, in any significant way, the fundamental relationship between the American public and his FBI.

Throughout his career Hoover tried to defend the bureau's public image whenever popular culture tried to fit it into the ritualistic formulas of crime entertainment. Such an accommodation to those conventions would have crippled his efforts to reform the popular attitudes that had made American law enforcement ineffective and anachronistic. Whenever Hoover saw popular culture turning the FBI agent into a conventional action detective, he tried to rescue the G-Man from his popular entertainment captors. One of the most ambitious of his rescue missions was his failed attempt to return the comic strip G-Man to the fold of FBI formula orthodoxy.

J. Edgar Hoover loved crime comics. He said they were "highly important influences in creating a public distaste for crime," and he let it be known that he derived "a keen inward satisfaction from seeing their flinty-jawed heroes prevail over evil."[1] One of his favorite comics was "Dick Tracy." Another was a strip called "Secret Agent X-9." Early in 1936 Hoover spotted something happening in "X-9" that he did not like. Slowly but surely the writers of "X-9" were turning their private eye into a G-Man. Maybe Hoover foresaw the comics doing the same thing to him that Hollywood had done to Homer Cummings. In any case he decided to act.

"X-9" began in 1934 as the Hearst chain's answer to the Daily News Syndicate's "Dick Tracy," but in the early going the strip suffered because the hero lacked a strong identity and a distinctive crime-fighting style.[2] Alex Raymond and Dashiell Hammett created the strip, but never made it clear whom X-9 was a secret agent for. He started as a millionaire playboy who moonlighted as a sort of free-lance avenger à la Lamont Cranston or (later) Bruce Wayne. He even had the traditional Oriental valet.

Raymond and Hammett abandoned the strip in 1935. The artwork was then taken over by Charles Flanders, the writing first by Leslie Charteris (famous for *The Saint*) and then by Robert Storm. Under Storm's direction X-9 began to display unexpected expertise with the microscope and the fingerprint powder. Even more unexpectedly, he acquired a boss in Washington. Early in 1936 he got rid of the valet, pinned on his badge, and stuffed some Justice Department identification in his wallet. Now the comics had their own FBI G-Man, and the FBI had an angry director. Around the same time the Hearst chain also inaugurated its own FBI strip, "The G-Man!", written by George Clark and Lou Hanlon. This strip made no attempt at realism. Its hero was the youthful Jimmie Crawford, perhaps based on Jimmy Christopher, hero of *Operation 5* pulp magazine, and his sidekick was his little brother, Junior.[3]

"Secret Agent X-9", on the other hand, was extremely realistic. It was a well-plotted, dramatically drawn strip with plenty of Hoover's beloved scientific deduction and hardly any rough stuff. The FBI got nothing but respectful, even worshipful, treatment, and there were regular flashbacks to Washington, where Hoover himself made stately appearances in the crime labs. All the pieces of Hoover's official FBI formula were there. The trouble was the way it was put together. Where Hoover liked to brag that the FBI was a "we" organization and that the whole bureau was the hero in every FBI case,[4] Secret Agent X-9 was at the center of every case, every scene, almost every frame, as independent and self-reliant as any proper American action hero. As befitted his title billing, he dominated everyone else in the strip: criminals, citizens, and fellow G-Men, even G-Men with the rank of director.

X-9 chose his cases because they interested him. He ran the investigations by himself and assembled the clues on his own, then evaluated them himself or flew to Washington to dope them out at the FBI crime lab. Then he hustled back to lead the raids and shootouts and make the big arrests. Other agents (also known by letter-number combinations), the crime labs, and even Hoover himself were simply resources at the disposal of the ace agent. The bureau was there when X-9 needed it, but

Secret Agent X-9 with "The Director." Copyright 1937, King Features Syndicate, Inc.

only when he needed it. It was merely one of his tools, like his gun, badge, and car.

In each of his cases X-9 always operated as a one-man gang. In a 1937 adventure, for example, X-9 goes to investigate a rash of murders on an Arizona Indian reservation (the same case Collier had written up for Hoover in 1931). He finds a death-threat note that he thinks might break the case. "I'm taking a plane to Washington," he tells his assistants, "there's a job of typewriting identification to do." In Washington at FBI headquarters, X-9 strides masterfully from lab to lab while "the director," unmistakably Hoover, with a stocky build, wavy black hair, and bulldog features, tags along behind his star. X-9 is always one idea ahead of the director, making Hoover play a somewhat dense Watson to X-9's Holmes: "A man threatens to visit Anne Long—didn't you set a trap?" Hoover asks. "No sir," X-9 explains patiently. "It would have tipped our hand."

Whenever a case calls for deep thinking and elaborate planning, X-9 does it. He tells the director only enough to make sure he gets the help he needs from headquarters. His telegrams to Washington are practically commands. "Planning ruse to force 'brains' behind gang to show his hand," he wires Hoover. "May need armed help."

Hoover had nothing against free-wheeling comic strip detectives—as long as they stayed out of the FBI. Dick Tracy could do whatever he liked—he could go his own way and make his superiors look like idiots—but that was the Chicago Police Department's problem. In Hoover's FBI "free-wheeling" was a dirty word. The real bureau had room for only one star.

If the country began giving credit for the FBI's successes to individual G-Man heroes, then Hoover's carefully-crafted bureau, his finely-honed law enforcement program, even Hoover himself—all would become irrelevant. That was the danger Hoover saw when the "X-9" writers began to turn their detective into a G-Man. To convert the comics to FBI orthodoxy, Hoover was going to have to launch his own FBI comic.

To lead the assault on Agent X-9, Hoover called once again on Rex Collier. He told Collier that he wanted him to write an authorized comic strip for the bureau. He already had an artist, Kemp Starrett, and an editor, Doug Borgstedt, all signed up, with distribution to be handled by the Philadelphia Ledger Syndicate. The result of this collaboration between the news media and the FBI was "War on Crime," which opened on May 18, 1936, in forty-five papers across the country.[5]

Hoover, the Ledger Syndicate, and the subscribing newspapers all gambled on Hoover's belief (or hope) that the bureau's popularity was driven by a different dynamic than the rules of fantasy identification that usually operated in pop hero-worship. Hoover boasted that "War on Crime" was

not one of those boom-boom things that have no other purpose than to act as a thriller. . . . There has been a tremendous reversal of opinion in this country concerning law enforcement and law officers, and just such things as . . . [this] G-man feature strip have done a lot to bring about the change. . . . Years ago every kid wanted to be a Dillinger. Now we have thousands of requests coming from young men wanting to join the Bureau of Investigation. Law and order is coming in for some glorification.

The value of this sort of thing to the growing boy cannot be overestimated. He is taught that the policeman can be and is his friend, and he learns to see crime in its true light—as something far from glamorous, something sordid and evil that must be stamped out.[6]

Relying on the theory that there was a fundamental difference between G-Man heroes and their action detective cousins, the publicity for "War on Crime" stressed the contrast between the official strip's authenticity and the fantasies served up by the competition: "Daily millions of readers are following fictitious thrillers and dime-novel desperadoes in their wild comic-strip adventures! Imagine, then, how this great public audience will welcome and support a strip whose characters are actual people, whose heroes are real G-Men, and whose villains are John Dillinger, Machine-Gun Kelly and Baby-Face Nelson." "War on Crime," the publishers promised, would have "REAL G-MEN VERSUS REAL GANGSTERS, not lurid tales of a fictitious underworld, but actual case histories showing the actual people involved . . . FACTS—NOT FICTION!"

The agreement Hoover worked out with the Ledger Syndicate called for every word and picture to be approved by Hoover and Associate

Director Clyde Tolson. In return, the bureau gave every episode of the comic an affidavit of authenticity: "True Stories of G-Man Activities Based on Records of the Federal Bureau of Investigation—Modified in the Public Interest." With Hoover's blessing the strip's advertising played up the comic's official connections. One ad had a picture of Hoover brandishing a machine gun, and a promotional flier had a shot of Hoover fingerprinting Rex Collier—"Just in Case!" read the caption.

"War on Crime" was based on Hoover's assumption that the bureau had become popular simply because the public admired its achievements. The strip's advertisements disregarded the extent to which the bureau owed its popularity to fantasy identification with the bureau. This was a tactical error, because fantasy identification is what links the hero and his public, while admiration, which is kin to envy, separates the hero from the hero-worshipper.

The producers of "War on Crime" were so sure of the public appeal of the "real" bureau that they were willing to do whatever Hoover wanted to hang on to their official endorsements. On May 15, 1936, the "War on Crime" editor wrote Rex Collier:

I want to impress upon you one thing—and that is that we of course stand ready to make any changes the F.B.I. thinks necessary on any strips.

Do not think for a minute that we are not fully aware that the entire success of this venture is based on its authenticity. WAR ON CRIME is produced with the consent and cooperation of the F.B.I., and if it is necessary to cut down on the clues, action or anything, we must comply and we will. Please emphasize to Mr. Hoover that his final wishes are law, Rex, and that he need have no fear that we are going to run away and go wild on the basis of his concessions to us. We know that there would be no quicker way of ruining the entire success of the strip. I am very anxious that Hoover and Tolson know this. . . . Perhaps you will have the opportunity to show them this letter.[7]

All the people involved in the "War on Crime" project, then—Hoover, Collier, and the Ledger Syndicate people—were determined to steer clear of the G-Man formula. The outcome of their experiment would help answer whether the popular image of politics is merely a reflection of the political process, or whether popular involvement with politics grows out of the political process's resemblance to the patterns and rituals of popular mythology. Does the politician become a popular hero because of what he does, or because the popular audience interprets his actions as the fulfillment of popular myths? Did Hoover and the FBI become heroes because, as they claimed, they did the job; they got the Machine Gun Kellys and the John Dillingers? Or did the public idolize them because their exploits fit the pattern of the popular action detective formula? If Hoover's success was independent

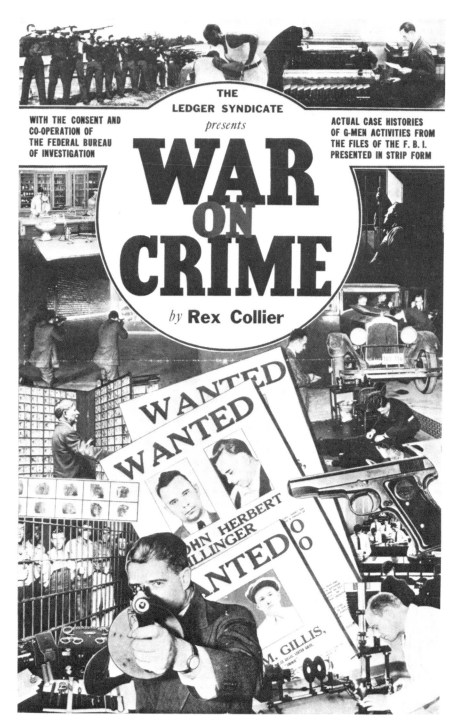

Above and right: Promotional flyer for War on Crime.

THE FIRST STRIP TO TAKE YOUR READERS *behind the scenes*

OF THE FEDERAL BUREAU OF INVESTIGATION!
NOT JUST ANOTHER THRILLER CRIME STRIP, BUT
AN AUTHENTIC PRESENTATION OF THE UNITED
STATES GOVERNMENT'S SCIENTIFIC AND RUTH-
LESS WARFARE ON ORGANIZED CRIME!

WAR *on* CRIME is part of a National educational movement to stamp out crime in America—a movement which has the 100% interest and backing of every law-abiding man, woman and child in our country!

Such a movement, to be effective, demands one thing . . . AUTHENTICITY! Accordingly, every word and fact in WAR ON CRIME has been checked and rechecked by officials of the Bureau of Investigation! For the first time, you are able to present to your readers in this dramatic form true facts of the most thrilling manhunts in history! Daily millions of readers are following fictitious thrillers and dime-novel desperadoes in their wild comic-strip adventure! Imagine them, how this great public audience will welcome and support a strip whose characters are actual people, whose heroes are real G-Men, and whose villains are John Dillinger, Machine-Gun Kelly and Baby-Face Nelson!

Real
G-MEN
Versus
Real
GANGSTERS

NOT LURID TALES OF A
FICTITIOUS UNDERWORLD,
BUT ACTUAL CASE HISTO-
RIES SHOWING THE ACTUAL PEOPLE INVOLVED

- **REAL NAMES**
- **REAL PEOPLE**
- **REAL PLACES**
- **REAL CASES**

FACTS—NOT FICTION!

Mr. Collier, the author, took the greatest precautions to insure accuracy in preparing his continuities. Not only did he secure all available data from the files of the Federal Bureau of Investigation, to whom all finished copy has been submitted, but also he gathered many significant facts from on-the-spot coverage of cases in which he obtained first-hand information of G-Men at work . . . personal human-interest facts which have no place in the terse records of G-Men activities . . . but inside facts the public is eager to discover.

Federal Bureau of Investigation
U. S. Department of Justice
Washington, D. C.

JOHN EDGAR HOOVER
DIRECTOR

Mr. Rex Collier,
The Evening Star,
Washington, D. C.

Dear Rex:

I have your request for certain material from the files of the Federal Bureau of Investigation for use in preparing an illustrated newspaper serial feature, depicting actual cases solved by the Bureau.

The idea of such a "strip" is a new one, and appears to have considerable promise as a factor in educating youth to the futility of crime, as well as in providing the public generally with a graphic portrayal of activities of the FBI in what you rightly call the "War on Crime."

I know through long association that you are thoroughly qualified to give an interesting and authentic account of FBI cases, some of the more important of which you have "covered" most creditably as a newspaperman.

I am very glad to cooperate with you in this new endeavor to the extent of making available to you the data you have requested. Your request that our experts check over each episode as you complete it, to insure accuracy, also is granted. I shall watch the progress of this enterprise with real interest.

With kindest personal regards, I am

Sincerely yours,

J. Edgar Hoover
John Edgar Hoover,
Director.

The author of WAR ON CRIME is
REX COLLIER

one of the best-known crime reporters in the newspaper business, and a member of the staff of the Washington Star since 1920. Unquestionably, there is no man better qualified or more suited to this work. From its very inception he has followed with active interest the fascinating career of J. Edgar Hoover, chief of the G-Men. The result of this has been the creation of a long-standing friendship between the two. As a specialist in crime reporting, he has come into possession of many colorful facts on G-Man activities. So well informed is he on the workings of the Federal Bureau of Investigation that two of his feature articles on the activities of the Bureau were published by the Department of Justice as official information booklets. As a feature writer in outstanding cases, Rex Collier covered the Lindbergh case from the beginning and scored many sensational "beats," including the first story of Jafsie's ransom payment to "John" and the first official details regarding the discovery of the baby's body.

As a feature writer he has covered such outstanding events as the Mississippi Flood in 1927, the Herbert Hoover Presidential campaign in 1928, and in 1929 he was a member of the Hoover "Good Will" party on its extensive South American tour.

We are proud to be associated with Rex Collier in producing this outstanding feature!

(below) Just in case! Rex Collier, author of WAR ON CRIME, is finger-printed by J. Edgar Hoover, director of the Federal Bureau of Investigation and chief of the nation's G-Men.

WAR ON CRIME opens with two weeks of preliminary strips on the inner workings of the F. B. I. immediately followed by the sensational Urschel kidnaping case! Following this come outstanding case histories on kidnaping, murder, bank robbery, extortion, piracy, forgery and racketeering, involving such notorious desperadoes as John Dillinger, Machine-Gun Kelly, Baby-Face Nelson, Harvey Bailey, Frank Nash, the Barker Brothers and other outstanding public enemies!

of popular mythology, he should have been able to make the popular culture G-Man into an accurate reflection of the real FBI; if Hoover actually owed his success to popular mythology, then he could retain his popularity only so long as his image continued to fit the expectations of the popular culture.

In spite of the avowedly realistic intentions of "War on Crime," the strip's writers and artists were not able to avoid using popular culture formulas in telling their story. The pressure of conventional expectations about the heroes of the law was so great that from the first episode to the last (the strip was dead by the end of 1936), "War on Crime" adapted itself to the demands of popular mythology. Each episode conformed to the routines of the action detective formula, with one fatal deviation. And that one stroke of originality was enough to doom Hoover's comic strip adventure.

The most graphic example of the adherence of "War on Crime" to the conventions of the action detective formula was the opening episode that introduced the strip during the first two weeks, beginning on May 16, 1936. It is normal procedure for every new comic book hero to be introduced with an episode known as the "origin story." This explains how the hero acquired his extraordinary powers and why he dedicated himself to the welfare of others instead of simply enjoying being the strongest, bravest, smartest, and best-looking man in the world.

Batman's origin story, for example, begins with the murder of Bruce Wayne's father and mother during a holdup. Bruce swears "by the spirits of my parents to avenge their deaths by spending the rest of my life warring on all criminals." Training himself for his crusade, "he becomes a master scientist, trains his body to physical perfection until he is able to perform amazing athletic feats," peers through microscopes, and hefts barbells. Then he chooses his disguise: " 'Criminals are a superstitious, cowardly lot, so my disguise must be able to strike terror into their hearts. I must be a creature of the night, black, terrible . . . a . . .' Just then a huge bat flies into the room. 'A bat! That's it! It's an omen. I shall become a bat!' And thus is born this weird figure of the dark—this avenger of evil—the Batman."[8] The final frame has Batman in full costume posed dramatically against the night skyline.

Batman's origin story fits a standard pattern. The comic strip hero makes his first appearance as a novice, sometimes as a boy, other times as an infant or a raw adult recruit. Then something happens—usually someone close to him is murdered—and he vows revenge, not just against his personal enemies, but against all criminals, declaring a war on crime. He trains himself for his new role, strengthening himself in mind and body, and adopts a heroic name, usually given to him by his antagonist in his first adventure. Then he sallies forth in a series of preliminary adventures before venturing into mortal combat with the

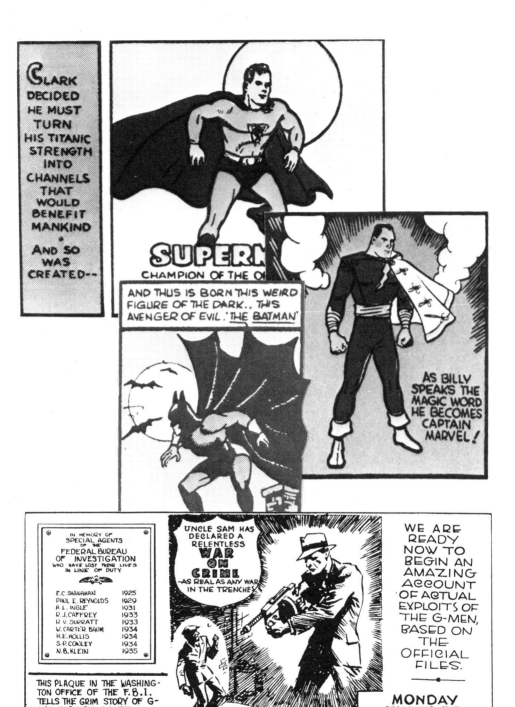

Classic poses from the origin stories of four fantasy heroes.

foe he was born to fight, the arch-villain, symbol of all evil. That villain defeated, the comic strip hero embarks on a career of battling new foes, each one also serving as the symbol of all crime, the subliminal message being that "crimes" may continue to occur, but "Crime" itself is now under control.

Superman does not have to go into training to get his superpowers. He arrives from "the doomed planet Krypton" and demonstrates his skills in a by-now-stereotyped sequence of sketches. "As the lad [given the name 'Clark Kent'] grew older, he learned to his delight that he could hurdle skyscrapers . . . leap an eighth of a mile . . . raise tremendous weights . . . run faster than a streamline locomotive . . . and nothing less than a bursting shell could penetrate his skin." In Superman's origin story the death of young Clark Kent's foster father reminds the boy that the elder Kent had told him years before that "this great strength of yours . . . [must be used] to assist humanity." Clark determines to "turn his titanic strength into channels that would benefit mankind. And so was created SUPERMAN, champion of the oppressed, the physical marvel who had sworn to devote his existence to helping those in need."[9]

Another function of origin stories is to supply their heroes with permanent motivation for their wars against crime. The audience has to know why fighting crime has become a kind of conditioned reflex with the comic strip hero. The simplest motivation is revenge, so the origin story usually serves up an atrocity that keeps the hero steamed up for the rest of his career. While Dick Tracy is proposing marriage to Tess Trueheart, for example, a bandit slaughters Tess's father. "Dick swears to avenge [this killing]," the caption reads, "and although not then on the police force, offers his services to the chief."[10]

"War on Crime" followed the same mythic pattern as these other adventure comics. The first frame shows a pair of idealized special agents in snap-brimmed hats gunning down a gang of brutish-looking thugs. "On a thousand fronts," reads the caption, "the crackle of government guns and the upraised hands of cringing desperadoes have marked Uncle Sam's 'WAR ON CRIME.' One by one America's public enemies have been sent to prison or, if they resisted with arms, to the morgue, by the courageous men of the F.B.I.—the G-MEN." This tableau of FBI men shooting down gangsters is the G-Man hero's characteristic pose, as much his trademark as Batman's crouch or Superman's profile in full flight. It is what has to be accounted for in the "War on Crime" origin story.

The next frame is a clue that the FBI story is going to be cloaked in mythology. A heroic portrait of J. Edgar Hoover appears over a caption that reads: "Directing this round-up of kidnappers, extortionists, bandits and other predatory criminals is a keen-eyed, broad-shouldered

lawyer, John Edgar Hoover, Federal Bureau of Investigation." Behind
Hoover's skull, as though emanating from his brain, float the two classic personae of the G-Man: a white-garbed scientist peering through a
microscope, and a stereotypical square-jawed special agent in a snap-
brimmed fedora.

The next two weeks' strips showed the G-Man evolving from an idea
in Hoover's brain into the machine-gun-wielding hero of the comic's first
panel. This is nothing less than the mythological enactment of the special
agent's metamorphosis from brainchild to G-Man. First, the artist
showed Hoover gaining control of the bureau in 1924. Before that epochal event, a caption states, the FBI was "an obscure agency steeped in
politics and burdened with inefficient agents, some with police records."

For the next few days the strip showed the fledgling G-Men going
through the kind of training that had turned Superman and Batman
into heroes. Instead of leaping tall buildings and outrunning locomo-
tives, the young G-Men learn how to prepare evidence; they study
jiu-jitsu, ballistics, X-rays, invisible ink, marksmanship, lie-detector
tests, and handwriting identification. They practice high-speed auto
chases and nighttime raids. Hoover's special pride and joy, the fingerprint collection, gets three full days.

Following the superhero pattern, the death of someone close to the
G-Men ends their training and calls them to their destiny, supplying
them with the revenge motive that will drive them on for the rest of
their careers. This is the Kansas City Massacre. The comic appropriated
Homer Cummings's interpretation of this crime: it was, says a caption,
"Gangland's bloody challenge to the law."

After this, "War on Crime" could end its origin story by displaying
the G-Man hero armed and ready for combat in his identifying pose: an
immense and spectral agent floating in the air in an other-worldly nim-
bus, his machine gun trained on a cowering crook. "We are now
ready," the origin story concluded, "to begin an amazing account of the
actual exploits of the G-Men, based on the official files." The stories
may have come out of the files, but the formula came right out of the
comic book adaptation of popular mythology.

The "War on Crime" origin story was not the only way the formulas
of detective comics crept into this avowedly realistic strip. The cases
that illustrated the bureau's history also followed mythological patterns.
The cases seem to have been unconsciously chosen to illustrate the
classic stages in the life story of the mythic hero: birth, training, acquisi-
tion of a heroic name, the call to destiny and, finally, the epic struggle
against a symbol of ultimate evil.

The G-Man hero's first case in "War on Crime" was that old standby,
Machine Gun Kelly's kidnapping of Oklahoma oilman Charles Urschel
in 1933. This was, to be sure, a notable case from the standpoint of

Above and right: The origin story of the G-Man hero in War on Crime.

WAR ON CRIME—Trained by Experts!

True Stories of G-Men Activities Based on Records of the Federal Bureau of Investigation—Modified in the Public Interest · Registered U. S. Patent Office · By Rex Collier

WAR ON CRIME—Practice Under All Conditions

True Stories of G-Men Activities Based on Records of the Federal Bureau of Investigation—Modified in the Public Interest · Registered U. S. Patent Office · By Rex Collier

WAR ON CRIME—Fingerprint Identification

True Stories of G-Men Activities Based on Records of the Federal Bureau of Investigation—Modified in the Public Interest · Registered U. S. Patent Office · By Rex Collier

WAR ON CRIME—World's Largest Collection!

True Stories of G-Men Activities Based on Records of the Federal Bureau of Investigation—Modified in the Public Interest · Registered U. S. Patent Office · By Rex Collier

WAR ON CRIME—Special "Public Enemy" File!

True Stories of G-Men Activities Based on Records of the Federal Bureau of Investigation—Modified in the Public Interest · Registered U. S. Patent Office · By Rex Collier

WAR ON CRIME—Prepared for "War"

True Stories of G-Men Activities Based on Records of the Federal Bureau of Investigation—Modified in the Public Interest · Registered U. S. Patent Office · By Rex Collier

MONDAY
BEGINNING THE
Urschel Kidnaping Case!

scientific crime solving and deductive reasoning, but Collier and Hoover seem to have chosen it as the first "War on Crime" adventure because of its mythic importance. For J. Edgar Hoover and his publicists the Urschel case was always "the case in which we got our name."[11] It was the adventure that lifted FBI agents above ordinary mortals and made them the stuff of legend by giving them their imagination-gripping nickname of "G-Men." Forty years later Hoover would still be describing the (possibly fictitious) scene of Machine Gun Kelly shouting, "Don't shoot, G-Men, don't shoot" at his FBI captors, supposedly the first time the agents had ever been so addressed. The episode would hardly have merited the overwhelming significance Hoover attached to it (the incident is a prominent feature of every authorized FBI book or movie) if Hoover, like the public, had not viewed the adventures of the bureau in the light of mythology.

Every mythic hero has to have a name to set him apart from the common herd as one destined for great deeds. It might be the Deity who gives the new name to the hero—Saul/Paul on the road to Tarsus, Simon/Peter as leader of the other apostles. Popular mythology sometimes conjures up a comic book god for a pop christening. Billy Batson, an orphan newsboy, wanders into an underground throne room where Shazam, "an ancient Egyptian Wizard" gives him the name of Captain Marvel while explaining the allegorical significance of Shazam's magic name: S for the wisdom of Solomon, and so on.[12] In popular culture the story's premise does not often permit divine intrusions, so another pop convention comes into play, which is for his first important enemy to give the victorious hero his new name. Cooper's Natty Bumppo, for example, gets his warrior's name of "Hawkeye" from a dying Mohawk. In the myth of the G-Man, Machine Gun Kelly plays the role of the dying Mohawk. The FBI agents who raided Kelly's room entered as ordinary detectives. Kelly's shout of panic turned them into the figures of romance. The hero now had his epic name.

The next case in "War on Crime" was another milestone in the development of the G-Man myth. The new hero now needed a mission worthy of his new name. Thus the next episode was the Kansas City Massacre, which Collier had already described in the origin story as "gangland's bloody challenge to the law," the beginning of the "war on crime." There was more symbolism here. This case gave the G-Man hero a personal stake in the war on crime—avenging the death of fallen comrades.

A popular culture hero cannot go into combat for merely legalistic reasons; he has to live by a personal code of chivalry. The Kansas City Massacre showed that he had such a code. The death of the FBI agents at Kansas City's Union Station also showed that the G-Man was no longer simply another cop. Criminals who attacked the G-Men were attacking symbols of the law itself, so the death of an agent called for vengeance by the entire G-Man clan. Murder of an agent was a personal affront to all G-Men and to the values they stood for.

The strip's Kansas City Massacre episode began like a chapter out of "Prince Valiant": "Accepting gangland's challenge at Kansas City, Director Hoover of the Federal Bureau of Investigation ordered a relentless hunt for the slayers of Agent Caffrey." Before long the FBI's prime suspect, Pretty Boy Floyd, begins to go to pieces under the relentless "G-heat," and he makes a "proposition to Uncle Sam": he will surrender if Hoover will guarantee his immunity from the "hot seat." Hoover's reply conforms to the rule that only poetic justice is sufficient to slake the action hero's thirst for revenge. "Tell Floyd for me," he says, "that we don't bargain with gangsters. . . . He is going to pay the full penalty for those murders at Kansas City." This tale of insult and revenge can end only with Floyd's death. The finale was titled "The Massacre Avenged," and showed Floyd going down before an impromptu firing squad of G-Men. Thus "the F.B.I. avenged completely the gory massacre at Kansas City."

The G-Man hero—born, trained, named, and blooded—was now ready for the greatest criminal the publicity mills of the thirties could produce: John Dillinger, "The Mad Dog of the Midwest," billed by "War on Crime" as the ultimate American criminal, the archetypal American bad man. In the myth of the G-Man the Dillinger case is the main event—Goliath to the G-Man's David, Hector to his Achilles, Grendel to his Beowulf—High Noon. The preliminary events over, the hero has to face the enemy champion in a battle to the death. Once Dillinger lies on a slab in the morgue the G-Man hero is a full-fledged mythic hero, ready for a perpetual crusade against the ungodly.

But this was not to be. Soon after the Dillinger episode "War on Crime" ran out of gas; it had vanished from the newspapers by the end of 1936. The G-Man hero had everything a popular culture hero needed except a personality, and it was no accident that his personality was a blank. Hoover let Rex Collier fit the FBI story into the patterns of popular culture mythology, but he refused to let the G-Man hero become the kind of free-wheeling operative he objected to in "Secret Agent X-9." Hoover intended "War on Crime" to demonstrate that organization, not individual heroics, was the FBI secret, so instead of a sharply-defined star agent who passed through the heroic life cycle to acquire audience recognition and identification, "War on Crime" had a collective hero: a crowd of anonymous FBI agents, all with the same square jaws and poker faces, all acting in unison, all taking orders at every turn from their director. "War on Crime" had the appearance of the action detective formula, but it was a myth without, properly speaking, a hero.

Collier and the Ledger Syndicate had not somehow gotten the urge to create a comic strip version of the collective novel. The rough drafts and page proofs for the comic show that Hoover and his officials kept a tight rein on Collier and his collaborators. Hoover would not permit Collier to give the field agent the self-reliance and independence appropriate to an American action detective hero. FBI agents could not be stars. They had to remain subordinate to Hoover in everything, and Hoover was a thousand miles away from the action, a sort of brooding off-panel presence, felt, but for the most part not seen.

Collier tried manfully to give readers someone to identify with in the strip, somebody with a name and a face. As far as was humanly possible, Collier gave them Hoover. The desk-bound director of "War on Crime" was repeatedly brought into the plot. Collier would cut from the heroics in the field back to strategy sessions in Washington, where Hoover was shown barking orders into a telephone. All the intercutting made hash of the plot and, even worse, it confused readers who were not used to identifying with a hero whose only weapon was a telephone that seemed to be growing out of his ear.

There was also a practical problem. Even though Hoover insisted on anonymity for the strip's field agents, at least one of them needed a name so that Hoover would not have to address his orders "to whom it may concern." In response to Collier's pleas headquarters said that if there had to be a field agent with an identity, it ought to be Hoover's roving personal representative, Sam Cowley.

Collier tried to go along with this, which was part of Hoover's promotion of Cowley as a rival to Melvin Purvis in the ace agent sweepstakes. The trouble was that Cowley had not figured in all the cases Collier was writing about, and Cowley was not in on the kill in some of the cases he had worked on. This made the use of Cowley as a source of continuity for the strip an added source of confusion. He was a hero who kept disappearing from the action when things got hot, only to show up when the fight was over, deliver a bloodthirsty sermon, and then disappear again. With the strip's continuity in tatters, Collier tried to make some sense out of the confusion by inventing a "generic" agent named Inspector Thomas Woodrow, "veteran nemesis of crime," carefully described as Hoover's personal representative in the field.

In the Kansas City Massacre episode, the disagreement between Hoover and Collier over how the star agent should be characterized reduced the strip to a shambles. Sam Cowley had not been involved in the initial stages of this case, nor was he present when Melvin Purvis shot Pretty Boy Floyd. The first draft of the episode had "Inspector Woodrow" in charge. Then Hoover demanded Collier make Cowley the star, so Cowley's name was substituted for Woodrow's in the episodes that had not yet appeared. Then Hoover, evidently reluctant to tamper with the facts in a case still fresh in the public's mind, told Collier to get Cowley out of Floyd's death scene. Once again the proofs were revised, and Woodrow's name was put back in. Finally Collier, in desperation, wrote his editor: "Since sending you the final week of the Massacre case I have gone over the whole case and find that the elimination of Cowley's name and substitution of Woodrow's in the last week may cause confusion. The facts are that Cowley was in general charge of the hunt, but was not at the scene of Floyd's slaying. Earlier in the story I have had Inspector Woodrow in charge of the round-up of Massacre murderers. At that time Cowley was not in charge—yet the F.B.I. wants to give Cowley credit for the final capture."[13] By this time Woodrow and Cowley were being shuffled in and out of the strip bewilderingly. At the bureau's insistence, for example, there was a picture of a plane overhead, with an agent on the ground gazing at it and saying, to no one in particular, "That must be Inspector Cowley and his squad. Washington ordered him to drop the Stoll case temporarily and take charge of the hunt for Floyd."

In a last-ditch effort to rescue the continuity of his strip Collier went through the proofs of the Massacre finale and crossed out all proper names. A line that first read, "Disregarding repeated demands of Inspector Cowley of the F.B.I. that he surrender" was changed to "Disregarding repeated demands of Inspector Woodrow of the F.B.I.," finally emerging as "Disregarding repeated demands of the F.B.I."

The result was that the reader of "War on Crime" had no one at all to identify with. The final absurdity was Floyd's death scene. In action detective formula stories—in all mythic adventures for that matter—the hero must personally kill the villain, and he must stay to pronounce the epitaph. In "War on Crime" the climactic line, "All right, men, fire," emerges out of a mob of anonymous agents. An adventure story ought to close with the hero standing over the body of the fallen villain; the best "War on Crime" could do was to assign "an Inspector" to strike this pose over Floyd's corpse.

In his history of the daily comic strips Ron Goulart guessed that "War on Crime" failed because its artwork, writing, and plotting were just too good for its audience.[14] They were not getting enough "Kapowie"'s and "Pow"'s. There was more to it than that. J. Edgar Hoover was trying to collaborate with American popular culture in the production of an official G-Man myth, but he was trying to do it on his own terms. American popular culture's response to Hoover's mythopoeic parsimony was what might have been expected. If Hoover's FBI denied the public an official G-Man hero, then pop culture would manufacture bogus G-Men. Thus while the FBI's officially sanctioned entertainment during the thirties was, without exception, short-lived and of limited popularity, American popular culture, and the comics in particular, swarmed with unsanctioned, bootleg G-Men—Secret Agent X-9, "G-Man," Captain America, The Shield, and dozens of lesser-known colleagues. This meant that almost from the beginning there were, not one, but two G-Men in American popular culture. The FBI agent sponsored by the bureau (in officially-sanctioned productions like "War on Crime," radio's "This Is Your F.B.I.," television's "The F.B.I." and Hollywood's *The F.B.I. Story*) had a personality as gray as his business suit. The G-Man created by the popular entertainment industry itself, however, was an updated version of the classic American gunfighter—lean, mean, and young, a lawman with style. At first he dressed in the regulation business suit, snap-brim hat and badge, but soon, faced with competition from Superman, Batman, and Captain Marvel, he began to jazz up his haberdashery and his crime-fighting style. He put on masks, capes, and electric-hued long johns and moved to more spectacular cases than the old Dillinger and Machine Gun Kelly melodramas. He also gave up square names like G-8 and X-9 and began operating as Captain America and The Shield, protecting America against a whole new cast of "international gangsters" like Hitler, Tojo, and Mussolini.

Hoover feared that if FBI entertainment adapted itself to the action detective formula, he, like Homer Cummings, would be upstaged by ace agents. This finally did come to pass in the comic strips, though not in Washington. As G-Man comics strayed further and further off the FBI reservation, the comic strip directors of the FBI receded just as far from the main action. Hoover was a fixture in adventure comics during the late thirties and early forties as a sort of gray eminence managing a stable of action heroes, but he did not figure as an action hero himself. He seemed to be an intermediary between the realms of out-and-out fantasy and newspaper reality, between heroes like Captain America and official America. He was comic book fantasy's connection to Washington—and Washington's link with fantasy.

Such was his role in the origin story of the most famous of all the FBI-inspired superheroes, Captain America.[15] Captain America was born in March, 1941. The origin story's first page set the stage: "As the ruthless war-mongers of Europe focus their eyes on a peace-loving country," a crew of saboteurs are preparing to dynamite "American Munitions, Inc." Back in Washington there are discouraging reports from the chief of staff: "I tell you, Mr. President, there's no stopping these vermin. . . . They're so firmly entrenched in our ranks that I hesitate to give a confidential report to even my most trusted aide." Roosevelt asks his cabinet: "What would you suggest, gentlemen, a character out of the comic books? Perhaps the HUMAN TORCH in the army would solve our problem! But seriously, gentlemen, something is being done. . . . Please send in Mr. Grover!" Enter J. Arthur Grover, head of the Federal Bureau of Investigation. Grover takes them to a secret laboratory, where they

The comic book G-Man's evolution into a fantasy hero.

watch FBI scientists exhibit their solution to the nation's security problem. The doctors take a frail young volunteer, rejected as unfit for military service, and inject him with "a seething liquid" that will turn him into "one of America's saviors." The military leaders "gape in awe" as "the serum coursing through his blood . . . [builds] his body and brain tissues, until his stature and intelligence increase to an amazing degree."

In the corresponding scene in "War on Crime," recruits are injected with the director's inspirational leadership by means of classroom lectures, firing-range instruction, and gymnasium workouts. Imparting the G-spirit via hypodermic needles has a certain flair the official comic strip lacks.

The volunteer's feeble muscles surge and grow. At last he towers like a mountain of flesh over his scientist-creators. "Behold," one of Grover's scientists announces, "the first of a corps of super-agents whose mental and physical ability will make them a terror to spies and saboteurs. . . . We shall call you CAPTAIN AMERICA, son! Because, like you . . . Americans shall gain the strength and will to safeguard our shores." At that moment the spies attack. They kill the serum's inventor, wound Grover, and smash the only bottle of Captain America serum. The Captain annihilates the spies, but the damage is done: instead of a legion of Captain Americas, there will be just one. He does not want to have to face Hitler completely alone, however, so he organizes a fan club called "Captain America's Sentinels of Liberty." Each member pledges "to uphold the principles of the sentinels of liberty and assist Captain America in his wars against spies in the U.S.A."

Captain America was the most famous of the fantasy G-Men spawned by the adventure comics. With his red, white, and blue leotard and his shield with its scarlet letter "A," he was also the most gorgeous. Almost as pretty was The Shield, billed as "The G-Man Extraordinary," who appeared a year before Captain America. Hoover made regular guest appearances in The Shield's adventures: in the first panel he might give the hero his assignment, in the last his medal. Like Captain America, The Shield was "no importation from another planet nor accidental freak of nature" but "the product of years of painstaking toil, the climax to brilliant scientific research." The Plastic Man was still another superhero G-Man, and he also had a stand-in for Hoover (FBI Chief Banner) for a boss.

Hoover's definitive role in American comic book mythology was established in still another superhero origin story, this one for "The Justice Society of America," a showcase for DC Comic's new and rising comic book heroes. The JSA first appeared in the Winter, 1940, issue of *All Star Comics*. Charter members were The Atom, The Sandman, The Spectre, The Flash, Hawkman, Dr. Fate, The Green Lantern, and Hour Man. Superman and Batman made occasional guest appearances.[16]

During their first meeting, while the costumed crime-fighters swap yarns about their favorite cases, The Flash steps out and returns an instant later. He has just been to Washington for a meeting with J. Edgar Hoover, and he has good news: "He wants all of us members of the Justice Society to come down and see him—all together! I thought next Thursday night would be okay. Incidentally," The Flash adds, "he's one swell guy."

Hoover's encounter with the Justice Society of America might represent popular mythology's final pigeonholing of the director and his real-life bureau. Neither of them would henceforth assume center stage in heroic adventures. Hoover would remain in the comics to send costumed crime fighters into the fray and to welcome them home; the official FBI would continue to appear, but only as a team of faceless and nameless avengers in the last panel of gangster comics to mete out poetic justice with their Tommy guns.

There would continue to be FBI comic books—dozens of them—throughout the forties, but Hoover and the FBI would lose their featured roles in the comics' documentary-style crime-and-punishment formula re-enactments of the great public enemies cases. In the famous series of *Crime Does Not Pay* comics that appeared in the late forties, Dillinger, Floyd, and Nelson rob, murder, and die as full-fledged stars, with the FBI merely appearing in the last panel to gun them down. When Hollywood began to turn out gangster movies again in the sixties, the FBI simply provided a car to keep the chase going until it was time for the villains to be exterminated.

It is hardly surprising that J. Edgar Hoover should have failed to make the comic strip G-Man follow the director's line. The thirties and forties were the most creative period in the history of the comics, precisely because artists like Hal Foster ("Tarzan") and Philip Nolan and Dick Calkins ("Buck Rogers") had discovered that the comics provided an ideal means for turning mythological material into popular entertainment. By the end of the 1920s the comics were no longer "the funnies." They were the popular audience's favorite vehicle for fantasy identification with heroic characters in epic adventures. Once the comics had broken their ties to realism, the adventure strips began to borrow other elements from myth while they discarded the dull fetters of probability. As heroes sailed through outer space and swung through jungle vines, they became projections of their readers' fantasy selves, selves freed from the limitations of youth, weakness, or ignorance.

With the comics functioning as one of depression America's main sources of ego-gratifying fantasy, Hoover was bound to fail when he tried to make the comics' action detective hero, the favorite fantasy hero of the depression, obey the prosaic rules and regulations that hemmed in the real-life FBI. Perhaps more significant than Hoover's predictable failure was the adventure comics' continued fascination with the pop culture G-Man despite Hoover's opposition and despite his efforts to "civilize" the action detective. This adds weight to the hypothesis that the basis of the FBI's pop culture appeal was the raw material the bureau provided as grist for the myth-making mill.

The further the pop culture G-Man strayed from Hoover's home turf of facts, files, and briefings, the more clearly he revealed himself as an essentially mythological figure. Whenever Hoover tried to manipulate public opinion by tinkering with the G-Man's mythological traits, he was depriving him of attributes a pop culture hero cannot give up without losing his popularity.

The record of Hoover's adventures in the comic strip field suggests that success in what Walter Bagehot called the "dignified" side of politics,[17] Murray Edelman's "symbolic uses of politics,"[18] occurs when the political leader makes his personality and actions conform to the formulas governing that area of popular culture most closely corresponding to his field of action. Since the formulas of crime entertainment require the presence of an action hero performing rituals of crime and punishment, a symbolic leader like Hoover prospers only as long as his image conforms to the formula; his popularity declines when his image deviates from it. Real-life crime-fighting interests the public only when it provides the same satisfactions offered by crime entertainment: an identification "in action and passion with heroes who struggle to uphold principles of social order. In this identification with leaders and causes," according to Hugh Dalziel Duncan, "anxiety, fear, and loneliness vanish."[19]

When real life furnishes dramas of crime and punishment (the Dillinger case, for example) that closely resemble rituals of crime and punishment, the public will insist on interpreting the principal figures as action heroes and formula villains whose encounters will be understood as popular mythology. When the image of the real-life crime-fighter deviates from the formulas—as did the image of the FBI in "War on Crime"—the public will reject this truth that does not satisfy to embrace a lie (or formula) that does.

9

Public Hero Number One:
J. Edgar Hoover and the Detective Pulps

$\mathbf{G}$-Man movies and comics show how popular culture assimilated
J. Edgar Hoover's FBI agents by turning them into conventional heroes
of popular myth and ritual. Hoover's own public image was also affected by popular culture's drive to ritualize and mythologize politics.
Hoover found that he, no less than his agents, had to conform to
popular expectations if he wanted to retain his popular appeal. Moreover, since Hoover refused to let his agents act like heroes, there was
additional pressure on him to act like an action detective himself so that
someone in the bureau would be maintaining the traditions of Old
Sleuth and Nick Carter.

The eventual result of popular culture's pressure on Hoover to live up
to public expectations was a spate of headline stories in the late thirties
about the director's personal action detective heroics. The cultural dynamics that pushed Hoover in this bizarre direction were an important
influence on Hoover's political career and historical role. Generally
remaining below the surface of the public consciousness, these forces
can be clearly discerned in the pages of the detective pulps, a popular
entertainment medium that developed a particular enthusiasm for the
bureau and its director during the thirties.[1]

The G-Man craze and the detective pulps were made for each other.
These 128-page magazines had taken the place of the nineteenth-
century story papers and dime novels as the American public's most
popular purveyor of formula adventures, and so it was only natural that
in the wake of Cagney's *G-Men* all the adventure pulps—*Argosy, Blue
Book, Real Detective, True Detective,* and many others—should feature
formula detective stories starring G-Man heroes. Finally two pulps dedicated almost exclusively to the exploits of the FBI appeared. One was

G-Men, which began in October, 1935, and stayed with the FBI until
the winter of 1953. The other was *The Feds,* which ran from December,
1935, until it folded in September, 1937. Both magazines tried to put
together a total G-Man experience for their readers—public enemy adventures, straight-from-the-shoulder inside stuff on crime fighting from
the director, tips on FBI training, techniques, and equipment—all presented as an escapist myth for young Americans. During its short life
The Feds tried to follow the FBI's own formula for popularization of
the bureau, while *G-Men* used the action detective formula as its guide.
As a reward for its loyalty, *The Feds* got Hoover's explicit approval and
endorsement, while its renegade rivals received his blanket condemnation of all "bang-bang" formula G-Man entertainment. Once more,
however, Hoover's attempts to alter the course of popular culture came
to nothing, as the public again showed its preference for crime entertainment that followed the well-worn paths of myth and ritual.

The FBI pulps, judging by their ads, were aimed predominantly at an
audience of teenage boys. A few older readers might pick up copies
("False Teeth—Sixty Day Free Trial" and "Stop Your Rupture Worries"), but advertisers evidently thought that FBI magazines were ideal
media for peddling products and services to young males. Some ads
began, "Hi There, Pimple Face" or "It's a Crime to be Skinny"; others
tried to calm the worries of would-be Casanovas ("*Sex Harmony and
Eugenics* in a plain wrapper"). Most of the ads in the FBI pulps—
indeed in all of the detective magazines—were aimed at youths caught
up in fantasies of ego-gratifying careers. There were ads from the National Radio Institute ("I'll send my first lesson free. It shows how *easy*
it is to learn at home to fill a GOOD JOB IN RADIO"), from the Aviation
Institute of the U.S.A., and from the old reliables, LaSalle Extension
University and International Correspondence Schools. Naturally some
ads gave the G-Man fan the chance to fill out a coupon to learn how to
"BECOME A SUCCESSFUL DETECTIVE."

These fill-in-the-coupon fantasies of future greatness (or at least ade-
quacy) in *G-Men* were interspersed throughout 128 pages of FBI lore.
The feature attraction was always a full-length novel starring Dan
Fowler, the magazine's own ace G-Man, together with a bonus assortment of special agent short stories. Along with the adventures of Fowler
and his lesser colleagues, *G-Men* offered comic strips, cryptography
lessons and puzzles, "exposés" of the racket-of-the-month by a "reformed public enemy," and chatter about the magazine's own G-Man
Club. Usually there was also a hard-hitting extract from one of
Hoover's speeches, normally a press release picked up out of the public
domain, although *G-Men* presented them as though they were written
specially for the magazine.

G-Men's Hoover pieces tended to be drawn from the director's more
hard-nosed harangues, with titles like "Partners in Murder—The Evils

G-Men Magazine *(1935–1953)*.

G-Men, *November, 1935.*

of the Parole System as Exposed by America's Greatest Crime Foe." In the November, 1935, issue Hoover blasted "sob sisters," "convict-lovers," and "uninformed and misinformed know-it-alls" who believed that "the individual is greater than society, that because any criminal can display or simulate even the slightest evidence of ordinary conduct, then indeed he must be a persecuted thing, entitled to be sent forth anew into the world to repeated robbery, plunder and murder."[2]

The monthly racket exposé carried a by-line intended to convey the impression that the author knew whereof he spoke. One house pen name was "Frankie Lewis, former public enemy and racketeer." A typical effort was "Passing the Queer—the Sensational Inside Story of Counterfeiting." According to Frankie, counterfeiting was a "swell" racket, "swell—if the G-Men don't get you sooner or later. But, brother, they sure as hell will." Frankie's reminiscences usually ended on a note of nostalgia for the good old pre-FBI days: "The G-Men have the underworld by the throat. Slowly, but surely, they're strangling it. It doesn't pay, brother. It might have been a good game once, but it doesn't pay any dividend now."[3]

G-Men had a regular comic feature called "Public Enemies," a crudely drawn three-page treatment of one of the FBI's more famous victims. The strip tended to dwell lovingly on the gangster's death agonies in a hail of FBI bullets: "They found Nelson's body the next day. Sixteen bullets had perforated his legs and a seventeenth had pierced his stomach, spleen and liver! Finis . . . Baby Face."[4]

G-Men's cryptography feature, "The Black Chamber," supposedly was the work of "M. K. Dirigo, World Famous Cryptographer." Over the years he provided lessons about pattern words, frequency charts, and grids. Each issue carried the names of readers who had solved the previous month's code, with the best solution winning a $15 prize.

Each feature assured the reader that simply by reading the magazine, thereby "informing" himself about the bureau, he was somehow helping the FBI fight crime. By learning what FBI agents had to learn, by listening to what J. Edgar Hoover had to say, and by reading about the bureau's famous cases, the reader could almost convince himself he had joined the FBI. To provide a tangible sign of his spiritual enlistment, *G-Men* set up a readers' club with a membership application in every issue:

Calling all readers—join the G-Men Club! There's a coupon on page 128—and this is our first announcement of our nation-wide organization to combat crime! Qualifications for membership are simply these:

You must promise to uphold the law and aid in its enforcement whenever possible. You must agree to back the Government Men in all their activities— and disseminate public opinion opposed to the gangster and the racketeer.

Members of the G-MEN CLUB are expected to learn all they can about Department of Justice activities and spread this knowledge on to others—discouraging crime by emphasizing the modern, scientific, sure-fire methods of today's manhunters.

The applicant had to sign this oath: "I promise to uphold the laws of the nation and to do all in my power to aid in their enforcement and to back the efforts of the Federal Agents in their fight on crime."[5] For sending in his coupon and a dime, the reader got a "valuable" bronze badge inscribed "G-MEN CLUB—Special Agent."

The magazine had a column called "Federal Flashes" filled with club news and letters from members:

I like your idea of a crime-fighting club and will do all I can to cooperate in your activities.

Thomas S. Peavey, Jasper, Oregon

I am 20 and a bugler serving in the Royal Marines. I'd like to be a member of your club, if possible.

L. F. Webb, H.M.S. Tamar, Hong Kong

There were letters that showed that at least some members were fairly serious about the organization:

Several ruffians in our neighborhood have been misusing the air-raid shelters, and in keeping with my oath to the G-Men Club, a companion and I decided to undertake a patrol to keep these shelters in good order. You know how important these shelters are to the lives and comfort of our fellow-countrymen. We have had very good results in this, cooperating with our local police.

W. O. Hebbes, Hants., England

Letters like this evidently worried the editors, and they warned G-Men Club members not to let their power go to their heads:

We are always glad to receive our readers into membership in our nation-wide organization to combat crime. G-MEN CLUB has no connection with any national or local law-enforcement agency—but is merely an association of readers of this magazine. Of course we do believe that our club is a real asset in helping law-enforcement and crime-prevention work. All readers must realize, however, that membership confers no special privileges in connection with law-enforcement bodies—it does, however, enable readers to join with thousands of other club members in working to stamp out crime.[6]

After *G-Men*'s nonfiction features had vicariously recruited the reader into the FBI, he was ready for the main event, the chance to identify with the magazine's ace G-Man, Dan Fowler, on a big case. The magazine worked hard to give young readers something to identify with in Fowler's characterization. "Well might Dan Fowler be a hero to a young special agent fresh from training school and on his first assignment," one story began. "Already," it continued, Fowler "was becoming almost a legendary figure in the Service—Dan Fowler, the Nemesis of the terrible Grey Gang, the slayer of its leader, Ray Norshire."[7]

Yet he was not a veteran, scarcely a year out of training himself. His features, too bold of outline to be handsome, were, in repose, not unlike those of the youthful Lincoln; he moved with a slight awkwardness that concealed a muscular power and agility beyond the ordinary. His grey eyes, set far apart in an indication of a generous spirit which his wide mouth bore out, were yet capable of going hard and cold as glittering steel—and the mouth could set in a line like a sword-slash above his jutting chin.

"His dead-or-alive look," Sally Vane called it—blond Sally Vane, whom Dan Fowler had known all his life, for whom a boyish affection had ripened into the full flower of love—love as strong and simple natures such as his give only once in life. And now, between these two, fate had forged another knot.

Dan Fowler's father, a county sheriff of long and honorable service, had gone down before the bullets of the Grey Gang, fighting gallantly to his death. And Sally's father, a brave policeman, had been murdered in cold blood by the same band of killers. Now in Sally Vane's heart burned the passion for revenge—not upon the Grey Gang, for they were no more—but upon the whole dark underworld.[8]

Every month readers accompanied Dan into the fictional director's office for the same kind of bracing uplift they got in the magazine's monthly feature by the real-life Hoover. Then Fowler and the readers got to use the same sort of techniques presented in the issue's factual articles. Readers joined Fowler for the same kind of action served up in *G-Men*'s comic strip histories of the bureau's crime wars. And they could definitely count on Dan Fowler for action: "Fiery, hateful, merciless hell! Lead whizzing through the air, finding its mark, sinking, tearing into unresisting flesh. The street slippery with blood; the air hideous with screams and the unceasing, merciless chatter of guns—tommies, gats, machine-guns—as thugs, truck-guards, and G-men fired all at once."[9]

During *G-Men*'s eighteen-year run Dan Fowler tracked down every variety of villain in the pulp magazine stockroom: evil circus freaks, Chinese silk thieves, Malay pirates, and the normal garden-variety spies and gangsters. Each month's story had its quota of surprises, but all were variations on the same basic plot, which might start like this:

In his office at Washington, the Director of the F.B.I. stared at a bright red pin stuck almost in the center of a huge map of the United States that covered one whole wall.

"Central City," he mused, half aloud. His eyes narrowed. "We've got to wipe out that mob, Fowler. Got to!"

Dan Fowler, ace operative of the Federal service, nodded understandingly.

"This thing is big," the Director went on. "How big yet, we don't know. That place is a sore spot on the face of the earth—how far its poison may spread unless we check it and check it quickly, no one can say."

"Let me at it, Chief," Fowler begged. . . . Dan had rarely seen his chief so thoroughly aroused before. His crusading anger reminded the young operative of the righteous wrath of the prophets of old as they thundered out against the wickedness of Babylon and Gomorrah.[10]

This time a criminal gang had taken over an American city. On another occasion a crime czar might have gotten control of a key industry, or the director might have spotted a pattern that connected scattered outbreaks of robbery and murder. In the standard Dan Fowler plot, whatever the outrage that got things going, behind it there was a conspiracy by a criminal genius to organize criminals across the country into an underworld army capable of a coordinated assault against the lawful order, exactly the idea that Hoover and Courtney Ryley Cooper had tried to refute with their theory of "the roots of crime." No ordinary criminal was worthy of the FBI's heavy artillery; for Dan Fowler to get involved, the enemy needed a status in the criminal world equivalent to the FBI's reputation as the country's top cops. Dan Fowler could not take on anything less than the entire "army of crime." Anything less was a waste of his time.

The head of this army of crime was always a mysterious and terrible genius whose identity was unknown to friend and foe. Stories of this sort captured their readers' attention by treating as actualities the submerged fears and paranoid suspicions of the popular imagination. At the beginning of one story, "King Crime," skeptics in the bureau suspect that King Crime is only "a myth . . . a spook, a scapegoat—there's no such person. . . . People like to think up stories like that when they can't find any explanation for the things criminals do."[11] (This was what Hoover always said, and what the official FBI formula maintained.) In Dan Fowler's cases, however, the people who thought up "stories like that" were right, and so were the multitudes who believed in conspirational explanations of public events. In the world of Dan Fowler there was, behind all the depredations of lesser crooks, a single, sinister personality totally committed to the destruction of everything holy. The plot device of a crime king also let Fowler accomplish something that would have been impossible if crime were not an organized conspiracy—exterminate evil with a single burst of his machine gun. And since these crime czars were projections of the public's secret fears, the criminal geniuses' entrances were usually accompanied by *misterioso* effects:

The room was in darkness . . . something clicked at the far end of the room. Every man present knew what it meant. Their leader had arrived. There was a second click; a sort of greenish light appeared behind a wire screen which completely cut off the end of the room where the dumbwaiter shaft was. Against this greenish glow they saw a bulky, seated figure—a dark shadow, cowled and robed like a Grand Inquisitor, a shadow which utterly dominated the room.

The shadow was—King Crime.

No man there had ever seen more of him. No man could have identified him had he met him on the street. He was just—King Crime. The mysterious, terrible King Crime, in whose gift lay riches, whose word was life or death.[12]

By C. K. M.
SCANLON
Author of "Tong War," "Big Shot," etc.

One of the men went down as Fowler

fired from the shadow of the prison walls (Page 55)

CHAPTER I

Murder for Sale

HE was of medium height, medium weight, had medium brown hair and a medium complexion. He might have been actually named Mr. Medium. He was of the type which, when it turns to crime, becomes the despair of industrious detective officers seeking descriptions from the eye-witnesses. There was nothing about him to describe. Even his blue serge clothes were inconspicuous and ordinary. A thousand such as he pass any busy corner every rush hour. The house-dick in the lobby of the great hotel didn't waste a glance on him as he walked toward the elevators; didn't even see him. The elevator boy wouldn't have remembered the floor at which he got off, if questioned ten minutes later.

All of which goes to show what human ingenuity can do with the idea of protective coloring, so helpful to hunted wild things. Mr. Medium might very well become an object of police attention at any moment, if his affairs went wrong. He might need his protective coloring.

For Mr. Medium was a salesman, a broker, if you please—of murder.

He went down a corridor, turned a corner, opened a door and walked into the living room of a suite—without knocking. Two men awaited him one a nervous, hard-eyed, swarthy young man with an evil droop to his eyelids, the other burly and gruff voiced.

"Well, gentlemen?" said Mr. Medium, dropping into a chair and wav

The F. B. I. Plays The Ace of Special Agents in a G-Man Deal at Nokomis!

G-Men, *March, 1936.*

Compared to other supervillains, King Crime's ambition of taking over Central City was modest indeed. Underworld crime kings in Dan Fowler adventures were usually bent on conquering the world, or at least the United States. Ambitions on that order were the rule in pulp G-Man adventures. Operator 5 (Popular Publication's ace agent) had "to save the United States from total destruction in every story, every month." His writer recalled that "when I was called in to start the series they already had a cover illustration, . . . the White House was being blown up."[13] All the heroes in the more fantastic variations on the action detective formula had to cope with these underworld Napoleons. In 1937, for instance, The Shadow worked on a case called "The Crime Oracle." This villain was known as "The Head," and that was all he was: a talking head on a pedestal issuing orders to his terrified gang, directing them in a plan to extend his criminal rule over the entire country.[14] One reason the FBI's officially sanctioned entertainment never succeeded as well as unofficial G-Man adventures was that Hoover prohibited his writers from exploiting the idea of a criminal underworld. This meant unsanctioned writers could use more dramatic villains in their stories than the writers who followed Hoover's orders.

Since thirties popular culture regarded both the real and the fictional
FBI as the nation's last line of defense against an underworld takeover,
a budding crime czar's usual strategy in a Dan Fowler story was to lure
the bureau into a set battle where defeat would discredit the FBI, de-
moralizing the country by making it believe that further resistance was
hopeless. An example is a Dan Fowler adventure that appeared in October, 1937, called "Crime's Blackboard—A Racket Czar Organizes the
Mobs of a Nation into a Mighty Unit of Doom."[15] The story begins
with Fowler in a high state of excitement: nostrils flaring, pulse racing,
breath quickening. A lesser man might have put in for sick leave, but
not Fowler. These rabid symptoms were old hat to him: they simply
meant the veteran crime-buster had a new case, one worthy of "the
world's greatest man-hunter":

Organizing every top gang in every city in the United States! Whipping the
wolves into line so that they actually pulled together as a unit in sufficiently
large jobs! Hijacking a truck here; robbing a bank there; looting a jewel house
in another place; kidnapping a prominent person in still another! Then subtly
combining the secondary stages of such crimes so that they all ran together in
deadly, tangled confusion, with the very participants not knowing all the ramifications! The man who could do that was the most dangerous individual on
earth.[16]

Fowler's mind races through the evidence to a hair-raising conclusion: behind this crime wave there lurked a plot that could succeed only
by crippling the nation's anticrime elite. The unknown enemy's next
move would be against the FBI itself.

The scene shifts to Akron, Ohio, where the mayor, district attorney,
and police chief are meeting with a delegation of leading citizens for a
seminar on law enforcement. Their guest is the "crisp, dynamic, hard-
hitting" Director of the Federal Bureau of Investigation. His presence
reassures the group: a tire tycoon whispers that "at least for a little
while we can feel safe. . . . no one would try anything while the head of
the Federal Bureau himself was in town."[17]

At the very moment the Director is giving his pep talk about "Cooperation Against Crime," the leaders of the local underworld are having their
own conference. Their guest speaker is a beautiful mystery woman from
the East Coast named Madge Forester, "tall, slender, but delicately, gor-
geously mature . . . with something very cold and very sinister in her
eye."[18] She is the personal representative of the mysterious 'Big Boss" in
New York. His orders are to kidnap the son of the same tire tycoon who
had found The Director's presence in Akron so reassuring.

The news throws the mob into a panic. They plead with Madge for a delay. One crook begs her not to make them do it "while the Chief of the G-Boys himself is in the burg!" Nothing doing; the snatch has been planned precisely because the Director is in town:

I've told you the reason for that, honey. . . . The Bureau is the toughest thing we've got to fight. Anything that hurt the Gs would help us. And don't think this won't hurt! Son of one of America's richest men kidnapped right from under the nose of the Chief of the F.B.I.! That'll give the Bureau a knock it will take years to live down. It'll hit 'em where they live, honey. And if the Gs don't catch up with the snatchers—which they won't with the chief planning the getaway—the Bureau will never have quite the same rep again. You get it?[19]

They get it.

This kidnapping is just the sort of move Fowler had predicted: not simply a crime, but a blow at the source of the Bureau's power—its reputation. The kidnapping is a "gesture of contempt for the F.B.I. and all it represented. Also a shrewd blow calculated to give the Bureau the worst possible publicity and cripple its powers forever. The G-Men depended heavily on public help and favor. This would blast both for a long time."[20]

The public's reaction to the kidnapping proves that the Big Boss knows his popular culture. With headlines screaming "RUBBER MAGNATE'S SON KIDNAPPED UNDER NOSE OF G-CHIEF—HEAD OF F.B.I. WATCHES GANG STEAL RUBBER KING'S SON,"[21] confidence in the bureau begins to crumble. "Smalley felt a little hysterical. . . . The chief of the Federal Bureau of Investigation was in town. The papers had played up the visit big. His lips curled. Hell of a lot of good the F.B.I. was when such things as this could happen! An over-ballyhooed bunch of parlor policemen!"[22]

Faced with this crisis, the Director huddles with Fowler to map out the FBI's counter-strategy. "The G-Men had their work cut out for them, all right. The G-Men, under the leadership of their iron-jawed Chief who was facing, politically and every other way, the most significant crisis of his career."[23] Despite the seriousness of the situation, the Director remains calm: "The Chief sat quietly in his hotel suite, with his arms flat and in repose on the arms of his chair. Other men might pace jerkily, or drum with their fingers, or fiddle with their hands, when under pressure. The Chief didn't. Urgency only produced a little more repose in the man. A dynamic repose, however."[24]

Eventually, of course, the bureau cracks the case. A clue here, a clue there, some quick thinking, some fast shooting, and once again Fowler has his man. Back in Washington the Director can relax, his reputation intact, his bureau still the scourge of the underworld: "But under the smile was the pride almost of a father, backed by the deeper pride of a man who had dedicated his life to the service of his country for those who served under him with equal faithfulness. The man walked to a picture on his wall. It was a score of fine-looking men, the latest crop of new agents to leave the Washington training course. The Director quietly saluted them. A few would die in service before the year was out. 'To the F.B.I.' he whispered, while his salute endured."[25]

The widespread belief, which Hoover shared, that the bureau's reputation was its greatest weapon, let the G-Man pulps claim that they were working for the public good by glorifying the FBI. To hear J. Edgar Hoover on the subject, however, the G-Man craze was more of an irritation than a pleasure. In 1936 Hoover was raked over the coals by the Senate Appropriations Committee because some senators suspected Hoover of inspiring this publicity, perhaps even using taxpayers' money for the purpose. He defended himself by claiming he had no control over most FBI entertainment, did not like much of it, and had complained about some of it. On the subject of the pulps, he had this to say: "There are many magazine articles that are particularly objectionable. . . . You see the so-called lurid portrayal of the work of the G-Men. As a matter of fact, a very small portion of our time is devoted to shooting. We refer to it as 'bang bang' publicity. We are not in favor of it."[26] A few years later one of Hoover's spokesmen went even further. "Some people who are not familiar with the situation," he said, "have intimated that Mr. Hoover likes publicity. That is a common human failing, but one that Mr. Hoover does not share."[27]

That last statement seems somewhat exaggerated, but the point is that Hoover did distinguish carefully between G-Man idolatry that followed the official line and that which departed from it, and he did lash out at the heretics. Hoover's heavy-handedness with his critics was proverbial—letters to a writer's publishers and editors, leaks about a critic's background, rebuttals fed to friendly reporters. He treated loyal writers more tenderly, but the whip-hand was still there.

Since the G-Man pulps sold the illusion of participating in the FBI's crusades, authenticity was a valuable commodity and Hoover's endorsement was the ultimate guarantee that a story was authentic. Hoover could and did award his endorsement to publishers who followed his directions, and he withheld it from others. Since everyone was competing to have the most official G-Man publication, Hoover's endorsement was worth having (or at least publishers thought it was worth having).

The FBI pulp that did get Hoover's endorsement was *The Feds*. If the director was actually using "luridness" as his criterion, he would have been hard put to distinguish between *The Feds* and *G-Men*. *The Feds'* stories were every bit as bloody as the ones in *G-Men*. The difference was that instead of a full-length G-Man adventure like *G-Men*'s Dan

G-MEN vs. CRIME!

THE *Feds*

10¢ · **SEPT. 1937**

REG. U. S. PAT. OFFICE

ARE YOUR FINGER PRINTS ON FILE?

How J. Edgar Hoover's F.B.I. Can Help You Protect Yourself and Your Family—Another special article with official photographs

MURDER
ON
PARADE

An amazing novelette
of the U.S. Naval Academy

Gripping Novelettes and
Stories of Secret Service,
Postal Inspectors, Coast
Guard, Mine Bureau,
F. B. I. and other

Despite Hoover's endorsement, The Feds *lasted only from 1935 to 1937.*

Fowler novel, *The Feds* had lengthy, highly detailed nonfiction essays on various aspects of the bureau's operations, which were nothing more than scissors-and-paste jobs culled from FBI handouts, illustrated with bureau photographs and graphics, and enlivened with hefty chunks of the director's speeches.

The FBI articles in *The Feds* closely followed the FBI formula C. R. Cooper had invented in *Ten Thousand Public Enemies*. *The Feds* claimed that

the whole story of the success of Hoover's men does not rest alone in their brilliant attacks upon organized crime. This handful of men, with the whole United States to cover, with mobility that has never yet been matched by any other organization dazzles the nation again and again by some brilliant coup which brings behind bars an outstanding public enemy—public "rat" to Hoover and his men. . . . And every agent is in on these battles, from their Chief, Hoover, through the district heads and to the newest rookie. . . .

Behind this, however, stands the excellent training which these men receive. . . . In other words, everything that can be done to train men to battle crime has been done with Hoover's men. They are fit for their task, and the record which they have made for themselves—a record which surpasses that of *any* law enforcement organization, in modern or ancient times—speaks for itself.

Since the inception of the F.B.I.'s present work under the leadership of Hoover, America need not fear for its law enforcement.[28]

It was not quite true that *The Feds* had no star agent to pit against the other magazines' Dan Fowlers. *The Feds'* answer to Dan Fowler was J. Edgar Hoover himself. The magazine realized, however, that Hoover was going to need a handle with a little more pizzazz than "The Director" if he were going to compete against brutes like Doc Savage, The Shadow, or for that matter, Dan Fowler, "The World's Greatest Man-hunter." *The Feds'* solution was to bill Hoover as "Public Hero Number One." Each month's full-length FBI piece started off with a rave about the director: "John Edgar Hoover, as director of the Federal Bureau of Investigation and as America's popular Public Hero No. 1, is the world's leader in law enforcement circles. He is Crime Battler No. 1 in this country as well as all over the world. The methods he uses should be worth considering."[29] Each month the magazine focused on another of Hoover's "methods," with plenty of gush about the director's genius in thinking it up.

Evidently *The Feds'* approach was what the director wanted because the magazine got regular encouragement from "Public Hero No. One" himself. One of Hoover's letters (which was of course, proudly re-printed) informed the editors that "I am particularly happy that such a comprehensive and true story of the activities of the Federal Bureau of Investigation has been presented to the reading public. It is one of the most comprehensive and intelligently written articles about the work of our Bureau which I have had the opportunity to read."[30]

Despite Hoover's plugs *The Feds* failed for the same reason that all the Bureau's efforts to control popular entertainment would fail. Instead of giving young readers an action hero to identify with in formula adventures, the magazine gave them the boss of the action heroes. Even more unpardonably, the magazine told the kids that they ought to look up to Hoover because he was a great teacher. Kids did not buy pulp magazines for a chance to identify with teachers.

The Feds made another mistake. Instead of letting readers imagine themselves as one of the G-Men they had been reading about in the newspapers, *The Feds* made them realize that, as far as Hoover was concerned, readers were only civilians. Instead of trying to involve the readers in the excitement of formula adventure, the magazine published insulting commentary like this: "Here is explained another phase of F.B.I. work which protects you and your family, and adds to the prestige of John Edgar Hoover, Public Hero No. 1."[31] Popular culture does not create heroes just to be protected by them. The public wants those heroes to lead them into danger, to provide them with adventure, to give them thrills, not security. Magazine buyers are not interested in

The Feds, *September, 1937.*

ARE YOUR FINGERPRINTS ON FILE?

Here is explained another phase of F. B. I. work which protects you and your family, and adds to the prestige of John Edgar Hoover, Public Hero No. 1

(Illustrated with Official Photographs)

THERE are two ways of combating crime. One way is to go after the criminal and get him red-handed after the crime is committed, and, by building up a solid case, secure conviction. The other way is to get the interest and enthusiasm of the public so aroused that they will all take a deep interest in crime, and thus prevent its beginning by giving all the cooperation possible to the law-enforcement agencies.

John Edgar Hoover, as director of the Federal Bureau of Investigation and America's popular Public Hero No. 1, is the world's leader in law-enforcement circles. He is Crime Battler No. 1 in this country, as well as all over the world. The

methods he uses should be worth considering.

And John Edgar Hoover, as befits a man of his capabilities, and the leader of the F.B.I., uses *BOTH* methods!

His F.B.I. men go out in the field and combat crime by investigation, or by gunfire, if necessary! And they also go out in the field and bring home the lesson of crime prevention to every one in this country and what is more furnish the means of combating crime in such a way that every citizen can do his part.

The whole story of the success of Hoover's men does not rest alone in their brilliant attacks upon organized crime. This handful of men, with the whole United

The seal of the Department of Justice, of which the F. B. I. is a branch.

reading about somebody else's adventures—they want to be able to pretend they are having those adventures themselves.

By the standards of successful action pulps, everything *The Feds* did was wrong. Instead of involving readers in adventures, the magazine distanced them from the action. Instead of describing the FBI as the spearhead of a crusade that demanded the participation of the whole country, the magazine treated the public as an audience—an enthusiastic audience—but nothing more than an audience. All Hoover wanted, *The Feds* said, was "to get the interest and enthusiasm of the public aroused so that they will all take a deep interest in crime, and thus prevent its beginning by giving all the cooperation possible to law-enforcement agencies."[32] But pulp magazine readers did not want to cooperate with the G-Men. They wanted to *be* G-Men.

Since *G-Men* magazine had an FBI club, *The Feds* tried to have one, too. Even this was mishandled. Instead of sending readers membership cards, badges, and equipment to help them track down and capture suspicious-looking playmates, *The Feds* asked readers to sign and mail a letter to Hoover: "I would like to have my identification recorded in your CIVIL IDENTIFICATION DIVISION. Please send me the official cards which I will properly fill out and return to your Bureau."[33] While successful G-Man entertainment was giving Americans the chance to imagine themselves as members of the FBI, having the same kinds of adventures as the real G-Men, Hoover's favorite magazine was urging them to become card-carrying members of—the public! If that was the best the real FBI could offer, the public would stick with the make-believe G-Men.

The Feds glorified Hoover because the only way entertainment that followed the FBI formula could give the public a hero was to turn the director himself, the only G-Man permitted by regulations to have an identifiable face and name, into an action detective. Popular culture's delusion that J. Edgar Hoover was the perfect embodiment of the action detective ideal was foreshadowed in a G-Man adventure series that ran in 1935 in *Blue Book,* one of the quality (15¢) pulps.

The hero of this series was ace agent James "Duke" Ashby. Ashby's adventures were standard action detective routines without any of the fantastic features that made the Fowler stories readable and unintentionally funny. The stories were filled with the sort of procedural details that fascinated Hoover. Between cases Ashby relaxed by reciting passages from the (real) FBI handbook: "You are a soldier in the front-line trenches. You are fighting a force that threatens to overwhelm your country. That fact justifies any sacrifice you may be called upon to make."[34] Like Dan Fowler, Ashby liked to imagine himself getting killed on the job so that he would get his name inscribed on the bronze "Killed in Action" plaque in Hoover's office.

Blue Book gave its G-Man series an elaborate origin story that revealed "Duke" Ashby as an idealized version of J. Edgar Hoover. "I first met Special Agent Ashby," wrote Robert R. Mill, "in the offices of J. Edgar Hoover, Director of the Bureau of Investigation. . . . Special Agent Ashby is typical of the men commanded by Mr. Hoover. For that reason he ceases to be a mere character of fiction and becomes a symbol of one of the most important eras in the history of law enforcement."[35]

The crime wave of the thirties, Mill explained, provided the FBI with a historic opportunity. "The result is history, chapters of which were written in the smoke that curled from blazing guns. . . . Today complete victory, if not an established fact, is well within the range of vision. . . . That fact entitles the special agent to walk in the paths of the frontiersman, the explorer, the soldier and other epic characters of history."[36]

Mill claimed he had written his G-Man stories as a public service. "The very nature [of the G-Man's work] . . .has made of the special agent a romantic figure of mystery. He walks alone, shuns publicity, and remains a man apart."[37] Mill wrote that he had decided it would do the public good to know what these romantic figures of mystery were doing, and so he went to Washington, where Hoover let him poke around headquarters and the branch offices:

With this as background, I sat at a desk with Mr. Hoover, hoping to obtain the finishing touches. The picture of Special Agent James Ashby was almost complete. It needed only a touch of the crusader, which all these men have. That is what drives them into the service. It is what holds them there. It was the power that motivated the men whose names now appear on a tablet which bears the inscription "Killed in the Line of Duty."

Looking at that man before the desk, it was very easy to supply that touch. Then Special Agent Ashby came to life. He was as real as the man at the desk. The G-Men all helped to give him to me. . . . Mr. Hoover acted as his spokesman:

"All the decent people of the United States are our employers. The only reward we ask is your loyal support and understanding."

These stories are written with the sincere hope that they may play at least a small part in bringing that about.[38]

Hoover's repeated failures in popular entertainment finally taught him that the public was simply not interested in an FBI image that did not cater to its need for fantasy, so beginning in mid-1936 Hoover began to follow the lead of *The Feds* and *Blue Book* by offering himself to the public as an action hero, the "Number One G-Man." No longer content with posing as the Washington-based strategist and long-distance coordinator of the anticrime crusade, Hoover took to the field himself. No more was he simply the trainer of the G-Men, sending them out on assignments while he remained behind in Washington issuing orders and interpreting evidence. Now it was Hoover himself who was leading raids and making arrests, just like Dan Fowler and Secret Agent X-9.

Today the public might raise its eyebrows at a forty-year-old bureaucrat charging about the country waving a pistol and a pair of handcuffs. In the late 1930s nobody, except for a few die-hard FBI-haters, thought it was strange at all. By flamboyantly reshaping his own image to fit the specifications of the action hero, Hoover was giving the public what was missing from official FBI entertainment—a G-Man who could operate with the same personal freedom as the action detectives in unsanctioned special agent entertainment. If the public was too simple-minded to appreciate the intricacies of the FBI's bureaucratic crime-fighting technique, then Hoover would give them something they could understand—real-life crime-and-punishment entertainment in which all the FBI roles—strategist, scientist, and street-fighter—were played by one self-reliant hero, J. Edgar Hoover.

The first, and most highly-publicized, of the director's "own" cases (as Bureau publicity titled them) was his arrest of Alvin Karpis in 1936.[39] Karpis was a member of the Ma Barker gang, which was responsible for a spectacular series of robberies and kidnappings from 1931 until 1935. On January 16, 1935, FBI agents killed Ma Barker and her sons. That left Karpis as the last surviving big-name bandit of the gangster era, public enemy number one. With Dillinger, Floyd, Nelson, and the Barkers all dead, Karpis was Hoover's last chance to do what the public expected of an action detective hero—to meet a criminal popular culture had turned into a symbol of all crime in hand-to-hand, one-on-one combat.

Alone now, Karpis underwent extensive plastic surgery and tried to continue his career. After several small robberies, he looted an Erie Railroad mail car carrying a factory payroll in November, 1935. This was spectacular enough to make the media compare Karpis to the legendary Jesse James. The publicity ante was now large enough for the director to deal himself in. At the same time the success of "Secret Agent X-9" against "War on Crime" was showing Hoover what the public expected of a G-Man hero, the director passed the word throughout the bureau that Karpis was "his" man. When Karpis was located, Hoover was going to make the arrest himself.

Hoover had his first chance in March, 1936. He got word that Karpis was hiding in his favorite "good town," Hot Springs, Arkansas, so he collected his top assistants and headed south on a chartered plane. By the time Hoover got the raid organized, however, Karpis had fled, probably tipped off by local police.

On April 30, 1936, Hoover finally got another tip: his agents had Karpis trapped in a New Orleans apartment. Cautioning them to avoid further leaks and not to notify the local police, Hoover rushed to Loui-

ALVIN KARPIS

G·MEN & HEROES OF THE LAW

G·MEN ANSWER PUBLIC ENEMY NUMBER-1. 103

Hoover personally arrested Alvin Karpis, "The Director's Man," in 1936.

ana on an all-night plane. Here is Hoover's version of what happened: "I had told the boys how desperate he was, and had given them all a chance to back out if they wished to. Not one made a move. Then I told them they could put on bullet-proof vests if they wished to. Not one made a move."

As the G-Men moved into position around Karpis' hideout, the gangster and a friend stepped out of the apartment and into their car. "I told the special agent who was driving to step on the gas, but just as we started a mounted policeman came gallumphing down the street on a big white horse, floppity-floppity-flop. We had to let him go by. He might not have understood what all the shooting was about and charged in on the wrong side. Then, as we started again, a child on a bicycle crossed our bow. We couldn't risk injuring the child, so we stopped again. Finally, we closed in on the gangsters and made the capture. At last, we had in our hands the most dangerous public enemy in the United States. 'Put the cuffs on him, boys,' I said."[40] It turned out that nobody had remembered to bring cuffs, and Karpis's hands had to be tied with an agent's necktie.

The spectacle of the chief of the nation's leading law enforcement agency leading a raid against a major criminal and making the arrest himself was front page news. Hoover played the action hero role to the hilt by giving out tough-guy interviews about the case. Under the headline "HOOVER ORDERS 'STICK 'EM UP!'" in the *New York Journal,*

Hoover said this: "Stammering, stuttering, shaking as though he had palsy, the man upon whom was bestowed the title of public enemy number one folded up like the yellow rat he is. There was no betrayal of Karpis by his pals or others. The man who said he'd never be captured quit like the yellow rat he is and the rest of gangland is at heart. Why, we don't rank the yellow rats. It is you fellows who do that for us, but if you want to know who I rank as Public Enemy No. One today, it is old man politics."[41] Follow-up stories assured the public that Hoover was continuing to supervise the case personally even after the capture. The bureau reported that the director escorted Karpis to the Saint Paul, Minnesota, prison, and that he himself conducted the "third-degree grilling" [sic] of the kidnapper.[42]

The public was naturally interested in learning what had gotten into the director. Hoover's enemies claimed that he had been embarrassed during the March, 1936, Senate Appropriations Committee hearings when one of his Senate critics taunted Hoover for never having made an arrest himself. Senator Kenneth McKellar of Tennessee wanted to know why Hoover "wasn't out risking his neck" like the G-Men in the movies. *Time* said that Hoover was "boiling mad" and had "returned to his office and demanded the latest reports on Alvin Karpis, the last of the Barker gang. Then he flew down to New Orleans [and] personally led the raiding squad into the Karpis hideout."[43]

The FBI itself claimed that the Hoover-Karpis feud had its origin in something far more portentous (and dramatic) than a little senatorial ribbing. The director had gone on the warpath because Karpis had challenged Hoover to personal combat, and that was something no hero could ignore. Shortly before the New Orleans raid, the bureau claimed, Karpis had vowed to kill Hoover and had passed word to the director by way of the underworld grapevine that "you got my pals, but I'll get you." Hoover's reply was that "we intend to knock off everybody who ever worked with this guy. It may run into 25 or 30 people."[44]

The day after Hoover arrested Karpis, Rex Collier ran a column in the *Washington Star* that elaborated on the death threat story:

John Edgar Hoover had planned to be present at the capture of Alvin Karpis ever since the gun-toting, boastful desperado threatened death to the Director some months ago.

Undismayed by the threats Hoover told friends that nothing would suit him better than a face-to-face meeting with "Old Creepy" as the nation's Number One Public Enemy is known to his pals.

When a friend expressed concern over the threats Hoover laughingly remarked that Karpis would never have warned him in advance if he had really intended to do him harm. "Anyway," he added, "that rat is too yellow—like all of his kind."[45]

A few weeks later the bureau added another dime-novel touch to the story. "Karpis' first plan," the bureau affirmed, "was to fly from city to city, killing the Special Agents in Charge of field offices. But he put this aside for an even better one. He sent word to Hoover that he intended to kill him, thereby avenging "Ma" Barker's death. The threat was not an idle one to Hoover."[46]

In the face of American popular culture's preference for action heroes who picked their own cases for their own reasons and finished off their enemies themselves, the FBI was finally giving the public a real G-Man who could do everything the make-believe G-Men were doing in the pulps and comic strips. As though in compensation for the bureau's emasculation of the regulation FBI agent in the entertainment it officially sanctioned, the bureau began to promote J. Edgar Hoover as a real action detective. Just as the pulps interpreted each month's case as an apocalyptic confrontation between the symbol of crime and the symbol of the law, a battle for the soul of society, one of Hoover's assistants contributed a symbolic interpretation of the Karpis case that could have come right out of Dan Fowler's adventure in "Crime's Blackboard": "We knew that the gang leaders and lone-wolf desperadoes were convinced that with the Director dead, there would be a letup in the campaign against them. We knew, too, from the wild boasting that Karpis was given to, that he believed he would achieve a kind of royalty status in the underworld if he could knock off the top man in the F.B.I. and get away with it."[47]

Once Hoover had gotten a taste of action, it was hard to keep him in his office. On May 7, 1936, Hoover flew to Toledo to lead a pre-dawn raid on the hideout of Harry Campbell, another member of the Karpis-Barker gang. When newsmen asked Hoover if he had led the raid himself, he replied, "I did," but then modestly added that "it was a 'we' job, not an 'I' job."[48]

On December 14, 1936, Hoover was finally able to do some shooting. His agents trapped a twenty-five-year-old bank robber named Harry Brunette in a New York City apartment on West 102d Street. They staked out the building and then sent for Hoover, who was in town on business. He ordered Brunette to surrender and then told his men to open fire. The shooting lasted for thirty-five minutes until a tear gas bomb flushed out Mrs. Brunette, who had been wounded in the thigh, and then Brunette himself. Hoover was able to make the arrests personally. When New York City police arrived, attracted by all the shooting, Hoover barred them from the action, telling them to direct traffic and handle the crowds of rubber-neckers. Soon the bureau's tear gas bombs set the building on fire and the fire department rushed to the scene. According to *Newsweek,* "Amid the hubbub, a flustered G-Man poked a sub-machine gun at a husky fireman. 'Dammit, can't you

Hoover in the Stork Club, New Year's Eve, 1938.

read?' growled the fireman, pointing at his helmet. 'If you don't take that gun out of my stomach I'll bash your head in.' "[49]

The raid got Hoover more action hero headlines: "25 G-MEN LED BY HOOVER CAPTURE BANDIT IN WEST 102ND ST" proclaimed the *New York Times*.[50] It also caused some complaints. The police commissioner said that the bureau had snatched an important criminal out of his jurisdiction after promising to share the arrest with the city police; he accused Hoover of risking public mayhem in the quest for "bigger headlines." Other city officials were quoted muttering about "heroics" and "small town stuff." Hoover took a lofty view of the controversy. "The important thing," he piously insisted, "was not how or why Brunette was captured but that this embryo Karpis or Dillinger is in custody and that the taxpayers got what they paid for, the apprehension of criminals."[51]

The climax of Hoover's career as an action hero came on August 24, 1939. For two years New York City and state police had been looking for Louis "Lepke" Buchalter, who headed the New York protection racket that virtually controlled the garment industry, as well as the nationwide hit squad known as "Murder, Incorporated." In 1937

Lepke went into hiding when combined federal and state rewards totalling $50,000 created the so-called "Big Heat": constant harassment of the underworld designed to force Lepke's associates to turn him in. Finally one of Lepke's friends convinced him that a deal had been worked out with the FBI to protect him from New York State Attorney General Thomas Dewey, who was waiting for Lepke with indictments for capital crimes. Federal charges, Lepke was told, would be limited to one narcotics offense carrying a ten-year sentence, but only if he surrendered himself to the FBI. The arrangement seemed plausible because Dewey was being promoted as a likely presidential opponent against FDR in 1940 and it was possible that Roosevelt was using Hoover to dim Dewey's reputation as the nation's leading racket-buster.

The break came when crime boss Albert Anastasia phoned columnist Walter Winchell to tell him Lepke was willing to surrender. Winchell knew how to put together a good story. He called Hoover and arranged for Hoover to be alone at Fifth Avenue and Twenty-Eighth Street at 10:15 on the evening of August 24. When Winchell pulled up in a borrowed car exactly on schedule, Hoover got in and Winchell introduced him to the other passenger. "Mr. Hoover," Winchell said, "this is Lepke." "Glad to meet you," Lepke said hopefully.[52] Actually there had been no deal. The federal government convicted Lepke on the narcotics charge, then turned him over to Dewey, who convicted him of murder and had him electrocuted in 1944.

An action hero was a celebrity, so Hoover's name began to appear regularly in the columns of celebrity columnists—Walter Winchell, of course, and Ed Sullivan. His diet, hobbies, and sporting activities were all covered in their columns, the thirties' equivalents of television talk shows for exposing celebrities to the public. These publicists taught Hoover how to live like a star. He did his drinking at the Stork Club and his vacationing at Palm Beach.

As Hoover's image changed from bureaucrat to action hero, his appearance also changed to meet the public's expectations. Before 1933 Hoover's publicity pictures showed a thin, pale, serious fellow with a camera-shy, inexpressive face and slicked-down hair. His props in these early pictures tended to be his desk, his papers, and his pen. Hoover's new man-of-action image demanded action poses, so in the late thirties Hoover had himself photographed holding machine guns, tennis rackets, and fishing rods, or striding manfully at the head of a grim-looking parade of agents. In 1944 the bureau began to circulate a publicity portrait that showed a relaxed, confident Hoover in a movie detective's three-piece suit. He was posed in front of a map of the country that showed the location of his agents, and he wore a jaunty smile that owed something to Cagney's self-assured leer. By then Hoover knew how to dominate the camera, and he looked like a man sure of his celebrity status and in complete control of his image. The blurb circulated with the 1944 portrait sounded like a pulp magazine's ballyhoo for a new adventure hero:

Tough, and looks it, is MR. J. EDGAR HOOVER, Director of the Federal Bureau of Investigation of America, the most efficient anti-crime organization in the world. This stockily built chief has a sensational record for bringing public enemies of all kinds, including the notorious kidnapping gangs, to justice. The prevention of sabotage and espionage have since the war become major tasks of the F.B.I., and as a result of the exploits of his men, Mr. Hoover is the hero of all American schoolboys. . . . Besides many articles in newspapers and magazines, he has written a book, "Persons in Hiding." Mr. Hoover has a pleasant personality; is a bachelor; fond of sports; and collects Chinese antiques.[53]

Under the impact of Hoover's personal heroics and attendant publicity the FBI's carefully crafted image was thrown out of balance. Hoover's action hero image reduced the rest of the FBI to the role it played in G-Man entertainment—a backdrop for the star agent. FBI publicity during the forties dwelt more on "color" stories about Hoover than on the FBI procedures that were the core of FBI publicity during the first phase of the bureau's build-up. By the early forties, perhaps discouraged by their failure to make the whole organization the hero of the bureau's adventures, Hoover's publicists seem to have succumbed to the popular audience's demand for heroes. Instead of the FBI, it was now J. Edgar Hoover himself they advertised as the nation's main defense against crime and sabotage.

This new and hard-boiled Hoover was the hero of Frederick L. Collins's authorized history of the bureau, *The F.B.I. in Peace and War* (1943). Even Hoover had to blush at some of Collins's flattery, and he chided him for "the sin of over-friendliness,"[54] the only sin Hoover tolerated in his associates. Collins's book (which was quickly turned into a popular radio show) described the FBI essentially as a stage upon which Hoover could demonstrate his greatness. Hoover was, Collins said, "the hero of the story . . . the man who represents the law . . . the protagonist of decency as against vice."[55]

In 1943 Hoover was forty-eight years old, not yet the squat bulldog of his later years, but even then a stocky guy with a physique like a fireplug. That was not what Collins saw. He saw an American action hero, and an American action hero was supposed to look like Joe Palooka. Collins's Hoover was "the exact antithesis of the professional office holder. The alert face beneath the close-cropped, slightly curling, thick black hair is round and young—the skin tight-drawn, the flesh firm, not a semblance of flabbiness or sag. The compact body, with the

Hoover as the action detective hero, from a 1944 publicity shot.

shoulders of a light heavyweight boxer and the waist of a tennis player, carries no ounce of extra weight."[56]

If readers' minds were so clouded by mythology that they would accept Collins's word portrait instead of the man they saw in the daily newspapers and weekly newsreels, then they would also have no trouble swallowing the rest of Collins's gush: "Bright of eye, rugged of countenance, sturdy of build, his physical movements quick and incisive, his mental reactions trigger fast, his words (few and to the point and marshalled by a trained and orderly mind) come with the speed and effectiveness of machinegun fire."[57]

Collins may have felt that he was making the director seem a little too warlike to be welcomed into genteel society, so he hastened to add that

this man is so human, his emotions so strong, his very righteousness so wrathy, that it is too bad that the dignity of his position doesn't permit him to break down oftener and let the public see him for what he is. We read the newspaper accounts of his stalking relentlessly through dark hallways into the hideaways of armed public enemies. We admire the courage of the man. Who could help admiring it? But we lay down the paper with the idea that here is a solemn fellow, who takes himself pretty seriously, and who insists that everybody else take him that way, too. As a matter of fact, he is just the opposite. Get him out for dinner when he has time for it—which is seldom enough these days—and he is the gayest companion imaginable.[58]

Hoover was never off duty, so he could not delight the public with his sparkling personality as often as Collins would have liked. "Hoover's peacetime working hours, when there wasn't anything especially doing, were from eight-thirty in the morning until around seven at night. When he was on a case, he often went forty-eight and seventy-two hours without sleep, and with nothing to eat but sandwiches."[59]

What was the rest of the bureau doing while Hoover was wolfing down sandwiches, piling up overtime and stalking relentlessly down dark hallways? How did they feel about slaving away in the shadows while Hoover hogged the spotlight? Were they a little jealous? Nothing of the kind:

The men love him. They know he is a hard taskmaster. They feel from time to time the weight of his heavy hand, the impact of his rigid standards of efficiency; they find themselves staggering sometimes under his everlasting drive. But they know he works harder than any of them, and dares as much. They plead with him not to expose himself to the dangers he insists on sharing with them. And if you want to know what they think of him as a man, and a gentleman—well, all you have to do is to get out your Bible and plagiarize the Beatitudes.[60]

Frederick Collins was able to write this drivel without self-consciousness, Hoover was able to edit it without embarrassment, and the public was able to read it without snickering, so they all must have understood that the director was no longer an ordinary mortal whose press releases had to stay within the bounds of credibility and taste. His action heroics had turned him into a figure of fantasy like the other action detectives of popular entertainment. He had become a projection of the public's needs and desires, so when Collins flattered Hoover, he was flattering every American who identified with the director. Collins and Hoover's other publicists could use the whole gamut of clichéd superlatives for Hoover—and Americans would swallow them all with the same eager suspension of disbelief that let them believe every action hero was, for as long as the entertainment lasted, all-powerful, all-knowing, and all-American.

Hoover's dual role as politician and pop culture hero was valuable to him in his jousts with rivals and in his postwar crusade to construct a patriotic creed for Americans out of his own political and cultural beliefs. On the other hand, his G-Man heroics undercut his avowed ambition of using the image of the bureau to spark a revitalization of American law enforcement. The medium, in this case Hoover's performance as the action detective hero, contradicted the message, which was that professionalism and science, not blood rituals, ought to be the basis of modern law enforcement. By the end of the thirties, the same law enforcement leaders who had admired Hoover's gospel of professionalism had become irritated and jealous of his headline-hogging heroics. Nor could Hoover sustain his action detective pose indefinitely. Eventually his advancing age and infirmities chained him to his desk, thus starving his image of the regular infusions of new adventures it takes to sustain a heroic reputation.

From the standpoint of Hoover's own ideas on professional law enforcement—indeed from the standpoint of ordinary common sense—his efforts to cast himself in the role of the action detective hero were completely irrational. The unconscious dynamics of popular culture had taken control of Hoover himself, just as they had captured the public image of his bureau. Once again popular culture was providing the spectacle of life struggling to imitate art.

10

The Junior G-Men:
The FBI and American Youth Culture

The curtain opened and out pranced a middle-aged actor in a Buster Brown suit. "Gee, but I'd like to be a G-Man," he sang in a squeaky voice, brandishing a toy pistol, "and go bang, bang, bang, bang."

> I'd put on disguises of all different sizes
> And would I win prizes
> For telling who spies-es.
>
> Just like Dick Tracy, what a he-man (and go bang, bang, bang, bang.)
> I'd do as I pleased, act high-handed and regal
> For when you're a G-Man there's nothing illegal.[1]

That was in Harold Rome's 1937 hit Broadway revue, *Pins and Needles,* the same year a not altogether approving editor noticed that "children no longer play cowboys and Indians or even cops and robbers. The game is G-Men and hoodlums, with the strongest kid impersonating Hoover."[2]

The FBI probably had even more of an impact on American kids during the depression and World War II than it did on their G-Man-infatuated parents. Kids not only could imagine themselves as FBI agents—they could also act out their fantasies in the playgrounds and vacant lots. And when the depression generation of kids entered post-war American business, government, and culture, the intensity of their childhood identification with the G-Men made it impossible for them to look at Hoover with eyes undazzled by hero-worship and nostalgia for lost youth. Hoover had established a relationship with future senators, congressmen and presidents (and their constituents) during the depression that made it psychologically impossible for them to criticize, correct, or oppose him, even when his late tendency to see communism behind every social or cultural change made him one of the principal roadblocks in the way of progress or honorable politics.

The same things that appealed to their parents also attracted depression youngsters to the FBI, but the emphasis was different. Older Americans were awed by the symbolic meaning of the FBI's great cases, whether they interpreted them in the light of the FBI's own publicity or by the G-Man formula. To adults the allure of the FBI was that it had taken over the role of the action detective hero in providing spectacular rituals of cultural solidarity. The kids, on the other hand, were fascinated by the bureau for its own sake—because of its training, its techniques, its weapons, and its cases. They did not care what it all meant.

Perhaps because American children had not yet been indoctrinated in the national myth of the self-reliant hero, what particularly fascinated kids about the FBI was the image it promoted of being one big team, a "we" organization, even though that was precisely the aspect of the FBI's official image that put off their parents. As one boy from Warwick, Rhode Island, wrote Hoover, "The only difference between the F.B.I. and the Boy Scouts is the F.B.I. carries guns and the Boy Scouts use a pen knife."[3] As far as American kids were concerned, Hoover's FBI was adults' closest approximation to a kids' gang. Hoover and his men seemed to be the only adults in America—except for baseball players and circus clowns—who were doing something that made sense to pre-pubescent America. Because kids saw the FBI as a grown-up kids' gang, their fascination with the bureau found its most characteristic expression in the phenomenon of the Junior G-Man Club.

J. Edgar Hoover apparently had nothing to do with starting the Junior G-Man Club craze of the thirties and forties. The kids (and the advertisers who were after their dimes and quarters) came up with the idea on their own. Nor did Hoover try to create any formal link between the real bureau and its youth auxiliaries. Junior G-Man clubs were born independent of bureau sponsorship, they flourished, and finally faded away, feeding the fantasies of a generation of American kids until the bureau and its director finally changed their public images after World War II to such an extent that they no longer had a part to play in youthful make-believe.

There were actually many different Junior G-Man clubs. Neighborhood kids organized thousands of them on their own initiative, then wrote to Hoover for his aid and advice on operating them:

Dear Mr. Hoover,

Please help me and my friends start an F.B.I. club. We need guns, bombs and other things to surprise the crooks.

KIDS' LETTERS TO THE F. B. I.

Selected by **Bill Adler**

Illustrated by Arnold Roth

For American youth of the thirties, the FBI was a grown-up kids' gang.

If you don't let us have this club, it would be like having a choice between law and crime, and saying you want crime.

> Your friends,
> Mickey, Herbie, Jeff, Ken
> Elmira, New York.[4]

Advertisers organized other clubs as publicity stunts to promote G-Man movies, G-Man radio shows, and G-Man magazines. By the early thirties there were many of them exploiting the national fascination with detective heroes. The most elaborate clubs were organized to help sell breakfast cereals.

One of the first of the breakfast cereal detective clubs was "Inspector Post's Junior Detective Corps," which Post Toasties had started by 1932. Inspector Post was nobody at all, just a cartoon sketch of a beefy character with a slightly moronic overbite and a brown fedora. Post Toasties ads showed the Inspector holding a secret agent's badge while he gave a pitch for his club and for Post Toasties:

Boys and girls! Inspector Post wants all of you to join his Junior Detective Corps. Send him the coupon under his picture and he will put your name on the roll of the Junior Detective Corps. He will send you a detective's badge. And an instruction book which will tell you how to find clues, how to do secret writing, and lots of other things detectives must know. The book also contains the secret code of the Junior Detective Corps and the secret pass word.

Just so Inspector Post will know you are helping to keep your body strong and your mind alert (you know a detective must be strong and quick) he also asks that you send with the coupon two tops from Post Toasties boxes. Post Toasties, you know, is *full* of quick energy—just what a detective needs.

Applicants had to take an oath before the inspector would send them their badges: "Inspector Post: I promise to ask my mother to have Post Toasties *often* for breakfast. I want to be strong and quick so that I will be a *good* detective."[5]

Inspector Post's Junior Detective Corps is particularly noteworthy because it later became a G-Man promotion, but there were many other clubs helping American kids play detective games long before anyone had heard of the FBI. There was a Quaker Puffed Rice's Dick Tracy Secret Service Patrol that gave kids the chance to "be a master detective like Dick Tracy." For a dime and four box tops, kids got a Dick Tracy Secret Code Book, the Patrol Pledge, a Badge, the Secret Detecto-Kit, and a chance to "amaze your friends." The "Genuine, Official Detecto-Kit" contained photographic negatives of Dick Tracy, Tess Trueheart, Pat Patton, and Dick Tracy, Jr., a photo developer (Secret Dick Tracy

Formula Q-11), a stylus for secret writing and an official Dick Tracy Secret Instruction Book. There was a Captain Midnight Club (Ovaltine), a Sky King Club (Peter Pan Peanut Butter), and a Lone Ranger Club (Cheerios); each had its own distinctive detective ring, flashlight ring, or magno-glo secret writing ring.[6] The clubs exploited every variety and permutation of kids' adventure fantasies, with mind-numbing packages of cowboy, airplane, and detective activity options.

The champion of all the kids' clubs was Ralston's Tom Mix Straight Shooters. Tom's peculiar charm was his incredible array of battle scars. Every Straight Shooters' ad had a chart of Tom's wounds: "Tom Mix has been blown up once, shot twelve times, and injured forty-seven times. . . . this chart shows the location of Tom Mix' injuries—'x' marks fractures; circles—bullet wounds; scars from 22 knife wounds are not indicated."[7] Straight Shooters could get all the standard premiums: decoder badges, secret manuals, and two-in-one compass and magnifying glasses ("ideal for detective work, nature study, school work and to start a camp fire"). The club's no-nonsense slogan was, "Lawbreakers always lose, Straight Shooters always win. It pays to shoot straight."

All the breakfast food clubs ran advertisements that provided samples of the kinds of adventures kids could expect if they joined. Whether the organization was a cowboy, detective, or space cadet club, the adventures tended to follow the same all-purpose formula. One Straight Shooter ad from 1937 had the Straight Shooters lend a hand to the FBI. "With Federal Agents closing in on them," the story began, " 'Big Shot' and his city gangsters are looking for a hideout in the mountains." The place they choose is the home of Jimmy and Jane, two of Tom Mix's Straight Shooters, who are taken hostage. The Straight Shooters escape by blinding the guard with a face-full of flour, then riding away on their horse, Tony, who has been trained to kick machine guns out of gangsters' hands. As he rewards the kids and Tony with special medals ("Thanks, governor . . . gee, these are the swellest medals I ever saw"), the governor of the state wonders where the kids got all their energy. Tom's reply: "Reckon that's because they eat Ralston. It takes a hot whole wheat cereal such as Ralston to keep you fit." Club members could send in for the same medal Tony and the kids had just won ("You'll be proud to wear it 'cause it shows you're a special pal of Tom's. Hurry! Send in right away.")[8]

Before, during, and after the Junior G-Man boom, the cereal manufacturers of America were arming and training youthful detectives, organizing them into posses, and sending them off in pursuit of imaginary desperadoes. When pop culture made heroes of the G-Men in 1935, it was only a short step more for copy writers to substitute a real name—the FBI—for imaginary ones, real heroes—the G-Men—for the Inspec-

*Capitalizing on the Junior G-Man craze, Post Toasties' Inspector Post (1932)
metamorphosed into Melvin Purvis (1936).*

tor Posts and Dick Tracys, and real gangsters—Pretty Boy Floyd or
John Dillinger—for their dime novel badmen. In 1936, therefore, Post
Toasties replaced Inspector Post with former ace G-Man Melvin Purvis.
Post's "Junior Detective Corps" became the "Junior G-Man Club," later
the "Melvin Purvis Law and Order Patrol." [9]

After leaving the bureau on July 12, 1935, to write his memoirs, Purvis
had gone to Hollywood; his opportunities there blocked by Hoover, he
endorsed Dodge autos and Gillette razors. Finally he arrived at Post
Toasties. To indicate their cereal's enlistment in the federal anticrime
crusade, Post replaced Inspector Post's face in the ads with Purvis's and
put a G-Man shield in his hand instead of Post's "secret operator's"
badge.

Like all the other breakfast cereal detective clubs, the Purvis outfit
ran sample adventure scenarios on the backs of cereal boxes and in

the comic sections of Sunday newspaper supplements. Though Post Toasties billed the ads as actual "Law and Order Patrol" cases, "taken from the files and published to prove that CRIME DOES NOT PAY," they followed the same fantasy formulas as all the other junior detective clubs. The ad for July 4, 1937, "The Clue of the Copper Screen," began with Purvis and his two secret operators, Laura and Jim, polishing off a breakfast of Post Toasties, while Purvis outlines the day's adventure for the kids: " 'We'll have another helping—and then we're going to tackle a tough case.... I've been called in to investigate a mysterious jewel robbery at "Harbor View," the big Tucker estate. We're going there right now. I intend to plant you two Secret Operators on the place as Mr. Tucker's niece and nephew so you can scout around for clues without arousing suspicion.' "[10]

Jim and Laura find that the thieves gained entrance to the Tucker mansion by cutting through a copper screen. In the gardener's shack on a neighboring estate they find metal shears with bits of copper on the blades. Returning to Purvis's crime lab, they and the "former Ace G-Man" run an experiment with an impressive-looking piece of equipment. A caption explains that "the Metal Detector is used to discover whether two pieces of metal come from the same original piece. Purvis put a piece of metal screen from the Tucker home and a scrap of metal from the shears in his Metal Detector. The Metal Detector proved that the metal on the shears came from the cut screen of the Tucker bedroom."[11]

Case now closed, the Law and Order Patrol huddle with their commander in the kitchen for his critique: "That was smart work, Laura and Jim! You did some quick thinking." Then they get their reward: "Now that we've put Moretta where shears won't do any good and the Tucker jewels are safe, let's all enjoy a big bowl of Post Toasties."[12]

Purvis promised the club's new members important cases just like "The Clue of the Copper Screen," and he offered them a chance to use the kind of crime-fighting science Hoover's publicity bragged about: "Get my new Secret Operator's shield and my Secret Operator's manual containing special instructions . . . codes and passwords . . . secrets of crime detection . . . and how to win promotion to higher ranks . . . also pictures of all my wonderful free prizes! To be a Secret Operator, just send me the coupon below, with two red Post Toasties box tops."[13] Purvis could supply all the equipment a special agent needed—microscopes, telescopes, notebooks, cap pistols, even official Law and Order Patrol baseball gloves. These ads suggest the possibility that one reason the FBI caught on with kids was that Hoover gave his agents gadgets that were grown-up versions of the novelties the kids got for their boxtops. In fact, some kids saw no reason why the real FBI should not give them crime-fighting equipment too. For example, they asked Hoover for pictures of the ten most wanted criminals for their scrapbooks. A boy from Gainesville, Georgia, wrote Hoover that "I need guns, radar, hankerchiefs, lie machine and a loud whistle. I am going to catch some crooks after school tomorrow."[14]

The Junior G-Men clubs' gimmickry was no different from the other kiddie corps', but only the Junior G-Men had a parent club in Washington, a big league team headed by a national hero adults could join only after an arduous and esoteric initiation. The FBI's image as a grown-up version of the kids' breakfast cereal clubs was certainly one reason for Hoover's popularity with the younger set.

In 1940 Hollywood capitalized on the FBI's youth gang image with its own Junior G-Men, the Dead End Kids (Huntz Hall, Frankie Darro and company) in a twelve-chapter Universal serial called, naturally, *Junior G-Men*.[15] They were pitted against an anarchist outfit called "The Order of the Flaming Torches," which was planning to destroy "secret national military projects." Their campaign against the Flaming Torches let the Dead End Kids perform some favorite Junior G-Man stunts—Morse code reflected off broken glass, escapes from the gang's hideout, a chance to pilot a plane. Two years later *Junior G-Men of the Air* pitted the kids against the Japanese fifth column operating under the scarifying code name of "The Order of the Black Dragonfly." The Dragonflies' specialty was oil-field sabotage. This time the kids got to parachute out of a plane for a big finish.

The Dead End Kids in Junior G-Men *(1940).*

During the thirties and forties there was always a G-Man adventure at the Saturday matinee. Secret Agent X-9 was featured in two movie serials: Scott Kolk starred in 1937, Lloyd Bridges in 1945. Dick Tracy joined the bureau for a fifteen-chapter Republic serial in 1939 *(Dick Tracy's G-Men)* with Ralph Byrd wearing the two-way wrist radio. The Black Falcon (in his black hood, black goggles, and black long underwear) was an FBI man in *Flying G-Men,* starring Ralph Paige (Republic, 1939). *G-Men vs. the Black Dragon* (1943) had Rod Cameron fighting the Japanese underground led by Nino Pepitone as Spy Master Haruchi. Haruchi had a secret suspended animation drug that let him return from the dead each time the FBI thought they had finished him off. In 1945 Kernan Kripps played a G-Man in *Federal Operator 99,* and after the war there were three more FBI serials: Clayton Moore in *G-Men Never Forget* (1948), Kirk "Superman" Alyn in *Federal Agents vs. Underworld, Inc.* (1949), and Walter Reed in *Government Agents vs. the Phantom Legion* (1951). By then the Junior G-Man fad was long over and the Feds were reduced to chasing truck hijackers.

The Junior G-Man serials ran the same kinds of giveaway promotions as the breakfast food clubs—fingerprint cards, badges, cardboard pistols and public enemy posters. Adult G-Man "B" pictures also used free FBI toys to attract the kids. G-Man giveaways helped promote *Federal Agent* (Bill Boyd), *When G-Men Step In* (Robert Paige), and *Federal Man Hunt* (Robert Livingston).

When Hoover bowed to pop culture pressure in 1936 and began to concoct an action detective image for himself, the kids were no less impressed than their elders, but Hoover's derring-do meant something different to them than it did to their parents. In the fantasy world of the Junior G-Men, Hoover corresponded to the kid in every gang, usually a little older, always a little tougher than the rest, who was the born leader the other kids followed. Because the Junior G-Men understood their relationship to Hoover in the light of their experience with their own older playmates, the kids idolized Hoover even more than did Hoover's most worshipful adult fans. They wrote him letters like this:

Dear Sirs,

Mr. Hoover is not my hero, Jesus is. But Mr. Hoover has done more toward helping to keep down juvenile delinquency, as well as other crimes, and he is my second hero.

Please do not tell Mr. Hoover that he is only my second hero because I DO NOT want to make him feel bad.

Yours,
Bert C.
Falls Church, Va.[16]

They even tried to curry his favor by informing on friends they suspected of disloyalty:

Dear Mr. Hoover,

There is a boy I know named Red Hopkins. He found a picture of you in a magazine and he cut it out.

Then he took your picture and put it on a poster and wrote WANTED below the picture.

I am not a squealer, but I think you should know about Red Hopkins.

> Sincerely,
> Mark K.
> Birmingham, Michigan.[17]

The childhood daydream of doing something so impressive that the leader of the gang would single him out as his best friend was the specialty of the *Big Little Books,* fat (1½ inches thick) little (4½ inches by 3¼ inches) volumes put out by the Whitman Publishing Company with text on the left hand page, and a single cartoon frame illustrating the text on the right. Depending on how well a kid could read the pictures could be used as a supplement or as a substitute for the text.

There were *Big Little Books* based on most of the popular comic strips (Mickey Mouse, Li'l Abner, and Blondie), the classics *(Moby Dick),* and popular children's series (Tom Swift and Frank Merriwell). *Junior G-Men and the Counterfeiters* appeared in 1937, starring two ten year-olds who have to take over an FBI case when Special Agent G-23 crashes his car on the boys' front lawn. "I'm helpless with this ankle," he tells them.

"Maybe you can give me a hand. . . . Would you two like to be G-Men, too—I mean Junior G-Men?"

"Junior G-Men!" Bill and Sam echoed together.

"First you must take the oath."

"Oath?" Bill was almost too thrilled to speak.

"Exactly. All G-Men have to take the oath. Now repeat slowly after me—'As a Junior G-Man I promise to uphold all the laws of the United States, to keep myself mentally alert and physically fit, and to aid in every way the enforcement of law and order.' "

Bill and Sam—as a swift lightning flash revealed—stood at attention, saluting an imaginary American flag. Solemnly they repeated the oath in unison.

"You are now drafted as Junior G-Men," the man declared.[18]

This qualifies the boys to get captured by gangsters, burn down the robbers' hide-out, explore caves, slither down ropes, and send messages

Above: From Junior G-Men and the Counterfeiters *(1937), by Morrell Massey. Copyright, 1937, Western Publishing Company, Inc. Reprinted by permission.*

Below: "Big Little Books" Junior G-Man titles from the mid-thirties.

by Morse code. The adventure finally over, they "sigh happily as the words of praise echoed in their ears—'You did a fine job as Junior G-Men.' "[19]

G-Man on the Crime Trail (1936), was based on "G-Man," Lou Hanlon's comic strip in the *New York Daily Mirror*. The Junior G-Man was Junior Crawford, kid brother of Jimmy Crawford, "Ace of the G-Men." After helping his big brother fight "Reds" and gangsters, he is tucked into bed dreaming about his brother's prediction that he will "grow up to be a G-Man like your brother."[20] Another variation on this formula was to give the reader a rookie agent to identify with instead of another kid: evidently as long as the story's hero was younger than anybody else in the plot, the fantasy would still work. In *G-Men on the Job* (1935) the hero was "Young" Bill Lee, billed as "Uncle Sam's youngest G-Man," just out of training and working on his first case.

There was one other thing about Hoover's FBI that dazzled depression kids. Not only was the FBI the apotheosis of a playground gang, with its heroic leader and array of fascinating euipment, but the bureau gave the Junior G-Men access to an almost endless assortment of scenarios for playtime adventures: the great public enemies cases. One way kids could get hints on how to use the FBI's exploits as scripts for Junior G-Man adventures was to buy G-Man bubble gum cards, which adapted FBI cases for youthful consumption and which shed more light on the differences between adult and youthful G-Man fantasies. Here is how the Dillinger case was rewritten for Junior G-Men consumption on one gum card:

The night of July 19, 1934, an ordinary small automobile pulled to the sidewalk in front of Chicago's North Side Biograph Theatre. In it was Number One G-Man Melvin Purvis. In nearby positions were fifteen more G-Men. A tip-off had been given—a tip-off from a woman, known only as The Woman in Red: John Dillinger, notorious Public Enemy Number One was going to take her to the "movies" that night!

Yes! There he goes!! Not the Dillinger Purvis expected. Slight, his hair dyed black, gold-rimmed spectacles, a new moustache and (believe it or not) his eyebrows plucked.

Patiently the G-Men wait.

Two hours later. Dillinger comes out. The Woman in Red is at his side. Now he is "on the spot." His daring woman companion is on the spot too. Will G-Men bullets mow her down, too? That is the chance she knowingly took. She dares not make a break. She must stick close. The G-Men are ready. They close in—quickly and apparently from nowhere. Dillinger whirls, reaches for his gun, makes a start from a nearby alley. Too late! Hot lead drops him in his tracks; a bullet in the head, another near the heart. The Woman in Red is unharmed. Dare Devils all! But again the heroic G-Men, defenders of the law, triumph over the public enemy.[21]

This card was from one of the six competing series of G-Man bubble gum cards that appeared during the thirties and forties. Each card told the gory end of one of the FBI's victims. The Dillinger card was number ten in National Chicle's twenty-four card series called "Dare-Devils." The flip side pictured the G-Men pouring tracer bullets into Dillinger's staggering body.

Gum Incorporated's "G-Men and Heroes of the Law" was the classiest of the six sets. It came out in 1936 with 168 cards numbered from 1 to 240, a so-called skip series with gaps designed to make kids keep buying to try to get the nonexistent numbers. The Dillinger card in this

"Dare-Devils" Dillinger gum card from the mid-thirties.
"G-Men and Heroes of the Law" Dillinger gum card.

set began like this: "Trailed for countless crimes, sneering at capture, blasting his way from every jail that held him, ruthless and calculating . . . John Dillinger, whose life seemed charmed against the bullets of the law." After lambasting the gangster for a few more lines, the card skipped ahead to Dillinger's death at the Biograph:

Crash! Crash! . . . Crash! . . . Crash! echoed four shots as the G-Men opened their deadly fire.

The outlaw staggered, cleared the sidewalk with a bound, turned into an alley a hundred feet away, as a 45-caliber bullet ripped through his breast. Another found its mark in the same spot. Another tore through his neck and brain, coming out over the right eye.

John Dillinger had met his match at last, the end that all killers sooner or later find before the unswerving aim of G-Men who take their trail and track them down![22]

That was the "True, 'Official' Story" of this case. The first card in the series had the true and official story of Pretty Boy Floyd:

A command to halt echoed across the field, followed by the deadly R-a-a-a-t—tat-tat-tat! Ta-ta-ta-t-t! of machine guns.

"Pretty Boy" Floyd plunged forward on his face, rolled over, flopped on his stomach, got to his knees, and fell.

He was dying as his pursuers rushed upon him with handcuffs ready.

G-Men had given him the penalty an outlaw's crimes deserve![23]

All the gum card condensations of FBI cases followed the same pattern. First they gave enough background on the criminal to give a kid a handle on the character he was going to play. Then they raced ahead to a highly detailed, almost choreographed, reenactment of the final shoot-out, exactly tailored to the requirements of kids choosing up sides for make-believe battles between G-Men and gangsters. The gum cards structured the FBI's cases to fit the familiar pattern of battles between cowboys and Indians, train robbers and posses, and, a few years later, GIs and Germans. The games were essentially running gunfights leading to a climax when the criminal, no escape left, gets his cue to act out a spectacular death scene with a display of staggers, jerks, and twitches while his pals pump a barrage of bullets into his gyrating body.

All the gum card collections were packed with adventure scenarios for pint-sized crime busters. Gum Makers of America's twenty-four card series was "True Spy Stories"—mostly fights between fictitious spies and the FBI, together with a few stories about counterintelligence agents from other friendly nations. There were also three series of "strip cards," perforated rows of five or six cards sold by themselves instead of in gum packages. These were never as popular as the gum cards

Pressner's Pretty Boy Floyd gum card.

because they were too light to be pitched against the curb. One strip set of ninety cards was called "American G-Men." Another, a black-and-white set, was "Crime Does Not Pay." The Pressner Company had a series in 1936 called "Government Agents vs. Public Enemies." Number 205 was "A Fight to the Finish," the story of Wilbur Underhill, an Oklahoma bandit the FBI called the "Tri-State Terror":

So dangerous, so fearless that even big shot gangsters wouldn't team up with him! He had the killer's lust for bloodshed, and after horrible murders, desperate robberies, and amazingly performed jail breaks and narrow escapes, he became America's Public Enemy Number 1. Federal Agents determined to stop his mad career.

After successfully robbing a bank he disappeared for some time. It was on a bitter cold and drizzly night in late December, 1933, that Wilbur Underhill was finally located in Shawnee, Oklahoma. A dog was standing at the side of his house of refuge. "Quick, men, we've got him and the place surrounded. Hurry before that dog warns him," commanded the leader of the G-Men.

The special agent in charge trained his machine gun on a window behind which the outlaw was barely visible. At the terse call·to surrender Underhill ruthlessly opened fire. The lawmen returned bullet for bullet. Underhill fell, but miraculously he was up again. Then he was seen to duck out of sight.

Suddenly, through the deadly fire of incessant pistols, automatics and machine-guns, Underhill dashed out of the front door. He slumped in a stumbling fall. But he staggered up and went on. Again the G-Men cut him down. Again he got up, and this time he vanished around a nearby house.

After a long search they found their dangerous enemy sprawled on a bed in a furniture store. Thirteen bullets had riddled his torn body. Yet he lived for a week. Lived to die slowly the death that must come to any man who murderously opposes law and order. The G-Men are always victorious.[24]

In formula stories the "detail" tends to accumulate at that point in the story designed to capture the reader's imagination. Adult and children's versions of the same G-Man story both followed the broad outline of the crime-and-punishment formula, but they lingered over different sorts of details. Stories for adults dwelt on the FBI's procedures: fingerprinting, ballistics, and sophisticated organizational methods. The receptivity of adult audiences during the thirties to this material shows they must have agreed with Hoover that the meaning of the FBI's cases was that the cases demonstrated the FBI's discovery of a crime-fighting method that really worked and that could be relied on to safeguard the nation from crime.

When the same stories were rewritten for kids, almost no attention was paid to the methods the bureau used to solve the case. The only

Secret writing and codes were standard Junior G-Man activities.

details the kids got were ones that helped dramatize the final shootouts, with the young reader imagining himself either as one of the G-Men pumping bullets into the quivering body of Dillinger, or as Dillinger himself. Adults wanted to know how and why the FBI had won its war with the gangsters, and so they were intrigued by the cat-and-mouse aspects of the cases; the kids simply wanted the bad guys to be really tough, the fights really exciting, the G-Men really victorious, and they really did not care what it all meant. This difference between adult and child psychology meant that while Hoover was able to use G-Man adventures in adult entertainment to promote his ideas about law enforcement and later his political ideas, the same approach would not work with the kids because they had no interest in rituals of social unity as affirmations of cultural values: the Junior G-Men simply wanted clubs, toys, and action. The FBI kid gangs simply offered kids a way to keep on doing what they wanted to do, but with one attractive improvement. When they pretended to be G-Men they were taking on identities that were real and highly-respected—even by big people. They were acting out fantasies that everyone in the country was taking seriously. There was just one thing they could not figure out:

Dear Mr. Hoover,

You are lucky to be the head of an organization like the F.B.I. which is so famous all over the world.

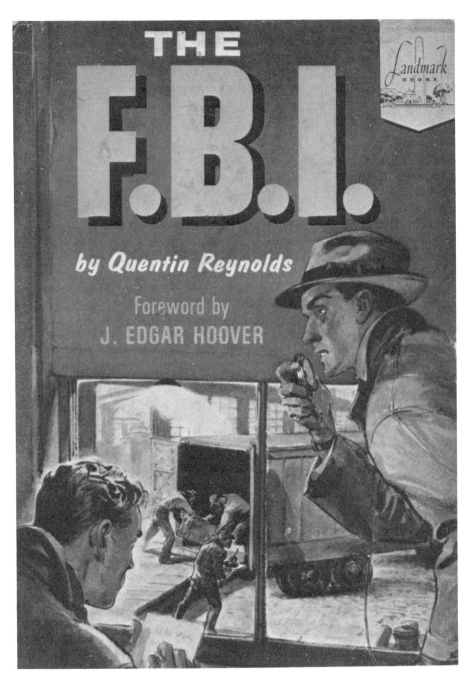

THE
F.B.I.

by Quentin Reynolds

Foreword by
J. EDGAR HOOVER

"When a young man files an application with the F.B.I., we do not ask if he was the smartest boy in his class. We want to know if he was truthful, dependable, and if he played the game fair. We want to know if he respects his parents, reveres God, honors his flag and loves his country." From Hoover's introduction to Quentin Reynold's F.B.I. (1954).

I am the head of a Jr. F.B.I. club in Chicago and nobody has ever heard of us.

Please write how we can get to be famous. We don't have much money to spend for advertising.

Sincerely,
Morris G.
Chicago, Illinois[25]

The G-Man boom of the thirties and forties made a deep impression on everyone who lived through it, but probably its most lasting effect was on children young enough to be caught up in the national mania for FBI role- and game-playing that constituted the Junior G-Man craze. The FBI's appeal to adults was fundamentally a matter of vicarious participation in remote events, with the audience several removes away from the real action. Kids, on the other hand, were able to act out their G-Man fantasies for themselves, and that hooked them on the FBI for life. Attorney General Ramsay Clark, for example, said that Lyndon Johnson was "really almost disqualified to be Hoover's boss. . . . Mr. Johnson was young enough to have grown up in the Dillinger days, and he liked that sort of thing."[26] When Hoover visited Austin in 1959, then-Senator Johnson grabbed him by the neck and dragged him outside, yelling at startled passers-by, "Come over heah, boys. I want you all to meet J. Edgar Hoover, America's Number One G-Man!"[27] Richard Nixon also went through his own Junior G-Man phase: when Hoover presented him with an honorary G-Man badge at a White House ceremony, Nixon recalled that he had filled out an FBI application after the war but had been rejected. (The bureau decided that Nixon lacked "aggressiveness.")[28]

It is hard to imagine the young JFK playing Junior G-Man, but Kennedy did worry about tangling with the hero of the kids from the other side of the tracks. According to one story, shortly after his inauguration Kennedy polled his closest associates on the first moves he should make as president. They urgently recommended that he fire Hoover and CIA Director Allen Dulles. Kennedy's response was to reappoint them both. Robert Kennedy later explained that the election had been so close that the new administration needed all the reassuring symbols it could get.

The Junior G-Man boom subsided during World War II, partly because the war gave Hoover's public relations a new mission of discouraging the public from participation in spy-hunting, but mostly because the situation that let the FBI rescue the country from the depression's cultural crisis by destroying a string of public enemies was unique and nonrepeatable. Along with the depression and World War II, then, the Junior G-Man phenomenon was one of the special experiences that separated the generation that had grown up during the thirties and forties from its children, part of the generation gap that divided the country during the sixties and seventies. As long as the now-grown-up Junior G-Men maintained their dominance over American culture, Hoover's place in the American political hierarchy was secure, but eventually, even in his case, the flesh had to grow weak. The precariousness of the FBI legend during the sixties and seventies could be seen almost every day during the FBI headquarters tour, as fifty-year-old fathers and grandfathers pointed out relics of Dillinger and Floyd to uncomprehending offspring, while the kids turned away in boredom from something that had been one of the most intense experiences of the previous generation's fantasy life.

11

The FBI in Peace and War:
The Shift in the Bureau's Image

World War II radically altered the FBI's public relations objectives. Before the war Hoover's publicity sought to encourage the public's participation in a crusade to reform American law enforcement. His wartime public relations discouraged the public from amateur saboteur-hunting and counterespionage, thereby preventing the sort of security hysteria that had wracked the nation during the First World War, a spy scare that had eventually helped destroy the old bureau when its role in aiding and applauding the grassroots spy hunters was exposed after the war.[1] FBI publicity's wartime goal of calming the public created another conflict between the bureau's official image and the pop culture G-Man advertised and exploited by popular entertainment. The gap between the bureau's wartime image and the expectations of popular entertainment's G-Man finally grew so wide that the director once again committed the bureau to a major entertainment production intended to steer the FBI's pop culture image back towards reality as defined and decreed by Hoover. The project was "This Is Your F.B.I.," the bureau-endorsed radio program that was Hoover's official conduit to American popular culture from 1945 until 1953.

In 1936 Hoover had been a novice when he launched his "War on Crime" comic strip, but by 1945 he had a decade of experience in dealing with reporters, film producers, and writers. By then he fully understood how difficult it was to steer American popular culture away from its beloved action detective formula in its handling of crime-and-punishment materials.[2] Hoover knew how particularly hard it was to work his will in the intensely competitive world of radio, the nation's most popular—and hence most intensely market-oriented—entertainment medium in the forties.

Hoover's struggles with the radio G-Men went back to July, 1935, when Phillips H. Lord paid a visit to the FBI's Washington offices.[3] Lord was the most successful producer in radio, and as the star of the "Seth Parker" show, he was one of the most famous men in the country. He had been producing and directing as well as starring in "Seth Parker," a program of New England music and humor that had run every Sunday night on NBC since 1929. Lord played a choirmaster and Sunday school teacher in a mythical Maine town called Jonesport. The show was so popular that some of the religious songs Lord composed for the show were collected in a *Seth Parker Hymnal* still to be found in some country churches. Lord went on from "Seth Parker" (which ran until 1939) to create hit shows like "We the People," "Mister District Attorney," "Treasury Agent," "Policewoman," and "David Harding, Counterspy."[4]

For a few months before he showed up at Hoover's office, Lord had been experimenting with a new format for "Radio Crimebusters," a crime show he was writing and producing for NBC. Lord told Hoover he wanted to capitalize on the Hollywood G-Man cycle by changing the policemen heroes of "Radio Crimebusters" into FBI agents, with plots based on cases from bureau's files. Hoover liked the idea. He told Lord to get some memos on interesting cases from Clyde Tolson and work up a few sample scripts.

A few days later Lord turned in his scripts and Hoover hit the roof: "They just wouldn't do. . . . Our men don't act that way."[5] He told Lord to get someone who knew the bureau and collaborate with him. Lord asked for some names, and Hoover suggested the two writers he usually worked with, Courtney Ryley Cooper and Rex Collier. Lord immediately replied that he could not stand Cooper, so he would take Collier, sight unseen.

Collier and Lord got to work on July 18, 1935, in an office in the Justice Department. The agreement between them gave Collier the primary responsibility of dealing with Hoover. Lord wrote:

We will sit down together and you will have a list of as many cases as it is convenient for you to jot down. In a very sketchy way you will tell me the general idea of each case and then, together, we will pick as many cases as seem to lend themselves to a good radio production. Then either one of us can call up the Department and read the names of the cases and ascertain if there is any objection to any of them being used. You are then to submit to me an outline of each case selected of sufficient content to be dramatized. . . . I will then take the case and break it down into radio script; writing the dialogue and setting the story up for production. I will then hand it over to you and sit with you to see if there are any reactions or questions, and, if not, then it is up to you to get it through Mr. Hoover. Our financial arrangement is that I will pay you $300.00 cash the same day that the script is cleared by Mr. Hoover.[6]

The outlines Collier wrote were based on the bureau's so-called "Interesting Case Memoranda." These "IC Memos" were, and still are, the FBI's standard method of providing a journalist with information about a case. Written by agents in the bureau's public relations department, an IC Memo not only gives the basic facts in the case—names and aliases together with details about the crime, the investigation, and the arrest—but also the bureau's opinion about what it was that made the case "interesting." If the reporter followed the bureau's lead, his story would turn into an illustration of one of the FBI's crime-solving techniques, rather than a simple cops-and-robbers story. In other words the I.C. Memo would prod the reporter to follow the FBI formula rather than the action detective pattern in writing up the case.

The cases Hoover gave Collier and Lord memos on were those Hoover and his publicists were using to build the FBI legend. They chose the Dillinger case for the first broadcast, followed by the Osage Indian case, the Machine Gun Kelly/Urschel case, the Ma Barker gang, Pretty Boy Floyd, the Jake Fleagle case, and several other highly publicized kidnappings and robberies.[7]

Phil Lord had his own ideas about the way this kind of material ought to be adapted for radio. The Phil Lord formula was the action detective formula expanded into a slick package of action and violence, heavy on the sound effects, punctuated with stern anticrime homilies that proclaimed there was a social purpose behind all the bloodletting and brutality. He liked to start his shows off with an ungodly cacophony of sound effects that were so raucous and flamboyant that they later gave rise to the cliché "coming on like gangbusters." According to radio historian Jim Harmon, Lord's opening sound effects in "Gangbusters" were "a capsule view of crime and punishment": "sirens howling in the night, the flaming chatter of submachine guns, and, finally, the marching tread of convicts headed for their cells" followed by an echo-chambered voice "Calling the Police! Calling the G-Men! Calling all Americans to war on the underworld!"[8] For Phillips H. Lord, an FBI case was simply going to be a new twist on the old action detective formula.

The opening sequence of the first "G-Men" episode was classic Phillips H. Lord:

ORCHESTRAL CHORD SUSTAINED

ANNOUNCER: Presenting the first of a new series of programs—G-Men.

ORCHESTRA PLAYS 15 seconds. Music softens.
WOMAN'S SHRIEK
MAN'S VOICE Stop her!!
Two quick shots.
DOOR SLAMS

ORCHESTRA UP FULL 15 seconds. STOPS
TWO SIRENS FADE IN AND OUT IN SUCCESSION.
Hollow-voiced Police calls.

POLICE   Calling cars 42, 23, 56, report immediately—Police head-
                quarters.—Calling all cars—cover all roads leading from the
                city for two black limousines—calling (fade) all cars—cover
                roads from city.

                ONE SIREN FADING IN AND OUT.

                THREE NEWSBOYS: EXTRA, EXTRA—all about the Dillinger gang.
                Read about Dillinger shooting way to freedom. Extra. Dillinger
                and Baby Face Nelson—

                CALLING OF NEWSBOYS FADES.[9]

The show had all the standard Phil Lord sound effects: jingling keys,
clanging jail doors, the thud of falling bodies, and racing engines. The
scenes had plenty of suspense and violence, and the plot followed the
classic ritual pattern of crime and punishment, right up to the final line:
"Dillinger's dead. . . . Crime doesn't pay—the G-Men never give up the
hunt."

Nevertheless, the show was not unadulterated Phillips H. Lord. Beginning with the Dillinger program, the original scripts show Lord
screaming for more action and individual heroics, the bureau responding with more and more instances of scientific crime detection and
bureaucratic crime-fighting. The show finally became a tug of war between Hoover and Lord over whether the show was to follow the
G-Man formula or the FBI formula, with Lord protesting that "the
material you gave me . . . is practically impossible to work with" because the FBI and Collier had left out all the "color." To Hoover the
scientific aspects of the show were what made it noteworthy, because
science, not racing engines, screaming sirens, or chattering machine
guns, was the trademark of Hoover's FBI. To Lord the FBI procedures—fingerprint searches, lab reports, and the like—were sheer
agony since they slowed down the action and killed the suspense. By the
final "G-Men" episode the action had all but disappeared, and the
show had been turned into a treatise on the FBI method. At that point
Phillips H. Lord disappeared, too.

That last episode of "G-Men" was the case of Eddie Doll, which the
bureau liked to treat as a tragic love story that illustrated one of
Hoover's points in *Ten Thousand Public Enemies:* that a criminal was
not "someone who could be detected a mile off, by his face, his manners, his clothing, his conversation, . . . crime is ever at your elbow,
vicious crime, dangerous crime, against which you cannot relax your
vigilance for an instant."[10] Whenever the bureau wanted to show the

relationship between big-time crime and the ordinary citizen, it dredged up the case of Eddie Doll, who had used the disguise of respectability to lure a "legitimate woman" into crime.

The Eddie Doll episode opened with a sober tribute to the FBI.[11] The exciting sound effects that had introduced the first shows had by now been vetoed by Hoover as "too sensational."

ANNOUNCER: The Chevrolet Motor Company presents—G-Men. The 1935 model criminal, scornful of law, monopolized the headlines of the American press not long ago. Large type recorded his escapades as he went from one crime to the next. He had a loose philosophy which, so long as it succeeded, captivated young minds. Godless, he believed in neither the sanctity of human life nor property. What he wanted, he took with the gun; whoever opposed him, he destroyed with the gun. Then a miracle happened. A giant eraser rubbed the outlaw and his henchmen out of the headlines. It cut their loud voices to a whisper. The eraser was the Federal Bureau of Investigation of the United States Department of Justice. Chevrolet Motor Company presents tonight the thirteenth episode in its radio series, G-Men, its broadcast in tribute to the Government's special agents for the record they have made in turning the country back into the hands of the lawabiding citizen.

Then the announcer turned the mike over to a subdued Phil Lord:

LORD: Good evening. This series of G-Men programs is presented with the consent of the Attorney General of the United States, Honorable Homer Cummings and with the cooperation of Mr. J. Edgar Hoover, director of the Federal Bureau of Investigation. Tonight's dramatization is based on the files of the Federal Bureau of Investigation and has such modifications as to names, places and incidents as are deemed essential to the public interest. . . .
It is now late at night, September 16, 1930, the gang's hideout at Lincoln, Nebraska.

The first two scenes established Eddie Doll as a bankrobbing wizard who never makes a mistake, never leaves a clue. First the show portrayed his meticulous plans for a "million dollar bank job," next the flawless execution of the robbery—no commotion, no shots, no sound effects at all until the engines of the getaway cars roar to a crescendo. And that was all the action the show was going to have, about five minutes' worth.

Almost the whole show was set in the "private office of Inspector

Haynes, Federal Bureau of Investigation, Washington." "Agent Dennison" marches into the Inspector's office:

DENNISON: (FADE IN) You sent for me, Inspector Haynes.

HAYNES: Yes—sit down, Dennison. You know, it may not be long before
               bank robbery will be under our jurisdiction—but, of course,
               now it isn't. This bank robbery in Lincoln, Nebraska, was one
               of the cleanest jobs ever done in this country. There isn't a clue.
               I wish we could enter the case—but we can't—however, any
               information we can get together will be appreciated by the local
               authorities. They've cooperated with us in the past—and I'd like
               to return the courtesy by sending them some information.

DENNISON: Not a clue—

HAYNES: Not one—BUT—we've got to work one out.

Haynes sends for his staff, who come in loaded down with files on the
case.

HAYNES: Sit down—all of you. Now—these bank robbers didn't leave a
               clue behind as to their identity—but when you haven't got a
               clue, you've got to make one. I've got here a complete report on
               how the robbery was executed. I want to check the "modus
               operandi" of this gang. Every musician has a definite individual
               musical touch—every painter has a style all his own—every
               criminal has his own individual approach to a crime. We know
               there are some dozen gangs of bank robbers in the middle west
               that haven't been caught—we know some recent gangs have
               been broken up—this robbery may have been committed by a
               leader who had his schooling from some gang that's already
               been caught. If we can find that one of the middle western gangs
               operates similar to the procedure used in this robbery, it'll be a
               nail to hang our hat on.

Haynes' staff begins to run down the list of gangs, while their boss
tosses them out, one by one, until one report catches his attention. He
speculates that a recently released gang leader, Edward Doll, might have
teamed up with members of the "Yates gang," a gang that has a style
similar to the Lincoln bank robbers. "Why do all of these facts fit
together so perfectly?" he asks his crew.

       Haynes pieces together more clues until he gets his big break—a
prison rumor that Doll has recently married a "Doris Mathews."
Haynes pounces on this clue in a display of reasoning that leaves his
straight man dazzled:

HAYNES: Um—that's the best tip we've had.

DENNISON: It's going to be a big job to examine all the marriage licenses in New York over a period of six months.

SMITH: They probably both got married under fictitious names.

HAYNES: That's a possibility but wait a minute—let's do some careful thinking. Doll meets a girl—now, why does he marry her?

DENNISON: Because he wants to live with her.

HAYNES: All right—now comes the question is he going to let her know who he really is. If she were the type of girl that he could take in as one of the gang—then she would be the type of girl who would live with him without marrying him. Right?

DENNISON: Yes.

HAYNES: All right—now—if she's not the gangster type of moll—then he doesn't want her to know who he is and he'd change his name. Right?

DENNISON: It's good reasoning.

HAYNES: All right—now, if he doesn't want her to suspect anything then he can't say to her when they're married that she must sign a fictitious name to the marriage license. He'd change his name— but that marriage license is going to contain her REAL name. We've got to find a license made out to Doris Mathews—

DENNISON: That's perfect reasoning, Inspector!

The buzz of admiration from Haynes' staff fades out and the scene shifts to New York City's marriage license bureau:

DENNISON: Whew—I've got to rest a minute. Six weeks of this—seven days and nights a week is beginning to tell.

HAYNES: (CHUCKLE) This is patience—this methodical research is part of our job nobody else ever stops to think about.

More of the same follows, with sound effects of shuffling cards and typewriters. Finally the marriage license turns up and with it the girl's Vermont address. This leads Haynes and Dennison (cooperation with the local police by now forgotten) to Doll's hideout and the arrest. Doll can't believe it: "How'd you find me—I didn't even make ONE false move." Haynes replies, "That's one of the things that HELPED us in finding you, Doll."

And that was that. Not a shot fired, not a car chased, not a thug slugged. The "G-Men" Doll episode had followed J. Edgar Hoover's FBI formula to the letter: an army of essentially anonymous agents reporting back to the big brains in Washington. No gangbusting heroics to distract anyone from the big story, which was that Hoover's scientific crime detection machine had the ability to fit these reports together, match them up against information in the files, until finally the answer to the "Who dunnit?" question would pop magically out of one of the FBI's newfangled automatic card-sorters.

At the end of the Eddie Doll case Lord announced that this had been the last official installment of "G-Men," and he began hinting about the new show he was planning:

Up to the present we have never asked for letters on this series, but on a radio program letters are the only way we know whether we have pleased you. If you would like to have this series started again—if you believe the presentation of this series will help make this country a better place to live in—I would greatly appreciate your writing to let me know. You can address the letters to Phillips Lord, care of the station to which you are listening, and if enough mail is received I am sure we can make arrangements to present another very similar series in the very near future. This is Phil Lord bidding you goodnight.

As far as the public was concerned, Lord's FBI show was a success. The ratings made it the second most listened-to half-hour show on the air. Nevertheless, the show lasted only thirteen weeks, and Hoover and Lord evidently parted with bad feelings on both sides.

Lord's daughter blamed the show's quick demise on the personalities of the two men; although Hoover tried to win Lord over with gestures like an honorary FBI badge, she felt that both Hoover and her father were too stubborn and headstrong to work together successfully.[12] Lord's egotism was legendary in the radio industry. According to radio historian Jim Harmon,

the manner in which Lord came up with new program ideas was a thing to see in itself. He would breeze in from a vacation of sun and sea on his island off the Maine coast and announce he had a couple of new ideas for radio series. "One is terrific, it's wonderful . . . typical Phil Lord idea . . . what everyone expects from radio's number one idea man," Lord is quoted as saying. His second idea was not such an explosive one, however. It would only make a good, solid type of show to run a few years, according to one published account of the meeting. "It's about the idea an *average* man would have." One of the newer writers on Lord's staff couldn't successfully stifle his snicker, and was fired on the spot.[13]

He liked to start off one of his promotions by billing it as an idea only "a genius like Phil Lord" could dream up. Since Hoover also considered himself an authority on just about any topic, it is reasonable to assume that they would clash. Rex Collier recalled that Lord chafed under the discipline of sticking to the facts of authentic cases; he wanted to shift to fictional cases, which Hoover would not permit.[14]

In reality, Lord's differences with Hoover ran much deeper than a personality clash between two strong-willed individuals. The ambitions of the industry and of the bureau in such cooperative ventures, while not diametrically opposed, were by no means identical. Lord wanted to exploit the FBI by simply tacking the G-Man badge, a hot commercial property, onto the old reliable action detective hero. He finally backed out of his partnership with the FBI because Hoover was making him do something he did not want to do: abandon the action detective formula.

In a very short time Lord was back on the air with another series, and that, of course, was "Gangbusters," one of the most phenomenally successful shows in radio history. His new show had all of the vicious hoodlums, trigger-happy cops, rousing sound-effects and "crime does not pay" morality that Lord gloried in and that Hoover had blue-penciled. "Gangbusters" was the greatest of Lord's many hits. It lasted on radio until 1952, when it made the switch to television for a short run under the title "Captured," starring former movie G-Man Chester Morris *(Public Hero Number One)*.

"Gangbusters" did not have official FBI endorsement, of course, but Lord made up for that by bringing in police officials as guest announcers for his fictitious cases (played by stand-ins, of course; flubs by amateurs were too high a price to pay for realism). Since Lord could no longer use Hoover's name on the show, he did something else that must have made Hoover's blood boil: he hired Colonel Norman Schwartz-kopf, head of the New Jersey State Police at the time of the Lindbergh case, as permanent announcer (also played by a stand-in). After what Lord had gone through working with Hoover, hiring one of Hoover's law enforcement rivals must have been intended as an insult.

Phil Lord's escape from the FBI reservation was quite a setback for Hoover's campaign to control the FBI's popular culture image. Lord went on for the next two decades presenting shows full of enough official-sounding language to make people think they were "official" productions. Their plots, however, were straight out of the detective magazines. Lord's personal favorite was the case of "Cardinella, the Devil." Radio historian Ron Goulart recalled that Cardinella "took mere children and, by threats of torture, forced them to rob and murder for him. . . . After he was hanged and pronounced dead . . . his gang tried artificial respiration and various restoratives on his body, freshly cut from the gallows. No wonder Lord loved it. This was merely a simple story of murder, torture, robbery and death—the perfect case for Phillips H. Lord." Another of Lord's favorites, according to Goulart, featured "a talking parrot turned stool pigeon. During a raid on a hangout of the Licavoli gang, the parrot was captured and turned over to Prosecuting Attorney Frazier Reams. He got the bird to talk, revealing many bits of information it had heard over the years, including names and phone numbers. Confronted with this information, gang leader Licavoli confessed. The heroic parrot was interviewed on *Gangbusters,* where it screamed right on cue, 'Licavoli!' "[15]

Lord called cases like these "authentic police case histories" presented "in cooperation with police and Federal law enforcement agencies across the United States." Each program ended with a famous feature designed to convince listeners that "Gangbusters" was still somehow an "official" operation:

Now "Gangbusters" Nationwide Clues, broadcast every week as a public service to assist American police in their war against the underworld: "Wanted by the F.B.I. on an Indian robbery charge . . . Frank Elmer Berman . . . 5 feet 11½ inches . . . 185 pounds . . . brown hair . . . brown eyes—five moles on right side of face . . . three moles on left side of face . . . tattoos: anchor, left forearm . . . heart, left wrist . . . watch for Frank Elmer Berman . . . considered dangerous." These are the clues on the most urgently sought persons in the United States tonight. If you have any information concerning these clues, notify your local police, F.B.I., or "Gangbusters" at once![16]

Lord's other hit crime shows also stuck close to the action detective formula. "Mr. District Attorney" began each week's adventures by repeating the oath of office: "And it shall be my duty, not only to prosecute to the limit of the law all those charged with crimes perpetrated within this county, but to defend with equal vigor the rights and privileges of all its citizens!"[17] "David Harding, Counterspy," started with "Washington calling David Harding, Counterspy; Washington, calling David Harding, Counterspy," followed by Harding's stalwart response, "Harding, Counterspy, calling Washington!" Lord had an announcement on each show that the "United States Counterspies" were "officially appointed to combat the enemies of our country both at home and abroad."[18]

Hoover learned enough from his experience with Lord to insist on different procedures and safeguards whenever he again teamed up with popular entertainment. After "G-Men," Hoover required that the man in charge be someone he knew well, someone who shared his philosophy and "believed" in Hoover: men like Rex Collier, Courtney Ryley Cooper, Jerry Divine (of "This is Your F.B.I.") and Jack Warner, whose studio produced *The F.B.I. Story* and television's "The F.B.I."

Rather than draw up formal contracts, Hoover would depend on a personal relationship with the man in charge to ensure compliance with the FBI's suggestions and requests. In exchange Hoover would let the show write its own ticket on FBI assistance and technical advice.

Perhaps because he had been burned by Phillips H. Lord, Hoover kept the FBI officially out of radio for the next nine years. In 1944, however, new circumstances made him try again to gain control over the radio G-Men. Hoover's wartime role as the country's chief spy-catcher made him and the bureau more famous than ever. In June, 1940, President Roosevelt gave the FBI responsibility for intelligence and counterespionage within the Western Hemisphere (except for the Panama Canal, which went to the navy along with the Pacific; the army got Europe and Africa).[19] This put Hoover in the public eye as the man in charge of the war against the Axis on the home front (or "F.B.I. Front," as he called it) and gave him a popular status only a little lower than Roosevelt and the military's top brass. The Number One G-Man was now Spy-Smasher Number One. In 1943 the *Saturday Evening Post* paid him this tribute:

> Public Enemies One-on-down
> Shudder as he goes to town.
> Saboteurs and other rats
> Reach in panic for their hats
>
> > He gets his man
> > He never fails
> > He clutters up
> > Our finest jails
>
> Spies who double-X this G-Man
> No relation to the Herbert C. Man
> Soon discover it's suicidal—
> And he doubles in brass as
>
> Boyhood's idol.[20]

In his history of the comics Jules Feiffer remembers that "F.D.R. and J. Edgar Hoover [were] the President and Vice-President as far as [wartime] comic books were concerned."[21]

J. Edgar Hoover made sure his wartime activities got all the publicity possible, and again he could justify this self-glorification as essential to the bureau's mission. In 1933 Cummings had used publicity to reassure the public that the New Deal had the crime problem under control. During the war Hoover had to demonstrate that the government had the spy menace licked. The FBI's victories over spies were a way of boosting home front morale, but they had another equally important objective: heading off the vigilantes.

The spy-smashing publicity that Hoover orchestrated during World

War II sought to discourge amateur spy-chasing by "mystifying" counterintelligence. FBI publicity made counterespionage out to be a complex, highly sophisticated task best left to experts scientifically trained for the job—in other words, the FBI. Hoover's publicity had to keep a fine balance between making spy-catching seem easy, which might give the public the impression that the government was taking the spy threat lightly, and making the problem seem too urgent, which might persuade patriotic organizations to take spy-smashing into their own hands. As usual Hoover's operation had both practical and symbolic overtones. He had to control enemy spies and he also had to control the public's reaction to those spies.

Hoover was especially alert to the danger of oversensationalizing counterintellingence because his first spy case, shortly before the war, had gotten out of control. Since 1933 the FBI had been monitoring the German-American Bund, and in 1936 Roosevelt ordered Hoover to put it under regular surveillance.[22] The Nazis' coup in Austria on February 16, 1938, made newspapers call on the government to tighten security and rein in the bund. In response, the army, navy and FBI announced, obviously on Roosevelt's orders, that they were cooperating in "the greatest spy hunt ever"[23] and that suspects were "undergoing a severe grilling" by the FBI.[24]

This was not enough for the American Legion, which announced on May 9 that it was planning its own spy hunt,[25] and on May 10 Martin Dies's House Rules Committee launched its own investigation of foreign "-isms."[26] With the public showing signs of losing confidence in the government's ability to cope with the security crisis, the bureau announced on May 12 that it had finished a twelve-volume report on Nazi espionage activities.[27] On June 20 the government used the FBI report to indict eighteen American Nazis, calling the case "the greatest peacetime spy ring in history."[28]

The Nazi spy trials were intended to cool off the spy fever but the strategy backfired. Instead of crediting the government and the FBI with cracking the "Nazi spy ring," the public made a hero out of the undercover G-Man who had infiltrated the Nazi apparatus, and hailed him for saving the country despite official indifference. This agent, Leon G. Turrou, author of a book called *How to Be a G-Man,* was a colorful character with a history of mental disorder. While the government's case was still being prepared, he sold his exposé memoirs to the *New York Post.* This got him bounced from the bureau with a personal rebuke from FDR.[29] Attorney General Cummings managed to have the *Post* enjoined from publishing Turrou's memoirs,[30] but the stay was short-lived, and Turrou made more headlines by accusing his superiors of a cover-up. "I never intended in any way to interfere with the administration of justice," he wrote, "but merely to reveal the sinister force behind this spy ring, which will not be revealed at the trial."[31] He charged that he had been fired because he "had scooped J. Edgar Hoover, Director of the Bureau, in the matter of publicity."[32]

The mass indictments of the Nazis did not quiet the Nazi spy scare. On the contrary, now the government was being accused of having failed to trace the mysterious Nazi network all the way up to the top.

At this point Warner Brothers charged in where G-Men supposedly feared to tread, rushing the movie version of Turrou's memoirs, *Confessions of a Nazi Spy,* into the theaters. The studio's publicity campaign tried to turn the film into the centerpiece of a patriotic crusade against the Nazis. Warner Brothers bragged that their movie "called a Swastika a Swastika." The audience was asked to sign cards that said, "I pledge myself to do everything in my power to combat the Nazi espionage activties which are endangering the democratic institutions of the United States." Edward G. Robinson, who played the character modeled on Turrou, said that "in making *Confessions of a Nazi Spy* I feel I am serving my country just as effectively as if I shouldered a gun and marched away to war." Advertisements warned the public that "he may live next door to you, even work in your office . . . but still you don't know him! He shows his hand, but he does not show his face. A foreign government is paying him to betray America! He is a Nazi spy! . . . It was our American duty to make this picture! It is your American privilege to see it."[33]

The Turrou fiasco caused a sharp shift in FBI public relations. Hoover's publicity since 1933 had tried to mobilize the nation to take part in the administration's anticrime crusade. After the Nazi spy fiasco FBI publicity shifted to the objective of keeping the public out of the spy hunt. In January 1940, Hoover published a magazine article that laid down the basic line for the bureau's wartime publicity. "There is no denying," he began in "Stamping Out the Spies," "that we have a distinct spy menace, that hundreds upon hundreds of foreign spies are busily engaged upon a program of peering, peeking, eavesdropping, propaganda and actual sabotage." He followed this with a series of case histories to prove that the FBI had the situation well under control, and to show that "this country was never so well prepared to combat espionage activities."[34]

"The F.B.I. has received thousands of letters from earnest citizens, asking how they may aid in the battle against spydom," Hoover continued. "The citizen should consider his particular task to be fulfilled when he reports his suspicions to the nearest F.B.I. office. After that . . . [his suspicions] should not become gossip. Idle talk can hamper proper investigation."[35]

He explained that too much public involvement could be even worse than too little. "In the wave of patriotism which, fortunately, is rising throughout the nation, are dangers of overzealousness. We must not stoop to un-American methods, no matter how great the provocation or how patriotic the aim. We should regard vigilantes or vigilante methods as abhorrent. . . . This is no time for hysteria, wild rumors, or hair-trigger prejudices. If a neighbor does not agree with your war views he isn't necessarily an enemy of America. The real spy is extremely careful about voicing opinions."[36]

The argument Hoover presented in "Stamping Out the Spies" became the FBI's line in all its wartime publicity: "The nation is better prepared today than in years gone by. An offensive has started. The combined attack by federal and state forces should be sufficient so far as investigations and prosecution are concerned. Beyond the efforts of these forces there is a need, of course, for the individual cooperation of all sincere and earnest Americans. But this cooperation should be limited to passing on to the proper officials all questionable facts or rumors which may come one's way."[37] The cartoon that accompanied the article illustrated the passive role the FBI was urging on the public: Uncle Sam's giant foot wearing a boot labeled "The F.B.I." was shown crushing the head of the "Spy Menace" snake. The flashlight beam lighting the way for the FBI represented "Public Cooperation."[38]

Throughout the war Hoover kept telling the public to stay out of the spy hunt. Another example of Hoover's efforts along these lines was a *March of Time* documentary released in 1942 called *The F.B.I. Front.*[39] The film was billed as having been made with "the official cooperation of the Federal Bureau of Investigation"; its purpose was to show "the role of the G-Man in wartime." The film was a documentary-style fictional drama showing how the prewar FBI, through "the foresight of F.B.I. Director J. Edgar Hoover," had infiltrated the German-American Bund so that when the war broke out, the bureau had been ready to round up the agents of "Hitler's most powerful weapon in the U.S., his hoped-for fifth column." The film included the obligatory dose of technological razzle-dazzle: code-breaking machines, black light gadgets for reading secret messages, and the like. There was also a tribute to the FBI's role in "coordinating all local law enforcement bodies into a uniformly trained police force prepared to meet the additional problems occasioned by the emergency."

Before the war a movie like this would have been intended to raise the morale of the anticrime movement, but now the message was, "Let the F.B.I. Handle It." The point of the film was its warning that

on no condition should a citizen attempt to prosecute an amateur investigation of his own. There are several reasons for this. The F.B.I., to begin with, is the best investigating source. The *March of Time* film, *The F.B.I. Front,* just released, should convince even the most skeptical that no layman could hope to compete effectively with the facilities and training of the men whose work is shown in the picture. . . . The lessons taught by the *March of Time* film *The F.B.I. Front* should not only set at rest the mind of the honest alien, but also calm the ambitions of any amateur sleuth who fancies himself an adequate substitute for the trained, scientific, and, above all, humane agents of the F.B.I.

Since the new goal of Hoover's wartime publicity was to dampen public enthusiasm for spy-catching, there could no longer be any justification for the kind of frantic headline chasing that marked the period when Hoover was trying to sustain the momentum of the Cummings anticrime crusade. His public relations goals no longer called for the sort of bureau involvement in popular entertainment that had seemed necessary when popular identification with the bureau had been an essential part in his plans for unifying the nation and reforming law enforcement. The success of Hoover's wartime propaganda in persuading the public to leave the job of spy-chasing to the "humane" agents of the F.B.I. probably reconciled him to leaving radio counterintelligence to Phillips H. Lord. As long as Lord didn't come right out and call his gangbusters and counterspies FBI agents, Hoover felt that the public, the adult public at least, would not confuse Lord's fantasy with reality. Lord came close to crossing those limits, however, when he gave Counterspy David Harding an assistant named Special Agent Peters, but the "Counterspy" plots were so fantastic that nobody could have confused them with actual counterespionage. "These are the cells," Harding would announce during a tour of Counterspy headquarters, "where we keep enemy spies before we take them out and shoot them."[40]

Hoover went back on the air with an official FBI radio program because of an unauthorized G-Man adventure show that had so much seemingly authentic bureau detail that the public could hardly avoid believing it was an official FBI production. This new show's action formula plots portrayed individual G-Man heroes saving the country from Axis threats each week; it thus directly jeopardized Hoover's hitherto successful effort to convince the public that security work was so far beyond the ability of individuals that it had best be left to bureaucrats like himself.

In 1943 Hoover had collaborated with Frederick L. Collins on a history of the Bureau called *The F.B.I. in Peace and War,* and he officially recommended the book "to all who wish to know the F.B.I."[41] After the book hit the best-seller lists, Collins double-crossed Hoover by selling the radio rights to CBS without the bureau's permission. "The F.B.I. in Peace and War" went on the air in 1944 and continued to run for many years on Thursday nights. It was a typical gangbuster-type show, but it had plainly labeled FBI agents as heroes, and it had a persuasively official-sounding title. Hoover was outraged. According to Louis B. Nichols, head of the bureau's public relations, the bureau considered Collins to be "a free-wheeler out to make money. The Bureau was very unhappy at the inaccuracy and sensationalism of his show."[42] Hoover's first move was to force the show to include a weekly announcement that it was "*not* an official program of the F.B.I." He also went to Congress to get control over all further commercial use of the bureau's name and seal. But that was not enough to satisfy the director.

Hoover felt that the show was doing serious damage to the bureau's program of keeping the public out of security work. "The F.B.I. in Peace and War" downplayed the scientific and bureaucratic side of counterintelligence. By making success in spy-hunting depend on the strength and brains of individual agent heroes, Collins's show put the search for enemy agents within the capacities of anyone with enough sense to tell a Berlin accent from Brooklynese. Hoover hurried to counter this impression with his own official program, "This Is Your F.B.I.," an FBI production from start to finish.[43] The bureau thought up the show, located an advertisement agency, Warwick and Legler, to act as producer, and obtained a suitable sponsor after Hoover rejected the ad agency's first choice. The show's FBI-approved writer-director, Jerry Divine, was known and trusted by Hoover. Ironically, he had learned his trade as an assistant to Phillips H. Lord, and had been the chief writer on Lord's "Mr. District Attorney."

The first episode of "This Is Your F.B.I." was broadcast at 8:30 P.M. on Friday, April 6, 1945, on what would later become ABC.[44] Hoover made a guest appearance on the first show. His message was, "The Bureau was created to protect the people of the United States from its enemies within and without and so they ought to be told what it was doing." The president of Equitable Life, the show's sponsor, also made a speech: "Whenever there has been an opportunity for The Equitable to serve the public interest, we have gladly undertaken that privilege. We believe that no medium more vital than this official F.B.I. broadcast could be used to bring the Society closer to its members and those who may become members in the future. . . . In nearly every form of security other than the services rendered by your F.B.I. The Equitable considers itself your partner and your friend." The show's slogan, intoned by veteran movie G-Man Frank Lovejoy, was that "to your F.B.I. you look for national security . . . and to the Equitable Society for financial security. These two great institutions are dedicated to the protection of you, . . . your home and your country."

The first episode of "This Is Your F.B.I." was titled "the story of a crime against the nation—Espionage!" It picked up "The F.B.I. Front" theme of "Leave it to the F.B.I." It, and the episodes that followed it, were almost obsessively nonsensational. There were no chases, no fights, no shooting. The script even specified that the music be "NOT

MISTERIOSO." Since the show was intended to cool down any antispy hysteria ignited by programs like "The F.B.I. in Peace and War," the show's thesis was that there was no glamor in spying or spy-chasing: "Spying is just like any other business. A spy gets paid so much a week to do so much work." It also tried to prove that catching spies was boring work, hardly worth the attention of anyone with anything else worth doing. The audience formed its first impression of the show's FBI heroes (played by Geoffrey Bryant and Karl Swenson) by hearing them complain about their long hours:

ROSS: You look bushed.

DAN: I am kind of.

ROSS: Why don't you try hitting the hay early?

DAN: Are you kidding? I was in bed at 11:30 last night. But starting at midnight, the phone rang every hour on the hour. My wife wishes she'd married a doctor instead of an F.B.I. agent.

ROSS: My wife's been wishing that for 15 years.

Then they get down to business, tracking down a spy who has been sending information about New York shipping to German agents in Switzerland. Every clue they turn up—aliases, writing styles, handwriting, typewriting—demands the kind of laborious evaluation possible only in an enormous organization that has every type of scientific facility. Solving the case involves absolutely no heroics; spy-smashing seems about as interesting as reading the phone book. Actually, the agents do read the New York phone book, though, mercifully, not on the air. Midway through the show, after monumental labor, they finally assemble their conclusions and send them off to Washington. Back comes a telegram from J. Edgar: not enough evidence; back to work. Now and then they punctuate the monotony with more complaints:

ROSS: It's a lot of work. There must be hundreds of these baggage declarations.

DAN: There are thousands of air raid wardens. And with dogs.

ROSS: O.K. Ever look for a needle in a haystack before?

DAN: Yes. But this time, we're going to find it!

After a little more of this, the announcer breaks in to say that the program could dramatize only a fraction of the work Dan and Ross had to do to solve the case: "Actually, Special Agents of the F.B.I. discovered that from February 1 to May 5, 1941, boats sailing from Lisbon brought 3,095 aliens and 1,786 citizens to the Port of New York.

Approximately 5,000 people. Approximately 5,000 baggage declarations to check. Approximately 5,000 samples of handwriting to check against the handwriting on the letters to Switzerland, to match, to examine, to scrutinize, to sweat over, pore over, work over."

By the time Ross and Dan finally nabbed their Nazi agent, any would-be spy hunters in the audience should have decided that riveting rivets or widgeting widgets was more fun than shadowing enemy agents—so he should get back to rivets or widgets and leave the spies to the FBI. Certainly that was the moral Frank Lovejoy extracted from all this in his closing remarks: "In times like this, in war time, the F.B.I. is more alert, more watchful than ever. It has a tremendous job to perform . . . partly because there are more spies, but also because there are more people who have bits of information, people who talk, and talk too much. In this country, espionage is under control." What the ordinary citizen ought to do, Lovejoy said, was to keep quiet and calm. "What you talk about in a public place may seem unimportant to you, but if it's anything connected with the war, you may be helping spies. You may be writing a letter to Tokyo or Berlin."

The FBI's image during the war as the final guarantee of American security was so well established by the bureau's wartime public relations that the static and monotonous quality of "This Is Your F.B.I." may well have been one of the show's biggest assets. If the men who really understood national security could be so calm about it, the show implied, then there was no reason for the public to get upset about the problem. The progam's air of quiet confidence may have been exactly what the public wanted from its government during the war years and the unsettled cold war era that followed. In any case "This Is Your F.B.I." was successful enough to stay on the air for eight and one-half years until 1953.

While "This Is Your F.B.I." continued to calm and reassure the public after the war that its security was in good hands, popular culture kept dispatching its own unauthorized G-Men to battle crooks and Communists according to the old action detective rules of war. The most popular unofficial rivals to "This Is Your F.B.I." were "Top Secrets of the F.B.I." and "I Was a Communist for the F.B.I."

It is hard to imagine anyone taking Mutual Broadcasting's "Top Secrets" seriously. Its only asset was its announcer, Melvin Purvis—billed as "The Former Ace Agent of the F.B.I. . . . and . . . The Man Who Got Dillinger." Purvis's announcing style gave the show its only suspense: he stumbled repeatedly over his lines, sometimes pausing eerily in mid-sentence as though he could not quite believe what he was reading. The "Top Secrets" writers seem to have had a good time with their show. They gave it a memorably corny intro: a death march version of the villain's theme from stage melodrama, then a long drawn-out "Shhhhh . . ." They also seemed to hope that if they said enough nice things about the FBI, Hoover would not get mad at the show for pretending to be official. Each episode claimed to be based on material "from the files of the F.B.I., the dramatic highlights in the fight against crime by the most efficient, the most scientific law enforcement organization in the world—based on actual cases."[45]

The "Top Secrets" adventures were pure pulp formula. Each week the show's FBI heroes tracked down, slugged, and jailed another gangster or spy. There was often a sort of camp humor when the show's G-Men, known as Smith and Jones "in the interest of security," broke into comic vaudeville routines:

SMITH: You'll be meeting the gentleman and the lady.

JONES: The lady? Got a picture? Hmmm.
        Too bad she's not.

SMITH: Not what, Mr. Jones?

JONES: Not a lady, Mr. Smith.

"Top Secrets" also tried to copy the "scientific law enforcement" formula of official FBI entertainment by giving the G-Men a new technical toy each week. One week it was a "vest pocket broadcasting station." According to Purvis's introduction, "the case of the vest pocket broadcasting station was one of the most interesting and unusual cases in modern scientific crime busting but it wasn't so because of the crime— that was old stuff—or because of the criminals—they were smart, but old stuff too—it was interesting and unusual because of the way the crime busting scientists of the F.B.I. cracked the case." The idea was to wire Agent Jones for a meeting with a narcotics dealer: "That was it— inside a truck a completely equipped radio receiving station—with a turntable for recording a conversation three blocks away or a mile away if it had to. And the broadcasting station—well, that was in Jones' vest pocket. A disc no bigger than a quarter, but complete down to a fine point, and in the lining of Jones' vest a wire that led from the pocket to the top button of his vest. Yes, that button was the microphone—but nobody would guess it in a million years—it looked just like the other five buttons."

The trouble was that the "Top Secret" writers could not figure out how to work the radio into the plot. Except for some vaguely authentic radio talk ("Give me a level"), they forgot about the gadget until the end, when Purvis claimed that the radio had some unexplained part in nabbing the narcotics king: "Yes, a vest pocket broadcasting station did that. But if anyone thinks that he can find it just by pulling at the top button of a vest here is something for the memory book. The gimmick can be anywhere. So can the agent of the F.B.I.—and what's more, he can be anybody."

"This Is Your F.B.I." and Hoover's public relations had made the public expect more than sleuthing and shooting when the FBI was on the prowl, so the "Top Secrets" writers knew they had to do something with science, even if they could manage only pseudoscientific nonsense. The fake G-Man programs used science as an obligatory stage prop because for a decade Hoover's publicists had made science the unique selling proposition of the Federal Bureau of Investigation. "Top Secrets"'s moronic use of science shows that Hoover's official public relations made it necessary for even formula action detectives to display some familiarity with science if they wanted to pass themselves off as G-Men.

By and large, however, unofficial G-Man entertainment in the forties and fifties flourished by using the plot conventions Hoover's FBI formula banished from official bureau productions. The most successful unofficial FBI program of the cold war era, "I Was a Communist for the F.B.I.,"[46] was in the tradition of the undercover G-Men first popularized in the 1935 G-Man movie cycle. The show was based on the adventures of actual FBI undercover informant Matt Cvetic. Each week Dana Andrews, playing Matt Cvetic, was sent on another illegal and dangerous mission by his Communist bosses. Each week Andrews had to avoid blowing his cover (which would also have blown the rest of the series) while thwarting whatever the Red rascals were up to that week.

Dana Andrews's introduction placed each week's adventure in the context of a continuing struggle against communism. Just as Homer Cummings had given the public enemies cases mythic significance as battles in the war against crime, this was another instance of the FBI's official publicity penetrating popular culture:

ANDREWS: Nine years isn't a long time to the average American living a normal life, but a Communist for the F.B.I. doesn't live a normal life. Nine years of fear and tension seems an eternity. The fear isn't all personal. The greatest fear is that those you are trying to protect will fail to recognize, refuse to realize that Communists are dedicated to the elimination of personal liberty wherever it exists. If you are one of those who has refused to believe, listen to my story with an open mind. It should open your eyes, because it is part of the story of Communism.[47]

Andrews used two voices when he read his lines. When he was Matt Cvetic, FBI informant, he spoke in the earnest all-American tones of radio heroes from Jack Armstrong to the Lone Ranger and Superman. When he was in his Communist cover, he seemed to drop a few dozen

The FBI's wartime image as a bureaucratic security blanket: a scene from the FBI-supervised House on 92nd Street.

IQ points, speaking with a sort of bone-headed truculence as though he resented every treasonous moment he had to spend with the comrades. The show's real Communists sounded like Peter Lorre and referred to guns as "rewolwers." At the end of each program, after stalling the Red timetable for another week, Andrews would sign off in his "decent" voice: "It's a lonely life being a Communist, but when you can't depend on friends and you can't afford enemies, you're forced to walk alone. We must remember that the price of liberty is eternal vigilance, but the danger we warn against is very real."

The big difference between the real and fake G-Men was pointed up every time Dana Andrews phoned his FBI control. The G-Men of "This Is Your F.B.I." were puppets controlled (and protected) by the director. Whenever Andrews phoned *his* director he always got the same discouraging response: "Sorry Matt. There's nothing we can do to help you. You're on your own." The real G-Men were never on their own.

Unauthorized programs like "The F.B.I. in Peace and War," "Top Secrets of the F.B.I.," and "I Was a Communist for the F.B.I." prove that popular culture after the war, despite Hoover's propaganda, still saw the

FBI agent as the action detective hero of the prewar G-Man movie cycle. Meanwhile, even though popular entertainment had paid little attention, the bureau emerged from the war with a set of public relations objectives quite different from those Hoover had promoted before Pearl Harbor. Despite Hoover's quarrels with the action detective G-Man hero, his prewar publicity had the same intent as the ostensible purpose of the pulp magazine and Hollywood G-Men adventures—to enlist the public's interest and participation in the FBI-led crusade against crime. Hoover and popular culture both emphasized the mythic significance of the bureau's big cases as rituals of crime and punishment; both gave the public adventure heroes to identify with—preferably the entire FBI organization or, failing that, Hoover himself as a somewhat ungainly substitute for the action detective hero of popular culture.

In its publicity during and after the war, however, the bureau began to promote itself as a symbol of security, as a reason for the public to stop worrying about the threat of crime and sabotage; the bureau thus denied itself the chance to operate in an arena of heightened public concern. It thus abandoned its dynamic role as American culture's representative in rituals of national solidarity in favor of a static role as a symbol of security and unity and, during the fifties, a repository of traditional American values. By moving away from crime and punishment rituals, the bureau's public image had to draw on the inherited capital of its prewar popularity without replenishing it. By casting itself as a symbol of unity and national values, the bureau made itself vulnerable in unexpected ways when significant numbers of Americans began to attack national unity as a mask for oppression, or when the bureau itself failed to live up to the moral values it claimed to represent.

12

One G-Man's Family:
FBI Public Relations During the Fifties and Sixties

At the end of World War II, J. Edgar Hoover was, as far as anyone could see, an immovable monument on the American scene. His FBI had won, to all appearances, a permanent place in American culture as the nation's symbol of security and its bulwark against crime and communism. By raising his ambitions to larger goals during the fifties and sixties—from law enforcement leadership to a defense of traditional American religious and capitalistic values against foreign and domestic heresies, however, Hoover loosened his grasp on the pop culture formulas that had made him and his men culture heroes.

After World War II, Hoover ceased to be satisfied with his and his bureau's roles as action detectives and symbols of national security. That was no longer enough. He had come to believe that what was now needed was nothing less than the revitalization of all the traditional American values that were being threatened by modern infidelity. He therefore turned the FBI into a symbol of patriotism, domesticity, and religiosity, a barrier, not so much against crime, as against the revolution in morals that was shaking the order and tranquility of the status quo.

America had made celebrities out of Hoover and his FBI during the depression because an incredibly popular entertainment formula had needed a new hero and had discovered the G-Man. During the fifties the gumshoe was on the other foot. Now Hoover's publicists had to search for a formula that would let them use the FBI to demonstrate that the neighborly virtues of traditional Americanism, and not the alien nostrums of socialism, liberalism or secularism, were the cure for what ailed the country. With the aid of the popular entertainment industry, Hoover finally did discover a formula that would do the trick, just in time for the national consensus that upheld those values to disintegrate during Vietnam and Watergate, just in time for the bureau itself to demonstrate to the country that it had betrayed the values it stood for in its zeal to protect them.

The FBI's search for a new formula to replace the old ritual of crime and punishment forced it to take temporary leave of the popular entertainment scene from 1953, when "This Is Your F.B.I." went off the air, until 1959, when Hoover unveiled the New Look G-Man in *The F.B.I. Story*. *Walk East on Beacon* (1952), the film dramatization of Hoover's *Reader's Digest* story about the atom bomb spies, was the last official FBI movie to appear until 1959, and *G-Men,* the most popular of all the G-Man pulps, went out of business in 1953.

The last episodes of "This Is Your F.B.I." demonstrate that the bureau's abandonment of the action detective formula had left FBI entertainment almost plotless, and the G-Man hero with nothing to do except radiate kindness and understanding. Take, for example, an episode towards the end of "This Is Your F.B.I." 's run called "The Face,"[1] which narrator William Woodson introduced as an examination of juvenile delinquency's causes and cures. "Without any question," Woodson began, "juvenile delinquency is the most serious law enforcement problem of the day. Youth has been in the vanguard of the criminal army in this country. The basic cause of juvenile delinquency is a lack of moral responsibility and for this the blame rests squarely on the parents of the country for it is in the home that the child must learn that others besides himself have rights and must learn the values that will help him grow into a decent, law-abiding citizen—a public servant and not a public enemy."

This sounds like an introduction to a hard-boiled drama about antisocial punks—but it is not. The program opened with Special Agent Jim Taylor being summoned to a local police station by a friendly sergeant, where a boy has been arrested for theft. Taylor asks, "Are we on the case officially?"

SERGEANT: No, Jim, there is no F.B.I. violation, but I thought you might try to talk a little sense into the youngster.

TAYLOR: O.K., I'll try.

The Sergeant introduces Taylor to "Bobby," whose face is disfigured by an ugly scar. As they enter his cell, the boy shouts, "Why don't you leave me alone? Why doesn't everyone leave me alone?" The sergeant replies, "Everybody did. That's why you're here. I asked Jim Taylor to come here to tell you a story."

Taylor's story is about a case he handled years before. A boy had been stealing packages from trucks, and a driver had gotten a good look at the thief, whose face was disfigured by a caved-in nose. "The driver said it was the strangest face he ever saw. At first he thought it was a monkey." The delinquent, Danny Auburn, was an orphan in the care of an older sister. He had quit school because his classmates had been laughing at his face, badly cut in a bicycle accident; they had been calling him "Monk." He told his sister, "I'll steal and I'll have money. Then I'll be important."

Narrator Woodson interrupted the story to interpret the action up to this point:

There is a moral in tonight's case brought to you from the files of the F.B.I.— the moral is that there is no quick cure to the problem of juvenile delinquency. The problem is deep-rooted and varies with each individual. It is the job of social workers, psychologists and those who come into contact with anti-social youth to burrow deep and find the causes of delinquency in each particular case—and then to treat the cause.

With Danny we are finding one possible cause for his delinquency. True, law enforcement officers are responsible for protecting society against its Dannys and Bobbys—and most of them are wise enough to know that the best way to do this is to effect a change in the attitude of the young offender toward life.

Taylor then tells how he interviewed Danny's sister, who told him that Danny's disfigurement had changed his personality. "So you see," she told Taylor, "he's not really to blame." Taylor agreed: "No, I guess everybody's to blame."

Taylor recalls that he went to his boss, who agreed with him that the boy deserved sympathy, and together they came up with a way to help Danny. Taylor called a friend who was "an outstanding plastic surgeon." Then Taylor went to see Danny:

DANNY: Why don't you take me to the zoo. Yeah, I'll do all right there. See me scratch myself. See the monkey.

BREAKS DOWN CRYING

TAYLOR: Take a look at this picture. Did you ever hear of plastic surgery? They can do wonderful things today. They can build a whole new face. A plastic surgeon drew this picture. My doctor friend says it can be you, and he wants to do it for nothing.

Taylor tells Bobby that "the doctor operated and did a wonderful job. The doctor is still alive, and we can speak to him about you." Bobby does not believe Taylor, so the G-Man turns to the sergeant:

TAYLOR: Tell him, Sergeant.

SERGEANT: Bobby, I'm the fellow in that story. I'm Danny Auburn.

William Woodson wrapped up the story with a moral:

And that's the story of two juvenile delinquents who were saved by the intervention of your F.B.I., who were returned to good standing in their communities because a doctor with a social conscience decided to work with law enforcement agencies to do his part to fight the menace of lawbreaking youngsters.

Off-hand you might have thought there was nothing a plastic surgeon could do
to combat juvenile delinquency—but there is something each of us can do if we
have the mind to do it—the mind and the heart.

It might be hard to enroll as a fighter against juvenile delinquency. It might cost
time or money, but if the future of the nation is of any importance to you, you
will enlist tomorrow in this war, this incessant war against a wave that is
creating criminals faster than the nation can build prisons to house them.

Let tomorrow be a day of dedication when you will dedicate youself to join the
ranks of those who are doing their part to ensure the future—their future and
yours.

When "This Is Your F.B.I." was not turning the G-Man into a social
worker, it was using him to instruct local cops on their responsibilities.
The show for October 31, 1947, had Agent Taylor tell a police officer,
"You went to the F.B.I. National Academy, Joe, so you know the rules.
The F.B.I. can't step into a local situation unless there's a federal law
under our jurisdiction that's been violated." Or else Taylor was lectur-
ing the public on the Constitution: "Your F.B.I. can never be a substitute for effective law enforcement on the local level. . . . The F.B.I. is an
investigative agency, not a vigilante group. Our job is your security, but
an even more important job is to protect your civil liberty."[2]

While the G-Man was absent from popular entertainment between
1953 and 1959, Hoover himself fronted for the bureau with an awe-
some schedule of lectures and articles, climaxed in 1958 by the best-
selling book of his career, *Masters of Deceit*.[3] This book contained
everything the director had ever thought or felt about the apocalyptic
battle between Christian America and the satanic forces of communism.

The book's twenty-nine printings were more a tribute to Hoover's
popularity than to the book's merits, however, because *Masters of Deceit* was a mess. It was a mess because Hoover and his ghost writers
(primarily Louis B. Nichols) knew exactly what they wanted to say—
that communism was bad, that America was good, that old-fashioned
American goodness should be the country's secret weapon against the
Reds—but they had no idea how to put that message across. They put
the book together by rummaging through the junkshop of pop culture,
picking up popular entertainment formulas at random, using them and
discarding them. There was nothing in the way of a controlling story

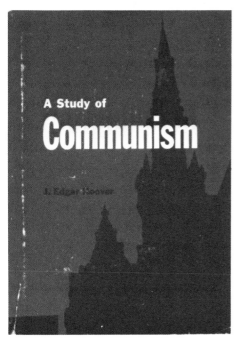

Hoover as popular culture's resident expert on communism: Masters of Deceit *(1958),* A Study of Communism *(1962),* J. Edgar Hoover on Communism *(1969).*

line to give coherence or direction to this juicy collection of Communist outrages. The bureau had not yet discovered a formula that would let the G-Man display the new moralistic symbolism Hoover had decreed for the hardy old hero.

Sometimes Hoover's men tried to fit the fight against communism into the format of a cops-and-robbers movie chase:

> Shortly before noon one day a top Party official drove east out of town. At the outskirts he doubled back, twice turning corners and coming to abrupt stops. Then, at speeds varying from forty to eighty miles an hour, he continued east for twenty-six miles. Turning around, he retraced his route at eighty miles an hour.
>
> He was "dry-cleaning" in a most dangerous and reckless fashion. . . . This type of fanatical communist, if so instructed, would not hesitate to lead a riot, steal vital military secrets, sabotage defense industries, or perform illegal activities. Here is the true communist at work, without concern for personal risk or safety.[4]

Despite the incongruity between the putative villainy of the Communist in this case and the less than terrifying evidence Hoover could submit of his depravity (speeding and reckless driving), a Communist was evidently so repugnant to Hoover that everything he did was a mortal sin. Otherwise Hoover could not have arranged this sequence of crime to begin with riots, move on to spying and sabotage, only to end in the false climax of "illegal activities."

Elsewhere Hoover's ghosts exploited the pornography of racism. They described a local NAACP leader opening a chapter meeting with a person-by-person loyalty oath to unmask Communist infiltrators. "All entered denials until he got to the back of the room where the state organizer for the Communist party was sitting with a white woman."[5] The phrase "white woman" was pointless unless the bureau assumed that this detail would trigger a response in the reader of emotional revulsion against miscegenation. Was Hoover now casting the G-Man as the white race's defender of racial purity?

The Crime Records Division's frantic search for formulas even led them to the conventions of horror films in an effort to describe otherworldly evils that lurked in the soul of the Communist. "The CPUSA," said Hoover, "is a freak [that] has grown into a powerful monster endangering us all." Again, "The W. E. B. DuBois Clubs are new blood for the vampire of international communism." Or, "Communism is cannibalistic. Its servants are periodically offered as sacrifices on the communist altar."[6]

Horror films were not the only "B" movies Hoover raided for formulas to use in *Masters of Deceit*. The book is also filled with the imagery of satanism and witchcraft. "At the age of sixteen, as he later said, Lenin ceased to believe in God. It is reported that he tore the cross from his neck, threw this sacred relic to the ground, and spat upon it."[7] It was out of this blasphemous ritual, according to Hoover, that communism was born. The initiation of Communists into the party's mysteries was, in the Hoover version, also tinged with diabolism. "In the presence of an eighteen-year-old girl [the obligatory Black Mass virgin?] and a dark-haired stooped old man [the Black Man?] Eric signed an application for party membership." Occurring even more frequently than this kind of explicit reference to the occult in *Masters of Deceit* (the very title conjures up the Olde Deluder) is satanic innuendo: Communist plots are "diabolic" plots, Communist glee is "diabolic" glee (peals of which echo through the Red underworld whenever clergymen like the Berrigans are "duped" by Communists), Communists are motivated by "diabolic" logic.

The popular culture of American Protestantism was one of Hoover's major resources in *Masters of Deceit*, providing him, for instance, with the revivalistic formula of repentance and forgiveness. What hope is there, Hoover asked, against this new barbarism that corrodes the nation's spiritual strength and tests its military defenses? "All we need is faith. . . . The truly revolutionary force of history is not material power but the spirit of religion."[9] Faith could protect the innocent from the seductions of communism just as it had rescued scores of Communists (now on the F.B.I. payroll) from the depth of Marxist degradation. Hoover reported that his files were filled with tales of Communists who told their confessor agents that a chance reading of an anti-Communist article by Hoover saved their souls: his word acted on them like Saul's thunderbolt. For revivalists from Jonathan Edwards to Billy Graham, the most convincing proof of God's presence and approval has been the crisis conversion. The convert is living proof that God (and civilization) is triumphing now and in the future will triumph completely, which may explain Hoover's well-known fondness for former Communists. "Loyal Americans," he said, "must accept their [former Communists'] sincere repentance as a return to the full scope of citizenship. All great religions teach that the sinner can always redeem himself [for a moment, at least, Hoover seems to be offering anticommunism as another "great religion"]. Who, then, shall sit in judgment on the ex-communist? Who dare deny him the promise held out to all those who repent of the evil they have done and who try to make amends . . . ? To deny that men can change is to deny the truths which have eternally guided civilized man."[10] The formulas of popular Christianity allowed Hoover to charge that communism was also a religion, though a false one: "Communism is more than an economic, political, social, or philosophical system. It is a way of life; a false, materialistic, 'religion.' It

THE J. EDGAR HOOVER
YOU OUGHT TO KNOW

BY HIS PASTOR

EDWARD L. R. ELSON

In the fifties Hoover promoted himself and the bureau as symbols of traditional Americanism.

would strip man of his belief in God, his heritage of freedom, his trust in love, justice, and mercy. Under Communism all would become, as so many already have, twentieth century slaves."[11]

The book is filled with allusions to popular religion. Hoover accused Communists of disrespect during sacred occasions: "There is seldom a religious quality to the music, eulogies, or the 'mourners' conduct." He knew that Communist grief is always feigned, since the Reds lack human emotions; to make sure the reader noticed their insincerity he placed quotation marks around the word "mourners." On another occasion he dragged in poor Mother Bloor's cadaver: "At the 'state funeral' of Mother Ella Reeve Bloor in 1951 the 'mourners' talked, laughed, and smoked."[12]

The vision of himself that Hoover revealed in *Masters of Deceit* was that of the defender of Christian civilization against the barbarian hordes from the East: "Communists are barbarians in modern dress, using both club and blood purge. . . . Communism has turned the values of Western Civilization upside down."[13] This notion led him to another source of imagery, Hollywood's historical epics. He peppered the book with references to these films: "Lenin introduced into human relations a new dimension of evil and depravity not surpassed by Genghis Khan or Attila."[14] Stalin was also an Attila. (Years later poor Mark Rudd and the SDS were "modern campus Attilas.") Why did

Hoover pick on Attila? Because Attila conjured up the scene of Christian Rome besieged by the barbaric hordes, while out of the gates a small, dignified band of clerics advances with a richly clad, stocky little figure in the lead, processional cross in hand. The barbarian recoils from the cross, and civilization is safe once more. And whom was Hoover imagining in the role of Pope Leo?

The one formula that seemed to be Hoover's favorite in *Masters of Deceit* was to let America be symbolized by the middle-class family, thus characterizing communism as an assault on the domestic circle. Heading the list of Hoover's charges against Marx, for example, was the charge that the Red patriarch was a bad provider and ran a sloppy household. Quoting from Gustav Meyer, Hoover reported that for Marx, "washing himself, combing his hair, changing his underwear and shirts are a rarity. . . . He is often lazy for days. . . . In the entire apartment there is not a single piece of clean and good furniture, everything is broken, tattered, and ragged; everything is covered with a finger-thick dust, everywhere there is the greatest disorder. . . . As for sitting down, that is a really dangerous matter. Here is a chair with only three legs; over there the children are playing at cooking on another chair which happens to be still unbroken. Sure enough, that is the one which is offered to the visitor, but without any effort to clean off the food. You sit down at the risk of ruining a pair of trousers. . . . Such is a faithful picture of the family life of the Communist chief, Marx."[15]

Hoover described the Communist family as a parody of a decent American household. "These youngsters are taught from their earliest years that God does not exist. One Communist mother in a Northern state taught her children that God was not real. She said that it was fun to watch Superman on TV but that a person must recognize that he doesn't actually exist. It's the same way, she said, with God."[16] According to Hoover, Communist children also lose, along with their religious beliefs, their respect for the law. "In one instance a Communist father denounced a federal law that restricted the activities of the Party. His teen-age son, confused by the statement, pointed out that the act was part of the law of the land. 'Son,' the father replied, 'if a law is bad, you do not have to obey it.' "[17]

Hoover charged that for the Communist the party had replaced the family. "The Party," he wrote, "is his school, source of friends, and recreation, his substitute for God. Communism wants the *total* man, hence it is *total*itarian. The Party, in the final analysis, has an interpretation for the whole of life. Nothing is untouched: science, psychology, sex, love, care of children, history, literature, the origin and end of life. Everything must be absorbed. Communism is a unitary, all-embracing, and absolute system."[18]

By the time the G-Man hero reappeared in American popular culture in 1959, Hoover had finally settled on the formula he wanted. The first piece of popular entertainment to feature this new myth of the G-Man was Mervyn LeRoy's *The F.B.I. Story* (1959), the film adaptation of Don Whitehead's authorized history of the bureau, which had been published in 1956 under the same title.[19] Whitehead's book was a history of the bureau and a wide-ranging survey of its operations grafted onto a casebook of FBI adventures. Whitehead was decidedly sympathetic to Hoover (who provided an FBI seal for the cover and an introduction), but *The F.B.I. Story* was not simply a puff job. It was a solid piece of journalism written by a two-time Pulitzer Prize winner, head of the *New York Herald Tribune*'s Washington bureau. The FBI furnished Whitehead with material and went over the manuscript with him, but according to the head of the bureau's Crime Records Division, who had gotten Whitehead to write the book, the bureau did not edit it.[20] Like many reporters who have covered the bureau, however, Whitehead was won over by the enthusiasm and dedication of the agents in the field and their Washington bosses; his thesis was that the bureau's successes and laudable ambitions were the real FBI story, not the instances when the bureau fell short of its own or Whitehead's expectations. After thirty-eight weeks on the best-seller lists and nation-wide serialization in 170 newspapers, Whitehead sold *The F.B.I. Story* to Warner Brothers at a meeting attended by Hoover and Louis B. Nichols, head of FBI public relations.[21]

If producer-director Mervyn Leroy, who had first gotten into gangster films in 1930 with *Little Caesar,* had simply filmed the book Don Whitehead had written, the result would have been an expanded news-reel documentary of the type Time-Life had done several times about the FBI for the *March of Time* series. But Warners intended its FBI film to be a major release aimed at the mass market family audience, and so it would have to be reshaped to suit the new conventions for mass entertainment that had developed during the fifties. The movie was, of course, going to need a hero, and because he was going to be a hero for the fifties, he was going to need a family. Therefore Mervyn LeRoy did not tailor Don Whitehead's book, subtitled a "Report to the People," to the dimensions of the action detective formula, though that was the solution that would have been natural during the thirties and forties. He turned this potential saga of the hard-fighting G-Men into a domestic drama.

Plenty of Whitehead's book survived the treatment scriptwriters Richard L. Breen and John Twist gave it. The tours of the FBI labs, the big cases, and the outline of the bureau's history were all still there in abbreviated form, but the meaning of it all was now something new and different. Don Whitehead had stayed with the original image of the FBI J. Edgar Hoover and his publicists had fabricated during the thirties—a relentless, irresistible, scientific crime-fighting team, educating the pub-

One G-Man's family: James Stewart and Vera Miles in The F.B.I. Story *(1959).*

lic and reforming American law enforcement while it led a nationwide movement against crime—and had used it to give his book theme and structure. Whitehead's book had stuck close to the by-now-familiar mythology of what the FBI had done, what it was doing, and what role it played in American life. The film version had bits and pieces of Whitehead's original theme, but the underlying concept of the FBI as the vanguard of a national "movement" against crime had been discarded. Whitehead's conception of the bureau's crusading spirit had provided his book with its dynamism. The movie replaced the crusade with group dynamics.

The group dynamics were the ups and downs of one FBI family, the Hardestys of Nashville. *The F.B.I. Story* was Special Agent Chip Hardesty's story; played by Jimmy Stewart, he solved all the film's big cases, bridged the historical gaps between the dramatic episodes, and gave new agents lectures that instructed the audience in FBI procedures and facilities. If Hardesty's role in the film had been limited to this, he would simply have been a "composite character," a dramatic device used by many writers to lend human interest to stories about large organizations; Sanford J. Ungar followed this practice in his 1976 history of the bureau, which has superseded Whitehead's.[22] But Jimmy Stewart had more than Dillinger, Nazis, and Communists to keep him busy. He also had Vera Miles.

Warner Brothers brought the old G-Man formula up to date by turning *The F.B.I. Story* into something that the *Saturday Review* called "One F.B.I. Man's Family." The dramatic fireworks in this picture were not the shootouts, which seemed to be mere interludes; the emotional high voltage was generated by the conflict between the two stars as the domestic tranquility of Hardesty's all-American brood was disrupted, time and again, by his FBI career.

The movie picked up the Hardesty story in 1924.[23] Chip's girlfriend Lucy (Vera Miles) refuses to marry him while he "works for that Bureau," stuck in a "dinky little rut" with nothing to show for his work except a payroll number. Chip is pretty disgusted with the bureau, too—it is corrupt, ineffective, and the ceiling fan in his office does not work—so he hops a train to Washington to turn in his badge.

Chip walks into FBI headquarters at a hallowed moment in the bureau's history. A new director has taken over, and Chip gets there just in time to hear Hoover promise his staff a new FBI with freedom from

The F.B.I. Story's *meticulous reenactment of the Kansas City Massacre.*

politics, new scientific procedures, and a spirit "dedicated not just to justice but to a love of justice." Chip pleads with Lucy to let him stay in the bureau and "study criminology" with the new director who "can make water run up hill." She relents, and Hardesty sets off to solve the bureau's first big cases, some of them conveniently moved from the pre-1924 years into the Hoover era, thus preserving the dramatic unities if not the record.

One familiar case sends Hardesty to the Osage reservation in Oklahoma, where he disguises himself as a prospector to solve that much-told tale of the early Hoover years. The climax of the story this time, however, is not the arrest that closes the case. Back in Nashville his wife has been expecting their fourth child, and on the night that Chip breaks the case, she loses the baby. This lets Stewart indulge in one of his characteristic mumbling outbursts: "The Bureau has no right to send people to hell-holes like Oklahoma with no schools, no churches." He swears he'll quit the bureau and give his wife the kind of home she deserves, but now she won't let him quit because now she is proud of his job, proud of Hoover's new FBI. The FBI is worth her little sacrifice, she tells him, and so he has to stick it out.

Every important milestone in FBI history is transformed into another Hardesty family crisis. When the G-Men get the right to carry weapons, it turns out that Mrs. Hardesty is afraid of guns. Stewart mulls that one over and then mumbles something to the effect that "craftiness can solve many a case but with hoodlums you sometimes need a good, hardworking, conscientious machine gun." Later on, under the strain of the perpetual gunfights of the gangster era, Mrs. Hardesty's nerves start to unravel. She leaves home to stay with her mother until Chip quits; she goes back to him when her family shows her newspaper clippings of Chip's cases with headlines like "F.B.I. WINNING GANGSTER WAR."

World War II is portrayed as an FBI–Hardesty family operation with only a little help from the army and navy. Pearl Harbor is bombed during another family crisis: Chip's daughter has forgotten her lines during a school assembly speech, and the news of the attack arrives just as Stewart is consoling her with the thought that her little tragedy won't be the biggest disaster she will ever face. Hardesty's wartime missions have him tracking Nazi spies in the jungles of South America, but the biggest scenes are on the home front. During a family chorus of "Oh, You Beautiful Doll" a telegram arrives with word that Hardesty's only boy is dead in action in the Pacific.

When the war is finally over, a new one begins for Chip Hardesty: "Now the enemy was Communism, which threatened labor and management, church and home." By this time he is high enough in the bureau to have his own private phone to Hoover. When Hardesty rounds up his Reds, the two spy-smashers congratulate each other with a "Good job, Hardesty—thank you, Mr. Hoover" routine. Back home Lucy Hardesty is a grey-haired grandmother who just nods and smiles when her ancient G-Man (by the chronology of the movie he would have had to be at least sixty) rushes off on new cases. At the end of the picture she has finally accepted the fact that when she married Chip Hardesty, she married more than a man: she wedded the whole FBI.

Audiences who went to see *The F.B.I. Story* expecting something like the old G-Man movies were a little puzzled by Warner Brothers' new breed of special agents. The *New York Times* complained the show was more concerned with "the joys and sorrows of the American home and the bliss of domestic security than the historic details of crime." The program seemed to treat the bureau's great cases as "occupational hazards" that were "sandwiched between such domestic obligations as getting the kids off to school and sitting down to a bowl of breakfast food. In short," the *Times* went on, "the F.B.I. agent is presented as a pillar of the American home, as much as—or even more than—a pillar of law enforcement and protection against Communist spies. . . . 'This country's growing and crime will grow with it,' one of the eager beavers says. . . . It sounds like a slogan: 'Be a G-Man and Give Your Family Complete Security.' "[24]

If the bureau's new commitment to domestic security (both national and familial) fit the movie G-Men of the fifties, then the FBI had not just updated the detective formula that had served it so well during the thirties and forties—it had traded it in for a new one, and it had done so voluntarily. According to Mervyn LeRoy, Hoover "and his men controlled the movie. . . . Everybody on that picture, from the carpenters and electricians right to the top, everybody, had to be okayed by the F.B.I. . . . I had two F.B.I. men with me all the time, for research purposes, so that we did things right."[25] If Hoover and the bureau did not actually dictate the way the book was adapted to film, it is certain that they passed on all the changes and approved them.

The F.B.I. Story downplayed the action-detective aspects of the old G-Man formula (which Hoover had called "the adventure of scientific law enforcement" in a thirties speech) and focused on a "nice-guy" characterization that would have been absurd in earlier G-Man heroes. The FBI of the fifties seemed to believe that the G-Man's role as the moral center of his family was more interesting (or at least more important) than his on-the-job heroics.

When Hoover plunged into his last major venture in mass entertainment in 1965, television's "The F.B.I.," he made this house-broken G-Man the star. "The F.B.I." opened and closed every episode with the bureau's official stamp of endorsement, the FBI seal, protected since 1954 against unauthorized commercial use along with the Forest Service's Smokey the Bear gimmick. Crawl credits at the end of each show thanked "J. Edgar Hoover and his associates for their cooperation in the production of this series." Once a month there was a mug shot of a top ten fugitive with an appeal for information on his whereabouts. Hoover himself never appeared on the program as a character, but the office of "The Director" was supposed to be next door to that of Efrem Zimbalist, Jr., the star agent. Hoover did make guest appearances to kick off each new season. At the beginning of the first program of the series' second year there was a clip of Hoover giving a Freedoms Foundation award to Ford, the show's sponsor. When L. Patrick Gray was trying to claim the director's chair, he also barged in as a guest announcer, but after he resigned in disgrace, his name was removed from the programs made during his short regime.

A viewer would have had to assume that in exchange for all the official trappings Hoover would have demanded some control. Actually Hoover made no attempt to conceal the fact that he and the bureau were completely in charge. Shortly after his death *TV Guide* published an article by Hoover saying that he had waited out some six hundred offers by producers eager to make an FBI television series before he was finally approached by men he was sure he could trust: Jack Warner of Warner Brothers, who had produced the unofficial *G-Men* in 1935 and

Left to right: Philip Abbott, Efrem Zimbalist, Jr., and William Reynolds in the crime lab on television's "The F.B.I."

Mervyn LeRoy's *The F.B.I. Story,* and James Hagerty, president of ABC, whom Hoover had gotten to know when Hagerty was President Eisenhower's press secretary.[26] ABC had also ingratiated itself to Hoover by buying the rights to *Masters of Deceit,* which, however, was never filmed. In his *TV Guide* article Hoover wrote that Warner, Hagerty, and the show's producer, Quinn Martin (of "The Untouchables") had agreed to give the FBI complete approval over scripts, personnel, and sponsorship.

Scripts for the show shuttled back and forth between Hollywood and Washington,[27] the bureau straightening out inconsistent character details and illogical plot elements, persistently requesting that FBI legal jurisdiction be clearly established to justify every move made by Zimbalist as Inspector Erskine. Crime Records also kept a sharp eye out for smut and gore. "Perhaps we are inclined toward Puritanism in an increasingly permissive world," Hoover explained, "but foremost in our minds from the beginning episode has been the fact that *The F.B.I.* is telecast into American homes at a 'family hour' on a 'family evening.' "[28] Probably nobody but the FBI's censors would have been aroused by a scene in which some nostalgic old ladies told Erskine that they liked "to remember the way it was." When Erskine smiled in sympathy, Crime Records protested that "this could be suggestive," so he had to wipe off the grin.

The bureau's revisions show keen attention to anything, no matter how farfetched, that could have reflected adversely on the FBI's reputation for decorum, thoroughness, and precision. One script with a Florida location mentioned hills: the bureau pointed out impatiently that "the highest hill in Florida was believed to be less than twenty feet." The same script tried to send a hunter out after ducks with a rifle: the bureau's good old boys made sure he had a shotgun before the cameras rolled.

The bureau forced the writers to tread a thin line between showing so few crime details that the shows became dull and implausible, or so many that the bureau would be open to the charge (from the rural bank presidents whose telegrams seemed to frighten Hoover) that the show was "a blueprint for crime." Above all, the bureau's censorship of "The F.B.I." shows Hoover's late sensitivity to charges that the bureau violated civil liberties. One script had Erskine order a person back from a fishing holiday to help in an investigation. "We would have neither the temerity nor the authority," the bureau protested to Martin, "to order this citizen to return from his fishing trip."

Sex and violence are the meat and potatoes of action detective shows; character and police procedure are the trimmings. After Hoover's men got finished scissoring "The F.B.I." there was very little left except characterization and procedure. Efrem Zimbalist, Jr., said that when television violence became controversial in the late sixties, headquarters

I LED 3 LIVES

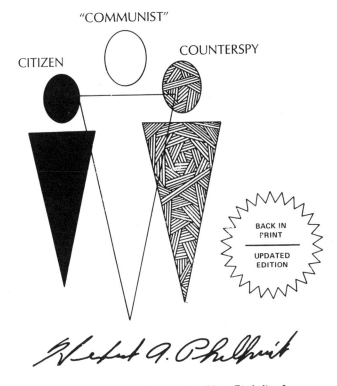

"COMMUNIST"

CITIZEN   COUNTERSPY

BACK IN
PRINT

UPDATED
EDITION

Herbert A. Philbrick

Foreword by Efrem Zimbalist, Jr.

Zimbalist was as much a symbol of the bureau in the sixties and seventies as Cagney had been in the thirties. This appeared in 1972.

put out a rule that "there would be no more deaths—immortality. We didn't kill anybody, I think, the last two or three years."[29]

Despite these restrictions "The F.B.I." was a success by conventional show business standards. Ratings made it the best-liked new show during its maiden season, and at the time of Hoover's death it was being watched by 40 million Americans every week, with overseas syndication bringing Inspector Erskine to fifty more nations from Canada to Singapore.[30]

Some of this success was owing to Zimbalist's considerable camera presence and to the sincerity he was able to bring to his role. Like many established Hollywood stars of his generation, Zimbalist was a staunch traditionalist in his cultural and political attitudes. His off-screen respect for guardians of traditional values buttressed Erskine's unfailingly noble physical, spiritual, and sartorial demeanor.[31] Another reason for the show's popularity was Crime Record's attention to detail, which kept the Quinn Martin organization on its toes. Even a politically unfriendly reviewer in the *Village Voice* called "The F.B.I." "one of the last vestiges of well-produced, well-acted entertaining engrossing television series left to the escapist adult. Politics, shmolitics, who can be fussy?"[32]

The professional slickness that let even the *Village Voice* tolerate "The F.B.I." as "escapist" was a symptom of what was wrong with the program; wrong, that is, if FBI entertainment was still supposed to dramatize the bureau's role in leading the nation and law enforcement against crime. Far from using entertainment to rouse the public in favor of strong law enforcement as it had during the thirties, the FBI of the sixties and seventies seemed more worried about offending someone. The show's highly publicized agreement to ban the words "Mafia" and "Cosa Nostra" was the most celebrated example of the bureau's eagerness to please everybody, but there were many others. Cartha DeLoach, the assistant director in charge of Crime Records, who was responsible for creating "The F.B.I.," claimed that Hoover ordered him seven times to cancel the show because of some ammunition it had given his enemies. "Each time I had to write a memo defending it." Hoover's timidity during his last years was the despair of DeLoach and other FBI brass who wanted to use aggressive public relations to keep the FBI at the head of the American law enforcement pack. "After a while Hoover lost his sense of daring," DeLoach recalled. "He would only go for sure winners. No longer was he creating an image for the Bureau, but only maintaining it."[33]

The timidity of detail in "The F.B.I." was less debilitating than the timidity of the show's overall format, which insulated the program from having any real impact on public opinion, probably out of fear of furnishing ammunition to the bureau's political enemies. Superficially "The F.B.I." seemed to be using the same action detective formula that the bureau had ridden to glory during the 1930s, but actually the show's formula was fundamentally different. The G-Man adventures of the thirties had taken the action detective of stage, screen, and pulp magazines—young, handsome, brash, brainy, and brawny—had smartened him up a bit, quieted him down a little, and had turned him into the legman for the FBI team. The G-Man had been different from other detective heroes in that he spent less time with girls, more time on the phone to Washington. He had also been more impressive than his private eye pals because he had the whole FBI organization, with all its files, labs, and machine gun ranges, backing him up. But what really set the G-Man apart from other adventure show detectives was the kind of crimes he solved, and what it was supposed to mean when he solved them.

G-Man adventures during the thirties had taken the action detective formula and had given it political significance. In the FBI's adventure programs of the thirties, the bureau entered cases because of a breakdown of local law enforcement. The criminals they chased were public enemies, national symbols of crime who had ignited public hysteria symbolized in the movies by mass protest meetings and montages of scare newspaper headlines. The G-Man was no ordinary detective: he was the embodiment of public wrath, symbol of the national determination to bring crime under control. The FBI offered its investigations as samples of what all law enforcement could be like if the nation's police accepted FBI leadership and coordination, and if an aroused public opinion cleaned up corrupt political interference with justice and supported professionalization of the police.

Hoover had crammed official FBI entertainment of the thirties full of propaganda supporting the New Deal's anticrime program, but G-Man entertainment of those years, despite all the "educational" content, was still basically a ritual of crime and punishment. Hoover simply made sure that when the crook went to his inevitable doom, the audience understood that justice had been done, but only because of the innovative methods the bureau had brought to crime fighting. The crime and punishment formula was an integral part of thirties G-Man entertainment because unless the FBI method was regularly field tested against important crooks, the public would have had no proof that it really worked.

In sharp contrast to the clear-cut political implications of thirties FBI entertainment, Inspector Erskine's adventures were securely contained within the fictive world of the television screen. Television's FBI was no longer a gangbusting outfit leading a national crusade against crime. It was another version of Chip Hardesty's family, with an off-screen patriarch ("The Director") and an on-screen father figure (Efrem Zimbalist, Jr.) with his surrogate family (Philip Abbott as Assistant Director Ward and William Reynolds as Special Agent Colby). Each week their smooth office routine of paper shuffling and chitchat about wives and kids was interrupted by a crisis in the form of a crime, and then the team pulled together to get things back to normal. No longer were the G-Men shooting it out with thinly fictionalized gangsters based on notorious real-life public enemies. Gone was the pervading sense of national crisis, the electric atmosphere of anticrime hysteria. Vanished too was the drama of epic conflict between public symbols of good and evil, the evangelical atmosphere of an FBI-led revival of American law enforce-

ment. The crimes the television G-Men solved were merely formal violations of the law with none of the meaty entanglements with contemporary headlines that had made the old-time G-Men dramas resonate
between fact and fantasy. In comparison with the G-Men of the thirties
and forties, Special Agent Chip Hardesty and Inspector Erskine were
symbols of the status quo, not a new America-in-the-making.

A skeleton of the old action-detective formula remained in *The F.B.I.
Story* and "The F.B.I.," but a new set of conventions had been superim-
posed on it. This was the domestic formula, a concoction with two
main ingredients—a warm, secure family group and an intrusion from
the outside that disrupted it. The characters' emotional energies (intellectual interests, too, if they had any) were directed inwards toward
other members of the family circle; the world outside was simply a
source of troubles, funny troubles for families like Lucy's and the Nel-
sons, more frightening ones for families in soap operas and "The F.B.I."
This domestic formula is perfectly suited to an audience whose interests
are overwhelmingly private in orientation, an audience that has turned
away from public affairs to immerse itself in the drama of private life.
Its bias is fundamentally apolitical or even antipolitical.

When westerns and detective stories were combined with the domestic formula they were, so far as social bite is concerned, defanged. The
classic cowboy stories gave America a myth of national origins that
demonstrated, as the Virginian said at the end of Owen Wister's epic,
how the nation had turned virgin land into "a whole lot more United
States." Even the most juvenile horse operas showed kids how cowboy
heroes brought law and order to the Wild West. The detective story,
too, made its social statement with its picture of society as the scene of
eternal warfare between the law-abiding and the lawbreakers. Even
when served up as pure escapism, then, the Western and detective formulas had rubbed up against tender spots on the national psyche.

During the fifties and sixties the crime show and the western were
brought up to date by having the domestic formula laid over them.
Sometimes the hero was given a real family ("Bonanza," "MacMillan
and Wife") but more often he had a surrogate family like Inspector
Erskine's, composed of friends and fellow cops ("Gunsmoke," "The
Mod Squad," "Ironside"). Sheriffs still had their showdowns with the
bad guys, cops still chased their crooks, but now these were merely
intrusions from the outside world that disturbed, only to clarify and
strengthen, the bonds between friends in a continuing drama of private
relationships. The domestic formula shifted the audience's attention
away from the work the FBI, as a symbol of the law, did in pacifying
society and reforming law enforcement to agents' behavior as ordinary
human beings: decent, moral, well-behaved—paragons of private, not
civic, virtue.

The FBI did not junk its old (and highly productive) entertainment formula for a new one just because of a shift in popular tastes, though the fifties' "togetherness" ideal may have encouraged producers like Mervyn LeRoy and Quinn Martin to trade in the bureau's old motto (Fidelity, Bravery, and Integrity) for *Kinder, Kirche,* and *Kuche.* Nor is the elderly Hoover's sentimentalization of the bureau as the family he never had a sufficient explanation for the change, though his petulant requirement that his birthdays and anniversaries be marked by gifts and ceremonies suggest he did see himself as patriarch of the special agent clan. The reason the FBI changed its entertainment formula in mid-century was that the only man who counted, J. Edgar Hoover, had changed his mind about what was wrong with the country and what had to be done to save it.

FBI entertainment was never intended exclusively as advertising for the bureau, although with its professed goals of recruiting new agents and encouraging the public to cooperate with G-Men in the field and to believe them in the witness box, it was advertising. J. Edgar Hoover encouraged mass media G-Man adventures because entertainment had an assigned role in the program he had mapped out for himself and the FBI. The public interpreted G-Man entertainment of the thirties in the light of the New Deal's anticrime program. FBI entertainment of the fifties and sixties has to be interpreted as expressing a point of view that Hoover was stating more explicitly in his public addresses and writings during those decades. Hoover abandoned the G-Man formula of the thirties because, in the light of his new analysis of what the country needed during the fifties, it had become irrelevant. This change in Hoover's thinking is obvious when his speeches of the thirties are compared to those of the fifties.

"Our country depends on the majesty of our laws," Hoover would say during the thirties. The fundamental cause of crime was "disrespect for the law." The public had lost respect for the law because, time and time again, it had seen that crime paid. The answer to crime was to prove that crime did not pay through dramatic action that everyone, young and old, literate and illiterate, could understand.[34] "Until the criminally-minded person . . . can be taught the inexorable lesson that he cannot get away with violating the laws of society without adequate punishment—until that day arrives, just so long will you have the constant menace of serious crime."[35]

Crime paid, Hoover insisted, because corrupt politics bred corrupt law enforcement, directly through political fixes of criminal investigations, indirectly by keeping policemen poorly educated and equipped. "Rid America of the renegade politician and you rid America of crime, for he is the ally of crime; he is the torchbearer of crime. Rid America of the venal politician and we become a free nation."[36] With all the force of a syllogism, then, the next step of Hoover's argument was that public opinion had to be aroused against crime, because only when the public apathy that tolerated corrupt politics and inefficient law enforcement was ended would the country be rid of the "renegade politician." "Crime will continue to increase until public sentiment crushes crime and public sentiment cannot crush crime until a public consciousness is aroused against all forms of crime."[37] Since G-Man entertainment helped raise the public consciousness, then, Hollywood and the pulp industry were doing the Lord's work as well as making money when they glorified the FBI. "Here is a holy cause," he intoned. "To combat crime there must be a constantly growing band of missionaries who shall go into the highways and byways carrying with them the fearlessness and the crusading spirit so badly needed in a hand-to-hand combat with a predatory beast. Its name is CRIME!"[38]

At this point Hoover would usually provide illustrations of how the FBI was forging new weapons to help win the crusade against crooks. Sometimes he would give his audience a peek into the mysteries of fingerprinting or of tear gas. Other times he would paint a glowing picture of the new gospel of police professionalism: "The primary purpose of the F.B.I. National Police Academy is to train selected officers in order that they may return to their respective police organizations and impart the training received at Washington, D.C., to the members of their local departments. . . . Certainly, here is the forerunner of a new day in law enforcement."[39]

Hoover was a thoroughgoing traditionalist and moralist, and so his speeches during the thirties were also filled with references to the need for moral education—in the home, church, and school—as an essential part of the anticrime campaign. Like the other New Deal warriors in the NRA and CCC, he appealed to flag and country to rally the public to his crusade. But even when he was preaching about personal values and morals, he argued that these were strengthened or weakened by the government's ability to uphold the law. Hoover's emphasis during the thirties was always on the bureau's militantly political goals. He labored to show that the FBI was building an institutional framework that would permit the nation to act effectively against crime.

Hoover's theory of crime fighting as a public crusade was what gave the FBI dramas of the 1930s their political impact. G-Man adventures took Hoover's ideas, decked them out in blood and guts, and set them out in a form that could be painlessly absorbed into national consciousness. This made G-Man entertainment part of the public political life of the thirties.

During the fifties and sixties the FBI's institutional structure was far more impressive than it had been during the thirties. The bureau itself had vastly expanded; the National Police Academy had its FBI-indoctrinated graduates in every major police force in the country, often as chiefs or other high-ranking officers, since the Academy diploma was a valuable aid to promotion. The FBI had become the power behind the scenes in the International Association of Chiefs of Police and the American Legion, while Hoover himself had crushed all serious rivals to his position as symbolic leader of American law and order.[40]

In speeches during his last twenty years Hoover dutifully ran through the statistics that proved the bureau's sterling performance, just as he had ever since he had taken over the FBI, but his heart was no longer in his obligatory lobbying for the bureau's annual appropriations. He began warming up when he got to flaying sob-sister parole officers, revolving-door courts, and the procedural labyrinths built by civil libertarians, pseudo-liberals, convict-lovers, and other heathens. But his rhetoric finally got red-hot only when he reached the cause that had become a crusade for Hoover during his last years—the moral reform of America.

Hoover's speeches and books towards the end were more like revivalists' sermons than reports by the country's top cop. A typical speech saw him slide into his subject by saying that "today, there are too many signs that Americans, as individuals, are pursuing the deadly course of irresponsibility which has led to the downfall of other nations and other cultures throughout the history of mankind."[41] Then he would catalogue the nation's slide into degeneracy: "Americans, in growing numbers, are developing a dangerously indulgent attitude toward crime, filth, and corruption. No one can deny that motion pictures are deliberately and defiantly pursuing an increasingly bold courtship with obscenity. No one can deny the role of the television industry in bringing lurid portrayals of violence and sadism into the living rooms—and even the nurseries—of our homes. No one can deny that sensual trash is moving closer and closer to children's books on the shelves of our newsstands and magazine stores."[42] Then the director would call America back to the old-time traditions and values: "Here and abroad, mortal enemies of freedom and deniers of God Himself conspire to undermine the fundamental forces which are the lifeline of our country's vitality and greatness, our most formidable weapons, in peace and war. . . . These are America's great bulwarks. They are under savage attack today, just as they were so severely tested nearly 200 years ago at Bunker Hill and at Valley Forge."[43]

Even when Hoover addressed professional law enforcement groups, his rhetorical climax tended to be a call for moral reform. In 1967 he told the Regional Conference on Crime Prevention of the Michigan Bar Association that "the flames of freedom . . . have been fed by the spiritual fuel which abounds only in a land where an abiding faith in God and recognition of Him as the true Author of Liberty prevail. America is strong because she is good. That strength and goodness stem from the

Boys and Girls
COLOR THE PICTURE AND MEMORIZE THE RULES

FOR YOUR PROTECTION, REMEMBER TO:

- Turn down gifts from strangers
- Refuse rides offered by strangers
- Avoid dark and lonely streets
- Know your local policeman

Federal Bureau of Investigation
United States Department of Justice

Top: A coloring sheet distributed by the bureau in the seventies.

Below: An FBI-endorsed board game of the seventies.

presence of God in all areas of national life. . . . The laws of Moses must remain . . . our National Creed."[44]

During the thirties Hoover's message was that modernized law enforcement would be able to save the country through science and institutional reforms like the FBI's National Police Academy. During the fifties and sixties Hoover no longer promised that tinkering with the law enforcement machinery would be enough: "Suppose every American," he wrote in 1958 in *Masters of Deceit* "spent a little time each day . . . studying the Bible and the basic documents of American history, government and culture? The result would be a new America, vigilant, strong, but ever humble in the service of God. . . . I thrill to think of the even greater wonders America could fashion from its rich, glorious, and deep tradition. All we need is faith, real faith."[45] The nation's number one G-Man had dropped his machine gun and picked up the cross. "Shall I make my child go to Sunday School and church?" he asked in an article in *American Mercury*. "Tell him, 'Junior, in our house we all go to church and Sunday School, and that includes you.' . . . The parents of America can strike a telling blow against the forces which contribute to our juvenile delinquency, if our mothers and fathers will take their children to Sunday School and church regularly."[46]

Hoover's shift from police professionalism and the national anticrime crusade to moral redemption as the cure for America's ills had made the action detective aspect of the G-Man formula unsuitable as a projection of his program. If faith and family solidarity were the answers, then the moral of the FBI message was getting the kids to eat their breakfast before they went off to school, and not shooting down John Dillinger and Pretty Boy Floyd. The message was contained in Inspector Erskine's unfailing politeness and decency in spite of provocation, and not in the number of "would-be crime czars" he put behind bars.

Entertainment formulas, of course, are not the whole answer to the FBI's rise and fall, but the bureau's public image always towered over its modest actual presence on the national scene (it still has only 7,800 special agents), and formula entertainment had an important part in building that image. It was the public's belief that the G-Men were the shock troops in a national crime crusade that had lifted the bureau above the level of ordinary political institutions, and the action detective version of the G-Man formula had helped create that perception.

During the fifties and sixties the FBI's reputation was no longer getting the constant puffs of official self-promotion that had kept it inflated over the years. J. Edgar Hoover's attention had shifted to higher concerns than gangbusting. Hoover's rhetoric, which overshadowed all rival crime-control theories during his lifetime, no longer used the institution of the FBI as a symbol of how the nation would be saved, and he no longer dramatized the bureau's big cases as symbols of the country's war against evil. The domestic version of the G-Man formula was an accurate reflection of the old director's new gospel, but it stripped the FBI of its dramatic symbolism of old as the one institution that stood between the nation and ruin. The domestic formula stressed the G-Man's private role as the embodiment of the ordinary decencies—defender of the faith, not public defender. It made a virtue out of ordinariness and left the FBI an ordinary institution, vulnerable as all ordinary institutions are to criticism, attack, and—worst of all—evaluation on the basis of performance, not political symbolism.

This new Bible-quoting choirboy image of the G-Man was actually a time bomb within the FBI's defenses. The old G-Man had been invulnerable—and so he helped keep the real FBI protected against criticism. As long as the G-Man was preeminently a man of action, only defeat on the field of battle could have discredited him. The conventions of American popular culture make it essentially irrelevant whether an action hero smokes, spits, or swears—as long as he gets the job done. Advertise the G-Man as a saint, however, and he can no longer redeem himself through action. He becomes vulnerable to every rumor of corruption. If the slightest whisper of immorality is proven true he is mortally wounded. His respectability is then transformed to hypocrisy, his moral message into sanctimoniousness.

By turning the G-Man into a symbol of morality Hoover made the bureau vulnerable to precisely the kind of allegations that began to surface during the 1960s. The old G-Man had never claimed to be a saint; if he were caught taking a shortcut around the Bill of Rights he could always redeem himself by catching another crook or smashing another spy ring. This sort of rebuttal was not available to the new G-man. The domesticated G-Man based his claim to popular respect on his righteousness, and so, according to the unforgiving logic of popular culture, with the first stain on his cloak of moral perfection he forfeited that claim.

13

Today's FBI

On October 25, 1981, eight years after Efrem Zimbalist's "The F.B.I." left the air, the bureau launched a new officially sanctioned prime-time show, "Today's FBI," with "a new breed of dedicated, young F.B.I. agents . . . fighting today's crime with tomorrow's weapons!"[1] In those eight years much had happened—to the country, to the FBI, and to the pop culture G-Man. There had been Watergate, the resignation of a president, and a blue-ribbon inquiry into government abuses of civil liberties. Also occurring during these years were the forced resignation of an acting FBI director; indictments and convictions of top FBI officials for Hoover-era illegalities; a series of self-effacing, almost invisible directors; and total rejection by the public of Hoover's carefully nurtured FBI legend. To put it bluntly, the G-Man was defunct. He had been fatally wounded by mid-1975, dead by the end of that year. The G-Man's reputation as the country's gangbuster and spysmasher was buried and all but forgotten. The FBI's pop culture image was now that of the phone tapper, the bedroom bugger, the blackmailer; the scandal monger, the racist, the character assassin; the poisoner of the well of intellectual and political freedom.

J. Edgar Hoover often feuded with popular culture over the bureau's pop image, but he had always been able to count on the public's overwhelmingly favorable attitude towards the bureau as a foundation for his attempts to manipulate public opinion. He never had to operate in the face of a public hostile towards the bureau and its mission. So what kind of G-Man did the bureau send out in 1981 to confront this unprecedentedly unsympathetic audience?

The show, canceled before the start of the 1982 season, betrayed a self-conscious awareness that it was skating on thin ice. Producer David

"Today's F.B.I." premiered on October 25, 1981.

William Webster hoped Mike Connors would be able to do for his image what Cagney and Zimbalist had done for Hoover's.

Gerber's G-Men, led by police drama veteran Mike Connors ("Mannix"), were careful to explain, justify, and apologize for every move they made, as though there were a posse of ACLU lawyers, PTA fussbudgets, and the editorial board of the *Nation* lurking just out of camera range, ready to push the "abort" button the first time an agent bumped into the Bill of Rights. When these newest G-Men bugged a child pornographer, they not only procured a warrant, but they referred to it every time the scene changed to make sure that anyone who tuned in late knew the FBI was clean. When an agent laid violent hands on a suspect, he got a letter of censure from Connors, no matter how much it pained him. The bureau evidently went through the show's scripts with scrupulous attention to anticipate any possible objections of the most punctilious civil libertarian.

The same kind of acute sensitivity to potential criticism and past complaints about the bureau explains the most remarked-upon novelties of the new series. "Today's FBI" did not simply staff its ranks with the usual roll call of ethnic and sexual minorities. It proceeded to use the raised consciousnesses of its women, its blacks, and its ethnics (there seemed to be no G-Gays) as a source of plot complications no less important than the basic routine of crime and punishment. The "Today's FBI" team of special agents included the Mediterranean-looking Joseph Cali, country-boy Richard Hill, a black, played by Harold Sylvester, and probably the most notable departure from the old FBI show, a female agent played by Carol Potter. The show was careful to stress the bureau's pluralism because it was trying to refute the stock (and accurate) charge that the bureau is an enclave of white male Christians.

"Today's FBI" made full use of the melting pot quality of its cast—Joe Cali ran into problems on cases by getting too emotionally involved, identifying with the sympathetic crooks and persecuting the more villainous ones. Carol Potter and other female agents agonized over their problems in trying to "have it all"—an exciting career and a family. The black agent complained that the bureau let criminals inflict more brutality on him on undercover assignments than it would permit white agents to suffer.

When the show's G-Men were not citing the legal sources of their jurisdiction or worrying about the problems of being black or female in the new FBI, they were tousling each other's hair, slapping each other on the back, squeezing each other's arms, and giving each other brotherly (or sisterly) hugs—the encounter-group generation playing cops and robbers. The new breed of G-Man was a human being, with his heart, psyche, and demographic status on his sleeve. These agents never stopped explaining their feelings or trying to understand one another's problems (as women, blacks, or mixed up G-Men). They were human beings first, agents second. Richard Hill would give Harold Sylvester a comforting hug after Sylvester was beaten up on an undercover assignment. Connors, acting on the advice of the psychologically-oriented Carol Potter, would pull the overly-emotional Joseph Cali off assignments when he got too involved: once when he started to see the world through the eyes of the Godfather-style crime family he had infiltrated; another time when his hatred for a ring of child pornographers edged him towards a violation of civil liberties. The drama in each episode grew out of the tension between the agents' instinctive reactions as ordinary people and their obligatory behavior as professional federal agents.

The bureau evidently considered the new G-Man's emotional openness a major selling point for the show, and also hoped that the public would react to its breathless revelation of this new FBI style as though it were a daring exposé that G-Men are human, too. "It's not the old F.B.I.," one of the stars told an interviewer. "The original series was very cut and dry: there were good guys and bad guys and they were easy to tell apart. This series is not intended to be a whitewash of the Bureau. 'Today's F.B.I.' will try to depict the genuine article—real agents facing complex and dangerous situations as both law enforcers and human beings."[2] According to Mike Connors, "Dave Gerber [the show's producer] told A.B.C. that he wasn't interested in putting on the program unless they could show the warts and blemishes as well as the good side of the F.B.I."[3] Evidently the agents' emotional outbursts were what he meant by "warts and blemishes."

"Today's F.B.I." agents also made a point of humbling themselves before the local cops. They never pulled rank on the locals. In fact, they emphasized that they were only assisting and were quick to defer to the locals' expertise when on their turf. Once when the agents locked themselves out of their car, they even called the city police for help.

The intensity of the relationships between the agents was the most noticeable feature of "Today's F.B.I.," obscuring the production quality and acting, which were clearly superior to the general run of television action entertainment.[4] Actually the group therapy element of Connor's FBI was a logical extension of the FBI "family" atmosphere that permeated the old show. The difference was that while the new show also stressed Connor's fatherly relationship with his agents, he was, in keeping with the times, more concerned with developing their awareness of themselves as autonomous individuals instead of submerging their personalities within the organization. "Today's F.B.I." was an uncritical participant in the culture of narcissism, which meant that agents had to find (and express at tedious length) justifications for themselves whenever they had to sacrifice their individual desires to group-oriented goals.

The show's producers were also conscientious in making sure their plots dealt with the day's most pressing crime concerns: labor racketeering, organized crime, child pornography, defense industry spying, civil rights, airplane hijacking, and lunatic religious cults. They even provided the kind of sexual titillation that would have been unthinkable on the old show—Connors once encouraged a scientist to have an affair with a beautiful blonde who had promised to be very nice to him if he gave her some defense secrets from his firm. The scientist fell in with Connors' scheme with gusto. Yet even with the professionalism of the production, the overall attention to detail, the generally fine acting, and favorable critical reaction, the show did not find a receptive audience.[5]

The show languished near the bottom of the ratings, during 1981 and 1982, doing particularly poorly in the 8:00 P.M. Sunday slot against its competition, "Archie Bunker's Place" (CBS) and "CHiPs" (NBC). After a few weeks of being battered by the competition, ABC began preempting the show regularly with movies and special events, using the show to fill in the gaps late in the evening, a move that suggested the network had given up on the program, since this was a sure strategy for losing whatever audience the show might have acquired. Halfway through the season word began to circulate that the show was being canceled, and when the 1982 season premiered, "Today's F.B.I." was yesterday's memory.

Viewers were perplexed by the show; they were confused by the lack of "action" (violence), by what appeared to be the forced and overdone camaraderie of the agents, by the sensitivity the agents showed for the feelings of local cops. Viewers were impatient with the show's laborious footnoting of the FBI's legal jurisdiction and the legality of its proce-

The calculatedly balanced cast of "Today's F.B.I.": from left to right, Joseph Cali, Mike Connors, Carol Potter, Harold Sylvester, and Richard Hill.

dures. But underlying all this dissatisfaction was the fact that viewers were simply not interested in what the show was trying to say.

The show actually operated on the same assumptions that had guided the old FBI show: that the public's attitude towards the FBI was overwhelmingly favorable, and that the bureau could rely on the public's involvement in the myth of the G-Man to hold the audience's attention while the bureau used the show to peddle Hoover's latest ideas. Thus the audience had hardly minded, though it probably did not pay much attention to, Hoover's use of "The F.B.I." to refute liberals' standard criticism of the bureau on matters of civil liberties and legal jurisdiction and his use of the show to promote Zimbalist's bureau as a symbol of patriotic Americanism.

"Today's F.B.I." updated its format, but it assumed that the public was still under the spell of the old G-Man myth, that the show could still count on a pre-sold audience that needed, at the most, to be reassured that the bureau is fair, contemporary, and humane. Unfortunately, the world is now a cold and unfriendly place for the pop culture G-Man.

What is the pop culture image of the FBI these days? To put it bluntly, it is an unmitigated disaster. Where the old FBI had been pop culture's defender of the nation, its spysmasher and gangbuster, the seventies had turned it into its prime symbol of a government at war with the nation's liberties. That had always been the counterculture's idea of the bureau, but during the seventies the general public also had swung over to that view. The G-Man began turning up as the villain in mainstream mass market movies, television, and the seventies version of the old pulp magazines, thrillers by writers like Irving Wallace and Robert Ludlum.

In the pulps of the thirties the FBI had been all that stood between the nation and criminals bent on taking it over. In Wallace's *R Document* of 1976, the *FBI* is the criminal conspiracy, and the FBI director himself the pulp villain, "the most dangerous individual on earth," who has to be defeated if the nation is to be saved. The director, an undisguised stand-in for J. Edgar Hoover, is plotting to manipulate the nation's fear of crime to permit a suspension of the Constitution. This will put him in charge of a "Committee on National Safety" that will rule the country by decree.

Wallace's FBI director is Vernon Tynan. Tynan is—and is not—J. Edgar Hoover. He is one of Hoover's protégés, who had left the bureau after Hoover's death rather than serve under Hoover's successors, only to be called out of retirement to take over the bureau. Tynan is modeled so closely after Hoover—the same "hooded eyes," "bulldog features," stocky build, the same rumors about an "unnatural relationship" with his inseparable associate director (meaning Clyde Tolson)—that Wallace is able to use the seventies' popular stereotype of Hoover to flesh out the characterization of his novel's demon director.

And he is a demon. He uses a call girl to blackmail the attorney general, who is an opponent of the proposed Thirty-fifth Amendment that will put the director in charge of the government. He plans the assassination of the president to create an emergency he can use to take power under this Thirty-fifth Amendment. He sets up concentration camps to hold the dissenters he intends to round up after he takes over.

All this would have been incredible, even by the tolerant standards of Irving Wallace's readers, had Wallace not been able to count on his readers' prior acceptance of popular culture's new devil theory about Hoover and the FBI, a theory that had become conventional wisdom by the time Wallace wrote his thriller. Wallace obviously did not feel that he had to fear stepping on the toes of any great number of Hoover's admirers. He portrays Tynan's capacity and appetite for evil as utterly superhuman. "Tynan is everywhere," a renegade FBI agent explains. "He picked up where J. Edgar Hoover left off. Remember Hoover's OC—Official and Confidential—files? Hoover had his gumshoes getting information on Muhammad Ali, Jane Fonda, Dr. Benjamin Spock, and at least seventeen high Government officials, Congressmen, newspapermen."[6]

Every time Wallace exposes another of Director Tynan's atrocities—the murder of the chief justice, for example—he silences any disbelief by comparing the crime to one of J. Edgar Hoover's alleged horrors. One scene seems intended to demolish the last illusions of Hoover's die-hard fans, if there were still any left. For the benefit of a ghostwriter hired to compose his biography, Tynan draws up a list of J. Edgar Hoover's achievements:

It was J. Edgar Hoover who introduced professionalism into law enforcement. He got rid of the Keystone Cop image . . . and he made the public respect us. . . . Just think of what J. Edgar Hoover did. . . . He nailed John Dillinger, Pretty Boy Floyd, Alvin Karpis, Machine Gun Kelly, Baby Face Nelson, Ma Barker, Bruno Hauptmann, the eight Nazi saboteurs who landed from submarines, Julius and Ethel Rosenberg, Klaus Fuchs, the Brinks' robbers, James Earl Ray—the list is a mile long. "Ten miles long," the ghost writer silently added.

He thought of the triumphs Tynan had conveniently left out. For most of his career Hoover had conveniently ignored the Mafia, refusing to believe in its existence. Not until 1963, when Valachi decided to talk, did Hoover recognize organized crime. Singed by this evidence of the Mafia, Hoover never referred to it by that name, preferring the euphemism La Cosa Nostra instead. Apologists would claim that the Old Man had ignored the Mafia because he was afraid that the underworld might bribe and corrupt his agents as they had the local police, and thereby ruin his scandal-free reputation. Cynics would insist he avoided the crime syndicate because investigations would take so long that they might lower his crime-statistics batting average. . . .

Hoover had called Dr. Martin Luther King, Jr., a notorious liar and had wiretapped his telephone to record details of his sex life. Hoover had called former Attorney General Ramsey Clark a jellyfish. Hoover had called Father Berrigan and other Roman Catholic antiwar activists kidnappers and conspirators before their cases had been presented to the grand jury. Hoover had slurred Puerto Ricans and Mexicans, insisting people of those two nationalities couldn't shoot straight. Hoover had bugged Congressmen, as well as nonviolent civil rights and antiwar protestors. He had even investigated a fourteen-year-old Pennsylvania boy who had wanted to go to summer camp in East Germany and an Idaho scout master who had wanted to take his troop camping in Russia.

[The writer] recalled a column by Pete Hamill that he had read. "There was no single worse subversive in this country in the past thirty years than J. Edgar Hoover. This man subverted our faith in ourselves, our belief in an open society, our hopes that men and women could live in a country free of secret police, of hidden surveillance, or persecution for political ideas."[7]

In 1937 it would have been hard to find a man in America more universally admired than J. Edgar Hoover; forty years later his reputation had totally collapsed. Whatever good he may have done was buried beneath the rubble of his ruined image. In the thirties Hoover was the hero who had come to save the public from the underworld enemies who were fastening their grip on the nation's vitals. In the seventies Hoover was a symbol of the invisible government whose tentacles were popularly supposed to be on the verge of strangling the few remaining free institutions in America. His G-Men now were symbolic villains who threatened the nation in the pages of pulp novels and on the movie screen.

Another highly successful thriller writer with a firm grasp on the public's fears and fantasies is Robert Ludlum. Ludlum equips his heroes with everything they need to succeed as fantasy figures for the upwardly aspiring middle class. They know about wines, good clothes, the best cars and stereos; they succeed at anything they attempt: writing a best seller, bedding down with a nationally famous newswoman, or outwitting and outfighting the CIA, FBI and KGB. His heroes also have self-confident opinions on the whole spectrum of current events and mores, always proffered in a way that implies that no reader with any pretensions to intelligence could possibly disagree. In Ludlum's hands the thriller formula becomes a veritable manual of style, instructing the reader on the attitude one ought to maintain towards any issue of current debate. Bach, Picasso, law and order, the Bill of Rights, Vietnam, or Danish modern furniture—all seem to cause anxiety in Ludlum's readers, so his heroes have to demonstrate the latest fashions in manners and ideas even while they thwart conspiracies against the commonweal. Ludlum's action detectives are arbiters of elegance as well as hard-boiled heroes. Ludlum and Wallace devote so many pages to opinions of their heroes on the major questions of the day because these writers think their readers identify with their heroes largely on the basis of the characters' political and cultural attitudes. In the mid-seventies, one of the opinions Ludlum and Wallace expected their readers to share with their heroes was a profoundly negative attitude towards Hoover and the Bureau.

Ludlum's 1977 thriller *The Chancellor Manuscript* revolves around a luridly imagined struggle to control J. Edgar Hoover's "blackmail files" immediately after his death in 1972. In Ludlum's story Hoover is assassinated by an ultrasecret power elite dedicated to "guiding" the nation when the pressures of democratic politics become too much for the public to bear. The villain of the story is a renegade member of this elite who intends to use the files to "make the system work" for disenfranchised blacks. The complexity of this plot and the difficulties of exposing it are incredibly convoluted—Ludlum has many faults as a writer but lack of invention is not one of them. *The Chancellor Manuscript*'s hero, who is a Ludlum-like writer of best-selling thrillers (his work in progress seems to be *The Chancellor Manuscript* itself) has many opportunities to instruct the reader on the scope of J. Edgar Hoover's sins: "senators and congressmen and cabinet members [were] made to toe the Hoover line or face the Hoover wrath, . . . Hoover's actions following the assassinations of both Kennedy and Martin Luther King [were disgraceful]. . . . The press is convinced he withheld damaging information from the Warren Commission. God knows how devastating it was; it might have altered the judgements at Dallas and Los Angeles, and Memphis. . . . Hoover's use of electronic and telephone surveillance . . . was worthy of the gestapo. No one had been sacrosanct; enemies and potential enemies had been held at bay. Tapes had been spliced and edited; guilt had come by remote association, innuendo, hearsay, and manufactured evidence."[8] The premise of the writer-hero of Ludlum's novel is that Hoover's blackmail files not only existed, but that he had used them, "systematically making contact with scores of subjects he believe[d] are in opposition to policies he favors, threatening to expose their private weaknesses if they do not retreat from their position."[9] The hero intends to use his book to expose Hoover as "a dangerous megalomaniac who should have been forced from office twenty years ago. A master whose tactics were more in tune with the policies of the Third Reich than those of a democratic society. I want people to be outraged by *J. Edgar Hoover's* manipulations."[10]

The unbridgeable distance between the G-Men C. K. M. Scanlon wrote about in thirties pulps and the FBI of Irving Wallace and Robert Ludlum cannot be explained merely as stemming from the differing political convictions of individual writers. Popular writers on Wallace's and Ludlum's level do not really have political convictions. They simply give the public back its own stereotypes with the dark tones blackened and the light tones whitened to create a melodramatic contrast between absolute good and evil. Popular fiction does not risk tampering with the public's sense of "what is." Pulp writers accept the popular wisdom and manipulate it to suit the conventions of formula entertainment. Writers like Wallace, Ludlum, and the staffs of the adventure pulps know their audiences. If they think that their audience worships the FBI, it is very strong evidence that the public, at least the greater part of it, actually does love the bureau. If they assume that the public now believes Hoover was a monster, then it may safely be assumed that the popular audience has in fact concluded that the late director actually was the kind of monster Wallace and Ludlum claim he was.

And just as the 1930s' glorification of the G-Man pervaded all the pop culture media, so did the vilification of Hoover and his FBI during the late seventies. In *Dog Day Afternoon*, for instance, the by-the-rulebook insensitivity of FBI agents made them, and not the film's flaky (and therefore human) crooks the heavies of the picture.

By the time "The F.B.I." went off the air in 1974, Hoover had been dead for two years (he died May 2, 1972) and the bureau's reputation, a reputation Hoover had built and guarded with fanatical vigilance during his forty-eight-year tenure, was in shambles. According to the Gallup pollsters, in 1965 nearly all Americans, 84 percent, gave the bureau a "highly favorable" rating. In 1970 the percentage was down to 71 percent, and in August, 1973, it had plummeted to 52 percent. To a certain extent, the bureau's slide simply paralleled a similar decline in the prestige of all establishment symbols (at each stage the polls reported that the public had more respect for the FBI than the military or the CIA, and about the same rating as for the local police). But for an organization that had devoted so much of its energy over the years to building a public image, and whose primary function, law enforcement leadership, depended on its standing with the public, this decline was particularly disastrous. In 1971 a poll conducted by a group friendly to Hoover and the FBI discovered that the tendency of American youth to identify with the FBI, always an important objective of the bureau's publicity, had almost disappeared: only 22 percent of the young respondents said they would like to be FBI agents; 69 percent said they would not.[11]

It would be plausible to blame this collapse in the bureau's reputation on the monotonous series of public relations disasters that occurred after Hoover's death, unrelieved by any compensating favorable achievements. The bureau's reputation reached its nadir during the Watergate investigations when L. Patrick Gray, Hoover's successor as head of the FBI (with the rank of acting director), admitted that he had burned documents Watergate burglar Howard Hunt had forged about President Kennedy's involvement in the assassination of South Vietnamese President Diem. At the same time it also became clear that John Dean had turned the acting director and the entire FBI into patsies during the Watergate cover-up. With the bureau's credibility in the eyes of the media and the public in tatters, the bureau was defenseless as devastating revelation followed devastating revelation: financial improprieties by high FBI officials, blunders during the assassination investigations, and in 1975 headlines about the most astounding story of all—Hoover's maniacal attempt to destroy Martin Luther King as a public figure and to drive him to suicide. In the end Hoover and the FBI had hardly a defender left.

A rout of these proportions never occurs all at once, and in retrospect the cracks and flaws that permitted the collapse of the G-Man image during the seventies were all too apparent. There was J. Edgar Hoover's news conference in December, 1964, when he called Martin Luther King, soon to be awarded the Nobel Prize, the "most notorious liar in America."[12] Not until later would the story of Hoover's war against King be fully documented, but Hoover's public stand against King for the first time pitted the FBI director not just against outcasts from the American consensus but against the millions of mainstream Americans who regarded the civil rights movement as a moral crusade and Martin Luther King as the keeper of the American conscience.

As the sixties wore on, Hoover, whose strength had always been his sure sense of the American moral consensus, seemed to lose his bearings as the government's Vietnam policy destroyed that consensus. The younger generation, at least the not inconsiderable portion which opposed the war, began to look upon the FBI, which was spearheading the government's efforts to enforce the draft laws and curtail the antiwar movement, as the country's preeminent symbol of oppressive authority. Hoover's tactics against the antiwar movement also made him a figure of dread to the student protesters' parents.

The elderly Hoover's inability to identify with the young led to public relations fiascoes that widened the gulf between the bureau and the younger generation. By the end, Hoover was no longer even trying to reach the young directly with stories about "the adventure of scientific law enforcement." Now he was sounding the alarm to older Americans about horrible goings-on in high schools and colleges, forgetting that the surest way to alienate a parent is to criticize his child.

One example of Hoover's ham-handed public relations style towards the end of his career was a pair of articles about the SDS that he published in *The P.T.A. Magazine* early in 1970.[13] Subtitled "A Study in Student Extremism," the articles did not confine themselves to the predictable exposé of "the extremist minority [which], though influential, represents only a numerical few of our young people."[14] At a time when vast numbers of young Americans were intensely involved in politics, whether they supported or opposed the Vietnam war, Hoover seemed to be questioning the loyalty of any student whose interests extended past campus affairs. "The vast majority," he wrote, "couldn't care less for slogans about fighting 'imperialism' and 'warmongers.' Many, it is true, are concerned about national issues such as the war in Vietnam, but in reality it is the immediate, at-hand issues inside the schools that, as one young lady told me, really 'turn kids on'—issues such as dress regulations (how short a skirt a girl is allowed to wear or how long a boy's hair should be), cafeteria service and/or food, disciplinary rules."[15]

Hoover's dire warnings about the subversive danger of "radicalism" in the schools touched off a furor from parents. Their reaction seems to have stunned the editors, who had endorsed Hoover's article by claiming that "nobody is better qualified to talk about extremism than F.B.I. Director John Edgar Hoover, long a bulwark against encroachments on our liberties, whether these stem from the left or the right."[16]

All but one of the responses blasted Hoover for smearing American youth. Mrs. William Klein of Cincinnati wrote that "many young people feel that Mr. Hoover has been persecuting the youth and black people of this nation. Are the youth and the black people really our enemies? I think not. . . . The P.T.A. should not widen the generation gap, but should lessen it with understanding."[17] Rebecca Williams of College Park, Maryland, was "appalled by your January issue. The P.T.A. publishes a responsible magazine not given to smear journalism, but on pages 2, 3, 4, and 5 of the January issue, John Edgar Hoover repeatedly associated violent actions by youth with activities by students concerned about their education, the Vietnam war, the draft, racism, the right to assembly, the right to select what they read, and the right to dress as they choose. . . . I call upon the P.T.A. to deny, and clearly, the implications that active, concerned students are part of the violent and extreme behavior in our society."[18] Other parents branded Hoover himself as an "extremist" and his writing as "propaganda." It was left to Truman Leon Kittle of Geneseo, Illinois, to hurl the final devastating insult at the man who thirty years before had been the idol of the nation's youth as "Public Hero Number One": "Hoover reminds one of the self-righteous parent who refuses to accept any blame for the actions of his unruly off-spring."[19]

As this PTA fiasco demonstrates, Hoover did not go without criticism and he had his public relations disasters during his lifetime, but on the whole none of the derogatory publicity did serious damage to the bureau's reputation until after his death. It should be remembered that although Hoover was certainly highly unpopular with the antiwar protesters and their sympathizers, the anti-Vietnam movement itself was even more unpopular in middle America, as Nixon's victorious campaign against "Acid, Amnesty and Abortion" proved.

The collapse of the G-Man myth cannot be explained simply as an inevitable result of the public's discovery of the "dark side" of the FBI after Hoover's death. Just about everything now held against the FBI (illegal investigative techniques, persecution of political nonconformists, nonfeasance in civil rights, and neglect of major crimes while pursuing trivial "statistical accomplishments" like recovering stolen autos) was common knowledge within informed circles long before Hoover's death, in some cases for decades before his death. Nevertheless, while Hoover was living, the public ignored the bad news about his FBI, crediting only reports that would buttress the heroic image of the G-Man. After his death that same public would come to believe any revelations, no matter how old or ill-proven, that would help support the stereotype of the FBI as an American Gestapo bent on exterminating constitutional liberties, or any charges that would help indict Hoover as a would-be dictator bent on extending his personal power over the entire state, a know-nothing intent on exiling legal dissent from the bounds of patriotic behavior.

The general public has never taken a balanced or temperate attitude towards the FBI. During the seventies popular culture reversed the principles of selective perception it had always followed in choosing the information it would use to construct its image of the FBI. In both instances, once the public had formed its image of the FBI, whether positive or negative, its psychological investment in the bureau was so great that the laws of cognitive dissonance came into play, causing information not in conformity with the chosen image to be rejected as irrelevant or erroneous. This means that to understand the public's change of heart towards the FBI, we must discover why the public discarded its old stereotype of the bureau and chose a new one, since it seems that the public first has to adopt a stereotype of a person or institution before it is able to choose the sort of information it will accept as believable.

Actually there was an enormous amount of discreditable information about the bureau that the public knew about the FBI before Hoover's death, but that it chose to ignore. During the very years of the bureau's greatest public relations triumphs, in fact, there had appeared a sizable volume of published material hostile to the FBI. This well-documented case against the FBI might be labeled its "countercultural image": everything that was ignored or suppressed to preserve popular culture's stereotype of the heroic G-Man.

To start at the beginning, there was the House of Representatives report of 1920 on the bureau's abuse of civil liberties during the Red Scare raids and deportations. In 1920, also, a prestigious committee of lawyers (including Zechariah Chafee, Roscoe Pound, Ernest Freund, and Felix Frankfurter) published their *Report upon the Illegal Practices of the United States Department of Justice*.[20] One year later the Federal Council of Churches issued its own condemnation of the bureau's role in the Red Scare; its charges that the bureau had shown contempt for civil liberties were also highly publicized.[21] The bureau's role (masterminded by Hoover) in the framing of Senator Burton Wheeler during the 1923–24 Teapot Dome scandal was also widely reported at the time, and statements detailing these bureau illegalities were read into the *Congressional Record*.

There was little new fuel for the countercultural image during the late twenties, but that was only because Hoover kept the Bureau out of sight from 1924 to 1933. As soon as the big publicity build-up began under FDR, the criticism also reappeared. In *Collier's* Ray Tucker poked fun at Hoover and the FBI in a satiric piece called "Hsst, Who Goes There"[22] that ridiculed Hoover's frantic efforts to find out if he was going to be reappointed by Roosevelt. According to Tucker, Hoover's agents were shadowing everyone in official Washington who might have information, up to and including outgoing President Hoover.

In November, 1934 (just after the Dillinger, Floyd, and Nelson cases, and just before the Attorney General's Crime Conference), William Seagle wrote a hard-hitting attack on Cummings and Hoover called "The American National Police: The Dangers of Federal Crime Control," which appeared in *Harper's*.[23] Seagle charged that the pressure on the administration to extend federal jurisdiction over crime had come primarily from big business (and other "admirers of Mussolini"). According to Seagle, this far right coalition had been responsible for whipping up the public hysteria over the "non-existent" crime wave. Using the example of state police forces, Seagle argued that the further removed the police were from the local situation, the more likely they were to be employed to repress local dissidents, particularly labor organizers and aliens: "The State police as a result of their activities against labor and radical groups have become known as 'the American Cossacks'. . . . For this reason organized labor has opposed the extension of State police systems. A Federal police force could be even less subject to restraint."[24] Seagle fleshed out his anti-FBI brief with a list of the bureau's violations of civil liberties from World War I to 1934; significantly, he treated these offenses as though they were matters of common knowledge, hardly a revelation to anyone who had been following the news. Seagle's conclusion was that elevating the FBI to the status of popular heroes would simply be demagoguery of the most pathetic variety, and futile to boot. The nation's love affair with the G-Men could be dismissed as nonsense ("Not for nothing have our statesmen read detective stories in their spare time") were it not for the ease with which the Right could use a sacrosanct FBI to repress workers and radicals. In 1935 Milton S. Mayer joined the attack on the FBI with a debunking *Forum* article titled "Myth of the G-Men."[25] Mayer examined the G-Man craze from every angle and pronounced it bunk. The crime wave, he said, was a mirage. John Dillinger, whose death the FBI had hailed as the signal of its victory in the "war on crime," was guilty of no federal offense more serious than interstate auto theft, not a crime condemning him to be shot on sight. He went on to question the very notion of a "national" crime problem. "Crime," Mayer wrote, "is local. Criminals are local, . . . only the local police know the ins and outs of a metropolitan underworld. Only the local police know the haunts of criminals and the friends of criminals. . . . No squad of bright young men can gallop in from Washington and solve the crimes of these men alone."[26] Mayer pointed out (accurately) that in the bureau's most celebrated case it was the local police who turned up the tip that led to Dillinger's death.

Mayer argued that the fundamental tenet of the FBI legend was suspect; he maintained that the capture of celebrated criminals made no contribution at all to solving the nation's crime problem: "Crime has never been scotched by capturing or killing criminals haphazardly. The war on crime is no more furthered by the killing of a Dillinger than by the jailing of a Capone for income-tax evasion. There are a thousand Dillingers who know better than to take up with a policeman's girlfriend and a thousand Capones who know better than to write checks. The Bureau of Investigation is designed to prune the criminal tree; the tree goes on flowering."[27] As an alternative to Hoover's crime-fighting strategy Mayer proposed an approach liberals and the Left would urge on an unpersuaded public throughout the decades of Hoover's popularity: "The right way to fight crime is to remove the environment in which crime breeds, a suggestion which has been made by the 'impractical theorists of every age.' "[28] For Mayer, as for most of Hoover's liberal and leftist critics in the decades to come, the FBI's gangbusting heroics simply gave the nation an excuse to avoid doing anything about the social and economic inequities that produce crime.

To understand the cultural forces that produced the "Myth of the G-Man," Mayer argued, one had to employ the theories of social psychology as it attempted to untangle the causes of mass delusion and political demagoguery: "Beneath the enthusiasm for the war on crime lay, after 4 years of national panic, the public's desperate need for a bogeyman. This is an old and inveterate failing of society beset by economic straits. In most of present-day Europe, the bogeyman is a political or religious minority; in this country he has taken the form of a moral minority—the criminal."[29]

In "Myth of the G-Man" Mayer managed to identify exactly what it was that made liberals, leftists, and reformers so uneasy about the FBI's popularity. Hoover's most enthusiastic supporters, Mayer charged, were "the shouting patriots, many of them legislators, capitalists and publishers. The spirit of such influential individuals is loosely called Fascist; simply, it is the spirit that seeks order at the expense of justice. It advocates 'treating 'em rough,' whether ' 'em' are laborers on strike, communists at talk, or criminals in flight."[30] The conviction that law-and-order slogans were really smoke screens for an attack on reform was probably what kept the Left from catching the G-Man fever that swept the rest of the nation. The Left was able to find many reasons to fear and dislike the FBI over the years, but the basic precondition for this hostility towards the bureau was that the

Left's inherent distrust of the law-and-order mentality caused reformers to pass through the years of the FBI's greatest popularity without joining in the applause.

Although the Left held itself aloof from the G-Man craze its attitude towards the bureau during the thirties was more one of an at times amused tolerance rather than active hostility. There were several reasons for this. The most important was that the bureau had not been involved in political intelligence since Stone and Hoover reformed the bureau in 1924; not until 1936 was the bureau to get back into its antiradical harness,[31] and it took several years for the Left to learn of this return to the bad old days. Moreover, even though Roosevelt and Hoover were, from the outset, primarily concerned with Communist subversion, the bureau's more publicized counterintelligence activities during the thirties were aimed at native Fascists and German sympathizers. Second, reformers concerned with racial justice and civil rights were favorably impressed by the FBI when compared to local and state police (this was an era when lynching was cherished by southern Democrats as indispensable to the preservation of the southern way of life).[32]

But leftist tolerance for the FBI ended in 1940 with a vengeance. In February, 1940, the FBI raided the New York headquarters of the Veterans of the Abraham Lincoln Brigade. The bureau also arrested twelve members of the Abraham Lincoln Brigade in Detroit and Milwaukee and charged them with violating the federal penal code by recruiting volunteers to fight in the Spanish civil war. Since the vanquished Spanish Loyalist government (for which these Americans fought) had attained the status of a sacred lost cause to the Left, the FBI raids were tantamount to an assault on the heart and soul of radical America. These arrests and indictments were dismissed in a few days by Attorney General Robert Jackson, but the episode alerted the Left to Hoover's re-activation (in September, 1939) of his infamous antiradical General Intelligence Division. With the liberal journals *The New Republic* and *The Nation* leading the attack, the Left laced into Hoover; in response he rallied his supporters in the middlebrow mass-circulation press. *The Nation* printed a reexamination of the country's experience with the GID-directed Red Scare of 1919–20 and proclaimed that the division's rebirth was cause for alarm and protest. In support of this contention *The Nation* quoted Hoover's report to the House Appropriations Committee in September, 1938, in which he said he was compiling information on the "press and groups engaged in . . . subversive activities, in espionage activities, or any activities that are possibly detrimental to the internal security of the United States."[33] What, *The Nation* asked, had Hoover meant by "subversive activities"? The answer was that it was anything Hoover wanted it to mean, a situation that was clearly dangerous to the magazine's constituency. The definition of *subversive* subscribed to by some of Hoover's right-wing and big-business fans, *The Nation* observed, was broad enough to include "the whole New Deal from Mr. Roosevelt on down." *The New Republic* joined in the attack by charging that "the glamour that surrounds [Hoover] conceals the growth of a power inconsistent with our conception of democratic institutions."[34]

Even some conservative reporters like Westbrook Pegler joined the attack on Hoover. Pegler wrote, in words that Robert Ludlum or Irving Wallace could have borrowed verbatim, that "the F.B.I. has more dirt on more Americans, including Senators, Representatives, labor leaders, Governors, Mayors, and members of some of the political families of the New Deal government, than the foulest whelp of an open-air grand jury bred to a professional blackmailer of the press, radio and screen could reefer up in a thousand and one nights under the goofy spell of the toxic weed."[35] Today hardly anyone would doubt that the "blackmail files" (the "Official and Confidential Files") did exist and were used, but in 1940 belief in their existence was confined to the Left, and such charges, indignantly denied by Hoover, were regarded as libels by the bureau's friends.

Hoover responded to these attacks in a fashion that was an ominous portent of his later attitude towards any criticism of the FBI: the whole affair was a Communist plot, and he used as evidence the undeniable and not-unexpected fact that the American Communist party was one of his most vociferous critics.[36] The furor calmed down this time when Roosevelt made clear that he was on Hoover's side. America's entry into the war finally furnished Hoover with a patriotic consensus supporting his counterintelligence work, but liberals and the Left did not forget their grudge against Hoover, and they kept popping away at the FBI. Later, after the Hoover-Nixon-McCarthy connection had gutted liberalism during the late forties and fifties, it could be seen in retrospect that the FBI's leftist critics had not been mistaken in their forebodings about the danger Hoover's popularity held for them.

By 1939 the Left began to be alarmed by the rise of anti-Communist demagogues like the House Un-American Activities Committee's Martin Dies. The non-Communist Left was terrified by the sort of anti-communism promoted by Dies and Hoover, and not just because conservatives had long been able to use the Red smear to put reformers on the defensive. *The Nation* observed that "America is dotted with incipient fascist groups, closely related to the open shop industrialists, the public utility interests, the monopoly forces. An airview of our social landscape would show a vast sprawling country, deeply furrowed by regional attitudes and differences, crisscrossed by internal feuds among the reactionaries themselves, pervaded by a loose invertebrate fear and insecurity that may at the proper time be drawn into the pattern of fascism. . . . The one course calculated to unite the various separate strands of fascist feeling into a single design [is] the sustained anti-Communist campaign."[37]

Throughout the forties *The Nation* kept on the offensive against Hoover, never overlooking a chance to tax him with his misdeeds. "One need not be very radical to be suspect to the F.B.I.," it charged in 1941. "The truth is that the F.B.I. is a stronghold of anti-New Deal elements which may yet play a sinister role in American history, that the Attorney General has no real control over it, that it runs true to the familiar rightist pattern of secret police agencies everywhere."[38] Whenever the applause for Hoover's Nazi-spy hunting prowess grew too ecstatic *The Nation* reminded liberals that the same talents Hoover employed against gangsters and Nazis could easily be turned against the Left, which was all one vast symphony in pink and red as far as Hoover was concerned.

The Left's fear and hatred of Hoover reached an even higher pitch after Truman's 1947 Loyalty Directive gave the FBI a veto over government hiring and firing. Leftists and liberals, nervous at the very least about their career prospects, tended to blame the FBI (and not Truman) for bringing about a situation in which, as *The Nation* observed, "The federal employee who holds vigorous and critical opinion on this subject [national security] does wisely in these times to keep it to himself. In Washington this is an era when yea-saying is the safest course and independence of thought is at a drastic discount."[39]

During the fifties Hoover's right-wing allies, armed with Hoover's files and support, launched a devastating attack on American reform. At the peak of the McCarthyite ascendancy, with Hoover draped in honors as the peerless symbol of Americanism and as the ultimate authority on national security and patriotism, Max Lowenthal published a massively documented history of the FBI's highhanded disregard for civil liberties and the chilling effect Hoover's career had had on freedom of thought.[40]

Lowenthal went back to 1908 and the first debates over the establishment of the FBI to demonstrate that Congress had greatly feared that the FBI might become an expandable framework for a governmental spy system. He then laid out the evidence, using documents already in the public record, to show that the worst fears of the FBI's early enemies had been amply confirmed. Lowenthal's 460 pages of text and 83 pages of citations proved that the FBI never lacked for outspoken critics, that the FBI's offenses against civil liberties were well known, and that there had always existed ample documentary proof of the bureau's crimes. The only evidence today's critics of the bureau possess that Lowenthal lacked is confirmation from the FBI's own internal documents that Lowenthal's charges were accurate. The facts themselves have never been in doubt.

Lowenthal refrained from drawing conclusions himself; instead he let the comments of prominent statesmen provide the damning generalizations. He quoted Congressman John J. Fitzgerald of New York in 1908 that he feared that the FBI would become "in time a Federal secret police."[41] He then documented how the FBI had in fact acted as a federal secret police during the White Slave Scare of 1910, the Slacker Raids of 1918, the Red Scare Raids of 1919 and 1920; he described the bureau's role in turning the public against the Russian Revolution; he recounted its antiradical and antilabor activities during the twenties; he provided evidence of its hostility towards civil rights, its harsh treatment of critics, its tireless self-promotion, and its illegal investigative techniques; he castigated Hoover for his dictatorial treatment of his own agents and his refusal to cooperate with other federal agencies or with local police. All told, Lowenthal's *Federal Bureau of Investigation* constituted a rigorously argued and documented brief for the leftist/civil libertarian case against the FBI, a marshaling of all the evidence that had been excluded by the mythologizers of the FBI legend.

The bureau erupted in a violent campaign against the book, furnishing reviewers with boilerplate denunciations of the book. It even had its allies in Congress haul Lowenthal before the House Un-American Activities Committee; but Lowenthal, an experienced and very successful lawyer, had no difficulty exposing the foolishness and hypocrisy of the bureau's attacks on his patriotism.[42]

In spite of the cogency and force of Lowenthal's attacks, however, the bureau could have spared itself its effort and concern. *The Federal Bureau of Investigation* was unread except in circles where the bureau already stood condemned. Lowenthal's book quickly attained the status of a classic of the Left, but the general public was simply not interested in bad news about the bureau, no matter how sensational or convincing. Thirty years later, feature writers could pay the rent by repackaging and updating Lowenthal's stories, but in 1951 nobody wanted to read exposés of the bureau.

As far as the public was concerned, the FBI was all that stood between America and the Reds, while for liberals the FBI was the cutting edge of the new emerging fascism. Mainstream America and the Left had come to inhabit two entirely different imaginative realities; the world view of each would seem a preposterous delusion to the other.

The next salvo against Hoover came from a familiar source. After pointing with alarm at Hoover for more than twenty-five years to little effect, *The Nation* commissioned Fred J. Cook to conduct a full-scale dissection of the FBI. Cook's study filled the entire October 20, 1958, issue of *The Nation;* six years later Cook published a much-expanded version of the piece in book form as *The FBI Nobody Knows.* Once again Cook leveled the standard charges against the FBI, already familiar to *The Nation's* subscribers and to Lowenthal's readers, and he collected an abundance of fresh material to buttress his argument that Hoover personally and the FBI institutionally bore primary responsibility for the McCarthyite hysteria which Cook charged had stifled social reform and intellectual debate and had stultified political life in the United States since the beginning of the cold war.

For Cook the great issues in postwar America were civil rights and McCarthyism (meaning right-wing use of the Red smear for partisan political purposes). In both instances Cook charged that Hoover had been the country's greatest offender against decency. In the first case the crime was one of nonfeasance; in the second, of malfeasance. "The great moral upheaval of 1963," Cook wrote, "stirred no wrath and indignation in the soul of the all-powerful master of the F.B.I."[43] On the contrary, Hoover showed every sign of opposition to the civil rights movement; certainly he took advantage of every opportunity to broadcast his reservations about its "excesses" and its supposed links with tabooed forms of dissent. Cook observed that "southern political leaders, with whom Hoover has maintained a long and loving rapport, persisted in trying to smear the Negro movement for equality and justice in the twentieth century with the Communist label. They intimated that the F.B.I. endorsed this view."[44] Hoover did nothing to correct this deception, though he possessed proof of its falsity. After Hoover's death the bureau felt sensitive enough about this charge to commission a made-for-television movie on its civil rights offensives against the Ku Klux Klan called "Journey into Fear."

For Fred J. Cook, *The Nation,* and their readers, Hoover's refusal to enforce the laws protecting the rights of civil rights protesters was despicable; his support for McCarthy and other Red-hunting zealots was terrifying. The result of the postwar anti-Communist hysteria, Cook wrote, was a "great changeover from an intellectually fearless and free society to a sheeplike and conformist one."[45] Cook scrutinized the great "spy" cases that provided the rallying points for the McCarthyites—the Coplon, Hiss, Rosenberg, Remington, and Harry Dexter White cases— and found that in all of them the most elementary principles of legal procedure and common sense had been abandoned in a frantic effort to provide fuel for a continued anti-Communist hysteria. The result was that the nation's political processes had come to be ruled by innuendo, suspicion, and terror—all taking a toll in heartbreak, ruined lives, and suicide—to say nothing of the social and economic miseries that went unrelieved because of the triumph of reaction, perhaps the most important outcome of McCarthyism. "In the production of this national evil that was to enthrone innuendo and make the word of the informer sacred doctrine," Cook wrote, "no man in America was to be more influential than J. Edgar Hoover. His role was basic; his interpretation of fact, unchallenged; his word, in effect, superior to that of any court in the land."[46]

Cook ended *The FBI Nobody Knows* with a chapter melodramatically titled "The Final Judgement." Its climax was a succinct summary of the Left's case against the FBI, a Dorian Gray portrait of Hoover that was the countercultural image of the G-Man:

The pattern makes it clear that, behind the scenes, loftily above the battle and unsmudged by the battle smoke, Hoover has been the heart and soul of the witch-hunt era. His persistent overestimation of the threat of domestic Communism has been a major factor in creating a national mood of hysteria and unreason. His predilection for the use of such imprecise terms as "fellow traveler" and "pseudo liberal" has fostered the technique, so beloved by the right, of splattering with the treason label all liberal ideas and liberal opponents. . . . Free discussion is essential in a democracy. . . . Repress that freedom, and you dilute the nation's most precious heritage. It is precisely here, in the final analysis, that the influence of the F.B.I. has been most baneful.[47]

The FBI Nobody Knows was well-written, thoroughly documented, and filled with the most provocative and sensational charges. Despite all this, however, his book had no discernible impact on the general public. In a 1958 review of Hoover's *Masters of Deceit* Cook complained that no matter how many times writers exposed the danger posed to liberty by Hoover and the FBI, the public neither noticed nor cared, so that each new instance of Hoover's villainy was a shattering blow to the people directly affected. "It is a shock that, unfortunately, seems destined to be repeated again and again before America re-learns the art of looking ideas in the face and considering them on their merits without fear of the bugaboo. If [the publication and popularity of] Mr. Hoover's *Masters of Deceit* does nothing else, it has served as a convincing demonstration that this time is not yet."[48] The lack of any discernible public reaction to Cook's revelations in *The Nation* in 1958 or in his book in 1964 was still one more convincing demonstration that the "time was not yet" for the public to take seriously the countercultural image of the FBI.

By the end of the sixties, however, the growing tendency to question authority was having some effect on Hoover's sacrosanct image. In 1968 the first book by a disaffected agent appeared. This was *Inside the F.B.I.*, by Norman Ollestad,[49] followed in 1970 by William Turner's *Hoover's F.B.I.: The Man and the Myth*.[50] These two books portrayed the bureau as an insane asylum with grown men acting like children in an effort to obey the nonsensical regulations of a self-infatuated and senile director. But these books probably did not indicate a shift in mainstream popular culture's attitude towards the FBI; this flippancy and outrage instead revealed the increasing influence of the counterculture during the sixties as it grew to numbers that made books specially spiced to its taste a profitable sideline for publishers.

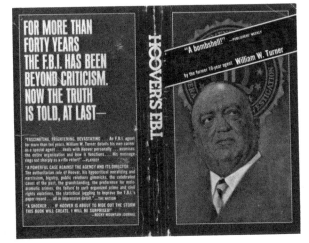

As Hoover's career drew to a close, there still existed, as there had throughout his life, two entirely different images of the FBI, each one self-consistent and dramatically complete. The first was the mainstream image of the heroic pop culture G-Man whose biography has been traced in this book. The other was the countercultural G-Man, the demonic inversion of pop culture's hero. This G-Man represented a repressive secret police working to crush social and political change in America with trumped-up charges of Communist subversion. This G-Man would use any means necessary to stamp out dissent or nonconformist behavior, recognizing no constitutional restraint or limit of common decency. For the counterculture, the face of the pop culture G-Man bore the frightening features of American fascism.

The two images of the G-Man were absolutely disjointed. An American who believed in one of them had to reject the other as a fraud. The Left's Hoover and pop culture's Hoover were not simply different evaluations of the same person—they were projections of two entirely different sets of cultural attitudes. Pop culture's G-Man represented the government protecting Americans against threats at home and abroad; the counterculture's Hoover was the government at war with its citizens, it was the state as a repressive instrument sworn to the service of capitalism, imperialism, and racism.

For each of these two audiences, there were two different G-Man myths, two different legends of the FBI. For the mainstream pop culture, of course, the highlights of the G-Man myth were the great gangster cases of the thirties and the atom spy trials of the early cold war. For the counterculture, the key episodes in the FBI legend were the bureau's "framing" of Remington, Hiss, Coplon, and the Rosenbergs. All of these cases, particularly the Hiss and Rosenberg cases, have been kept alive by liberals and radicals aware of the real damage these symbolic cases did to American reform. For many American reformers, this damage could be repaired only by proving the innocence of the principals in these political trials, or, at the very least, destroying the cases against them. Historian Allen Weinstein, whose *Perjury: The Hiss-Chambers Case* concludes that Hiss was not framed, that he did steal secret documents, and that he was guilty of the crime of perjury, argues that for *Nation* editor Carey McWilliams establishing Hiss's innocence was "somehow pivotal to invigorating American liberalism."[51] Weinstein concludes that the undying controversy over the Hiss case can be understood only by interpreting the "cold war iconography" of "Alger Hiss as Myth and Symbol."[52]

According to the countercultural Left, the great issues in the history of the four decades spanned by Hoover's public career were those of

Opposite: Bureau exposés: Max Lowenthal's The Federal Bureau of Investigation *(1950), Norman Ollested's* Inside the FBI *(1968), and William W. Turner's* Hoover's FBI *(1970).*

economic and racial justice. From this point of view, the FBI's great rituals of national unity were diversions, smoke screens that obscured the country's real problems. The FBI's gangster wars created a false consciousness that helped the ruling class build bridges over the contradictions that otherwise could have forced real change on the country. Thus the Left's characteristic attitude towards the FBI's most cherished cases was either derision (the gangster cases) or disbelief (the spy trials).

The G-Man craze of the thirties never included the Left because the events that formed the leftist imagination during the thirties were not the gangster wars; the Left's enthusiasm was for the great labor battles that organized the steel and auto industries. The Left was caught up in the excitement of the New Deal's cultural and economic efforts, in the civil rights battle, in the world struggle against fascism (particularly the Spanish civil war), and the lingering aftereffects of the great cause of the twenties, the Sacco-Vanzetti case. In every instance the FBI's role was either peripheral or adversarial. The Left may have moved from a neutral attitude towards the bureau to one of reflexive hostility as a psychological defense mechanism. America's orthodox political culture is so monolithic and one-dimensional that an almost automatic sense of oedipal guilt may be aroused whenever an American makes the rebellion against authority that is prerequisite to a commitment to social change. In this situation imputing wrongdoing to society in its authoritarian aspect is a way of liberating oneself from this sense of guilt. Since the FBI was the most visible symbol of the authoritarian state, the counterculture's myth of the malevolent G-Man, of the demonic Hoover, could satisfy its psychological need to justify its disloyalty to the status quo. Thus the Left's compulsion throughout Hoover's career and long afterwards to seek out and publicize the crimes of Hoover's bureau can be understood as an effort to confirm a theory in which the Left had made a heavy emotional investment before the evidence was in.

The Left's hostility towards the FBI as the symbol of the authoritarian state it was rebelling against rendered it immune to the G-Man craze; in the same manner mainstream America's psychological investment in the image of the protective FBI meant that the Left's charges against the bureau, even its proof of misconduct, had no effect on popular culture's enthusiasm for the G-Man. The most telling demonstration of popular culture's lack of interest in evidence of wrongdoing by the FBI throughout Hoover's career was its reaction to the unfolding story of the Martin Luther King scandal.

The FBI's investigation and persecution of King began in earnest in 1962; it persisted (in attempts to tarnish King's name) even after King's death in 1968. Knowledge that King was being unfairly and illegally harassed by the FBI was widespread as early as 1964; almost everything we now know about this disgraceful episode was a matter of public

The counterculture's Hoover according to David Levine. Copyright 1978, David Levine. Reprinted by permission.

record and available by 1969 to persons who took the trouble to inform themselves. The new information David J. Garrow's definitive 1981 study of the affair adds to the record is the strong evidence he uncovered that the FBI honestly did believe that King was unduly influenced, perhaps even controlled, by Communist party member advisors. The assumption, particularly by the bureau's leftist critics, had been that the so-called "Communist influence" aspect of the case had been a subterfuge, and that it had been King's criticism of the FBI's performance in protecting civil rights workers that had aroused Hoover's wrath.[53] Nevertheless, despite the sensational nature of the story, the public refused to pay attention to the Hoover-King affair. Whenever circumstances moved the story into the news, it made fresh headlines, as though the public were learning about it anew, as though it had wiped the previous charges from its memory. Hoover's top lieutenants had been trying to peddle salacious King material to the press since 1964, so within the Washington press corps the bureau's anti-King operation was common knowledge. In May, 1968, Drew Pearson published the story about the FBI's wiretap on King's phone. In June, 1969, the King wiretaps again made headlines when the bureau had to describe them in court testimony during Muhammad Ali's draft evasion case. Despite the grave seriousness of this effort by the bureau to intimidate King, Garrow reports that "the public arguments spent themselves within several weeks. Not until six years later [1975], when the Senate Select Committee on Intelligence Activities, headed by Idaho Democrat Frank Church, attempted a thorough probe of past misdeeds by American intelligence agencies, did public attention return to the Bureau's activities against Dr. King and the SCLC."[54]

If the public ignored a story in 1969, only to treat it as a sensational revelation six years later, the only possible explanation is that sometime between 1969 and 1976 the public had changed, at least in its assumptions governing what it would consider to be news. There is even stronger evidence than this that the public's basic assumptions *had* changed between 1969 and 1976. King's assassination in 1968 immediately led to charges, rejected by the general public, that Hoover was somehow responsible for his death. These charges, first advanced by the countercultural Left (by William Kunstler, for one) immediately after King died, were thoroughly investigated and were found to be utterly false. David Garrow, the most tireless investigator of the Hoover-King relationship, has concluded that "suggestions that the F.B.I. had anything to do with King's assassination are totally baseless, and are convincingly disproven by each and every careful study of the details of the event. People who continue to propound or believe such rumors are, in their own way, prisoners of the 'paranoid style' of thought. . . . While some proponents of the F.B.I. conspiracy theory may well have acted largely out of self-interest, many others who have accepted the idea have reflected only gullibility and ignorance."[55]

It is certainly possible to see self-interest, gullibility, and ignorance all at work whenever the public turns history and current events into moral melodrama. In any case, the FBI's purported responsibility for the King assassination at first conformed only to the counterculture's image of the FBI, so while it was believed by the Left, it was rejected by the public. Sometime in the early seventies, however, the public changed its mind and, in spite of the evidence, began to swallow the theory of an FBI assassination plot. The public's new desire to believe the worst of Hoover was revealed in Abby Mann's 1978 six-hour television docudrama "King." This dramatization portrayed Hoover "as a harassing racist psychopath fighting the specter of black insurrection." It presented the "clear implication that the F.B.I. was to some degree involved in the King assassination." The new attitude towards the bureau was revealed in one of the show's character's comments on official denials of the FBI's responsibility for the assassination: "They'll never make me believe it was coincidental."[56]

The FBI's record of illegal wiretaps, buggings, and burglaries were also well known to the informed public long before the Church committee made them part of the official record in 1975.[57] They had even

David Garrow, The F.B.I. and Martin Luther King, Jr. *(1981).*

formed the premise of a Nero Wolfe mystery aimed at the elite (or at least literate) public in 1965, Rex Stout's *The Doorbell Rang.*

Stout's plot seems to have been based on Fred J. Cook's account of the FBI's attempt to repress Max Lowenthal's *Federal Bureau of Investigation* in 1950. Wolfe's client, appalled by the public's indifference towards the bureau's misdeeds, had distributed copies of Fred Cook's *The F.B.I. Nobody Knows* to the country's power elite, thereby arousing Hoover's wrath. Wolfe neatly mousetraps the FBI by enticing it into a burglary of his office; he traps the G-Men there, strips them of their guns and credentials, then extracts a promise of immunity from the bureau for his client. The story ends with Hoover himself ringing the portly detective's doorbell. "Let him get a sore finger," Wolfe decides.[58]

So when did the public begin to pay attention to the seamy side of the G-Man's image? When did the G-Man change from hero to villain in popular culture? When did the counterculture's image of the demonic

FBI win the public's belief? When did Wallace and Ludlum start reading Fred J. Cook?

A cultural shift of this sort, no matter how momentous, might be supposed to take place gradually and imperceptibly, at a glacial pace. In the case of the FBI's public image, however, it is possible to locate a precise date when the public's attitude shifted from approval to hostility and alarm.

That shift had certainly taken place by December, 1975, when *Time* magazine ran a cover story with the title "The Truth About Hoover."[59] As is so often the case with *Time*'s major reports, the story was really about a cultural change that had already taken place. None of the "facts" that made up the "truth" about Hoover were new, though they had recently been dusted off by the Church committee. What was new was the readiness of the general public (*Time*'s readers) to give credit to the old Left-liberal charges that had been ignored for so long; what was new was the public's use of these old facts as a reason for rejecting the "old truth" about Hoover and its willingness to adopt instead a "new truth." *Time*'s "news," then, was not that there were new "facts" about Hoover, but that the public had now decided to pay attention to some old facts.

"The legend is crumbling," *Time*'s story began; "there had always been a few blemishes . . . but now [December, 1975], under congressional and journalistic scrutiny . . . a darker picture is coming into view."[60] The specific charges: that Hoover had made public relations the first priority of the bureau, that he had placed his bureau at the disposal of each succeeding president for political intelligence work, that he was vindictive, a racist, that he "trampled on the rights of citizens." After describing Hoover's campaign to repress citizens who were trying "to express grievances against their government," *Time* turned its attention to Hoover's personal failings; charges that he was maybe a little gay, that he probably was (by the end) a little senile, that he certainly was a little crazy. This last charge *Time* supported with a familiar collection of FBI administrative horror stories, weird things Hoover himself had done, weird things his sycophantic agents had done to placate him.

The counterculture image of the FBI, which was what *Time* was reporting as the revealed truth about Hoover, had always been constructed out of a complementary pair of beliefs. The first was the well-worn litany of FBI misdeeds, which *Time* dutifully recounted. The second was a disposition to deride the bureau's proudest accomplishments. As though to drive the final nails in the G-Man hero's coffin, *Time* went down the list of the G-Men's greatest spy and gangster cases, cases it had once celebrated, jeering at each one as overblown (the gangster cases) or underdocumented (the spy cases).

The real story behind this new truth about Hoover was the reason

Time's 1975 "truth" about Hoover was everything the magazine had ignored about him during his lifetime. Reprinted by permission from Time, The Weekly Newsmagazine; *copyright 1975, Time, Inc.*

why the public was now willing to cast aside its old admiration for Hoover and to join his enemies in desecrating his memory. "Certainly the post-Watergate morality casts a harsher light on official conduct that was once not questioned,"[61] was *Time*'s stab at explanation, adding that Hoover had preserved his legend by blackmailing his enemies and by laboring to promote the careers of his powerful friends.

Time was clearly at a loss to provide a convincing explanation why all the old anti-Hoover stories, which it and the rest of the mass media had routinely spiked over the years, had suddenly become hot news. Why had they not been hot news all along? *Time* could not address this question because the magazine swims in the same current of public opinion it tries to chronicle, so while *Time* is useful for recording the flow of popular symbols, stereotypes and assumptions, it does not stand far enough outside the culture to notice the underlying dynamics that ultimately determine its own editorial policies.

The myth of the G-Man was certainly dead by the date of *Time*'s story, December, 1975. The actual date was probably somewhat earlier. In July, 1975, former agent Joseph L. Schott published an irreverent collection of gags about the bureau, *No Left Turns*. For Schott, his readers, and for his mainstream publisher (Praeger), the bureau was no

Left: Until Watergate, charges against the bureau like the ones in Investigating the FBI *(1973) were shrugged off by the popular culture.*

Right: By 1975 the pop culture G-Man was either a criminal or, as in ex-agent Joseph Schott's book (1975), a clown.

longer to be taken seriously: it was a laughingstock whose only dramatic use was, as Warren Hinckle pointed out in his *New York Times* review, to serve a preposterous setting for *M.A.S.H.*-style theater of the antiestablishment absurd.[62]

The date of the G-Man legend's death was probably even earlier than that. It is safe to assume that the public had grown disenchanted with the heroic FBI image by the time ABC pulled Zimbalist's "The FBI" off the air, and that was in September, 1974.

If the legend was dead by the end of 1974, it was surely still alive, though perhaps not too robust, just two and one-half years earlier when Hoover died on May 2, 1972. *Time,* which was soon to discover the "truth" about Hoover, eulogized him then as "one of the greats." A few months later Nixon's "Acid, Amnesty and Abortion" victory over McGovern showed that the majority of Americans, silent or otherwise, still ranged themselves on the side of traditional values and the institutions like the FBI that protected those values despite, or even because of, the counterculture's assaults on the establishment.

This means that the death of the G-Man legend had to be sometime between November, 1972, and September, 1974. It would therefore seem that the public changed its mind about the G-Man and Hoover's FBI as part of the revolution in attitudes toward symbols of authority that accompanied the Watergate investigations, the impeachment hearings, and finally, Nixon's resignation.

If the Watergate crisis made the public change its mind about Hoover and the FBI after so many years of uncritical adoration, then that third-rate burglary must have fundamentally reversed some of popular culture's most cherished assumptions. Judging by what happened to the FBI's popular image, the public seems to have abandoned its traditional identification with the symbols of government. Mainstream popular culture seems to have interpreted Nixon's resignation as an authoritative validation of the counterculture's long-standing charge that the government was really a treacherous conspiracy against the republic.

To evaluate the Watergate crisis as a cultural revolution is only to follow the lead of the major actors in the politics of the Nixon era. It was part of their political style to interpret their acts in cultural terms, as struggles between contrasting systems of values and outlooks; hawks and doves, hardhats and longhairs, the "work ethic" and the "welfare ethic."

In his analysis of Watergate, *Breach of Faith,* Theodore H. White wrote that "all great political conflicts, everywhere, are underlain by a struggle of culture, as men begin to see their places in the world differently, as their 'consciousness' is 'raised' to new perceptions and indignations."[63] In White's drama the symbol of the "embattled old culture" was its most visible and militant defender, Richard Nixon. Ranged against him was a coalition so large and diverse that it eventually grew to include elements of nearly every political persuasion. Within this anti-Nixon Watergate coalition, however, Nixon's enemies in the counterculture had a status out of all proportion to their actual numbers. Even though the counterculture comprised only a small segment of the victorious anti-Nixon forces, Nixon's fall seemed to prove that the counterculture's alienated analysis of American politics had been right all along. Nixon's resignation, with its attendant demoralization of the old elite, suddenly made the counterculture respectable and, even more important for opinion- and taste-makers, stylish. Watergate converted popular culture, at least the elite molders of popular culture, into a counterculture, and made the counterculture popular.

For the FBI one of the most painful effects of popular culture's post-Watergate apostasy was the collapse of the case against the political

The only power he couldn't control was his own.

Tonight, ABC News Closeup presents some dramatic new evidence that adds to the controversy about J. Edgar Hoover's 48-year reign over the FBI. How did Hoover compromise America's national security during World War II? Why did he withhold information vital to the investigation of John F. Kennedy's assassination? Marshall Frady takes a penetrating look at this enigmatic man. And the police agency he ran.

ABC NEWS CLOSEUP ⊙ Tonight 10:00PM ⑦

Hoover's image in popular culture today. From a 1979 story on the FBI, and an ad for a 1982 television special. Sketch, left, copyright 1979 William Robinson.

Left that Hoover and the Right had woven out of the great loyalty trials of the forties and fifties, and the rise of new suspicions that those trials had been frame-ups. For example, the historian of the Hiss case, Allen Weinstein, thinks that "for many Americans a rapid and perhaps irreversible transformation of the Hiss Case's symbolism began during Watergate."[64] The public also began to wonder about the other iconic cases of the FBI's anti-Communist crusade. Writing in 1975 about the Rosenberg trial, Daniel Yergin said that Watergate

corrupted our faith in the sanctity and essential goodness of our institutions. One refuge of those troubled by this case [against the Rosenbergs] has always been the assumption that the government would not lie, that law enforcement agencies would not fabricate evidence; we can no longer accept such assumptions. [Recently] a whole torrent of disturbing information about FBI practices has come out; its agents, it seems, have not shied away from forging letters, faking death threats, planting informers who functioned as agents provocateurs, even kidnapping in the "interests of national security." How much further would the bureau have moved into illegality and fabrications when the spy mania was at its height and J. Edgar Hoover was in total control?[65]

To true believers in the American civic religion of politics, Richard Nixon's greatest crime was this hemorrhage of faith in government, this popular defection to the counterculture. Theodore H. White wrote that Nixon had "blasted the fundamental faith that bound ordinary Americans of whatever origin . . . to each other and the country—and destroyed the myth which held that they made the laws and that the President they elected would faithfully execute them."[66]

When White spoke of the "myth" of American politics, he meant the faith that the people and their government were one. The loss of this myth, via Nixon's "breach of faith," infected middle America with the suspicion and disbelief that had previously been confined to the countercultural Left. The counterculture's image of the villainous G-Man, therefore, now came to play the same symbolic role in the melodramas of the popular imagination that it long had performed in the nightmares of the Left.

The new pop culture image of the G-Man as villain was part and symbol of the suspicion of government that White held was the most pernicious result of Watergate. "Suspicion of government," White wrote, "is instinctive in human nature—and healthy, if not carried too far. In a democracy like America, the folklore of this atavistic suspicion has set up the Constitutional safeguards against government's abuse of power." On the other hand, according to White, there had always been those among whom "this suspicion . . . [became] morbid."[67] White's theory was that American politics had worked so well so long because this morbid suspicion of government had been confined to the lunatic fringe. This lunatic fringe had believed that government was "the conspiracy that takes away from them what they have earned. They fear and hate the imagined conspiracies of men in government. What Richard Nixon did was to convince them they were right."[68] More than that, Watergate convinced much of mainstream America that the counterculture's paranoia about government had been right.

Popular culture today is interested in news and entertainment about institutions like the FBI only as fuel for its near-paranoid suspicion of government, and it was into this suspicion that "Today's F.B.I." crashed. Ovid Demaris complained at the conclusion of his oral biography of Hoover that "in the wake of Watergate, there is . . . a gullibility gap, a disposition to believe anything bad about anybody."[69] There was

SOREL

IN 1935 I PAID 15¢ TO SEE "G-MEN". JAMES CAGNEY PLAYED AN FBI AGENT. HE WAS COCKY, COURAGEOUS AND INCORRUPTABLE.

IN 1946 I PAID 50¢ TO SEE "NOTORIOUS". CARY GRANT PLAYED AN FBI AGENT. HE WAS SUAVE, COURAGEOUS AND INCORRUPTABLE.

IN 1948 I PAID 80¢ TO SEE "STREET WITH NO NAME." LLOYD NOLAN WAS AN AGENT WHO SCRUPULOUSLY FOLLOWED THE LETTER OF THE LAW.

IN 1952 I PAID $1.25 TO SEE "BIG JIM McLAIN." JOHN WAYNE PLAYS AN AGENT WHO'S CHASING COMMIES, BUT HE NEVER BURGLES OR FAKES EVIDENCE.

NOT LONG AGO I PAID $3.00 TO SEE "THE FBI STORY." JAMES STEWART PLAYS A LONG-TIME AGENT WHO HAS NEVER BURGLED, BUGGED, BRIBED, OR EMBEZZLED.

WHOM DO I SEE ABOUT GETTING A REFUND?

also a disposition not to be particularly interested in a drama that featured as a hero someone like the G-Man who has been assigned the role of villain in the contemporary melodrama of an evil government at war with a virtuous and long-suffering citizenry.

The final irony in the long history of the pop culture G-Man was that "Today's F.B.I." not only had to face a public prejudiced against it by the counterculture's suspicion of authority, but that it also had to look up from its position at the bottom of the ratings to see "Sixty Minutes" (CBS) reigning as the highest-rated show on television, a program whose substance and style perfectly epitomized popular culture's conversion to the counterculture's suspicion of authority.

Today's FBI of Director William Webster remains a powerful and, to many, a troubling force in American life and politics, but it no longer can shape public opinion by representing American values. It no longer stands in the publicity spotlight orchestrating rituals of national solidarity. That power was lost with the death of the G-Man hero, a legend born fifty years ago out of the country's will to believe in its leaders and itself, a legend that died when the nation's suspicion of authority finally replaced its faith in its government. With that loss of faith the FBI's grip on American popular culture, after all those years of Dillinger and Floyd, Cummings and Hoover, Jimmy Cagney and Jimmy Stewart, of radio shows and comics and Junior G-Men, had finally come to an end.

NOTES
BIBLIOGRAPHY
INDEX

NOTES

Introduction

1. The FBI did not begin gathering national crime statistics until 1930 and its figures are not complete enough to be significant until 1933, so it is impossible to say anything with certainty about crime trends during the early depression. Informed guesses based on crime trends in cities that did maintain records suggest that serious crime in America rose to a peak in 1918 and then steadily declined until the 1940s, when it began a slow rise that finally exploded around 1960 with the phenomenal rise in the crime rate we are experiencing today. See the discussion of crime trends in *The Challenge of Crime in a Free Society: A Report by the President's Commission on Law Enforcement and Administration of Justice* (New York: Avon, 1968), pp. 101–5.

2. See Roland Barthes, *Mythologies* (New York: Hill and Wang, 1972), p. 129 for a more extended analysis. Myth, according to Barthes, tries to justify the way things are by showing that they have to be that way, since the temporal is an eternal reenactment of a timeless drama.

3. This is roughly equivalent to John Cawelti's definition in *Adventure, Mystery and Romance: Formula Stories as Art and Popular Culture* (Chicago: Univ. of Chicago Pr., 1976).

4. Richard Slotkin suggests that this battle be interpreted in the light of the myth of the struggle between "Moira" (the unconscious, the impulse, self-gratification) and "Themis" (the conscious, the rational, and the law), an idea he derived from J. L. Henderson's *Thresholds of Initiation* (Middletown, Conn.: Wesleyan Univ. Pr., 1967). See Richard Slotkin, *Regeneration Through Violence* (Middletown, Conn.: Wesleyan Univ. Pr., 1973).

5. *The Nation* 211(Nov. 28, 1970):6.

1. The Public Enemy and the American Public

1. This discussion is based on John Kobler, *Capone* (New York: Putnam, 1971).

2. Chicago's reform mayor publicly asked whether the city "was still abiding by the code of the Dark Ages: Or is this Chicago a unit of an American commonwealth? One day we have this O'Banion slain as a result of a perfectly executed plot of assassination. . . . In the meanwhile his followers and their rivals openly boast of what they will do in retaliation. They seek to fight it out in the street. There is no thought of the law or the people who support the law." Kobler, p. 135.

3. A sign of the gangster's success in establishing himself as an accepted part of the social scene was his offer to Chief Justice McGoorty of the Illinois Criminal Court in 1930. Capone offered to quit labor racketeering if allowed to sell his beer unmolested. The judge replied that "the time has come when the public must choose between the rule of the ganster and the rule of law." *Literary Digest* 107(Nov. 22, 1930):11.

4. Kobler, p. 314.

5. Ibid., p. 316.

6. Ibid., p. 250.

7. The school was the Medill School of Journalism, and the list included Benito Mussolini, Charles Lindbergh, Admiral Richard E. Byrd, George Bernard Shaw, Bobby Jones, President Herbert Hoover, Mohandas Gandhi, Albert Einstein, Henry Ford, and Al Capone. Kobler, p. 313.

8. The reports from the *Register* and the *Guardian* were quoted in the *Literary Digest*'s press summary, "Gangland's Challenge to Our Civilization," 107 (Oct. 25, 1930):8.

9. Kobler, p. 277.

10. Herbert Hoover gave the job of prosecuting Capone to the Treasury Department because the administration did not think it could win a case against Capone for his more serious crimes. Elmer L. Irey, boss of the Treasury's Intelligence Unit, said that "the job of putting Alphonse Capone in jail presented some rather obvious problems. In the first place, the city of Chicago, Cook County, and the state of Illinois, whose citizens had so much of their blood spilled by Alphonse, had shown no disposition to do anything but admit they were shocked. . . . When some irate citizens put on enough pressure to knock off a gambling joint or dim one of Al's innumerable blazing red lights, two things happened. The citizens got slugged or worse, and nobody knew nothin' about nothin'." Irey said that "we couldn't get enough evidence to convict Capone of bootlegging before a jury composed of my own nieces and nephews." Elmer L. Irey, *The Tax Dodgers* (Garden City, N.Y.: Garden City Pub., 1948). The Justice Department also ran away from Capone. J. Edgar Hoover's Bureau of Investigation seemed to duck any major role in the case so that it would not have to share in the blame for what was likely to be a humiliating failure.

11. Quoted in *The Literary Digest, 111(Oct. 31, 1931):6.*

12. See John William Ward, "The Meaning of Lindbergh's Flight," *American Quarterly* 10(Spring, 1958):3–16.

13. *New York Herald Tribune*, Mar. 3, 1932, p. 16.
14. *Literary Digest 112(Mar. 12, 1932):7.*
15. *New York Times*, Mar. 3, 1932, p. 1.
16. Ibid., Mar. 7, 1932, p. 11.
17. Ibid., Mar. 3, 1932, p. 8.
18. *Literary Digest* 113(May 28, 1932):7.
19. *New York Times*, Mar. 3, 1932, p. 8.
20. *Literary Digest* 113(May 28, 1932):6.
21. M. E. Tracy, "Laws and Lawless," *New York World Telegram*, May 14, 1932, p. 17.
22. *Literary Digest* 113(May 28, 1932):6.
23. *New York Evening Post*, May 13, 1932, p. 8.
24. *Literary Digest* 113(May 28, 1932):6.
25. Ibid., p. 7.
26. Ibid.
27. *New York Times*, Mar. 4, 1932, p. 9.
28. Ben Hecht, *A Child of the Century* (New York: Ballantine, 1970), p. 447.
29. Ian Cameron, *A Pictorial History of the Movies* (London: Hamlyn, 1975), p. 42.
30. Andrew Bergman, *We're in the Money* (New York: Harper, 1972), p. 8.
31. Others were *Gunsmoke, The Secret Six, Hell Bound, The Good Bad Girl, The Lawless Women, Gentlemen's Fate, Enemies of the Law, Homicide Squad, The Tip-Off, The Ruling Voice,* and *Bad Company.*
32. Lincoln Kirstein, quoted by Bergman, p. 11.
33. Bergman, pp. 3–4.
34. The movie was finished by October, 1931, though not released until 1932. For background on the problems Hughes had with censorship see the *New York Times*, May 13, 1932, sec. 8, p. 4.
35. The story about the connection between bad teeth and crime ran in the *New York Times*, Mar. 6, 1931, p. 46; the glandular theory was in the *Times* of Feb. 9, 1931, p. 16; tobacco and coffee were blamed in the *Times* of May 5, 1930, p. 25.
36. *New York Times*, Sept. 1, 1933, p. 1.
37. Ibid., Aug. 15, 1933, p. 1.
38. Ibid. Dec. 7, 1930, p. 3.
39. Ibid., Sept. 15, 1931, p. 3.
40. *Literary Digest* 109(Apr. 4, 1931):13.
41. The *New York Times* ran a feature article on this law on Jan. 3, 1932, sec. 9, p. 15.
42. Ibid., Oct. 10, 1933, p. 29.
43. For example, see the reaction to the sentencing of a Mrs. St. Clair to life for shoplifting, ibid., Feb. 7, 1930, p. 1.
44. Ibid., Aug. 15, 1933, p. 1.
45. Gordon Evans Dean, "Outlawry," *The Panel* 10(Mar.–Apr., 1932):13.
46. *New York Times*, Aug. 25, 1931, p. 1.
47. Ibid., Feb. 28, 1931, p. 1.
48. Ibid., Apr. 10, 1932, p. 22.
49. Ibid., July 11, 1932, p. 9.

50. Nathan Douthit, 'Police Professionalism and the War Against Crime in the United States, 1920s–30s," in G. L. Mosse, ed., *Police Forces in History* (Beverly Hills: Sage, 1974), p. 319.

51. *New York Times,* Feb. 28, 1930, p. 2.

52. Ibid., Mar. 23, 1930, sec. 2, p. 9.

53. Ibid., Mar. 13, 1931, p. 2.

54. Ibid., Dec. 19, 1930, p. 18.

55. Ibid., Oct. 28, 1931, p. 22.

56. *Literary Digest* 109(May 23, 1931):11.

57. Ibid., 107(Dec. 6, 1930):7.

58. Ibid.

59. *New York Times,* Aug. 22, 1931, p. 116.

60. *Literary Digest* 107(Dec. 6, 1930):9.

61. For a detailed discussion of this dispute, see Max Lowenthal, *The Federal Bureau of Investigation* (New York: Sloan, 1950), pp. 3–13.

62. For these speeches, see ibid., chap. 2.

63. This account follows Willard B. Gatewood, *Theodore Roosevelt and the Art of Controversy* (Baton Rouge: Louisiana State Univ. Pr., 1970), chap. 8.

64. Quoted by Lowenthal, p. 15.

65. Ibid., p. 19.

66. Howard Sackler's play *The Great White Hope* has a fictional account of this episode.

67. Lowenthal, chap. 4; chaps. 14–23; Robert K. Murray, *Red Scare* (New York: McGraw, 1964).

68. See Lowenthal, p. 83.

69. J. Edgar Hoover, "Fifty Years of Crime: Corruption Begets Corruption," in *Vital Speeches,* 5(June 1, 1939):509.

70. For accounts of the FBI's involvement in the Teapot Dome scandal, see Don Whitehead, *The F.B.I. Story* (New York: Random, 1956), pp. 63–66.

71. For Stone's mandate to Hoover, see Whitehead, p. 68.

72. Ron Goulart, *Line Up, Tough Guys* (Nashville: Sherbourne Pr., 1966), p. 73.

73. *New York Times,* May 28, 1933, sec. 2, p. 3.

74. Bergman, p. 113. Chapter 9 of *We're in the Money* is a perceptive analysis of the "mob" cycle of films.

75. Quoted in Bergman, p. 115.

76. Bergman, p. 118.

2. The Crime War of the Thirties

1. Carl Brent Swisher, "Biological Note" in *Selected Papers of Homer Cummings* (New York: Scribner's 1939), p. xiv.

2. See Murray, *Red Scare,* for a general account. Also see *Report upon the Illegal Practices of the United States Department of Justice* (Washington, D.C.: National Popular Government League, 1920).

3. This exchange is quoted in Lowenthal, p. 191.

4. Quoted in Lowenthal, p. 172. Walsh published his analysis of the raids in *Cong. Rec.*, 67th Cong., 4th sess., 1923, 64, pt. 3:3005–15.
5. Lowenthal covers this episode, pp. 289–93. Hoover's side of the story is in Whitehead, *F.B.I. Story*, pp. 63–65. By implication Hoover blamed all the wrongdoing in the bureau on a rogue agent named Gaston Means, so that Hoover's firing of Means represented a symbolic cleansing of the bureau and a demonstration of Hoover's own probity.
6. See Carl Brent Swisher, "Biographical Note," in Cummings, *Selected Papers*, pp. xi–xvi.
7. Ibid., p. xi.
8. Franklin Delano Roosevelt, *The Public Papers and Addresses of Franklin D. Roosevelt*, 3 vols. (N.Y.: Random, 1938), 2:15; James MacGregor Burns begins his discussion of the inauguration with the words: "It was like a war." *Roosevelt: The Lion and the Fox* (New York: Harcourt, 1956), p. 165.
9. Burns, p. 192; Jonathan Mitchell, "The Versatility of General Johnson," *Harpers* 169(Oct., 1934):585–96.
10. Leo O. Rosten, "Men Like War," *Harpers* 171(June, 1935):192, 195.
11. Warren I. Susman, "The Thirties," in *The Development of an American Culture* (Englewood Cliffs: Prentice, 1970), is a brilliant synthesis of the events and developments of the decade that uses the nation's desire for solidarity as the key to the period.
12. Roosevelt is quoted by Burns, p. 183. Burns argues that "the extent to which Roosevelt took the role of bipartisan leader during 1933 and 1934 has not been fully appreciated by scholars." Burns calls Roosevelt's policies during those years a " 'middle way' incorporating main lines of action of previous administrations, both Democratic and Republican, reflecting ideology and interests all across the long spectrum of Roosevelt's bipartisan support, and exploiting, of course, the atmosphere of crisis and fear" (p. 609).
13. *Selected Papers*, pp. 101–2.
14. Ibid., p. 122.
15. Homer Cummings, "Modern Tendencies and the Law," speech before the American Bar Association, Aug. 31, 1933, *Selected Papers*, p. 99.
16. Homer Cummings, "Criminal Law Administration—Its Problems and Improvements," speech before The Daughters of the American Revolution, Apr. 15, 1935, *Selected Papers*, pp. 26–27.
17. *New York Times*, June 3, 1933, p. 6.
18. Ibid., July 4, 1933, p. 30.
19. Ibid., Oct. 8, 1933, sec. 1, p. 1.
20. The speech was extensively covered by the press, and the *New York Times* story (Sept. 12, 1933, p. 3) carried the headline "Government, to Survive, Must Crush Menace of Armed Underworld."
21. Ibid., July 18, 1933, p. 7.
22. Ibid., Oct. 8, 1933, sec. 2, p. 2.
23. Ibid., Aug. 2, 1933, p. 5. One such call came from the assistant attorney general of the state of Illinois.
24. Charles Francis Coe, in the *New York Times*, July 13, 1933, sec. 8, p. 2.

25. Ibid., July 2, 1933, p. 2.

26. Ibid., July 28, 1933, p. 1.

27. Ibid., July 30, 1933, p. 2.

28. Ibid., July 3, 1933, p. 1.

29. See Murray Edelman, *The Symbolic Uses of Politics* (Urbana: Univ. of Illinois Pr., 1967), pp. 73–94, for a discussion of the ways in which a leader's acceptance of responsibility reassures his followers even when he fails to deliver as promised. "Willingness to cope," Edelman argues, "is evidently central. Any action (by a leader) substitutes personal responsibility for impersonal causal chains and chance" (p. 79).

30. *New York Times,* July 4, 1933, p. 30. In his news release Cummings specifically stated that Keenan would be "assuming charge of the nation's drive against organized crime." *New York Times,* July 27, 1933, p. 1.

31. There was no doubt in the public mind about who was leading the crime war. This was the point stressed by Patricia Collins, a lawyer who had worked in the Justice Department from 1935 on, when she was interviewed in 1975. "Mr. Cummings was a mighty figure. He really was a gigantic man." Miss Collins was then asked, "You mean that he was the star, not Hoover?" and she replied, "Yes, you bet. . . . For a man with legal competence, vision, imagination and stature, I don't think we've had any Attorney General who really reached Homer Cummings. . . . He was a giant of a man, he really was." Ovid Demaris, *The Director* (New York: Harper's Magazine Pr., 1975), p. 134.

32. *New York Times,* June 18, 1933, p. 1.

33. For example, see the story in the *New York Journal,* Oct. 22, 1934, p. 1.

34. *New York Times,* July 14, 1933, p. 3.

35. Ibid., Sept. 29, 1933, p. 1; *Washington Star,* Sept. 28, 1933, p. 1.

36. Homer Cummings, "Office Memorandum to Special Assistant Joseph B. Keenan," Aug. 1, 1933, *Selected Papers,* p. 29.

37. *New York Times,* Oct. 13, 1933, p. 1.

38. There were a vast number of stories about Alcatraz at the end of 1933 and early in 1934. See "America's 'Devil's Island'—and Some Others" in *Literary Digest* 119(Oct. 28, 1933):34. *Real Detective* called the idea of an American Devil's Island in San Francisco Bay a "joke" because a high school girl had recently swum from the island to the mainland. The magazine called for the prison to be located on a remote Pacific atoll. It went on to discuss the symbolic importance of such a location: "This is war time. The Roosevelt administration is fighting against fear, against depression, against moral decay. It is fighting, likewise, against the octopus of crime. . . . Against this flood of crime must be erected effective barriers. The first important blockade will have to be speedier and more impartial justice. And the second will have to be a new form of punishment that will terrify all potential wrong-doers and take out of circulation those individuals who, by the repeated perpetration of crime, have proved that they deserve no place in normal society. . . . America needs an isolated penal colony if it is ever to shake off the tentacles of the crime octopus." *Real Detective,* Jan. 1934, p. 26.

39. Homer Cummings, "A Twelve Point Program," *Selected Papers,* pp. 37–38.

40. *New York Times,* Apr. 24, 1934, p. 1. Keenan said (in the same story) that the Justice Department hoped "to get him dead."
41. Ibid., May 19, 1934, p. 1.
42. The surrender of New York mobster Dutch Schultz to the authorities on Nov. 30, 1934, was widely taken as a symbol of the healthy terror the Department of Justice had instilled in the country's criminals. One editorial had the headline: "WISE MR. SCHULTZ—HE KNEW THAT FEDERAL AGENTS GET THEIR MAN" and the story:

When the federal authorities announced that they were out to get Dutch Schultz, New York's elusive beer-runner and racketeer, Mr. Schultz wisely came in and gave himself up.

The Federal men mean what they say.

Mr. Schultz knew that.

He remembered what they did to John Dillinger.

He no doubt reflected on their relentless hunt for Baby Face Nelson, a hunt that cost two of their agents' lives—and Nelson's.

He concluded that discretion was the better part of valor in dealing with them and he is now behind bars.

The mere word that the Department of Justice was on his trail was enough, and this in spite of the fact that if Dutch is convicted and sent to the Federal Penitentiary, the chances are that he will serve out his term.

Paroles and pardons are rare from those institutions. Politics, pull and sentiment are of little account. Ask Mr. Alfonse Capone—he knows.

Mr. Schultz's ignominious surrender places the New York City and State Police in a pretty poor light.

However, it's all over now—thanks to the hardboiled reputation that the Department of Justice has built up for itself. (*New York Evening Journal,* Nov. 30, 1934, p. 44).

43. Once again, Cummings was responding to a suggestion often made during the pre-Roosevelt depression days and the early days of the New Deal. For example, on June 28, 1933, the district attorney of Nassau County (N.Y.) asked Cummings to call a conference of the nation's DAs, governors, and police chiefs. He wanted Cummings to "arrive at a method of combining all the law enforcement groups of the nation." *New York Times,* June 28, 1933, p. 28.
44. *New York Times,* Dec. 11, 1934, p. 2. The *Times* carried the full text of Roosevelt's speech.
45. Cummings' intentions are fully covered in *Selected Papers,* pp. 50–60.
46. *New York Times,* Dec. 12, 1934, p. 2.
47. *Selected Papers,* p. 55.
48. Ibid., p. 53.
49. Cummings had been talking about this institute for a long time; this description is from his radio address, "How the Government Battles Organized Lawlessness," May 12, 1934, *Selected Papers,* pp. 91–92.
50. Cummings repeatedly used such phrases as "intimate and friendly cooperation" to describe the type of linkage he was after. (*Selected Papers,* p. 44). Again, in 1937 Cummings explained that he had sought "to develop in the Department of Justice a structure and a technique predicated upon coopera-

tion with state and local agencies toward the accomplishment of our common end—the progressive control of crime in the United States." (*Selected
Papers,* p. 48). He liked to describe the future role of the Justice Department as a "nerve center of helpful impulses and a clearing house of useful
information." (*Selected Papers,* p. 92).

51. Editorial cartoons following the Crime Conference showed the prestige
Cummings's campaign had given to the Justice Department. One typical
image had Uncle Sam wearing a Justice Department badge (*New York
Evening Journal,* Dec. 14, 1934, p. 2). Another cartoon showed a pirate
ship labeled "Organized Crime" hiding behind a smoke screen labeled "Po-
litical Corruption" while overhead there flew a warplane with the marking
"Federal Government Pursuit." The caption was "Above the Smokescreen."
(*New York Evening Journal,* Dec. 14, 1934, p. 2).

52. Once popular culture had made J. Edgar Hoover's position secure, he successfully blocked Cummings's Bureau of Crime Prevention as a threat to his
bureau's central position in the crime control establishment. One of
Hoover's assistants remembers that Hoover was able to get Cummings's
public relations officer, Henry Suydam, fired for pushing too hard for the
Crime Prevention Bureau. That Cummings was disturbed by Hoover's success in blocking the bureau can be inferred from a wistful speech Cummings
made shortly before he retired: "I must confess quite frankly to you that I
have been troubled by the comparatively inconsequential advances in the
basic matter of crime prevention. . . . The origins of crime are primarily
local, and the sources many. There will ever remain thousands of separate
problems for thousands of separate communities. At the same time I am
convinced that the federal government has a definite responsibility which it
cannot afford to shirk. It was this conviction that led me to advocate, over
and over again, the creation of a crime prevention unit in the Department
of Justice that would serve as a nerve center of helpful impulses and a
clearing house of useful information. . . . Ultimately such a unit will be
created and, in years to come, some person reviewing the struggle will make
a vigorous speech expressing well-warranted indignation that the step was
not taken sooner. But we must not be too impatient. These things take
time." "Federal Law and the Juvenile Delinquent," July 29, 1938, *Selected
Papers,* pp. 93–94.

3. Hollywood and Hoover's Rise to Power

1. Tom Wicker, "What Have They Done Since They Got Dillinger?" *New
York Times Magazine,* Dec. 28, 1969, p. 5.

2. For an introduction to the theory of the relationship between crime and
punishment and cultural solidarity, see Emile Durkheim, *The Division of
Labor in Society* (New York: Free Pr., 1964; published in France in 1893),
pp. 70–110, and *The Rules of Sociological Method* (New York, Free Pr.,
1964; published in France in 1895), pp. 64–75. A notable attempt to apply
this theory to a problem in American cultural history is Kai Erikson, *Wayward Puritans* (New York: John Wiley, 1966).

3. Memo from J. Edgar Hoover to Homer Cummings, Feb. 1935. Furnished to the author by the FBI.

4. *G-Men,* a product of Warner Brothers studios, was directed by William Keighley. The screenplay was written by Seton I. Miller, based on a story by Gregory Rogers. The cast included James Cagney, Margaret Lindsay, Ann Dvorak, Robert Armstrong, Barton MacLane, and Lloyd Nolan.

5. Press release, Department of Justice, Mar. 23, 1933. Furnished to the author by the FBI.

6. This and the following series of quotations are from the Press Book for *G-Men,* which is on Reel 35 of the Press Book Collection at the Library of the Performing Arts, New York Public Library.

7. *Motion Picture Daily,* Apr. 27, 1935, p. 1.

8. For a discussion of *G-Men*'s success, and a cultural interpretation of the film, see Bergman, pp. 83–88.

9. J. Edgar Hoover, Apr. 1935; quotation from a form letter furnished to the author by the FBI.

10. *Hearings of the Senate Appropriations Committee on the Department of Justice Appropriations for 1937,* pp. 162–63. The exchange is quoted by Lowenthal, pp. 390–91.

11. Additional support for this theory may be seen in the fact that after Cummings left the Justice Department, J. Edgar Hoover reversed his opinion of *G-Men.* In 1949 Warner Brothers reissued *G-Men* to celebrate the twenty-fifth year of Hoover's directorship, this time with Hoover's blessings. Hoover gave his close friend Jack Warner permission to use the FBI seal during the introductory credits immediately following the studio logo, and to add a spoken prologue linking the bureau to the film. See Carlos Clarens, "Hooverville West: The Hollywood G-Man, 1934–1945," *Film Comment* 13(May–June 1977):10–16. Clarens assumes that Warner Brothers publicity was accurate in claiming that "Hoover . . . supplied a few technical advisors and passed approval on the leading man" although the evidence does not support this (p. 13).

12. *New York Times,* Dec. 12, 1934, p. 21.

13. Bergman, p. 85.

14. Louis B. Nichols, interview with the author, June 26, 1975. Nichols entered the Bureau in 1934 and soon afterwards went to work in the Research Division, which handled the FBI's public relations. He became head of the Research Division (afterwards the Crime Records Division) in 1938, and remained in charge of FBI public relations until his retirement in 1957. From 1951 until 1957 he was assistant to the director, the number three position in the bureau (under Hoover and Associate Director Clyde Tolson). During his years in the FBI Nichols arranged for the production of many official films that promoted the Bureau's "we" image, including *Persons in Hiding, The House on 92nd Street,* and *Walk East on Beacon.*

15. Schott's *No Left Turns* (New York: Praeger, 1975) is the funniest of all the many "exposés" turned out by former agents.

16. Quotes are from the *G-Men* script in the film archive collection at the State Historical Society of Wisconsin, in Madison. This collection has a special strength in materials relating to Warner Brothers and RKO films.

17. Louis B. Nichols, interview with the author.
18. *G-Men* press book.
19. Of the dozens of books devoted to the thirties gangsters, John Toland's *The Dillinger Days* (New York: Random, 1963) is the best.
20. Melvin Purvis, *American Agent* (Garden City, N.Y.: Doubleday, 1936). Purvis was the special agent in charge of the bureau's Chicago office during the Dillinger, Floyd, and Nelson cases.
21. Murray Schumach, *The Face on the Cutting Room Floor* (New York: William Morrow, 1964), p. 172.
22. Jack Alexander, "The Director-1," *The New Yorker,* 13(Sept. 25, 1937):21–22.
23. The argument that there really were "ten thousand" public enemies is given in Courtney Ryley Cooper's authorized book about the Bureau, *Ten Thousand Public Enemies* (New York: Blue Ribbon, 1935). These ten thousand were supposedly the especially dangerous criminals whose capture required special care, equipment, arms, and press releases.
24. *Literary Digest* 125(May 11, 1935):30.
25. *New York Times,* Apr. 24, 1934, p. 1.
26. Quoted in William W. Turner, *Hoover's F.B.I.: The Man and the Myth* (New York: Dell, 1971), p. 114. The producer was Quinn Martin, who put together "The FBI" for television.
27. *The Nation* 211(Nov. 28, 1970):6.

4. The G-Man and the Censors

1. Press book for *Public Hero Number One,* microfilm in the Library of the Performing Arts, New York Public Library.
2. Schumach, p. 17.
3. Ibid., p. 20.
4. Quoted by Robert Sklar in *Movie-Made America* (New York: Random, 1975), p. 134.
5. Herbert Blumer and Philip M. Hauser, *Movies, Delinquency and Crime* (New York: Macmillan, 1933), pp. 13–14.
6. Ibid., p. 15.
7. Sklar, p. 137.
8. Henry James Forman, *Our Movie Made Children* (New York: Macmillan, 1933), p. 213.
9. Garth Jowett, *Film, The Democratic Art* (Boston: Little, 1975), p. 227.
10. Schumach, p. 84.
11. *Commonweal* 20(May 18, 1934):58.
12. Schumach, pp. 86–87.
13. Quoted in Olga J. Martin, *Hollywood's Movie Commandments* (New York: H. W. Wilson, 1937), p. 114.
14. Ibid., p. 120.
15. Ibid.
16. Ibid., p. 121.
17. Ibid., p. 122.

18. Ibid., p. 123.
19. Ibid., p. 122.
20. Ibid.
21. Ibid., p. 120.
22. August Vollmer and Alfred E. Parker, *Crime, Crooks and Cops* (New York: Funk, 1937), pp. 259–60.
23. Report to the IACP by Peter J. Siccardi, president, quoted in Martin, p. 112.
24. Quotes are from sound tracks of films in the collection of the Library of Congress.
25. Quoted in Martin, p. 113.
26. Douthit, p. 332.
27. Vollmer and Parker, pp. 246–47.
28. Martin, p. 135.
29. O. W. Wilson, "Police Administration," in the *Municipal Year Book* (Chicago: International City Manager's Association, 1936), pp. 82–83.
30. Martin, pp. 134–35.
31. Ibid., p. 132.

5. The G-Man and the Public

1. Pioneering efforts to trace the history of the action detective include Edmund Pearson, *Dime Novels* (Port Washington, N.Y.: Kennikat, 1968; first published in 1929); Mary Noel, *Villains Galore* (New York: Macmillan, 1954); Ron Goulart, *An Informal History of the Pulp Magazine* (New York: Ace, 1973); and George Orwell, "Raffles and Miss Blandish," in *The Collected Essays, Journalism and Letters of George Orwell* 1(London: Secker and Warburg, 1968):461–93; idem., "Boys' Weeklies," in *The Collected Essays, Journalism and Letters of George Orwell* 3(London: Secker and Warburg, 1968):212–24.
2. Edmund Wilson, "Why Do People Read Detective Stories?" "Who Cares Who Killed Roger Ackroyd?" and "Mr. Holmes, They Were the Footprints of a Gigantic Hound," all reprinted in *Classics and Commercials* (New York: Farrar, 1950), pp. 231–37; 257–65; 266–74.
3. William O. Aydelotte, "The Detective Story as a Historical Source," in Francis M. Nevins, Jr., ed., *The Mystery Writer's Art* (Bowling Green, Ohio: Popular Pr., 1970), pp. 306–25.
4. Orwell, p. 151.
5. Pearson, *Dime Novels*, pp. 191–97.
6. Ibid., pp. 138–90.
7. Ibid., pp. 209–15; Robert Clurman, ed., *Nick Carter, Detective* (New York: Dell, 1965).
8. Pearson, *Dime Novels*, pp. 142–43.
9. Ibid., p. 141.
10. Ibid., pp. 142–43.
11. Goulart, *History*, p. 28.
12. Clurman, p. 11.

13. Press Book for *Public Hero Number One,* microfilm copy in the Library of the Performing Arts, New York Public Library.

14. Press book for *Public Enemy's Wife,* microfilm copy in the Library of the Performing Arts, New York Public Library.

15. *The Newgate Calendar* of 1773, in 5 vols., was the definitive edition, the culmination of a long series of trial records intended for the general reader. This tradition may have begun with the *Tyburn Calendar* of 1700 and included the famous *Select Trials at the Sessions House in the Old Bailey,* published in 2 vols. in 1730.

16. This example is reprinted (in facsimile) in Julian Symons, *A Pictorial History of Crime* (New York: Crown, 1966), p. 42.

17. E. Z. C. Buntline, *The Mysteries and Miseries of New York: A Story of Real Life* (New York: E. Z. C. Buntline, 1848). For a discussion of this book and of Buntline's career, see Jay Monaghan, *The Great Rascal: The Life and Adventures of Ned Buntline* (New York: Bonanza, 1951).

18. There have been many reprint collections of articles from the *Police Gazette.* See particularly the edition edited by Gene Smith, which carries an informative introduction by Tom Wolfe. (New York: Simon and Schuster, 1972).

19. Principally in Emile Durkheim, *Division of Labor.*

20. Ibid., pp. 104, 79.

21. George Herbert Mead, "The Psychology of Primitive Justice," *American Journal of Sociology* 23(1918):591, quoted in Dennis Campbell, *Sociology and the Stereotype of the Criminal* (London: Tavistock, 1968), p. 25.

22. Durkheim, *Division of Labor,* p. 108; Emile Durkheim, *Moral Education* (New York: Free Pr., 1961; first published in France in 1925), p. 167.

23. A. R. Radcliffe-Brown, *Structure and Function in Primitive Society* (London, 1952), quoted in H. D. Duncan, "The Development of Durkheim's Concept of Ritual and the Problem of Social Disrelationships" in Kurt H. Wolff, ed., *Emile Durkheim* (Columbus: Univ. Of Ohio Pr., 1960), p. 98.

24. For a discussion of Wild and his times, see Gerald Howson, *Thief-Taker General: The Rise and Fall of Jonathan Wild* (New York: St. Martin's Pr., 1960).

25. "Waters" [William Russell], *Recollections of a Detective Police Officer* (London, 1856) has been reissued (London: Covent Gardens, 1973) with an informative introduction. See also A. E. Murch, *The Development of the Detective Novel* (Port Washington, N.Y.: Kennikat, 1968).

26. Howard Haycraft, *Murder for Pleasure: The Life and Times of the Detective Story* (New York Appleton, 1941), p. 29.

27. Symons, *Crime,* p. 16.

28. See James D. Horan, *The Pinkertons* (New York: Crown, 1968). One of Arthur Conan Doyle's Sherlock Holmes novels, *The Valley of Fear,* was based on information given to Doyle by Allan Pinkerton when they were fellow passengers on a transatlantic steamer. Pinkerton told the story himself in *The Mollie Maguires and the Detectives,* which was published as vol. 6 in *Allan Pinkerton's Detective Stories* (New York: Carleton, 1877).

29. Orwell, p. 149–50.

30. William Ruehlmann, *Saint with a Gun: The Unlawful American Private Eye* (New York: New York Univ. Pr., 1974), pp. 91, 98–9.

31. Lotte Bailyn, "Mass Media and Children: A Study of Exposure Habits and Cognitive Effects," *Psychological Monographs* 61(1959):35.
32. Ibid., p. 33.
33. Ibid., p. 35.
34. Ibid., p. 30.

6. The FBI Formula and the G-Man Hero

1. Whitehead, *F.B.I. Story*, p. 68.
2. J. Edgar Hoover, "Criminal Identification," *Annals of the American Academy* 145(Nov. 1929):205–13.
3. See *Washington Post*, Oct. 13, 1929, p. 17.
4. Rex Collier, letter to the author, Apr. 20, 1976.
5. Conversation with the author, Jan. 27, 1976.
6. This case was featured in the radio show "G-Men," Don Whitehead's *F.B.I. Story*, the "Secret Agent X-9" comic strip, and the movie *The F.B.I. Story*. The story was also told twice by Courtney Ryley Cooper, first in *Enemies* (New York: Blue Ribbon, 1935) and later in "The King of the Bandits," *American Magazine* 125(June 1938):51–52; 146–48.
7. *Newsweek*, Aug. 12, 1933, p. 16.
8. Alexander, "Director-1," p. 24.
9. Drew Pearson, *Diaries* (New York: Holt, 1974).
10. Rex Collier and L. B. Nichols, conversations with the author, June 26, 1975.
11. Courtney Ryley Cooper, "Getting the Jump on Crime," *American Magazine* 116(Aug., 1933):23–25; 100–101.
12. Ibid., p. 100.
13. Ibid., p. 25.
14. Ibid., p. 100.
15. Ibid., p. 24.
16. Ibid., p. 25.
17. Ibid., p. 100.
18. J. Edgar Hoover, "Crime Trap," *American Magazine* 116(Nov., 1933):64–66; 94–98.
19. This slightly expanded version appeared in *Enemies*, p. 124.
20. "Crime Trap," p. 64.
21. Courtney Ryley Cooper, "Behind the Guns of Crime," *American Magazine* 117(Jan., 1934):101.
22. Ibid.
23. Cooper, *Enemies*.
24. Ibid., pp. 5,6
25. Ibid., pp. 3,4.
26. Ibid., p. 356.
27. Ibid., p. 6.
28. Ibid., p. 17.
29. Ibid., p. 126.

30. Courtney Ryley Cooper, "The Roots of Crime," *Saturday Evening Post,* Dec. 22, 1934, p. 13.
31. Ibid., p. 57.
32. Cooper, *Enemies,* p. 46.
33. Ibid., p. 178.
34. Ibid., p. 351.
35. Ibid., p. 352.
36. For instance see "The Statistical G-Man" in Turner, *Hoover's F.B.I.,* or read Schott, *No Left Turns.*
37. Douthit, pp. 332–33.
38. Cooper, *Enemies,* pp. 355–56.
39. Vollmer and Parker, p. 254.
40. Ibid., p. 260.
41. Sanford J. Ungar, *F.B.I.* (Boston: Little, 1976) p. 383.

7. The FBI Formula and John Dillinger

1. U.S. Congress, *Select Committee to Study Governmental Operations with Respect to Intelligence Operations, Final Report,* 94th Congr., 2d sess., S. Rept. 94-755, bk. 3, p. 932.
2. William C. Sullivan, quoted by Ovid Demaris in *The Director,* p. 83.
3. Alexander, "Director-1," p. 31.
4. William C. Sullivan, quoted by Demaris, p. 83–84.
5. Louis B. Nichols, interview with the author, June 26, 1975.
6. Alexander, "Director-1," p. 21.
7. A scene in *The F.B.I. Story* showed the Dillinger target, and it has also appeared frequently in other FBI movies.
8. This account is based primarily on John Toland, *The Dillinger Days.* Another reliable account is Robert Cromie and Joseph Pinkson, *Dillinger: A Short and Violent Life* (New York: McGraw, 1962).
9. J. Edgar Hoover, *Persons in Hiding* (Boston: Little, 1938), p. 303.
10. Quoted by Toland, p. 245.
11. Quoted by Cromie and Pinkson, p. 169.
12. Purvis, pp. 265–66.
13. *Time,* Apr. 23, 1934, p. 18.
14. Toland, p. 257.
15. Cromie and Pinkson, p. 169.
16. Ibid., p. 223.
17. *Time,* May 7, 1934, p. 18.
18. Whitehead, *F.B.I. Story,* p. 104.
19. Quoted by Milton S. Mayer, "Myth of the 'G-Men'," *Forum* 94(Sept. 1935):145.
20. *The New York Times* headline for Apr. 24, 1934, was, "NEW DILLINGER KILLINGS STIR THE PRESIDENT AND HE ASKS QUICK ACTION ON CRIME BILLS."
21. *Washington Star,* June 29, 1934, p. 1; July 9, 1934, p. 1; July 21, 1934, p. 1.
22. Toland, p. 307.

23. *Time,* May 7, 1934, pp. 18–21.
24. Quoted by Cromie and Pinkson, p. 88.
25. Quoted by Toland, p. 320. Whitehead has the identical quote (p. 105) but does not credit it to Purvis. Andrew Tully, *The F.B.I.'s Most Famous Cases* (New York: Morrow, 1965), p. 107, makes history follow the FBI line by giving these words to Sam Cowley.
26. Purvis, pp. 275–76.
27. *New York Daily Mirror,* July 24, 1934, p. 1.
28. Ibid., p. 2.
29. Ibid., p. 6.
30. Ibid., July 25, 1934, p. 1.
31. Cromie and Pinkson, p. 204.
32. *New York Evening Journal,* July 24, 1934, p. 26.
33. *San Francisco Chronicle,* July 23, 1934, p. 1.
34. Toland, p. 328.
35. *New York Evening Journal,* July 24, 1934, p. 1.
36. William C. Sullivan, quoted by Demaris, p. 81.
37. *New York Evening Journal,* July 24, 1934, p. 10.
38. Ibid., p. 1.
39. *Washington Star,* Sept. 2, 1934, p. 1.
40. *Time,* Oct. 29, 1934, p. 11.
41. *New York Evening Journal,* Oct. 23, 1934, p. 10.
42. *Washington Star,* July 23, 1934, p.3.
43. Ibid., July 25, 1934, p. 4.
44. Ibid., July 23, 1934, p. 1.
45. The series ran in the *Star* July 26–31.
46. *Washington Star,* July 26, 1934, p. 3.
47. Ibid.
48. Ibid., p. 1.
49. *New York Evening Journal,* Sept. 28, 1934, p. 1.
50. Ibid., p. 2.
51. J. Edgar Hoover, *Persons in Hiding* (Boston: Little, 1938), pp. 85, 98–99.
52. Louis B. Nichols, quoted in Demaris, p. 71.
53. All quotations are from a copy of the script furnished the author by the FBI, and from correspondence owned by Rex Collier.
54. All quotations are from page proofs of the comic strip owned by Rex Collier, and from letters and memos in his possession.
55. "War on Crime" page proofs.
56. J. Edgar Hoover, "The Adventure of Scientific Crime Control," Kalamazoo College, June 14, 1937. Reprinted in *Vital Speeches* 3(July 1, 1937):559–62.
57. Jay Robert Nash and Ron Offen, *Dillinger, Dead or Alive?* (Chicago: Henry Regnery, 1970). The quotation is from Nash's crime encyclopedia, *Bloodletters and Badmen* (New York: Warners, 1975), p. 167.
58. J. Edgar Hoover, memo in possession of the FBI.
59. Robert Shea and Robert Anton Wilson, *Illuminatus!* 3 vols. (New York: Dell, 1975).
60. *New York Times,* Mar. 7, 1976, Travel Section, p. 29.

8. The Comic Strip G-Man

1. Alexander, "Director-1," p. 20.
2. Background on Secret Agent X-9 can be found in Ron Goulart, *The Adventurous Decade: Comic Strips in the Thirties* (New Rochelle, N.Y.: Arlington House, 1975), and *Nostalgia Comics* 1 (n.d.).
3. Goulart, *Decade,* p. 90.
4. Louis B. Nichols, conversation with the author, June 26, 1975.
5. This discussion of "War On Crime" is based on interviews with the writer, Rex Collier, and on materials lent by Mr. Collier to the author.
6. Ledger Syndicate promotional flyer for "War On Crime" (n.d.), in possession of the author.
7. Doug Borgstedt to Rex Collier, May 15, 1935.
8. See the reprint of the Batman origin story in Jules Feiffer, *The Great Comic Book Heroes* (New York: Bonanza, 1965), pp. 69–70.
9. See the reprint of the Superman origin story in Feiffer, pp. 57–58.
10. See the synopsis of the Dick Tracy origin story in *Limited Collectors Edition Presents Dick Tracy* (Chicago: Chicago Tribune, 1975), inside cover.
11. For example, in his introduction to Andrew Tully's *The F.B.I.'s Most Famous Cases* (New York: Morrow, 1965), Hoover wrote, "Machine Gun Kelly occupies an . . . important place in the F.B.I.'s history, for he tagged our Agents with the indelible nickname of 'G-Men' on September 26, 1933, while surrendering at Memphis Tennessee" (p. x). Actually the term "G-Men" was not in general circulation until after the Cagney movie appeared in spring, 1935, though Rex Collier had begun using it in his Dillinger stories in July, 1934; this may mean that Hoover began promoting its use around that time. Certainly the term "G-Men" does not appear in any of the first newspaper accounts of Kelly's capture.
12. See the synopsis of the Captain Marvel origin story in Feiffer, p. 68.
13. Rex Collier to Doug Borgstedt, June 8, 1936.
14. Goulart, *Decade,* p. 90.
15. The Captain America origin story is reprinted in Feiffer pp. 163–70.
16. Jim Harmon, "A Swell Bunch of Guys," in *All Color For A Dime,* ed. Dick Lupoff and Don Thompson (New York: Ace, 1970), p. 179.
17. Walter Bagehot, *The English Constitution* (Garden City, N.Y.: Doubleday, 1966; first published in 1867), esp. pp. 63–69.
18. Murray Edelman, *The Symbolic Uses of Politics* (Urbana: Univ. of Illinois Pr., 1964), esp. pp. 4–21.
19. Hugh Dalziel Duncan, *Symbols in Society* (New York: Oxford, 1968), p. 237.

9. Public Hero Number One

1. For information on the history of the pulps, see Goulart, *History;* and Bill Blackbeard, "The Pulps," in *Handbook of American Popular Culture,* ed. by M. Thomas Inge (Westport, Conn.: Greenwood, 1979)1:195–224. Also see Tony Bluestone, ed., *The Pulps* (New York: Chelsea House, 1976);

Quentin Reynolds, *Fiction Factory* (New York: Random House, 1955); Frank Gruber, *Pulp Jungle* (Nashville: Sherbourne Pr., 1967); and Harold Hersey, *Pulp Wood Editor* (New York: Frederick A. Stokes, 1938).

2. J. Edgar Hoover, "Partners in Murder," *G-Men*, Nov., 1935, p. 88.

3. Frankie Lewis, "Passing the Queer," *G-Men*, Nov., 1935, pp. 106, 110.

4. Clayton Maxwell, "Public Enemies," *G-Men*, Nov., 1935, p. 105.

5. "Federal Flashes," *G-Men*, Nov., 1935, p. 122.

6. Ibid., Mar., 1936, p. 120; Jan., 1937, p. 122; July 1941, pp. 106–7.

7. C. K. M. Scanlon, "Bring 'Em Back Dead," *G-Men*, Nov., 1935, p. 16.

8. Ibid., p. 16.

9. C. K. M. Scanlon, "Give 'Em Hell," *G-Men*, Jan., 1937, p. 77.

10. Ibid., p. 22.

11. C. K. M. Scanlon, "King Crime," *G-Men*, Mar., 1936, p. 28.

12. Ibid., p. 37.

13. Frederick C. Davis quoted by Goulart, *History*, p. 85.

14. Maxwell Grant, "The Crime Oracle," *The Shadow Magazine*, June 1, 1936.

15. C. K. M. Scanlon, "Crime's Blackboard," *G-Men*, Oct., 1937, pp. 12–13.

16. Ibid., p. 71.

17. Ibid., p. 33.

18. Ibid., p. 38.

19. Ibid.

20. Ibid., p. 41.

21. Ibid.

22. Ibid., p. 40.

23. Ibid., p. 42.

24. Ibid.

25. Ibid., p. 81.

26. Quoted by Max Lowenthal, *The Federal Bureau of Investigation* (New York: Sloan, 1950), p. 392.

27. Ibid.

28. "Are Your Fingerprints on File?" *The Feds*, Sept., 1937, pp. 9–10.

29. Ibid., p. 9.

30. *The Feds*, Sept., 1937, p. 8.

31. "Are Your Fingerprints on File?" p. 9.

32. Ibid.

33. *The Feds*, Sept., 1937, p. 8.

34. Robert R. Mill, "Shock Troops of Justice," *Blue Book*, Sept., 1935, p. 6.

35. Ibid., inside front cover.

36. Ibid., p. 4.

37. Ibid., p. 5.

38. Ibid.

39. Hoover gave his own account of the capture in *Persons in Hiding*, pp. 70–72, and in Frederick L. Collins, *The F.B.I. in Peace and War* (New York: Putnam, 1943), pp. 286–87.

40. Collins, p. 287.

41. *New York Evening Journal*, May 2, 1936, p. 1.

42. Ibid.

43. *Time,* Aug. 8, 1949, p. 15.
44. *New York American,* Aug. 21, 1935, p. 1.
45. *Washington Star,* May 2, 1936, p. 12.
46. Ibid., May 16, 1936.
47. Ralph De Toledano, *J. Edgar Hoover: The Man in His Time* (New Rochelle, N.Y.: Arlington, 1973), p. 130.
48. *New York Evening Journal,* May 8, 1936, p. 1.
49. *Newsweek,* Dec. 26, 1936, pp. 16–17.
50. *New York Times,* Dec. 15, 1936, p. 1.
51. Ibid.
52. The story has been often retold; e.g., see De Toledano, p. 145.
53. FBI press release, 1944.
54. J. Edgar Hoover, Introduction to Collins, p. xv.
55. Ibid., p. 220.
56. Ibid., p. 283.
57. Ibid.
58. Ibid., pp. 285–86.
59. Ibid., p. 287.
60. Ibid., p. 290.

10. The Junior G-Men

1. Harold Rome told me that FBI agents often came to his theater just to hear this song, which goes on to satirize the director's fondness for the Stork Club and Palm Beach. Copyright 1937, Harold Rome; used with permission.
2. Kenneth G. Crawford, "J. Edgar Hoover," *The Nation* 144(Feb. 27, 1937):232.
3. Bill Adler, *Kids' Letters to the F.B.I.* (Englewood Cliffs, N.J.: Prentice-Hall, 1966).
4. Ibid.
5. 1932 Sunday Comic Supplement advertisement in possession of the author.
6. Reprinted in *Radio Premiums Illustrated,* ed. Rex Miller (Mt. Vernon, Ill.: Supermantics, 1971).
7. Ibid.
8. Ibid.
9. Ibid.
10. Ibid.
11. Ibid.
12. Ibid.
13. Ibid.
14. Adler.
15. For synopses of these and the following serials, see Ken Weiss and Ed Goodgold, *To Be Continued* (New York: Bonanza, 1972).
16. Adler.
17. Ibid.
18. Morrell Massey, *Junior G-Man and the Counterfeiters* (Racine, Wis.: Whit-

man, 1937), pp. 55–56.

19. Ibid., p. 424.

20. George Clark and Lou Hanlon, *The G-Man on the Crime Trail* (Racine, Wis.: Whitman, 1936), p. 424; another variation was to make a Junior G-Man hero out of the son of a G-Man: Warren F. Robinson, *The "G" Man's Son at Porpoise Island* (Chicago: Goldsmith, 1937).

21. Number 10 in the "Dare Devils" card series, n.d.

22. Number 10 in the "G-Man and Heroes of the Law" card series (Gum, Incorporated, 1936).

23. Number 1 in the "G-Men and Heroes of the Law" card series.

24. Number A 205 in the "Government Agents vs. Public Enemies" card series (M. Pressner, 1936).

25. Adler.

26. Ramsay Clark, in Demaris, *The Director,* p. 232.

27. Schott, p. 172.

28. Turner, *Hoover's F.B.I.,* p. 91.

11. The FBI in Peace and War

1. For accounts of the FBI's World War I activities, see Murray, *Red Scare,* passim; John Higham, *Strangers in the Land* (New York: Atheneum, 1973), pp. 211–12; Lowenthal, pp. 22–265; R. G. Brown et al., *Illegal Practices of the Department of Justice* (Washington, D.C., 1920; New York: Arno Pr., 1969).

2. For many instances of the pressure Hoover exerted on writers to project the "proper" image of the FBI, see Ungar, pp. 368–90.

3. Much of the following is based on the author's interview with Rex Collier, Jan. 27, 1976.

4. See Lord's obiturary in the *Portland (Me.) Press-Herald,* Oct. 21, 1975.

5. Rex Collier to author, Jan. 27, 1976.

6. Phillips H. Lord to Rex Collier, July 23, 1935. I am grateful to Rex Collier for making this agreement, and other correspondence between himself and Lord, available to me.

7. The complete list of subjects: John Dillinger (July 20), Baby Face Nelson (July 27), Osage Indians (Aug. 3), Martin Durkin (Aug. 10), Cannon Extortion (Aug. 17), Bremer Kidnapping (Aug. 24), Urschel Kidnapping (Aug. 31), Urschel Kidnapping—Machine Gun Kelly (Sept. 7), Tri-State Gang (Sept. 14), Fleagle Brothers (Sept. 21), Pretty Boy Floyd (Sept. 28), Boettcher Kidnapping (Oct. 5), Eddie Doll (Oct. 12). Source: FBI memo, dated Sept. 23, 1935.

8. Jim Harmon, *The Great Radio Heroes* (New York: Ace, 1967), p. 33.

9. All quotes are from a copy of the script in the possession of the author.

10. Hoover, *Persons in Hiding,* p. 280.

11. All quotes are from a copy of the script in the possession of the author.

12. Phillippa Lord in a conversation with the author, July 27, 1976.

13. Harmon, *Radio Heroes,* p. 40.

14. Rex Collier to the author, Jan. 27, 1976.

15. Harmon, *Radio Heroes,* pp. 34–35.

16. Quote is from the tape of a "Gangbusters" episode in the possession of the author.

17. Quote is from the tape of a "Mr. District Attorney" episode in the possession of the author.

18. Quote is from the tape of a "David Harding, Counterspy" episode in the possession of the author.

19. Ungar, p. 103.

20. *Saturday Evening Post,* Apr. 17, 1943, p. 34.

21. Feiffer, p. 48.

22. For the story of the FBI's pre-World War II counterespionage activities, see Whitehead, *F.B.I. Story,* pp. 157–70; Collins, pp. 211–26; Fred J. Cook, *The F.B.I. Nobody Knows* (New York: Macmillan, 1964), pp. 240–44, 252–57. Also see *Final Report of the Select Committee to Study Governmental Operations with Respect to Intelligence Activities,* 94th Congr., 2d sess., S. Rept. 94–775, book 3, pp. 391–422.

23. *New York Journal-American,* Feb. 22, 1938, p. 3.

24. Ibid., Feb. 28, 1938, p. 1.

25. Ibid., May 9, 1938, p. 4.

26. Ibid., May 10, 1938, p. 1.

27. Ibid., May 12, 1938, p. 2.

28. Ibid., June 20, 1938, p. 1.

29. Ibid., June 24, 1938, p. 1.

30. Ibid., June 23, 1938, p. 2. Turrou's memoirs were published in book form as *The Nazi Spy Conspiracy in America* (New York: Random, 1939).

31. *New York Journal-American,* June 23, 1938, p. 2.

32. Ibid., July 1, 1938, p. 1.

33. All quotations are from the press book for *Confessions of a Nazi Spy* in the microfilm collection of the Library of the Performing Arts, New York Public Library.

34. J. Edgar Hoover, with Courtney Ryley Cooper, "Stamping out the Spies," *American Magazine* 129(Jan. 1940):20.

35. Ibid., p. 83.

36. Ibid.

37. Ibid., p. 84.

38. Ibid., p. 21.

39. All quotations are from the publicity release "News Items from the March of Time's *The F.B.I. Front*" in the *F.B.I. Front* file in the Library of the Performing Arts, New York Public Library.

40. Harmon, *Radio Heroes,* pp. 44–45. Hoover evidently ignored the children's program, "Junior G-Men," which began in 1936.

41. Collins, p. xv.

42. Louis Nichols, interview with the author, June 26, 1975.

43. There were a few one-shot or local official FBI radio shows between 1935 and 1945. For example, the biographical series "The March Thru Life" broadcast a show about Hoover written by John B. Kennedy on WABC

(New York) on Mar. 31, 1941. WGY (Schenectady) ran a series of adventures called "The F.B.I. in Action" in 1943. Agents from the FBI's Albany office appeared as narrators, and the show was endorsed by Hoover.

44. Quotes are from the script in the possession of the author. For Hoover's remarks about the program, see *Radio Daily*, Mar. 21, 1945.

45. Quotes are from a tape in the possession of the author.

46. A movie with the same title was released in 1951 with Frank Lovejoy as Matt Cvetic. See Lovejoy's copy of the script in the Library of the Performing Arts, New York Public Library.

47. Quotes are from a tape in the possession of the author.

12. One G-Man's Family

1. Quotes are from tapes in the possession of the author.

2. Quotes are from tapes in the possession of the author.

3. J. Edgar Hoover, *Masters of Deceit* (New York: Holt, 1958; all quotes are from the Pocket Books edition, 1959).

4. Ibid., p. 270.

5. Ibid., p. 230.

6. Ibid., pp. 48,176.

7. Ibid., p. 24.

8. Ibid., p. 100.

9. Ibid., p. 314.

10. Ibid., p. 120.

11. Ibid., p. vi.

12. Ibid., p. 148.

13. Ibid., p. 301.

14. Ibid., p. 32.

15. Ibid., pp. 16–17.

16. Ibid., p. 106.

17. Ibid., p. 107.

18. Ibid., p. 161.

19. Whitehead, *F.B.I. Story*.

20. Louis B. Nichols, quoted by Demaris, *The Director*, p. 68.

21. New York *Herald Tribune*, Feb. 6, 1957, p. 10.

22. Ungar, *F.B.I.*

23. This discussion of *The F.B.I. Story* is based on the print of the film in the collection of the Library of Congress.

24. Bosley Crowther, *The New York Times*, Oct. 4, 1959, section 2, p. 1.

25. Mervyn LeRoy, quoted in Demaris, *The Director*, p. 69.

26. J. Edgar Hoover, "How J. Edgar Hoover Felt About TV's 'The F.B.I.,'" *TV Guide*, May 20–26, 1972, pp. 28–30.

27. This analysis of the FBI routine for processing "The F.B.I." scripts is based on interviews with members of the bureau's Crime Records (now called External Affairs) Division, and on an examination of scripts and memos in the possession of the FBI.

28. Hoover, "TV's 'The F.B.I.'," p. 30.
29. Quoted by Demaris in *The Director*, p. 71.
30. Estimates on the size of the show's audience vary according to the source and the year concerned. The high figure is Hoover's own, given in his *TV Guide* article. *Variety*, Feb. 16, 1969, gave a figure of 25 million per week, and listed 43 foreign countries as the overseas market.
31. Demaris, *The Director*, pp. 77–78, quotes Zimbalist on the actor's admiration for Hoover. Turner, in *Hoover's F.B.I.*, pp. 115–16, tells of some of Zimbalist's off-screen work for the FBI, which included speeches at the FBI National Academy, an appearance on the NET debate program "The Advocates," and honorary chairmanship of a national pro-FBI lobby called "Friends of the F.B.I."
32. *The Village Voice*, Feb. 8, 1968, pp. 25,27.
33. Cartha DeLoach, interview with the author, Mar. 10, 1975.
34. "Education Against Crime," speech to the Chicago Boys Club, Nov. 9, 1936, reprinted in *Vital Speeches* 3(Dec. 1, 1936):109–13. While Hoover, of course, did not write his own speeches, he treated them with the utmost seriousness. He customarily had his assistant directors cull his invitations to select the forums that would have the most impact. Then a conference of assistant directors, presided over by Hoover, would discuss what ought to be in the speech, after which several of the assistant directors, usually including Louis Nichols, chief of FBI publicity during the thirties, would prepare a draft. Hoover would edit these speeches minutely, so that the final speech reflected not only his ideas, but his feelings and style. Preliminary drafts of Hoover's speeches in the possession of the FBI show revisions in Hoover's hand that sometimes amount to completely new versions. The description of the speechwriting process is from an interview with Louis Nichols by the author, June 26, 1975.
35. J. Edgar Hoover, "The Influence of Crime on the American Home," *Radio Round Table Forum*, Mar. 11, 1936, reprinted in *Vital Speeches* 2(Mar. 23, 1936):390–94.
36. Hoover, "Education Against Crime."
37. J. Edgar Hoover, "Combating Lawlessness: America's Most Destructive Disease," speech delivered before the Association of American Life Insurance Presidents, New York City, Dec. 3, 1937; reprinted in *Vital Speeches* 4(Feb. 15, 1938):269–72.
38. Hoover, "Education Against Crime."
39. J. Edgar Hoover, "Problems of Law Enforcement: Crime Rests at the Doorstep of the American Home," speech to the annual convention of the International Association of Chiefs of Police, San Francisco, Oct. 10, 1939, reprinted in *Vital Speeches* 6(Nov. 1, 1939):54–57.
40. See Ungar, pp. 282–83, 434–36, for stories of Hoover's behind-the-scenes maneuvers in the American Legion and IACP, the last with mixed success.
41. J. Edgar Hoover, "Our Heritage of Greatness," speech delivered before the Pennsylvania Society and the Society of Pennsylvania Women, New York City, Dec. 12, 1964. FBI press release.
42. J. Edgar Hoover, "Keys to Freedom," speech delivered before the national convention of the Catholic Youth Organization, New York City, Nov. 16,

1963. FBI press release.

43. Ibid.

44. J. Edgar Hoover, "Faith, Freedom and Law," speech delivered before the Regional Conference on Crime Prevention of the Michigan State Bar Association, Rochester, Mich., Jun. 8, 1967. FBI press release.

45. J. Edgar Hoover, *Masters of Deceit,* pp. 311–14.

46. J. Edgar Hoover, "Should I Force My Child?" *American Mercury 86(Feb. 19, 1958):19.*

13. Today's FBI

1. Advertisement in *T.V. Guide,* New York Metropolitan Edition, Oct. 24–30, 1981, A-41.

2. Joe Cali, quoted in *Providence Sunday Journal Program Guide,* Sept. 20, 1981, p. 8.

3. Mike Connors, quoted by Bob Lardine, "This 'F.B.I.' Is Just Too Perfect," *New York Daily News,* Dec. 29, 1981.

4. Interviews in a College of Staten Island media class conducted by the author.

5. For example, see John J. O'Connor, " ' Today's F.B.I.'—Off to An Impressive Start," *New York Times,* Oct. 25, 1981, p. 31.

6. Irving Wallace, *The R Document* (New York: Simon, 1976), p. 251.

7. Ibid., pp. 57–58.

8. Robert Ludlum, *The Chancellor Manuscript* (New York: Dial, 1977), p. 120.

9. Ibid., pp. 126–27.

10. Ibid., p. 128.

11. Ungar, p. 493.

12. David Garrow, *The F.B.I. and Martin Luther King, Jr.* (New York: Norton, 1981), p. 122.

13. John Edgar Hoover, "The S.D.S. and the High Schools: A Study in Extremism," *The P.T.A. Magazine* 64(Jan. 1970):2–5; John Edgar Hoover, "The S.D.S. and the High Schools: Part 2," *The P.T.A. Magazine* 64(Feb., 1970):8–9.

14. Hoover, "The S.D.S. and the High Schools: Part 2," p. 8.

15. Hoover, "The S.D.S.: Extremism," p. 5.

16. Ibid., p. 3.

17. "Opinions by Post," *The P.T.A. Magazine* 64(Mar., 1970):19.

18. Ibid., pp. 19–20.

19. Ibid., p. 20.

20. *Report upon the Illegal Practices of the Department of Justice.* (Washington, D.C.: National Popular Government League, May 1920).

21. *The Deportation Cases of 1919–20* (Federal Council of Churches: Interchurch World Movement), presented before the Senate Judiciary Committee.

22. Ray Tucker, "Hsst, Who Goes There?" *Colliers* 92(Aug. 19, 1933):15,49.

23. William Seagle, "The American National Police," *Harpers* 169(Nov. 1934):751–61.

24. Ibid., p. 760.
25. Mayer, "Myth," pp. 144–48.
26. Ibid., p. 147.
27. Ibid., p. 148.
28. Ibid.
29. Ibid., p. 145.
30. Ibid., p. 146.
31. See Whitehead, *F.B.I. Story,* 18, esp. pp. 157–67, for an account of this.
32. For example, see "The Shape of Things," *The Nation* 143(July 18, 1936):59.
33. "Our Lawless G-Men," *The Nation* 150(Mar. 2, 1940):296; see also "Sequel to a Melodrama," *The Nation* 150(May 11, 1940):584–85; "Card for Mr. Hoover," *The Nation* 150(Mar. 23, 1940):380.
34. "Investigate the American OGPU," *The New Republic* 102(Mar. 11, 1940):330.
35. Quoted in Cook, *F.B.I. Nobody Knows,* p. 249.
36. Ibid., p. 247; " 'Plot' Against Hoover," *The Nation* 150(Mar. 9, 1940): 323.
37. "Mr. Dies Goes to Town," *The Nation* 147(Sept. 3, 1938):216.
38. "Why Tap Wires," *The Nation* 152(Mar. 8, 1941):258.
39. Thomas Sancton, "Dossiers for the Millions," *The Nation* 167(Sept. 25, 1948):336.
40. Lowenthal, *The Federal Bureau of Investigation.*
41. Ibid., p. 3.
42. "Dangerous Thoughts: The F.B.I. Reviews a Book," 172(*The Nation,* Jan. 27, 1951):86.
43. Cook, *F.B.I. Nobody Knows,* p. 405.
44. Ibid., pp. 405–6.
45. Ibid., p. 390.
46. Ibid., p. 271.
47. Ibid., pp. 422–23.
48. Fred J. Cook, review of Hoover's *Masters of Deceit* in *The Nation* 186(May 24, 1958):478–80.
49. Norman Ollestad, *Inside the F.B.I.* (New York: Lancer, 1968).
50. Turner, *Hoover's F.B.I.*
51. Allen Weinstein, *Perjury: The Hiss-Chambers Case* (New York: Knopf, 1978), p. 517.
52. Ibid., pp. 505–23.
53. Garrow, chap. 2.
54. Ibid., p. 202.
55. Ibid., p. 229.
56. John J. O'Connor, "TV: 6-Hour 'King,' Drama of Civil Rights," *New York Times,* Feb. 9, 1978, p. C–20.
57. *Final Report of the Select Committee to Study Governmental Operations with Respect to Intelligence Activities,* 94th Cong., 2d sess., 1976, S. Rept. 94-755. The hearings were held late in 1975 and early 1976.
58. Rex Stout, *The Doorbell Rang* (New York: Viking, 1965), p. 186.
59. "The Truth About Hoover," *Time,* Dec. 22, 1978, pp. 14–22.

60. Ibid., p. 14.
61. Ibid., p. 14.
62. Joseph L. Schott, *No Left Turns,* (New York: Praeger, 1975); Warren Hinckle, "Review of No Left Turns," *New York Times,* July 13, 1975, pp. 4–5. The 1978 film *The Secret Files of J. Edgar Hoover* also took an absurdist approach.
63. Theodore H. White, *Breach of Faith: The Fall of Richard Nixon* (New York: Atheneum, 1975), p. 331.
64. Weinstein, *Prejury,* p. 548.
65. Ibid., pp. 548–49.
66. White, *Breach of Faith,* p. 335.
67. Ibid., p. 335.
68. Ibid., pp. 335–36.
69. Ovid Demaris, *The Director* (New York: Harpers Magazine Pr., 1975), p. 329.

BIBLIOGRAPHY

Probably no institution in recent American history has been the subject of such massive and partisan publicity and study as Hoover's FBI. Compounding the problem raised by the sheer bulk of this material is the evanescent and highly perishable nature of much of it. Daily newspaper accounts of fast-breaking cases, news photos of Hoover and his prize catches, weekly installments of FBI entertainment on radio, television, and the comics—this constituted Hoover's FBI for generations of Americans; and not only is much of this material scattered and lost, but without an imaginative recreation of its emotional impact on the public at the time it is just so much flat seltzer. In addition to contemporary treatment of the FBI in the popular press, on radio, television, and film, I have found the following works helpful, organized beneath five headings: theoretical approaches to the cultural function of crime and punishment; popular crime entertainment and studies of its cultural function; materials dealing with the popular audience's historical fascination with real-life criminals and lawmen; FBI publicity produced by Hoover's highly prolific publicists and published under Hoover's name; finally, studies of Hoover and the FBI, journalistic and scholarly, friendly and unfriendly and, in by far the smallest category of all, objective.

1. Theoretical Approaches

The FBI's role in American culture has to be evaluated in the context of the contributions that politics, law enforcement, mass communications and popular entertainment make to cultural solidarity. I have found these works helpful in formulating the theoretical approach I have followed in this book.

Andenaes, Johannes. *Punishment and Deterrence.* Ann Arbor: Univ. of Mich. Pr., 1974.

Ashmore, Harry S. "Government by Public Relations." *The Center Magazine* 4(Sept.–Oct., 1971):21–28.

Bagehot, Walter. *The English Constitution.* Garden City, N.Y.: Doubleday, 1966.

Barthes, Roland. *Mythologies.* New York: Hill and Wang, 1972.

Blumer, Herbert. "Society as Symbolic Interaction." In *Human Behavior and Social Processes,* edited by Arnold M. Rose. Boston: Houghton, 1962.

Brett, Dennis T. *Crime Detection.* Cambridge: National Book League, 1959.

Campbell, Dennis. *Sociology and the Stereotype of the Criminal.* London: Tavistock, 1968.

Cipes, Robert M. *The Crime War: The Manufactured Crusade.* New York: New American Library, 1968.

Cummings, Sir John. *A Contribution Towards a Bibliography Dealing with Crime and Cognate Subjects.* Montclair, N.J.: Patterson Smith, 1970.

De Fleur, Melvin L. *Theories of Mass Communication.* New York: David McKay, 1966.

Duncan, Hugh Dalziel. "The Development of Durkheim's Concept of Ritual and the Problem of Social Disrelationships." In *Emile Durkheim,* edited by Kurt H. Wolff. Columbus: Univ. of Ohio Pr., 1960.

————. *Symbols in Society.* New York: Oxford Univ. Pr., 1968.

Durkheim, Emile. *The Division of Labor in Society.* New York: Free Pr., 1964.

————. *Moral Education.* New York: Free Pr., 1961.

————. *The Rules of Sociological Method.* New York: Free Pr., 1964.

Edelman, Murray. *The Symbolic Uses of Politics.* Urbana: Univ. of Illinois Pr., 1964.

Erikson, Kai. *Wayward Puritans.* New York: John Wiley, 1966.

Freud, Sigmund. *Group Psychology and the Analysis of the Ego.* New York: Norton, 1959.

Gardiner, John A., and Mulkey, Michael A., eds. *Crime and Criminal Justice.* Lexington, Mass.: Heath, 1975.

Gay, Peter. "Law, Order and Enlightenment." In *Is Law Dead?,* edited by Eugene V. Rostow. New York: Simon, 1971.

Gibbons, Don C. et al. "Gauging Public Opinion about the Crime Problem." *Crime and Delinquency* 18(Apr., 1972):134–46.

Gordon, George N. *Persuasion: The Art and Practice of Manipulative Communication.* New York: Hastings House, 1971.

Grupp, Stanley F. *Theories of Punishment.* Bloomington: Indiana Univ. Pr., 1972.

Harris, Richard. *The Fear of Crime.* New York: Praeger, 1969.

Hatch, Elvin, ed. *Theories of Man and Culture.* New York: Columbia Univ. Pr., 1973.

Hirsch, Herbert. *Violence as Politics*. New York: Harper, 1973.

Hirsch, Selma. *The Fears Men Live By*. New York: Harper, 1955.

Isaacs, Harold R. *Idols of the Tribe: Group Identity and Political Change*. New York: Harper, 1975.

Jay, Martin. *The Dialectical Imagination*. Boston: Little, 1973.

Klapp, Orrin E. *Heroes, Villains and Fools: The Changing American Character*. Englewood Cliffs: Prentice, 1962.

————. *Symbolic Leaders: Public Dramas and Public Men*. Chicago: Aldine, 1964.

Larsen, Otto N., ed. *Violence and the Mass Media*. New York: Harper, 1968.

Lasswell, Harold D. *World Politics and Personal Insecurity*. New York: Free Pr., 1965.

Lippmann, Walter. *Public Opinion*. New York: Free Pr., 1965.

Lopez-Rey, Manuel. *Crime: An Analytical Approach*. New York: Praeger, 1970.

Malinowski, Bronislaw. *Crime and Custom in Savage Society*. Cambridge: Cambridge Univ. Pr., 1966.

Mead, George Herbert. "The Psychology of Punitive Justice." *American Journal of Sociology* 23(1918):577–602.

Menninger, Karl. *The Crime of Punishment*. New York: Viking, 1969.

Miller, Walter B. "Ideology and Criminal Justice." *Journal of Criminal Law and Criminology* 64(June, 1973):141–62.

Morris, Norval, and Hawkins, Glenn. *Letter to the President on Crime Control*. Chicago: Univ. of Chicago Pr., 1977.

Mount, Ferdinand. *The Theatre of Politics*. New York: Schocken, 1973.

Nevins, Francis M., Jr., ed. *The Mystery Writer's Art*. Bowling Green, Ohio: Popular Pr., 1970.

Nisbet, Robert A. *Emile Durkheim*. Englewood Cliffs: Prentice, 1965.

Radcliffe-Brown, A. R. *Structure and Function in Primitive Society*. Glencoe, Ill.: Free Pr., 1952.

Radzinowicz, Leon, and King, Joan. *The Growth of Crime*. New York: Basic, 1977.

Radzinowicz, Leon, and Wolfgang, Marvin E., eds. *Crime and Justice*. New York: Basic, 1977.

Ranulf, Svend. *Moral Indignation and Middle Class Psychology*. New York: Schocken, 1964.

Reckless, Walter C. *The Crime Problem*. New York: Appleton, 1967.

Schur, Edwin M. *Our Criminal Society: The Social and Legal Sources of Crime in America*. Englewood Cliffs: Prentice, 1969.

Silberman, Charles E. *Criminal Violence, Criminal Justice*. New York: Random, 1979.

Slotkin, Richard. *Regeneration Through Violence.* Middletown, Conn.: Wesleyan Univ. Pr., 1973.

Smelser, Neil J. *Theory of Collective Behavior.* New York: Free Pr., 1962.

Wills, Garry. *Nixon Agonistes.* New York: Signet, 1971.

Wilson, James Q. *Thinking about Crime.* New York: Random, 1977.

Wolff, Kurt H., ed. *Emile Durkheim.* Columbus: Univ. of Ohio Pr., 1960.

2. Crime Entertainment Formulas

Popular entertainment featuring the FBI followed formulas that have a long history in popular culture. The following works survey this field and lay the groundwork for an analysis of the function FBI entertainment played in American culture.

Aisenberg, Nadya. *A Common Spring: Crime Novel and Classic.* Bowling Green, Ohio: Popular Pr., 1979.

Altick, Richard D. *Victorian Studies in Scarlet. Murders and Manners in the Age of Victoria.* New York: Norton, 1970.

Armchair Detective Magazine.

Aydelotte, William O. "The Detective Story as a Historical Source. In Nevins, Francis M., ed. *The Mystery Writer's Art.* Bowling Green, Ohio: Popular Pr., 1970.

Bailyn Lotte. "Mass Media and Children: A Study of Exposure Habits and Cognitive Effects." *Psychological Monographs* 61(1959).

Bergman, Andrew. *We're in the Money.* New York: Harper, 1972.

Blackbeard, Bill. "The Pulps." In *Handbook of American Popular Culture,* ed. by M. Thomas Inge, 1:195–224. Westport, Conn.: Greenwood, 1979.

Bluestone, Tony, ed. *The Pulps.* New York: Chelsea House, 1976.

Blumer, Herbert, and Hauser, Philip M. *Movies, Delinquency and Crime.* New York: Macmillan, 1933.

Cameron, Ian. *A Pictorial History of the Movies.* London: Hamlyn, 1975.

Cawelti, John. *Adventure, Mystery and Romance: Formula Stories as Art and Popular Culture.* Chicago: Univ. of Chicago Pr., 1976.

Clarens, Carlos. *Crime Movies: From Griffiths to the Godfather.* New York: Norton, 1980.

Clark, George, and Hanlon, Lou. *The G-Man on the Crime Trail.* Racine, Wis.: Whitman, 1936.

Clurman, Robert, ed. *Nick Carter, Detective.* New York: Dell, 1965.

Confessions of a Nazi Spy. Library of the Performing Arts, New York Public Library, Press Books for Movies, 1939.

Conners, Bernard F. *Don't Embarrass the Bureau.* New York: Bobbs, Merrill, 1972.

Daniels, Les. *Comix: A History of Comic Books in America*. New York: Outerbridge and Dienstfrey, 1971.

Davis, David Brion. *Homicide in American Fiction, 1798–1860*. Ithaca: Cornell Univ. Pr., 1957.

Dean, Graham M. *Agent Nine and the Jewel Mystery*. Chicago: Goldsmith, 1935.

FBI Front. Library of the Performing Arts, New York Public Library, Press Books for Movies, 1942.

The Feds Magazine.

Feiffer, Jules. *The Great Comic Book Heroes*. New York: Bonanza, 1965.

Forman, Henry James. *Our Movie Made Children*. New York: Macmillan, 1933.

G-Men. Library of the Performing Arts, New York Public Library, Press Books for Movies, 1935.

G-Men Magazine.

Gabree, John. *Gangsters: From Little Caesar to the Present*. New York: Galahad, 1973.

Gage, Nicholas. *Bones of Contention*. New York: Berkeley, 1974.

Goulart, Ron. *The Adventurous Decade: Comic Strips in the Thirties*. New Rochelle, N.Y.: Arlington House, 1975.

———, ed. *The Hard-boiled Dicks: An Anthology and Study of Pulp Detective Fiction*. Nashville: Sherbourne Pr., 1965.

———. *An Informal History of the Pulp Magazine,*. New York: Ace, 1973.

———. *Line Up, Tough Guys*. Nashville: Sherbourne Pr., 1966.

Grant, Maxwell. "The Crime Oracle." *The Shadow Magazine*, June 1, 1936.

Gruber, Frank. *Pulp Jungle*. Nashville: Sherbourne Pr.,1967.

Harmon, Jim. *The Great Radio Heroes*. New York: Ace, 1967.

———. "A Swell Bunch of Guys." In Lupoff, Dick, and Thompson, Don, eds. *All in Color for a Dime*. New York: Ace, 1970.

Haycraft, Howard. *Murder for Pleasure: The Life and Times of the Detective Story*. New York: Appleton, 1941.

Hecht, Ben. *A Child of the Century*. New York: Ballantine, 1970.

Hersey, Harold. *Pulp Wood Editor*. New York: Frederick A. Stokes, 1938.

Inge, M. Thomas, ed. *Handbook of American Popular Culture*. 3 vols. Westport, Conn.: Greenwood, 1979–81.

Johannsen, Albert. *The House of Beadle and Adams*. 2 vols. Norman: Univ. of Oklahoma Pr., 1950–62.

Jowett, Garth. *Film: The Democratic Art*. Boston: Little, 1975.

Klapper, Joseph T. *The Effects of Mass Media*. Glencoe, Ill.: Free Pr., 1960.

Knight, Stephen. *Form and Ideology in Crime Fiction*. Bloomington: Indiana Univ. Pr., 1980.

Limited Collector's Edition Presents Dick Tracy. Chicago: Chicago Tribune, 1975.

Ludlum, Robert. *The Chancellor Manuscript.* New York: Dial, 1977.

Lupoff, Dick, and Thompson, Don, eds. *All in Color for a Dime.* New York: Ace, 1970.

Margolies, Edward. *Which Way Did He Go?* New York: Holmes and Meier, 1982.

Martin, Olga J. *Hollywood's Movie Commandments.* New York: H. W. Wilson, 1937.

Massey, Morrell. *Junior G-Man and the Counterfeiters.* Racine, Wis.: Whitman, 1937.

Miller, Rex, ed. *Radio Premiums Illustrated.* Mt. Vernon, Ill.: Supermantics, 1971.

Murch, A. E. *The Development of the Detective Story.* Port Washington, N.Y.: Kennikat, 1968.

Noel, Mary. *Villains Galore.* New York: Macmillan, 1954.

Nostalgia Comics 1(n.d.).

Nye, Russel B. *The Unembarrassed Muse.* New York: Dial, 1960.

Orwell, George. "Boys' Weeklies." In *The Collected Essays, Journalism and Letters of George Orwell,* 3:212–14. London: Secker and Warburg, 1968.

———. "Raffles and Miss Blandish." In *The Collected Essays, Journalism and Letters of George Orwell,* 1:461–93.

Pearson, Edmund. *Dime Novels.* Port Washington, N.Y.: Kennikat, 1968.

Public Enemy's Wife. Library of the Performing Arts, New York Public Library, Press Books for Movies, 1935.

Public Hero Number One. Library of the Performing Arts, New York Public Library, Press Books for Movies, 1935.

Reynolds, Quentin. *Fiction Factory.* New York: Random, 1955.

Robinson, Warren F. *The "G" Man's Son at Porpoise Island.* Chicago: Goldsmith, 1937.

Ruehlmann, William. *Saint with a Gun: The Unlawful American Private Eye.* New York: New York Univ. Pr., 1974.

Scanlon, C. K. M. "Bring 'Em Back Dead." *G-Men Magazine,* Nov., 1935, p. 16.

———. "Crime's Blackboard." *G-Men Magazine,* Oct., 1937, pp. 12–13.

———. "Give 'Em Hell." *G-Men Magazine,* Jan., 1937, p. 77.

———. "King Crime." *G-Men Magazine,* Mar., 1936, p. 28.

Schumach, Murray. *The Face on the Cutting Room Floor.* New York: William Morrow, 1964.

Shadoian, Jack. *Dream and Dead Ends: The American Gangster/Crime Film.* Cambridge: M.I.T. Pr., 1977.

Sklar, Robert. *Movie-Made America*. New York: Random, 1975.

State Historical Society of Wisconsin at Madison. *Film Archive Collection.*

Stout, Rex. *The Doorbell Rang*. New York: Viking, 1965.

Thompson, Don, and Lupoff, Dick, eds. *The Comic-Book Book*. New Rochelle, N.Y.: Arlington House, 1973.

Wallace, Irving. *The R Document*. New York: Simon, 1976.

Weiss, Ken, and Goodgold, Ed. *To Be Continued*. New York: Bonanza, 1972.

Wilson, Edmund. "Mr. Holmes, They Were the Footprints of a Gigantic Hound." In *Classics and Commercials*, pp. 266–74. New York: Farrar, 1950.

———. "Who Cares Who Killed Roger Ackroyd?" In *Classics and Commercials*, pp. 257–65. New York: Farrar, 1950.

———. "Why Do People Read Detective Stories?" In *Classics and Commercials*, pp. 231–37. New York: Farrar, 1950.

3. Crime as Entertainment

America's fascination with the FBI and its great cases has to be seen as a special instance of the mass society's centuries-old interest in notable crimes and criminals. This field is so vast that no bibliography of the popular culture of true crime can be regarded as exhaustive or even representative, but the following sampling provides some indication of the scope and nature of our culture's enthusiasm for crime.

"Are Your Fingerprints on File?" *The Feds*. Sept., 1937, pp. 9–10.

Berlin, Normand. *The Base String: The Underworld in Elizabethan Drama*. Rutherford, N.J.: Fairleigh Dickinson Univ. Pr., 1968.

Buntline, E. Z. C. *The Mysteries and Miseries of New York: A Story of Real Life*. New York: E. Z. C. Buntline, 1848.

Byrnes, Thomas. *1886 Professional Criminals of America*. New York: Chelsea House, 1969.

Chandler, David Leon. *Brothers in Blood*. New York: Dutton, 1975.

Commonweal 20(May 18, 1934):58.

Crosland, Jessie. *Outlaws in Fact and Fiction*. London: P. Owen, 1959.

De Quincey, Thomas. "Murder Considered as One of the Fine Arts." *Blackwoods*, Feb., 1827; Nov., 1839.

Dixon, Franklin W. *The Hardy Boys Detective Handbook*. New York: Grosset and Dunlap, 1959.

Dumas, Alexandre. *Celebrated Crimes*. New York: P. F. Collier, 1910.

Eldridge, Benjamin, and Watts, William B. *Our Rival the Rascal*. Montclair, N.J.: Patterson Smith, 1973.

"Federal Flashes." *G-Men Magazine*, Nov., 1935, p. 122.

Gardner, Arthur R. L. *The Art of Crime*. London: Phillip Allen, 1931.

Gilbert, Michael Francis. *Crime in Good Company*. London: Constable, 1959.

Griffiths, Arthur George Frederick. *The History and Romance of Crime from the Earliest Times to the Present Day*. London: Grolier, ca. 1908.

Hammer, Richard. *Playboy's Illustrated History of Organized Crime*. Chicago: Playboy, 1975.

Henderson, Bruce, and Summerlin, Sam. *The Super Sleuths*. New York: Macmillan, 1976.

Hibbert, Christopher. *The Roots of Evil: A Social History of Crime and Punishment*. Boston: Little, 1963.

Horan, James D. *The Pinkertons*. New York: Crown, 1968.

Howson, Gerald. *Thief-Taker General: The Rise and Fall of Jonathan Wild*. New York: St. Martin's, 1960.

Hynd, Alan. *Murder, Mayhem, and Mystery: An Album of American Crime*. New York: A. S. Barnes, 1958.

Lawes, Lewis E. *Twenty Thousand Years in Sing Sing*. New York: Long and Smith, 1932.

Lewis, Frankie. "Passing the Queer." *G-Men Magazine*, Nov., 1935, pp. 106, 110.

Lustgarten, Edgar. *The Illustrated Story of Crime*. Chicago: Follett, 1976.

McKelway, St. Clair. *True Tales from the Annals of Crime and Rascality*. New York: Random, 1951.

Martin, Olga J. *Hollywood's Movie Commandments*. New York: H. W. Wilson, 1937.

Maxwell, Clayton. "Public Enemies." *G-Men Magazine*, Nov., 1935, p. 105.

Mencken, August. *By the Neck: A Book of Hangings*. New York: Hastings House, 1942. (Foreword by H. L. Mencken).

Monaghan, Jay. *The Great Rascal: The Life and Adventures of Ned Buntline*. New York: Bonanza, 1951.

Nash, J. Robert. *Bloodletters and Badmen*. New York: Warners, 1975.

Newgate Calendar. London, 1773.

Orwell, George. "Decline of the English Murder." In *Shooting an Elephant*, pp. 156–60. New York: Harcourt, 1950.

Pearson, Edmund Lester. *The Autobiography of a Criminal*. New York: Duffield, 1930.

———. *Books in Black and Red*. Freeport, N.Y.: Books for Libraries Pr., 1969.

———. *Dime Novels*. Port Washington, N.Y.: Kennikat, 1968.

———. *The Evil That Men Do*. Garden City, N.Y.: Doubleday, 1929.

———. *Five Murders*. Garden City, N.Y.: Doubleday, 1928.

———. *Investigation of the Devil*. New York: Scribner's, 1930.

———. *Masterpieces of Murder*. Boston: Little, 1963.

————. *Murder at Smutty Nose.* Garden City, N.Y.: Doubleday, 1926.

————. *Sketches in Murder.* New York: Modern Library, 1938.

Pinkerton, Allan. *The Mollie Maguires and the Detectives.* New York: Dover, 1973. First published in 1877.

Powers, Richard Gid. "Crime in Popular Culture." *Journal of Popular Culture* 9(Spring, 1976):743–47.

Reader's Digest. *Great True Stories of Crime, Mystery and Detection from the Reader's Digest,* Pleasantville, N.Y.: Reader's Digest, 1965.

Roughead, William. *The Art of Murder.* New York: Sheriden House, 1943.

————. *Bad Companions.* New York: Duffield and Green, 1931.

————. *Burke and Hare.* London: W. Dodge, 1921.

————. *Enjoyment of Murder.* New York: Sheriden House, 1938.

————. *The Evil That Men Do.* Garden City, N.Y.: Doubleday, 1929.

————. *The Fatal Countess.* Edinburgh: W. Dodge, 1924.

————. *The Murderer's Companion.* New York: Readers's Club, 1941.

————. *Nothing But Murder.* New York: Sheridan House, 1946.

————. *Rascals Revived.* London: Cassell, 1940.

————. *The Rebel Earl.* New York: Dutton, 1926.

————. *Tales of the Criminous.* New York: Cassell, 1956.

————. *Trial of Captain Porteous.* New York: Dutton, 1909.

Select Trials at the Sessions House in the Old Bailey. London, 1730.

Simpson, Helen et al. *The Anatomy of Murder.* New York: Macmillan, 1937.

Smith, Gene, and Smith, Jayne Barry, eds. *The Police Gazette.* New York: Simon, 1972.

Smyth, Frank, and Ludwig, Miles. *The Detectives: Crime and Detection in Fact and Fiction.* Philadelphia: Lippincott, 1978.

Social Science Program: Crime Detection. Garden City, N.Y.: Doubleday, 1970.

Symons, Julian. *A Pictorial History of Crime.* New York: Crown, 1966.

Thorwald, Jurgen. *The Century of the Detective.* New York: Harcourt, 1964.

Tracy, M. E. "Laws and Lawless," *New York World Telegram,* May 14, 1932, p. 17.

Van Every, Edward. *Sins of America as "Exposed" by the Police Gazette.* New York: Frederick A. Stokes, 1931.

"Waters" [Russell, William]. *Recollections of a Detective Police Officer.* London: Covent Gardens, 1973. (First published in 1856.)

Walker, Peter N. *Punishment: An Illustrated History.* New York: Arco, 1973.

Watson, Colin. *Snobbery with Violence: Crime Stories and Their Audience.* New York: St. Martin's, 1972.

Wolfe, Harry Ashton. *The Thrill of Evil.* London, Hurst and Blackett, 1928.

4. The Public Files of J. Edgar Hoover

The prodigious industry of J. Edgar Hoover's ghost writers and the enthusiasm of the public (or at least of the media) for his words makes it a difficult task to locate all the works to which he put his signature. The following includes his books, articles, and reprinted speeches. It does not include his great number of interviews, letters to the press, press releases, and non-reprinted speeches.

Books

J. Edgar Hoover on Communism. New York: Random, 1969.

Masters of Deceit. New York: Holt, 1958.

Persons in Hiding. Boston: Little, 1938.

A Study of Communism. New York: Holt, 1962.

Articles and Addresses

"Abolish Parole Abuses." *Forum* 100(Aug., 1938):71–73.

"Adventure of Scientific Crime Control, The." Speech delivered at Kalamazoo College, June 14, 1937. *Vital Speeches* 3(July 1, 1937):559–62.

"Amazing Mr. Means, The." Edited by C. R. Cooper. *American Magazine* 122(Dec., 1936):24–25+.

"America: Freedom's Champion." *Address delivered Oct. 18, 1960. Vital Speeches* 27(Jan. 15, 1961):197–200.

"American Ideal, The." Speech delivered at Freedom's Foundation Annual Awards, Feb. 22, 1957. *Vital Speeches* 23(Mar. 15, 1957):327–28.

"American's Challenge." Address delivered Oct. 9, 1962. *Vital Speeches* 29(Dec. 1, 1962):98–101.

"Basis of Sound Law Enforcement, The." *Annals of the American Academy* 291(Jan., 1954):39–45.

"Battle on the Home Front, The." Speech delivered at Annual Meeting of the International Association of Chiefs of Police, Aug. 9, 1943. *Vital Speeches* 9(Sept. 15, 1943):734–36.

"Beware of Frauds in Uniform." Edited by F. L. Collins. *Colliers* 110(Dec. 26, 1942):11+.

"Big Scare." *American Magazine* 132(Aug., 1941):24–25+.

"Bla Bla, Black Man." Edited by C. R. Cooper. *American Magazine* 122(Sept., 1936):32–34+.

"Blaster." *Reader's Digest* 49(Sept., 1946):99–103.

"Boy Who Wanted To Go Fishing, The." Edited by C. R. Cooper. *American Magazine* 122(Nov., 1936):54–55+.

"Brains Against Bullets." *American Magazine* 117(Feb., 1934):68–69+.

"B-r-e-a-k-i-n-g the Communist Spell." *American Mercury* 78(Mar., 1954):57–61.

"Bull Market in Stock and Bond Thefts." *Nation's Business* 58(Mar., 1970): 28–32.

"Buzzards in Disguise." Edited by C. R. Cooper. *American Magazine* 124(Nov., 1937):42–43+.

"Camps of Crime." Edited by C. R. Cooper. *American Magazine* 129(Feb., 1940):14–15+.

"Case of the Faceless Spy." *Reader's Digest* 78(Jan., 1961):61–64.

"Challenges of Crime Control." Address delivered Apr. 10, 1956. *Vital Speeches* 22(July 1, 1956):572–76.

"Citizenship." Address delivered June 16, 1959. *Vital Speeches* 25(Aug. 15, 1959):656–58.

"Combating Lawlessness: America's Most Destructive Disease." Speech delivered before the Association of American Life Insurance Presidents, New York City, Dec. 3, 1937. Reprinted in *Vital Speeches* 4(Feb. 15, 1938):269–72.

"Communism and the Schools." *U.S. News and World Report* 37(Nov. 26, 1954):130–31.

"Communist Gains among Youth." *U.S. News and World Report* 59(Nov. 1, 1965):46.

"Communists Are after Our Minds." *American Magazine* 158(Oct., 1954): 19+.

"Communist Threat in the U.S., The." *U.S. News and World Report* 30(Mar. 30, 1951):32–37.

"Courage of Free Men, The." Speech delivered at the Freedoms Foundation, Feb. 22, 1962. FBI press release.

"Crime of the Century, The." *Reader's Digest* 58(May, 1951):149–68.

"Crime's Family Doctor." Edited by C. R. Cooper. *American Magazine* 121(May, 1936):28–29+.

"Crime's Family Doctor." Edited by C. R. Cooper. *American Magazine* 121(May, 1936):28–29+.

"Crime's Law School." Edited by C. R. Cooper. *American Magazine* 130(Nov., 1940):55+.

"Crime's Leading Lady." Edited by C. R. Cooper. *American Magazine* 123 (Feb., 1937):54–55+.

"Crime's Masquerader." Edited by C. R. Cooper. *American Magazine* 123 (May, 1937):50–51+.

"Crime's Mouthpiece." Edited by C. R. Cooper. *American Magazine* 122(Oct., 1936):22–23+.

"Crime Trap." *American Magazine* 116(Nov., 1933):64–66+.

"Crime Wave We Now Face." *New York Times Magazine,* Apr. 21, 1946, pp. 1–6.

"Criminal Identification." *Annals of the American Academy* 145(Nov., 1929): 205–13.

"Criminals Are Home Grown." *Rotarian* 56(Apr., 1940):16–18.

"Dangerous Freedom." *American Magazine* 145(Jan. 1948):19+; same abridged in *Reader's Digest* 54(Mar., 1949):92–94.

"The Deadly Menace of Pseudo Liberals." *American Mercury* 86(Jan., 1958): 7–11.

"Death in Headlines." *Collier's* 102(Aug. 13, 1938):9–11+.

"Due Notice." *Harper's* 199(Dec., 1949):16.

"Education Against Crime." Speech delivered before Chicago Boys Club, Nov. 9, 1936. *Vital Speeches* 3(Dec. 1, 1936):109–13.

"Enemies at Large." *American Magazine* 137(Apr., 1944:17+.

"The Enemy's Masterpiece of Espionage." *Reader's Digest* 48(Apr. 1946):1–6.

"Enemies Within Our Gates." Edited by C. R. Cooper. *American Magazine* 130(Aug., 1940):18–19+.

"Enforcing the Laws." *U.S. News and World Report* 57(Dec. 21, 1954):36–40.

"Errand Boy of Crime, The." Edited by C. R. Cooper. *American Magazine* 121(June, 1936):22–23+.

"Faith, Freedom and Law." Address delivered before the Regional Conference on Crime Prevention of the Michigan State Bar, June 8, 1967. FBI press release.

"Faith in Freedom." Address delivered before the Brotherhood of the Washington Hebrew Congregation, Dec. 4, 1963. FBI press release.

"The Faith to Be Free." Address delivered on receiving the Criss Award, Dec. 7, 1961. FBI press release.

"F.B.I. and Civil Rights: J. Edgar Hoover Speaks Out." *U.S. News and World Report* 57(Nov. 30, 1964):56–58.

"F.B.I. Chief Speaks Up." *Senior Scholastic* 85(Dec. 2, 1964):21–22.

"FBI Director Hoover Tells How Communists Work in the U.S." *U.S. News and World Report* 28(June 23, 1960):11–13.

"FBI Laboratory in Wartime." *Science Monthly* 60(Jan., 1945):18–24.

"FBI's J. Edgar Hoover Reports on a Turbulent Year." *U.S. News and World Report* 69(July 27, 1970):24.

"FBI's War on Organized Crime." *U.S. News and World Report* 60(Apr. 18, 1966):102–104.

"FBI Warns about the Christmas Trade No Business Wants." *Nation's Business* 55(Nov., 1967):44–46.

"50,000 Communists." *U.S. News and World Report* 28(May 12, 1950):60.

"Fifty Years of Crime: Corruption Begets Corruption." Speech delivered before the National Fifty Years in Business Club, May 20, 1939. *Vital Speeches* 5(June 1, 1939):505–509.

"Fingerprint Everybody? Yes." *Rotarian* 50(Jan. 1937):16–17+.

"Fingerprinting School Children." *Scholastic Life* 21(Sept., 1935):2–3.

"First Pan American Congress on Criminology." *Bulletin of the Pan American Union* 78(Nov., 1944):605–608.

"Focus on Tomorrow." *School and Society* 100(Feb., 1972):84–86.

"Fortune in the Grave." *Reader's Digest* 49(July, 1946):83–87.

"Foreword" to Collins, Frederick L. *The F.B.I. in Peace and War.* New York: Putnams, 1943.

"Foreword" to Cooper, Courtney Ryley. *Ten Thousand Public Enemies.* New York: Blue Ribbon, 1935.

"Foreword" to Corey, Herbert. *Farewell, Mr. Gangster!* New York: Appleton, 1936.

"Foreword" to Jeffers, H. Paul. *Wanted by the F.B.I.* New York, Hawthorne, 1972.

"Foreword" to Jones, Ken. *The FBI in Action.* New York, New American Library, 1957.

"Foreword" to Tully, Andrew. *The FBI's Most Famous Cases.* New York: William Morrow, 1965.

"Foreword" to Whitehead, Don. *The FBI Story.* New York: Random, 1956.

"From J. Edgar Hoover: A Report on Campus Reds." *U.S. News and World Report* 58(May 31, 1965):84.

"God and Country, or Communism?" *American Mercury* 85(Dec., 1957):7–13.

"Gun Crazy." Edited by C. R. Cooper. *American Magazine* 125(Mar., 1938):36–37+

"Gunman's Love." Edited by C. R. Cooper. *American Magazine* 124(Sept., 1937):28–29+.

"Hitler's Spying Sirens." *American Magazine* 138(Dec., 1944):40–41+.

"Hitler's Spies Are Experts." With F. L. Collins. *Collier's* 111(Apr. 24, 1944):12+.

"Hoover Answers Ten Questions on the FBI." *New York Times Magazine,* Apr. 16, 1960, pp. 9+.

"Hoover's Warning: Be Alert to Fanatics." *U.S. News and World Report* 55(Dec. 19, 1963):14.

"How Communists Operate." *U.S. News and World Report* 29(Aug. 11, 1950):30–33.

"How J. Edgar Hoover Felt about TV's 'The F.B.I.' " *TV Guide,* May 20–26, 1972, pp. 28–30.

"How Safe Is Your Daughter?" *American Magazine* 144(July, 1947):3+.

"How Safe Is Your Youngster?" *American Magazine* 159(Mar., 1955):13+.

"How Red China Spies on U.S." *Nation's Business* 54(June, 1966):84–88.

"How the Nazi Spy Invasion Was Smashed." *American Magazine* 138(Sept., 1944):20–21+.

"How to Fight Communism." *Newsweek* 29(June 9, 1947):30–32.

"How to Keep Your Car." *Good Housekeeping* 146(Mar., 1958):154.

"How U.S. Reds Use Pseudo Liberals as a Front." *U.S. News and World Report* 40(Apr., 13, 1956):138–39.

"How Wise Is a Crook?" *American Magazine* 116(Dec., 1933):36–38+.

"I Challenge Your Right to Drive." *National Business Woman* 38(Feb., 1959): 26.

"Influence of Crime on the American Home, The." Speech delivered before the Round Table Forum, Mar. 11, 1936. *Vital Speeches* 2(Mar. 23, 1936):390–94.

"Interval Between, The." *Christianity Today* 14(Dec. 19, 1969):3–5.

"J. Edgar Hoover's Farewell: Let Me Be Remembered as a Man Of Fair Play." *U.S. News and World Report* 73(Aug. 7, 1972):80+.

"J. Edgar Hoover Speaks Out." *Nation's Business* 60(Jan., 1972):32–33.

"J. Edgar Hoover Speaks Out: Reds in the Negro Movement." *U.S. News and World Report* 56(May 4, 1964):33.

"Jokers Worse Than Saboteurs." *Science Digest* 15(Feb., 1944):81–83.

"Keys to Freedom." Speech delivered before the national convention of the Catholic Youth Organization, Nov. 16, 1963. FBI press release.

"King of the Bandits." Edited by C. R. Cooper. *American Magazine* 125(June, 1938):51–52+.

"Law Enforcement and the Citizen." Speech delivered before the New York Chamber of Commerce, Feb. 7, 1935. *Vital Speeches* 1(Feb. 25, 1935):335–39.

"Law Enforcement Views: Education for Leisure." *Education* 71(Oct., 1950): 92–98.

"Man's First Need." *American Mercury* 80(Mar., 1955):47.

"Man I Want My Boy to Be, The." *Parents Magazine* 15(Feb., 1940):23.

"Man with the Magic Wallet, The." Edited by C. R. Cooper. *American Magazine* 123(Mar., 1937):41–45+.

"Meanest Man I Ever Knew, The." Edited by C. R. Cooper. *American Magazine* 123(Apr., 1937):41+.

"Modern Problems of Law Enforcement." Speech delivered at the national meeting of the International Association of Chiefs of Police, July 9, 1935. *Vital Speeches* 1(July 29, 1935):682–87.

"Money or Your Life!" Edited by C. R. Cooper. *American Magazine* 123(June, 1937):42–43+.

"Morality for Violence." *Christianity Today* 16(Apr. 28, 1972):3–9.

"Mothers, Our Only Hope." With F. L. Collins. *Woman's Home Companion* 71(Jan., 1944):20–21.

"My Most Memorable Christmas." *Coronet* 33(Dec., 1952):37.

"National Police Force? No Says FBI Chief Hoover, A." *U.S. News and World Report* 58(Apr. 12, 1965):20.

"Nation's Call to Duty, A." Speech delivered at the St. John's University Law School, June 11, 1942. *Vital Speeches* 3(July 1, 1942):554–56.

"Negro in the FBI." Edited by S. Booker. *Ebony* 17(Sept., 1962):29–30.

"New Left Terrorism: A Warning." *U.S. News and World Report* 66(Jan. 13, 1969):12–13.

"New Tricks of the Nazi Spies." *American Magazine* 136(Oct., 1943):28–29+.

"Now: Instant Crime Control in Your Town." *Popular Science* 190(Jan., 1967):67–69.

"Our 'Achilles' Heel.'" Speech delivered at the annual convention of the American Legion, Sept. 30, 1946. *Vital Speeches* 13(Oct. 15, 1946):10–11.

"Our Common Task: When Crime Occurs There Has Been a Failure Somewhere." Speech delivered at the annual meeting of the International Association of Chiefs of Police, Oct. 3, 1955. *Vital Speeches* 22(Nov. 1, 1955):41–44.

"Our Heritage of Greatness." Speech delivered before the Pennsylvania Society, and the Society of Pennsylvania Women, New York City, Dec. 12, 1964. FBI press release.

"Patriotism and the War Against Crime." Delivered before the Daughters of the American Revolution, April 23, 1936. FBI press release.

"The Perpetuation of Our American Heritage." Speech delivered at the annual convention of the American Legion, Sept. 19, 1957. *Vital Speeches* 23(Oct. 1, 1957):747–50.

"Photography in Crime Detection." *Scientific American* 162(Feb., 1940):71–74.

"Physical Science in the Crime Detection Laboratory." *Smithsonian Reports* 1939:215–22.

"Police Brutality: How Much Truth, How Much Fiction?" *U.S. News and World Report* 59(Sept. 27, 1965):116–17.

"Policing a Nation at War." *Popular Science* 140(Feb., 1942):98–191.

"Problems of Law Enforcement: Crime Rests at the Doorstep of the American Home." Speech delivered at the annual convention of the International Association of Chiefs of Police, Oct. 10, 1939. *Vital Speeches* 6(Nov. 1, 1939):54–57.

"Portraits in Courage." Edited by J. Conniff. *Today's Health* 50(Mar., 1972): 30–34.

"Postwar Crime Wave Unless. . . ." *Rotarian* 66(Apr., 1945):12–14.

"Punish the Parent?" *Rotarian* 89(Oct., 1956):24–26.

"Real Public Enemy No. 1, The." Edited by C. R. Cooper. *American Magazine* 121(Apr., 1936):16–17+.

"Reconversion of Law Enforcement, The." Speech delivered at the annual convention of the International Association of Chiefs of Police, Dec. 10, 1945. *Vital Speeches* 12(Feb. 1, 1946):253–56.

"Red Fascism in the United States Today." *American Magazine* 142(Feb., 1947):24–25+.

"Red Spy Masters of America." *Reader's Digest* 58(May, 1951):83–87.

"Respectable Eddie." Edited by C. R. Cooper. *American Magazine* 122(July, 1936):34–35+.

"Reversing the Crime Trend." *U.S. News and World Report* 65(Aug. 26, 1968):36–37.

"Rising Crime Wave, The." *American Magazine* 141(Mar. 1946):23+.

"Roots of Crime, The." Edited by C. R. Cooper. *American Magazine* 207(Dec. 22, 1934):12–13+.

"SDS and the High Schools: A Study in Student Extremism." *P.T.A. Magazine* 64(Jan., 1970):2–5; 64(Feb., 1970):8–9.

"Science at the Scene of the Crime." *Scientific American* 155(July 1936):12–14.

"Sex Books and Rape: FBI Chief Sees Close Links." *U.S. News and World Report* 64(Mar. 11, 1968):14–15.

"Should I Force My Child?" *American Mercury* 86(Feb. 19, 1958):18–19.

"Stamping out the Spies." Edited by C. R. Cooper. *American Magazine* 129(Jan., 1940):20–21+.

"Slickers in Slacks." With F. L. Collins. *Collier's* 112(Oct. 16, 1943):24+.

"Spy Trap." Edited by R. M. Grant. *Popular Mechanics* 80(Dec., 1943):1–5+.

"Spy Who Double Crossed Hitler, The." *American Magazine* 141(May, 1946):23+; same abridged in *Reader's Digest* 48(June, 1946):19–22.

"Story of Crime in the U.S., The." *U.S. News and World Report* 65(Oct. 7, 1968):61–68; same with title "Violence." *Vital Speeches* 35(Nov. 1, 1968): 42–48.

"Student Riots in San Francisco." *U.S. News and World Report* 49(July 25, 1960):68–71.

"Tales the Bullet Tells." *Scientific American* 160(Jan., 1939):22–23.

"The Test of Citizenship." Speech delivered before the annual convention of the Daughters of the American Revolution, Apr. 18, 1940. *Vital Speeches* 6(May 1, 1940):440–43.

"Third Degree, The." Edited by C. R. Cooper. *American Magazine* 129(May, 1940):38–39+.

"These Fighters Against Youth Crime Need Your Help." *Reader's Digest* 78(Apr., 1961):145–46.

"They Make Your Hometown Safer." *American Magazine* 160(Aug., 1955): 26–27+.

"Third Front Against Juvenile Crime." *New York Times Magazine*, Feb. 27, 1944, pp. 8+.

"Traitors Must Die!" With F. L. Collins. *Collier's* 112(July 17, 1943):13+.

"Trigger Finger Clue." *Reader's Digest* 50(June, 1947):65–68.

"True Costs of Crime, The." *National Education Association Journal* 25(Dec., 1936):286.

"Turbulence on the Campus." *P.T.A. Magazine* 60(Feb., 1966):4–6.

"Twin Enemies of Freedom." Speech delivered Nov. 9, 1956. *Vital Speeches* 23(Dec. 1, 1956):104–7.

"Two Edged Sword." *NEA Journal* 51(Feb., 1952):31.

"$200,000 Rat Trap." Edited by C. R. Cooper. *American Magazine* 122(Aug., 1936):40–41+.

"U.S. Businessman Faces the Soviet Spy." *Harvard Business Review* 42(Jan., 1964):140–46.

"U.S. Communists Hide Deeper." *U.S. News and World Report* 36(Feb. 19, 1954):77–78+.

"U.S. Communists Today." *American Mercury* 78(May, 1954):80–84.

"U.S. Unrest as FBI Chief Sees It." *U.S. News and World Report* 68(Jan. 12, 1970):8.

"Underground Tactics of the Communists." *Coronet* 29(Dec., 1950):40–44.

"Uphold Our Laws." *Scholastic* 57(Nov. 3, 1950):5.

"Vital Role in Building a Stronger America." *P.T.A. Magazine* 57(Feb., 1963):18.

"War Against Crime Is Your War." *Reader's Digest* 93(Nov., 1968):17–18+.

"Warning from J. Edgar Hoover." *U.S. News and World Report* 59(Sept. 13, 1965):20.

"We Mollycoddle Criminals." *U.S. News and World Report* 59(Aug. 9, 1965):67.

"What J. Edgar Hoover Did about White." *U.S. News and World Report* 35(Nov. 27, 1953):117–23.

"What J. Edgar Hoover Says About Pressure Groups." *U.S. News and World Report* 57(Dec. 7, 1954):45.

"What Makes an FBI Agent?" *Coronet* 38(June, 1955):110–14.

"When a Child Is Missing." *Parents Magazine* 38(Mar., 1963):67+.

"When Criminals Are Set Free Too Soon." *U.S. News and World Report* 58(May 17, 1965):21.

"When Reporting Subversive Activities." *American City* 65(Oct., 1950):157.

"Who's to Blame for the Rising Wave of Crime?" *U.S. News and World Report* 52(Jan. 1, 1962):34–37.

"Why Crime Is Dropping." *U.S. News and World Report* 39(Sept. 30, 1955):45.

"Why Reds Make Friends with Businessmen." *Nation's Business* 50(May, 1962):78–80+.

"Why U.S. Uses Ex-Reds as Informants." *U.S. News and World Report* 39(Oct. 14, 1955):106–107.

"Wild Children." *American Magazine* 136(July, 1943):40–41+.

"Worthwhile Guidance in the Making of Good Citizens." *National Parent Teacher* 51(Nov., 1956):24.

"You Can Help Stop Juvenile Crime." *American Magazine* 159(Jan., 1955):15+.

"You Versus Crime." *Rotarian* 81(Nov., 1952):10–12.

5. The FBI in Public Print

The following list of scholarly studies and journalistic comment on Hoover and the FBI includes the most widely circulated attacks and defenses. None of these accounts provides the answer to the question some readers still might have about J. Edgar Hoover's most personal of preferences. The fact is that the people who really know are not saying, and that the people who are saying really do not know. For what it is worth, Ovid Demaris, listed below, has given the topic about all the treatment it deserves.

"Above and Below the Battle." *The Nation* 137(Nov. 8, 1958):330.

Adler, Bill. *Kids' Letters to the F.B.I.* Englewood Cliffs, N.J.: Prentice, 1966.

"After J. Edgar Hoover: What's Ahead for the FBI." *U.S. News and World Report* 72(May 15, 1972):39–41.

Alexander, Jack. "The Director-1." *The New Yorker* 13(Sept. 25, 1937):20–25.

———. "The Director-2." *The New Yorker* 13(Oct. 2, 1937):21–26.

———. "The Director-3." *The New Yorker* 13(Oct. 9, 1937):22–27.

———. "Why All This G-Man Publicity?" *Reader's Digest* 31(Dec., 1937):42–45.

Alsop, Stewart. "Watergate and the Liberals." *Newsweek* 81(June 25, 1973):96.

American Friends Service Committee. *Anatomy of Anti-Communism.* New York: Hill and Wang, 1969.

Anderson, Jack. With Les Whitten. "Hoover's Blackmail Tactics." *New York Post Magazine,* Jan. 12, 1976, p. 5.

———. "Hoover's Other Side." *New York Post Magazine,* Feb. 4, 1976, p. 5.

———. "Hoover's Wrath." *New York Post Magazine,* Jan. 7, 1976, p. 5.

———. "This Is Your FBI." *New York Post Magazine,* Nov. 7, 1975, p. 5.

Anderson, Paul Y. "Behind the Dies Intrigue." *The Nation* 147(Nov. 12, 1938):499–500.

———. "Investigate Mr. Dies!" *Nation* 147(Nov. 5, 1938):471–72.

"Anti-missive Missive." *Newsweek* 69(Feb. 6, 1967):32.

"Aw, Give J. Edgar A Degree!" *The Nation* 195(Sept. 22, 1962):142.

"Bag Job Snow Job." *The New Republic* 184(May 2, 1981):12.

"Battle of the Bugs." *Time* 88(Dec. 13, 1966):19.

Bentley, Eric, ed. *Thirty Years of Treason: Excerpts from Hearings Before the House Committee on Un-American Activities, 1938–1968.* New York: Viking, 1971.

"Better Not to Think of It." *The Nation* 192(Apr. 15, 1961):315.

Biographical Sketch of John Edgar Hoover. Washington, D.C.: FBI, July 15, 1936.

"Biography of W. H. Ferry." *The Nation* 195(Nov. 24, 1962):338–39.

"Brother Mole: The FBI and the Socialist Workers Party." *The Nation* 223(Nov. 6, 1976):452.

Brown, R. G. et al. *Illegal Practices of the Department of Justice.* New York: Arno, 1969. Originally printed in 1920.

Buckley, William F., Jr. "Defense Fund: Harassment of the FBI." *National Review* 29(July 8, 1977):793.

———. "Public Justice Versus J. Edgar Hoover. *National Review* 23(Nov. 19, 1971):1322.

———. "Shocking Report of Mr. Hoover." *National Review* 27(Mar. 28, 1975):360–61.

"Bugging." *National Review* 18(Dec. 27, 1966):1306–7.

"Bugging Hoover." *Time* 97(Aug. 26, 1971):17–18.

"Bugging J. Edgar Hoover." *Time* 97(Apr. 19, 1971):15–16.

"Bulldog vs. Jellyfish." *Newsweek* 76(Nov. 30, 1970):23+.

"Bureau of Vituperation." *Time* 96(Nov. 30, 1970):11.

Burns, James MacGregor. *Roosevelt: The Lion and the Fox.* New York: Harcourt, 1956.

"Can G-Men Violate the Law." *The New Republic* 102(Apr. 1, 1940):429.

"Card for Mr. Hoover." *The Nation* 150(Mar. 23, 1940):380.

Carpozi, George. *Red Spies in the U.S.* New York: Trident, 1968.

Catton, Bruce. "Red Herring and White." *Nation* 177(Nov. 28, 1953):445.

Cerf, P. "J. Edgar Hoover's First Job." *Good Housekeeping* 143(Sept., 1956): 176.

Challenge of Crime in a Free Society: A Report by the President's Commission on Law Enforcement and Administration of Justice, The. New York: Avon, 1968.

"Chartering the FBI." *The Nation* 229(Oct. 6, 1979):294–301.

"Christian Virtue." *The Nation* 203(July 11, 1966):37.

Clarens, Carlos. "Hooverville West: The Hollywood G-Man, 1934–1945." *Film Comment* 13(May–June, 1977):10–16.

"Clearing It with Hoover." *The New Republic* 156(Feb. 4, 1967):9.

Cohn, Roy M. "Could He Walk On Water?" *Esquire* 78(Nov., 1972):117–19+.

Collins, Frederick L. *The F.B.I. in Peace and War.* New York: Putnam, 1943.

Comfort, Mildred. *J. Edgar Hoover: Modern Knight Errant: A Biographical Sketch of the Director of the FBI.* Minneapolis: T. S. Denison, 1959.

"Common Sense on the FBI." *The Nation* 222(May 22, 1976):610–12.

"Confidential Informants." *Commonweal* 63(Oct. 21, 1955):51–52.

"Congress Should Investigate." *The New Republic* 102(Mar. 25, 1940):393–94.

Considine, Bob. "Duties of FBI Have Enormous Scope." *New York Journal American,* May 13, 1959, p. 1.

———. "FBI Director is Married Only to His Work." *Washington Evening Star,* May 13, 1959, p. 1.

———. "FBI Girds the Globe." *New York Journal America.* Feb. 12, 1959.

———. "Mr. G-Man Reviews His 35 Years as Nemesis of Crime." *New York Journal American,* Feb. 10, 1959, p. 1.

———. "We Never Give Up Is Keystone of FBI." *New York Journal American,* Feb. 11, 1959, p. 1.

"Conspiracy Group Denies Charges, Denounces Hoover." *Christian Century* 87(Dec. 16, 1970):1508.

Cook, Fred J. "Boris Morros: Hero of a Myth." *The Nation* 186(Jan. 25, 1958):70–74.

———. "FBI." *The Nation* 187(Oct. 18, 1958):221–80.

———. *The F.B.I. Nobody Knows.* New York: Macmillan, 1964.

———. "The Ghost of a Typewriter." *The Nation* 194(May 12, 1962):416+.

———. Review of Hoover's *Masters of Deceit. The Nation* 186(May 24, 1958):478–80.

Cooper, Courtney Ryley. "Behind the Guns of Crime." *American Magazine* 117(Jan., 1934):22–23+.

———. "Getting the Jump on Crime." *American Magazine* 116(Aug., 1933):23–25+.

———. "The Roots of Crime." *Saturday Evening Post,* Dec. 22, 1934, p. 13.

———. *Ten Thousand Public Enemies.* New York: Blue Ribbon, 1935.

Corey, Herbert. *Farewell, Mr. Gangster! America's War on Crime.* New York: Appleton, 1936.

"Corrupt, Stupid and Indecent: Burglaries of the Socialist Workers Offices." *The Nation* 222(Apr. 10, 1976):418–19.

Craft, J. "J. Edgar Hoover: The Compleat Bureaucrat." *Commentary* 39(Feb., 1965):59–62.

Crawford, Kenneth G. "J. Edgar Hoover." *The Nation* 144(Feb. 27, 1937): 232–34; 144(Mar. 6, 1937):262–64.

Crawford-Mason, C. "America's Top Cop Takes Aim at a Tough Target: Modernizing and De-Hooverizing the FBI." *People* 12(Dec. 24, 1979):94–95.

Cromie, Robert, and Pinkston, Joseph. *Dillinger: A Short and Violent Life.* New York: McGraw, 1962.

Crowther, Bosley. "The F.B.I. Story." *New York Times,* Oct. 4, 1959, Sec. 2, p. 1.

Cummings, Homer S. *Selected Papers of Homer Cummings.* New York: Scribner's 1939.

"Dangerous Thoughts: FBI Index." *The Nation* (May 13, 1950):449.

"Dangerous Thoughts: The F.B.I. Reviews a Book." *The Nation* (Jan. 27, 1951):86.

Davidson, Bill. "J. Edgar Hoover: Master of the Hunt." *Reader's Digest* 52(Apr., 1948):107–10.

Dean, Gordon Evans. "Outlawry." *The Panel* 10(Mar.–Apr., 1932):13.

"Death Penalty for Kidnapping." *The Nation* 137(Aug. 16, 1933):172–73.

Deedy, John. "J. Edgar, Dan and Phil." *Commonweal* 93(Dec. 18, 1970):290.

De Ford, Miriam Allen. *The Real Ma Barker. New York: Ace, 1970.*

Demaris, Ovid. *The Director.* New York: Harper's Magazine Pr., 1975.

———. "Office Politics of J. Edgar Hoover." *Esquire* 82(Nov. 1974):142–50+.

———. "Private Life of J. Edgar Hoover." *Esquire* 82(Sept. 1974):71–77+.

"Dementia Unlimited." *The Nation* 170(Apr. 29, 1950):388.

De Toledano, Ralph. *J. Edgar Hoover: The Man in His Time.* New Rochelle, N.Y.: Arlington House, 1973.

Diamond, S. "Kissinger and the F.B.I.: Harvard Years." *The Nation* 229(Nov. 10, 1979):449+.

"Dirty Business." *The Nation* 203(Dec. 26, 1966):690–91.

Donner, F. J. *The Age of Surveillance: The Aim and Methods of America's Political Intelligence System.* New York: Random, 1980.

———. "Hoover's Legacy." *The Nation* 218(June 1, 1974):678–99.

———. "Thank You, Mr. Director." *The Nation* 209(Oct. 27, 1969):448–49.

Douthit, Nathan. "Police Professionalism and the War Against Crime in the

United States, 1920s–30s." In G. L. Mosse, *Police Forces in History*. Beverly Hills: Sage, 1974.

Elliff, John T. *Crime Dissent and the Attorney General: The Justice Department in the 1960s.* Beverly Hills: Sage, 1971.

——. *The Reform of FBI Intelligence Operations.* Princeton: Princeton Univ. Pr., 1979.

"Emma Goldman." *Ramparts* 10(Feb. 1972):10–12+.

Ernst, Morris L. "Battle Against the Party." *Saturday Review* 41(Mar. 8, 1958):14.

"Eye on the FBI." *The New Republic* 169(Sept. 8, 1973):14–15.

FBI Annual Reports.

"FBI Chief vs. the Attorney General." *U.S. News and World Report* 65(Sept. 30, 1968):14.

"FBI Dirty Tricks: Revelations from Cointelpro Files." *Time* 110(Dec. 5, 1977):30.

"FBI Gets High Rating Despite Some Egghead Slurs." *Saturday Evening Post* 234(Apr. 8, 1961):10.

"FBI Head on Delinquency." *America* 97(June 8, 1957):296.

"FBI's Hoover: What the Fight Is All About." *U.S. News and World Report* 70(Apr. 19, 1971):89.

"FBI Kept Secret Files on Congressmen, Presidents." *Senior Scholastic* 106(Apr. 10, 1975):17.

FBI Law Enforcement Bulletin.

"FBI's Security Watch." *Newsweek* 35(Jan. 30, 1950):16+.

"FBI vs. Jean Seberg: Blasting a G-Man Myth." *Time* 114(Sept. 24, 1979):25.

Federal Council of Churches: Interchurch World Movement. *The Deportation Cases of 1919–20.*

Feldman, Harold. "Oswald and the FBI." *The Nation* 198(Jan. 27, 1964):86–89.

Felt, Mark. *The FBI Pyramid: From the Inside.* New York: Putnam's 1979.

Final Report of the Select Committee to Study Governmental Operations with Respect to Intelligence Activities. 94th Cong., 2d sess., S. Rept. 94-755.

"Fight for Secrecy of FBI Files." *U.S. News and World Report* 26(June 24, 1949):40–41.

"Fight over the Future of the FBI." *Time* 101(Mar. 26, 1973):17–20.

"File on J. Edgar Hoover." *Time* 98(Oct. 25, 1971):14–16.

"Filling Hoover's Shoes." *The New Republic* 168(Mar. 17, 1973):10–11.

Flynn, J. T. "Who's Behind Hoover?" *The New Republic* 102(Mar. 11, 1940):345.

Footlick, J. K., and Marro, A. "G-Man and Klansman." *Newsweek* 86(Aug. 25, 1975):74–75.

Fraser, Gerald. "F.B.I. Files Reveal Moves Against Black Panthers." *New York Times,* Oct. 19, 1980, p. 1+.

"The 'Front' on Trial." *The Nation* 150(May 4, 1940):556–57.

"Full Circle: Tackling the Catholics." *The Nation* 211(Dec. 14, 1970):613–14.

"G-Man Hoover's Nazi Plot." *The New Republic* 102(Mar. 18, 1940):364–65.

"G-Man Hoover's Spy Hunt." *The New Republic* 102(June 10, 1940):778–79.

Gage, Nicholas. "Has the Mafia Penetrated the F.B.I.?" *New York Times Magazine.* Oct. 2, 1977. Pp. 14–16+.

Galbraith, John K. "My Forty Years with the F.B.I. *Esquire* 88(Oct., 1977): 122–26+.

Garrow, David. *The F.B.I. and Martin Luther King, Jr.* New York: Norton, 1981.

Gatewood, Willard B. *Theodore Roosevelt and the Art of Controversy.* Baton Rouge: Louisiana State Univ. Pr., 1970.

Gawloski, Joseph J. *Bureaucratic Expertise and J. Edgar Hoover.* Master's thesis, John Jay College, 1975.

Goldstein, R. J. "Internment Camps for Citizens: The FBI's Forty Year Plot." *The Nation* 227(July 1, 1978):10–16.

Grafton, Samuel. "The Red Scare: A Case History." *The Nation* 140(Apr. 24, 1935):476–78.

Hall, R. "Freedom of Information: Insouciance at the FBI." *The Nation* 220(June 14, 1975):721–22.

Halperin, Morton et al. *The Lawless State: The Crime of the U.S. Intelligence Agencies.* New York: Penguin, 1976.

"Hammer and Splinter: FBI Infiltration of the Socialist Workers Party." *The Nation* 223(Sept. 18, 1976):228–29.

"Handcuffs on the FBI?" *Newsweek* 50(Sept. 2, 1957):21–22+.

Harris, Richard. "Reflections: Crime in the F.B.I." *The New Yorker* 53(Aug. 8, 1977):30–32+.

Harrison, Richard. *The CIA and the FBI.* London: F. Miller, 1956.

"Harry Truman vs. Hoover, Brownell." *Life* 35(Nov. 30, 1953):34–35.

Hart, Jeffrey. "Jean Seberg and the Media Myth-Makers." *Saturday Evening Post* 253(May–June 1981):30+.

"Heil Hoover." *New Republic* 153(Sept. 4, 1965):9.

"Heat on Hoover." *Senior Scholastic* 98(May 10, 1971):17.

Hentoff, Nat. "Sing No Sad Songs for the FBI." *Village Voice,* May 24, 1976, pp. 39–40.

Higham, John. *Strangers in the Land.* New York: Atheneum, 1973.

"Hoover and His FBI: An Era Ends." *Newsweek* 79(May 15, 1972):26–28+.

"Hoover and the Berrigans: East Coast Conspiracy to Save Lives Organization." *America* 123(Dec. 12, 1970):509.

"Hoover-Berrigan-Wills." *National Review* 23(June 1, 1970):578.

"Hoover-King Meeting." *Newsweek* 64(Dec. 14, 1964):22+.

"Hoover: Sacred and Profane." *National Review* 23(May 4, 1971):461.

"Hoover's Closet: Cointelpro." *Time* 104(Dec. 2, 1974):28.

"Hoover's Conspiracy." *Commonweal* 93(Dec. 18, 1960):291+.

"Hoover's FBI: Time For a Change?" *Newsweek* 77(May 10, 1971):28–32+.

"Hoover's Political Spying For Presidents." *Time* 106(Dec. 15, 1975):10–12.

"Hoover's Successor." *The Nation* 202(Mar. 7, 1966):254–55.

"Hoover's Woes." *Newsweek* 77(Apr. 12, 1971):39.

"Hoover: The One Who is in the Department of Justice." *Newsweek* 2(Aug. 12, 1933):16–17.

"Hoover the Vulgarian." *The Nation* 199(Nov. 30, 1964):394.

Horowitz, Irving L. "Reactionary Immorality: The Private Life in Public Testimony of John Edgar Hoover." *Trans-Action* 6(June 1969):64–70.

"In Defense of J. Edgar Hoover." *Time* 85(Mar. 5, 1965):41.

Irey, Elmer L. *The Tax Dodgers.* Garden City, N.Y.: Garden City Pub., 1948.

"Inside J. Edgar Hoover's X-Rated Files." *Time* 108(Dec. 6, 1976):24.

"Investigate the American OGPU." *The New Republic* 102(Mar. 11, 1940): 330.

"J. Edgar Hoover." *Commonweal* 81(Dec. 4, 1964):341.

"J. Edgar Hoover." *Current Biography,* 1940, pp. 400–402.

"J. Edgar Hoover and the FBI." *Newsweek* 64(Dec. 7, 1964):21–26.

"J. Edgar Hoover Collection: Proposal for Collection of FBI Files on Americans." *The Nation* 221(Dec. 27, 1975):677.

"J. Edgar Hoover: The Man Who Walked Alone." *Newsweek* 42(Nov. 30, 1953):28–29.

John Edgar Hoover, Director, Federal Bureau of Investigation, United States Department of Justice. FBI press release, Apr. 1, 1967.

Jeffers, H. Paul. *Wanted by the FBI.* New York: Hawthorne, 1972.

Johnson, G. W. "Cop Becomes a Cato." *The New Republic* 147(Sept. 10, 1962):14.

Jones, Ken. *Wanted by the FBI.* New York: NAL, 1957.

Justice Department Career of J. Edgar Hoover. FBI press release. May 3, 1972.

Kelley, Clarence M. "Is the F.B.I. Obsolete?" Address delivered May 18, 1977. *Vital Speeches* 43(July 15, 1977):478–81.

———. "Perspectives of Power: The F.B.I. Today and in the Future." Address delivered May 8, 1976. *Vital Speeches* 42(June 15, 1976):514–17.

"Knives Sharpening." *National Review* 16(Dec. 15, 1964):1094.

Knebel, F. "Cop and the Man." *Look* 19(May 31, 1955):29–33.

———. "How Hoover Rules the FBI." *Look* 19(June 14, 1955):77–81.

Kobler, John. *Capone*. New York: Putnam, 1971.

Kuhn, Ferdinand. *The Story of the Secret Service*. New York: Random, 1957.

Kunstler, William M. "FBI Letters: Writers of the Purple Page." *The Nation* 227(Dec. 30, 1978):721+.

Laing, A. "How I Didn't Shoot Eisenhower." *The New Republic* 169(Aug. 18, 1973):12–13.

Lardine, Bob. "This 'F.B.I.' Is Just Too Perfect." *New York Daily News*, Dec. 29, 1981.

Lasky, Victor. "Liberals Suddenly Discover Hoover." *Human Events*, Apr. 7, 1973, p. 9.

"Leaning on the FBI: Political Pressure Long Before Watergate." *Newsweek* 81(June 25, 1973):25.

"Least Wanted." *The New Republic* 63(Nov. 28, 1970):5–6.

"Leave It to the Experts." *Time* 80(Aug. 17, 1962):18.

"Let Him Go." *The Nation* 198(May, 18, 1964):499.

Levine, J. "Hoover and the Red Scare." *The Nation* 195(Oct. 20, 1962):232–35.

"Life and Times of the FBI Man." *Time* 101(Mar. 26, 1953):20.

"Life Imitates Art." *Time* 73(Dec. 18, 1964):73.

Lippard, Lucy R. "They've Got FBEyes for You." *Village Voice*, Nov. 4–10, 1981, p. 114.

"Long Reign of J. Edgar Hoover." *Time* 99(May 15, 1972):18–19.

Look, the Editors of. *The Story of the FBI with an Introduction by J. Edgar Hoover: Official Picture History of the Federal Bureau of Investigation*. New York: Dutton, 1947. Revised 1954.

Louderback, Lew. *The Bad Ones: Gangsters of the 30s and Their Molls*. Greenwich, Conn.: Fawcett, 1968.

Lowenthal, Max. *The Federal Bureau of Investigation*. New York: Sloan, 1950.

MacCormick, Austin. "A Quartet on Crime." *The Nation* 142(Apr. 15, 1936):487–88.

McIlhany, William H. *Klandestine*. New Rochelle, N.Y.: Arlington House, 1975.

McWilliams, Carey. "The Oppenheimer Case." *The Nation* 178(May 1, 1954):373–77.

———. "Senator McCarthy's Sixth Column." *The Nation* 178(May 22, 1954):434–36.

———. "White House under Surveillance." *The Nation* 174(Feb. 16, 1952): 150–52.

Mabie, J. "J. Edgar Hoover: Crime's Nemesis." *Christian Science Monitor*, July 29, 1936, p. 3.

Malin, Patrick Murphy. "The First Freedom." *The Nation* 172(June 2, 1951): 520–22.

Marro, A., and Goldman, P. "J. Edgar Hoover's Secret Files." *Newsweek* 85(Mar. 10, 1975):16–17.

"Matter of Mutual Advantage." *Time* 89(Feb. 3, 1967):19–20.

Maund, Alfred. "We Will All Stand Together." *The Nation* 182(Mar. 3, 1956):168.

Mayer, Milton S. "Myth of the G-Men." *Forum* 94(Sept., 1935):144–48.

———. "Special Agent." *Progressive* 40(Dec., 1976):40–41.

Meir, A. "Above the Law: FBI and the Socialist Workers Party." *The Nation* 228(Apr. 7, 1979):355–56.

Messick, Hank. "Schenley Chapter." *The Nation* 212(Apr. 5, 1971):428–31.

Mill, Robert R. "Shock Troops of Justice." *Blue Book.* Sept., 1935, p. 6.

Mitchell, Jonathan. "The Versatility of General Johnson." *Harper's* 169(Oct., 1934):585–96.

Moley, Raymond. "Faith of the FBI." *Newsweek* 61(Mar. 4, 1963):88.

"Morris, McGrath and Hoover." *The Nation* 174(Apr. 12, 1952):338–40.

Moyers, Bill. "LBJ and the FBI." *Newsweek* 85(Mar. 10, 1975):84.

"Mr. Dies Goes to Town." *The Nation* 147(Sept. 3, 1938):216.

Murtaugh, A. L. "Crazy SOB: An Agent's View." *The Nation* 220(Apr. 8, 1975):467–68.

Murray, Robert K. *Red Scare.* New York: McGraw, 1964.

Nash, Jay Robert, and Offen, Ron. *Dillinger, Dead or Alive?* Chicago: Henry Regnery, 1970.

Navasky, Victor S. "FBI's Wildest Dream: Campaign Against Martin Luther King." *The Nation* 226(June 17, 1978):716–18.

———. "Government and Martin Luther King." *Atlantic* 226(Nov., 1970):43–52.

———. *Kennedy Justice.* New York: Atheneum, 1971.

———, with Buckley, J. L. "J. Edgar Hoover Was a Superadministrator, but What Is His Legacy?" *Saturday Review* 55(May 27, 1972):25–29.

———, with Paster, Darrell. *Law Enforcement: The Federal Role.* New York: McGraw, 1976.

Nelson, Jack, and Ostrow, Ronald J. *The FBI and the Berrigans: The Making of a Conspiracy.* New York: Coward, McCann, 1972.

"New Kind of Government Sleuth in Washington." *Literary Digest* 84(Jan. 24, 1925):44–46.

"Next Mr. Hoover." *The Nation* 196(Feb. 16, 1963):131.

Ninety-Nine Facts about the FBI. Washington, D.C.: U.S. Government Printing Office, 1976.

"Not Quite Invulnerable." *The Nation* 212(Feb. 8, 1971):164.

O'Connor, John J. " 'Today's F.B.I.'—Off to an Impressive Start." *New York Times*, Oct. 25, 1981, p. 31.

———. "TV: 6-Hour 'King,' Drama of Civil Rights." *New York Times*, Feb. 9, 1978, p. C-20.

"Of Hoover and Clark." *Time* 97(May 3, 1971):16–17.

"Off Hoover's Chest." *Newsweek* 64(Nov. 30, 1964):29–30.

Ollestad, Norman. *Inside the F.B.I.* New York: Lancer, 1968.

"Omnipotent Cop." *New Republic* 143(Oct. 24, 1960):4.

O'Neill, Hester. "Thirty Years on the Job." *American Boy* 36(May, 1954):2–4+; 36(June, 1954):2–4+.

———. "FBI's Scientific Detective Work." *American Boy* 36(June, 1954):4–8+.

———. "J. Edgar Hoover's School Days." *American Boy* 36(July, 1954):8–9+; 36(Sept., 1954):8–9+.

"Ordeal By Spies: Harry Dexter White Case." *Christian Century* 70(Dec. 2, 1953):1382–84.

Ottenberg, Miriam. "What's ahead for the FBI?" *Look* 29(Feb. 23, 1965):27–29.

"Our Lawless G-Men," *The Nation* 150(Mar. 2, 1940):296.

"Our Titled Crook Catcher." *Business Week*, Nov. 11, 1950, p. 140.

Overstreet, Harry, and Overstreet, Bonaro. *The FBI in Our Open Society*. New York: Norton, 1969.

"Pandora's Box at the FBI: Files on Public Figures." *Time* 105(Feb. 3, 1975): 11–12.

"Paranoia in Power." *Harpers* 249(Oct., 1974):32+.

"Passing the Bug." *Newsweek* 68(Dec. 26, 1966):19–20.

"Past Dirty Tricks: White House Misuse of the F.B.I." *Time* 102(Aug. 27, 1973):15–16.

Payne, Cril. *Deep Cover*. New York: Newsweek Books, 1979.

Pearson, Drew. *Diaries*. New York: Holt, 1974.

Perkus, Cathy, ed. *Cointelpro: The FBI's Secret War on Political Freedom*. New York: Monad, 1976.

"Perils of Omnipotence." *The Nation* 201(Nov. 1, 1965):291.

Phelan, James. "Hoover of the F.B.I." *Saturday Evening Post* 238(Sept. 25, 1965):23–28+; 247(Dec., 1975):30–35+.

Philbrick, Herbert. *I Led Three Lives*. Washington, D.C.: Capitol Hill, 1972.

Pincus, W. "Misusing the FBI." *The New Republic* 168(Feb. 24, 1973):17–18.

"Plot Against Hoover." *The Nation* 150(Mar. 9, 1940):323.

Pogrebin, L. C. "Have You Ever Supported Equal Pay, Child Care, or Women's Groups? The FBI Was Watching You." *Ms* 5(June, 1977):37–44+; 5(Oct., 1977):37–44+; 5(Oct., 1977):7–8+.

"Politics and the FBI." *The Nation* 217(Sept. 10, 1973):196–97.

"President Nixon's Eulogy of J. Edgar Hoover." *U.S. News and World Report* 72(May 15, 1972):112+.

"Project 'Cointelpro': Hoover's Program of Counterintelligence Against the New Left." *The Nation* 218(Feb. 9, 1974):165.

Purvis, Melvin. *American Agent.* Garden City, N.Y.: Doubleday, 1936.

"Red Images." *Newsweek* 60(Oct. 29, 1962):23–24.

Redlich, Norman. "Spies in Government: The Bentley Story." *The Nation* 178(Jan. 30, 1954):85–87+.

————. "Spies in Government: The Jenner Report." *The Nation* 178(Feb. 6, 1954):109–10+.

Report upon the Illegal Practices of the United States Department of Justice. Washington, D.C.: National Popular Government League, 1920.

Reynolds, Quentin. *The F.B.I.* New York: Random, 1954.

Roane, S. "Encounter with a G-Man." *Progressive* 43(July, 1979):66.

Robb, Linda B. J. "I Remember J. Edgar Hoover." *Ladies Home Companion* 89(July, 1972):92+.

Robin, A. "Living Legends." *Today's Health* 39(Feb., 1961):61.

Rogers, James T. *Four Tough Cases of the F.B.I.* New York: Holt, 1968.

Roosevelt, Franklin Delano. *The Public Papers and Addresses of Franklin D. Roosevelt.* 3 vols. New York: Random, 1938.

Rosten, Leo G. "Men Like War." *Harpers* 171(June, 1935):192+.

Ruckelshaus, W. D. "Inside Report on the F.B.I." *New York Times Magazine,* Aug. 19, 1973, p. 7+.

St. George, A. "Cold War Comes Home." *Harpers* 247(Nov., 1973):68–70+.

Safire, William. "Exposing FBI Surveillance." *Current* 155(Oct., 1973):33–35.

Salmans, S., and Lesher, S. "It All Began with FDR: FBI's Political Intelligence Gathering." *Newsweek* 86(Dec. 15, 1975):27–28.

Sancton, Thomas. "The Case of Alger Hiss." *The Nation* 167(Sept. 4, 1948): 251–52.

————. "Dossiers for the Millions." *The Nation* 167(Sept. 25, 1948):336–37.

Sann, Paul. *Kill the Dutchman!* New York: Popular, 1971.

"Save Hoover Drive." *The Nation* 213(July 5, 1971):5–6.

Scherer, G. H. "What's Behind the Smear Campaign?" *American Mercury* 89(July, 1959):141.

Schneir, W., and Schneir, M. "Socialist Workers: Square Target of the FBI." *The Nation* 223(Sept. 25, 1976):272–77.

Schorr, Daniel. "Chilling Experience: FBI Investigation of Daniel Schorr." *Harpers* 246(Mar., 1973):92–97.

Schott, Joseph. *No Left Turns.* New York: Praeger, 1975.

Seagle, William. "The American National Police." *Harpers* 169(Nov., 1934): 751–61.

"Sequel to a Melodrama." *The Nation* 150(May 11, 1940):584–85.

Shannon, William V. "The J. Edgar Hoover Case." *Commonweal* 81(Dec. 11, 1964):375–76.

"Shape of Things, The." *The Nation* 143(July 18, 1936):59.

Shaw, John F. "Heresy of John F. Shaw: A Purloined Letter." *The Nation* 212(Feb. 8, 1971):172–77.

Shaw, R. "Couple of Cops." *Commonweal* 23(Jan. 31, 1936):372–74.

Shea, Robert, and Wilson, Robert Anton. *Illuminatus!* 3 vols. New York: Dell, 1975.

Sheerin, J. S. "F.B.I. Smear." *Catholic World* 188(Feb., 1959):357–58.

"Sherlock." *Scholastic* 24(May 12, 1934):25.

Sidey, Hugh. "L.B.J., Hoover and Domestic Spying." *Time* 105(Feb. 10, 1975):16.

————. "Man Who Stayed in Power." *Life* 72(May 12, 1972):12.

Silver, Isadore. "FBI: A Relevant Motion." *Commonweal* 98(May 25, 1973): 276–77.

Simon, William E. "War on the FBI." *Saturday Evening Post* 250(Sept., 1978)44–46+.

"Sleuth School." *Time* 26(Aug. 5, 1935):10–12.

Smith, John Chabot. *Alger Hiss: The True Story.* New York: Holt, 1976.

"Split Hairs and Tapped Wires." *The Nation* 153(Oct. 18 1941):360–61.

Stapleton, John. "Inquiring Photographer: Have Recent Events Tarnished the Image of the FBI for You?" *New York Daily News,* May 4, 1978, p. 55.

"Still Time for Hoover to Retire with Honor." *Christian Century* 81(Dec. 2, 1964):1483.

Stone, I. F. "The New Inquisitor." *The Nation* 166(Jan. 3, 1948):6–7.

————. "XXX and the FBI." *The Nation* 157(Sept. 25, 1943):342–43.

"Strange Case of Miss X, The." *The Nation* 177(Dec. 12, 1953):491–93.

Sullivan, William C. *The Bureau: My Thirty Years in Hoover's FBI.* New York: Norton, 1979.

Susman, Warren I. "The Thirties." *The Development of an American Culture.* Englewood Cliffs, N.J.: Prentice, 1970.

"TRB from Washington." *The New Republic* 163(Nov. 28, 1970):4.

Theoharis, Athan G. "Abuse of Power: What the New Hiss Suit Uncovers." *The Nation* 227(Oct. 7, 1978):336–40.

————. "From the Cold War to Watergate: National Security and Civil Liberties." *Intellect* 103(Oct., 1974):20–26.

————. *Spying on Americans.* Philadelphia: Temple Univ. Pr., 1978.

"They Stand out from the Crowd." *Literary Digest* 117(May 19, 1934):14.

Toland, John. *The Dillinger Days.* New York: Random, 1963.

"Tonic of Irreverence." *The Nation* 186(May 17, 1958):431.

"Trials are for Courts." *The Nation* 182(May 19, 1956):421.

"Truman on Trial: Harry Dexter White Case." *The New Republic* 129(Nov. 30, 1953):6–15.

"The Truth about Hoover." *Time* 106(Dec. 22, 1975):14–16+.

Tucker, Ray. "Hsst, Who Goes There?" *Colliers* 92(Aug. 19, 1933):15+.

Tully, Andrew. *The F.B.I.'s Most Famous Cases.* New York: Morrow, 1965.

——. *Inside the F.B.I.* New York: McGraw, 1980.

Turkus, Burton B., and Feder, Sid. *Murder Inc.: The Inside Story of the Mob.* New York: Manor, 1972.

Turner, William W. "Crime Is Too Big for the FBI." *The Nation* 201(Nov. 8, 1965):322–28.

——. *Hoover's F.B.I.: The Man and the Myth.* New York: Dell, 1971.

Turrou, Leon. *The Nazi Spy Conspiracy in America.* New York: Random, 1939.

Ungar, Sanford J. *F.B.I.* Boston: Little, 1976.

U.S. Congress. House. Committee on Government Operations. Subcommittee on Government Information and Civil Rights. *Inquiry into the Destruction of Former FBI Director J. Edgar Hoover's Files and FBI Recordkeeping.* Washington, D.C.: 1975.

U.S. Congress. Select. *Senate Committee to Study Governmental Operations with Respect to Intelligence Operations, Final Report.* 94th Cong., 2d sess. S. Rept. 94-755, bk. 3, p. 932.

U.S. Task Force to Review the FBI Martin Luther King, Jr., Security and Assassination Investigations. *Report.* Washington, D.C.: 1977.

Villano, Anthony. *Brick Agent.* New York: Quadrangle, 1977.

Vollmer, August, and Parker, Alfred E. *Crime, Crooks and Cops.* New York: Funk, 1937.

Wainwright, L. "Must J. Edgar Go on and on? *Life* 56(May 22, 1964):25.

Ward, Paul W. "Hacking to Justice with Cummings. *The Nation* 141(July 3, 1935):14–16.

——. "Midsummer Spy Madness." *The Nation* 143(July 25, 1936):19–20.

Washington, I. L. "F.B.I. Plot Against Black Leaders: Cointelpro." *Essence* 19(Oct. 1978):70–73.

"Washington Icons." *The Nation* 209(Sept. 1, 1969):164–65.

"Watchful Eye." *Time* 54(Aug. 8, 1949):12–15.

Watters, Pat, and Gillers, Stephen. *Investigating the F.B.I.* Garden City, N.Y.: Doubleday, 1973.

Webster, William H. "Work of the F.B.I." Address delivered Apr. 20, 1979. *Vital Speeches* 45(June 15, 1979):521–24.

Weinstein, Allen. *Perjury: The Hiss-Chambers Case.* New York: Knopf, 1978.

Westin, Alan F. "Wire-Tapping: Supreme Court vs. FBI." *The Nation* 174(Feb. 23, 1952):172–74.

Whitehead, Don. *Attack on Terror: The FBI Against the Ku Klux Klan in Mississippi.* New York: Funk, 1970.

———. *The F.B.I. Story.* New York: Random, 1956.

———. "J. Edgar Hoover Sums It up: We're Fair and We Are Hard." *Washington Evening Star,* May 9, 1954, p. 1. May 16, 1954, p. 1. May 11, 1954, p. 1.

"Who Knew about the Bugging: RFK's Story and the FBI's." *U.S. News and World Report* 61(Dec. 26, 1966):32–35.

"Why Tap Wires?" *The Nation* 152(Mar. 8, 1941):257–58.

Wicker, Tom. "G-Man under Fire." *Life* 70(Apr. 9, 1971):39–45.

———. "Now That the Mighty Have Fallen." *New York Times,* Aug. 3, 1976, p. 29.

———. "What Have They Done since They Got Dillinger?" *New York Times Magazine,* Dec. 28, 1969, p. 5+.

Wilson, H. H. "Case For Effective Control." *The Nation* 212(Feb. 8, 1971): 169–72.

Wilson, James Q. "Buggings, Break-ins and the FBI." *Commentary* 65(June, 1978):52–58.

———. *The Investigators.* New York: Basic, 1978.

Wilson, O. W. "Police Administration." In *Municipal Year Book.* Chicago: International City Managers' Association, 1936.

Wise, David. *The American Police State.* New York: Random, 1976.

Wolfe, Alan. *The Seamy Side of Democracy.* New York: David McKay, 1973.

Wool, R. "Metamorphosis of a Hawk: Why an Ex-Navy Hero from Tennessee Attacked J. Edgar Hoover." *New York Times Magazine,* Apr. 25, 1971, pp. 22–23+.

Wright, Richard O., and Mollenhoff, Clark. *Whose F.B.I.?* LaSalle, Ill.: Open Court, 1974.

XXX. "Washington Gestapo." *The Nation* 157(July 17, 1943):64–66; 157(July 24, 1943):92–95.

INDEX